Be Still

A Daily Devotional to Quiet Your Heart

the Lord will fight for you; you have only to keep still.
EXODUS 14:14

www.walkingwithpurpose.com

Authored by Lisa Brenninkmeyer
Cover and page design by True Cotton
Production management by Christine Welsko

The recommended Bible translations for use in all Walking with Purpose studies are: The New American Bible, which is the translation used in the United States for the readings at Mass; The Revised Standard Version, Catholic Edition; and The Jerusalem Bible.

Copyright © November 2019 by Walking with Purpose Inc.
All rights reserved. No part of this book may be reproduced in any form by any electronic or mechanical means (including photocopying, recording, or information storage and retrieval) without permission in writing from Walking with Purpose.

Any internet addresses (websites, blogs, etc.) in this book are offered as a resource and may change in the future. Please refer to www.walkingwithpurpose.com as the central location for corresponding materials and references.

19 20 21 22 23 24 25 / 12 11 10 9 8 7 6 5 4 3 2 1

ISBN: 978-1-943173-27-3

Be Still: A Daily Devotional to Quiet Your Heart

Table of Contents

INTRODUCTION
Dedication 3
Introduction 5

MONTHS
January 7
February 41
March 73
April 107
May 139
June 173
July 205
August 239
September 273
October 305
November 339
December 371

APPENDICES
Topical Index 407
Old Testament Index 413
New Testament Index 416
Monthly Prayers for Children 420
Notes 425

For everything there is a season, & a time for every matter under **HEAVEN:**
— ecclesiastes 3:1

Dedication

For my mother, Jane Harris

You have passed on a spiritual legacy to me, a deposit of wisdom, that I mark as the greatest of gifts. It was you who introduced me to Jesus and tended to my heart in such a way that I never doubted His love and interest in every detail of my life. The hours you have spent listening and your steadfast presence whenever I have needed guidance and help have made it easy to believe that God cares for me in this same way, albeit even more perfectly. Never underestimate the power of your presence in my life. It has been my steady anchor, has made me the woman I am today, and has given me the confidence to pursue goals and dreams that I have been woefully unqualified for. You speak with a gentle wisdom, and I have been the beneficiary of that for decades. The vast majority of the words in *Be Still* first came to me from your mouth. Thank you for teaching me. Thank you for listening to God when He spoke to you about me. Thank you for challenging me to live a life that counts, to always keep my eyes on eternity. Thank you for being my example and for faithfully teaching the Bible to women, causing me to want to grow up to be just like you. Thank you for sharing with me the secret of the Christian life—that it's all really the work of the Holy Spirit. We are the glove; He is the hand. And so it is with the pages of this book: Any good in it is credited to Him, but I'm saving some credit for you, too. You were my first teacher, and I am still learning from you.

Introduction

What does it mean to live the good life? How can I be happy? What choices will get me there? I hope this book of short daily readings will help you answer those questions.

How our day unfolds and feels has less to do with our circumstances than with our mind-set. While we can't control which events we'll encounter, we can always decide what our attitude will be. Will we filter everything that happens through a lens of gratitude? Will we be kind to ourselves by seeing ourselves through God's eyes? Will we look at suffering as something that always has purpose?

More and more, I am convinced that getting our attitude in the right place has everything to do with how we start each day.

Saint Josemaria Escriva coined a phrase that I think is so compelling: *the heroic minute*. He writes:

> The heroic minute. It is the time fixed for getting up. Without hesitation; a supernatural reflection and . . . up! The heroic minute: here you have a mortification that strengthens your will and does no harm to your body. If, with God's help, you conquer yourself, you will be well ahead for the rest of the day. It's so discouraging to find oneself beaten at the first skirmish.[1]

I realize that reading the word *mortification* probably makes you want to run for the hills. Who wants to start the day with something that sounds unpleasant? But stay with me for a minute. How do you feel when you get up and are behind the eight ball before things have even begun? Your first movements are rushed, requests come at you and require your attention, and all you can think is that you have got to clear your head and get some coffee. It's starting the day reacting instead of responding. It's feeling under siege and not knowing exactly why. It's also entirely avoidable.

Giving God the first minutes of your day will pay dividends later. I promise you, He will multiply your time. You'll get more done and have a peaceful heart while doing it.

But it's not just a matter of hauling your body out of bed. Resetting your mind is the critical step if you want your day to be the best it can possibly be. Which begs the questions:

- Which mind-set will best equip me to face the day with inner strength and gratitude?
- How do I gain that mind-set?

Saint Paul talks about this in Romans 12:2: "Be transformed by the renewal of your mind, that you may prove what is the will of God, what is good and acceptable and perfect." We renew our minds by looking at things from God's perspective. This is something we need to do every day; otherwise our thoughts and emotions will be in the driver's seat and the ride will be anything but smooth. The best mind-set is God's, and we gain it by listening to Him. While few people hear His audible voice, we all can hear His voice speaking through Scripture.

Each of the readings in *Be Still* begins with a Bible verse, followed by a reflection on how we can apply it to our daily lives, and ending with a short prayer. The readings give your mind something to chew on for the day. If you actually apply what you read, you will make significant progress in the spiritual life. What I've written relates to the problems, heartaches, and searching that I've experienced over the years. As I've traveled and spoken to thousands of women, I've had the privilege of listening to them unburdening their hearts. I've found that our struggles are universal. We are not alone.

These writings aim to touch the heart, strengthen the will, and enlighten the mind. The goal is transformation—that what we read will impact how we live. If you have done any of the Walking with Purpose Bible studies, you'll recognize those lessons in the pages of this book. Some writing is new, some is adapted from the Bible studies, and it all can serve as an aid to starting your day with God's perspective.

But what if you can't start your day this way? No worries. Just look for the first pocket of quiet in your schedule. It always comes, but we usually don't notice because we've filled it with mindless scrolling through our social media feeds or checking our email. What might change if instead of grabbing your phone, you read *Be Still*? It'll just take a few minutes, but the impact of that choice will be felt throughout the day.

Much of what I've written speaks of God's unconditional love for you; every reading should be filtered through that perspective. When God asks us to get moving, or change a bad habit, or do something that feels out of our comfort zone, it is always because He wants what is best for us. He is not a cosmic killjoy. He is a good Father who wants His children to flourish.

Most will read *Be Still* according to the day's date. But there is also an index at the back of the book that will guide you to dates that focus on topics including anxiety, God's love, friendship, the spiritual battle, perseverance, loneliness, and more. A scriptural index allows you to see the dates when specific books of the Bible are featured. This is a helpful tool for personal Bible study. In addition, if you'd like to pray for a child in your life in a more intentional way, there is a monthly prayer list at the back.

May what you read travel from your mind to your heart, going beyond information to transformation. May you meet Jesus in these pages, and may your trust in Him grow. "Now to him who is able to keep you from falling, and to make you stand without blemish in the presence of his glory with rejoicing, to the only God our Savior, through Jesus Christ our Lord, be glory, majesty, power, and authority, before all time and now and forever. Amen" (Jude 24–25).

January

So whoever is in Christ is a NEW creation. The old things have passed away. Behold new things have come.
2 Corinthians 5:17

JANUARY 1

Mary, Mother of God

"And Mary said, 'Behold, I am the handmaid of the Lord; let it be to me according to your word.'" (Luke 1:38)

These powerful words were Mary's fiat—her yes to God. When God issued the invitation for Mary to be the mother of the Messiah, He didn't fill her in on all the details of His plan. Her yes required a leap of faith. What did she need to have faith in? She needed to have faith in the goodness of God. On the surface, God's plan appeared to be setting up her downfall. Conceiving a baby before being married would devastate her reputation and possibly end her engagement to Joseph. The angel didn't explain to Mary exactly how it was going to play out. But Mary knew God, and she trusted that His plan would be good.

We can know someone in different ways. I can say that I know the President in the sense that I know who he is. I can identify him and know some facts about him, too. But that's very different than when I say I know my husband. I know my husband intimately. There are things about him that I know from personal experience. Even when he acts in a way that might seem insensitive, I know he has a tender and generous heart. This allows me to look past certain circumstances and see the best in him. I'm far less likely to do that for the President, because while I know about him, I don't know him personally.

Mary knew God personally. She knew His character—His mercy, goodness, justice, holiness, strength, and generosity. These qualities of God had been revealed to her, not because she was so special (although she was), but because she was looking for them.

God has revealed Himself to you as well. Have you noticed? Or is it possible that you have attributed His generosity, goodness, strength, and mercy to another person instead of to Him? Or have you given fate the credit? God has been at work in your life. He has intersected you at critical moments of need and elated moments of joy. He has always been there, bringing you just what you need. But He often remains hidden, only to be found by those who seek Him.

How well you know God will greatly impact your ability to offer your own fiat to Him—your unreserved yes to His plan for your life. Are you not sure where to start? Start by asking Him to reveal Himself to you.

Dear Lord,
Help me to look for evidence of You throughout my day. May my glimpses of You increase my trust in You. Amen.

Be Still

JANUARY 2

"Remember not the events of the past, the things of long ago consider not; See, I am doing something new! Now it springs forth, do you not perceive it? In the wilderness I make a way, in the wasteland, rivers." (Isaiah 43:18–19)

I can respond to the higher number on my weight scale in a few different ways. One is to joyfully say, "There's just more of me to love!" Another is to puddle in a heap on the floor, cursing the woman at the coffee shop who introduced me to the eggnog chai latte. I can look back and regret every time I celebrated the holidays with a tasty morsel. Or I can look forward, lace up my shoes, and get going with some better habits starting now.

Many of us are starting the New Year with an awareness of all the things we should be doing better. Unfortunately, the best intentions can quickly become sources of discouragement as we encounter our weaknesses. We might look back and see false starts, failures, and ingrained bad habits. We consider our families of origin and feel disheartened when the very things we disliked in our parents are evident in our own lives. We may wonder if we'll ever change.

The prophet Isaiah challenges us to stop looking back. God is doing something new! The inspiration we feel to change in positive ways comes from Him. It's evidence that He is at work within us. "For God is the one who, for his good purpose, works in you both to desire and to work" (Philippians 2:13). No matter how much your life feels like a wilderness or a wasteland, God can bring the change you so desire.

Because of Christ, you can be different. Whatever your temperament, personality, or behavioral habits, you can become the woman God wants you to be. We are called to "be renewed in the spirit of our minds, and put on the new self, created in God's way in righteousness and holiness of truth" (Ephesians 4:23–24).

How does this transformation happen? Does it come from striving? Does it depend on our perfection? No, it doesn't. The answer is found in 2 Corinthians 3:18: "All of us, gazing with unveiled face on the glory of the Lord, are being transformed into the same image from glory to glory, as from the Lord who is the Spirit." The inner change happens as we contemplate Christ. As we sit in His presence, we soak up His love. We behold His glory, and in the process, we begin to reflect it.

Dear Lord,
Please transform me into Your likeness. Amen.

JANUARY 3

"Behold the Lion of the Tribe of Judah." (Revelation 5:5)

In the classic book *The Lion, the Witch and the Wardrobe*, Lucy is preparing to meet the lion, Aslan, who represents Jesus in the story. She's frightened at the thought and asks Mr. Beaver if Aslan is safe. He replies: "Who said anything about being safe? 'Course he isn't safe. But he's good. He's the King, I tell you.'"[2]

The same could be said of Jesus: He isn't safe. But He's good. The life He leads us to isn't predictable, easy, or comfortable. But it is fulfilling, peaceful, and purposeful. The key word is *full*. Being a friend of the real Jesus, following Him wherever He leads, always fills the emptiness that so many of us feel inside.

Are you tired of feeling empty? Are you longing for purpose? Do you need something (or someone) to pull together the mess in your life and create something full of meaning? Then ask Jesus to give you more of Himself. This is a prayer He just waits to answer with a resounding yes.

The Bible tells us that Jesus loves you so much that "even the hairs of your head are all numbered" (Luke 12:7). He knows everything about you—the good, the bad, the innermost secrets—and nothing diminishes that limitless love. While other people may evaluate you according to how you perform, what you achieve, or what you look like, Jesus cares for you simply because you belong to Him.

"God shows his love for us in that while we were yet sinners Christ died for us" (Romans 5:8). He didn't wait until we were all cleaned up and deserving of His mercy. He proved His love when we were still a hot mess. And while this love is broad enough to reach every person, it is also intensely personal. In the words of Saint Augustine, "God loves each of us as if there were only one of us." Can you respond to this love by offering Him your heart?

If you aren't ready to do that, perhaps you could start to pray, "Jesus, if You are real, please come and get me." He understands that you feel lost. He knows that finding Him in the midst of the confusion in your heart feels impossible. So invite Him to come. Ask Him to find you. This is a prayer He loves to answer, but you have to ask. No one can do it for you.

Dear Lord,
Please give me more of Yourself. I offer my heart in return. Amen.

Be Still

JANUARY 4

"From the end of the earth I call to you, when my heart is faint. Lead me to the rock that is higher than I." (Psalm 61:2)

There is a rock higher than you. His thoughts are not your thoughts, and His ways are not your ways. But He is not distant. He is very near, and utterly attentive to your cry. He hopes that you will pray big, bold prayers. He hopes that you will see His limitless power, and ask accordingly. But at the same time, He hopes you are able to humbly recognize that your mind is not equal to His. You are finite; He is infinite, and He knows better than you what is best.

Can you trust that your heavenly Father knows what is best for you? This is such an important question—so essential to our prayer life that it's included in the *Compendium of the Catechism of the Catholic Church*, 575: "Filial trust is tested when we think we are not heard. We must therefore ask ourselves if we think God is truly a Father whose will we seek to fulfill, or simply a means to obtain what we want. If our prayer is united to that of Jesus, we know that He gives us much more than this or that gift. We receive the Holy Spirit who transforms our heart."

In Psalm 37:4, we read the promise: "Take delight in the Lord, and he will give you the desires of your heart." Something very interesting happens when we delight in the Lord when we pray: The very desires that God wants us to have are birthed in our souls. Slowly but surely, we become more like Jesus as we begin to want what He wants, when He wants it, how He wants it. We are changed. We are transformed.

Take some time to share your desires with the Lord. Dream wildly. Pray boldly. But never lose sight of the fact that your heavenly Father loves you and will only give you good gifts. And only He knows which gifts are best.

Dear Lord,
Thank You for being so far beyond anything I can wrap my head around. I don't expect to figure You out. You know better than I what is best for me, and You give me nothing less than that. Amen.

JANUARY 5

"The Lord is near to all who call on him, to all who call upon him in truth." (Psalm 145:18)

Have you ever felt you just can't find the time to pray? We're so busy, and although prayer sounds good in theory and we have a strong sense that we'd be better people if we did more of it, we get up and get moving and there doesn't seem to be any room in the day to slow down and talk to God.

That's the reason we often give for not praying. But I don't believe it's truly the underlying issue. I'm not saying that our schedules aren't busy. I just believe that we make time for whatever is most important to us. If I'm honest, when I don't pray, it's usually because I simply don't feel like it. There's something else that I'd rather do. I think I'm going to feel more satisfied by doing something else.

We live in a culture that values productivity, results, and performance. Because prayer, just like love, can't be measured in that way, it's tempting to put it on the back burner. Sometimes it just feels more satisfying to check some things off the to-do list than to sit quietly in prayer.

Whether or not we feel like praying should not determine whether we pray. We shouldn't pray to get something from God; we should pray simply to be with Him. Our willingness (or unwillingness) to "waste" time with Him says a lot about how much we love Him.

Dear Lord,
I want to love You more, I truly do. But if I'm honest, spending time sitting with You is hard. I can't see You. I can't feel You. I ask You a question and I only hear silence. This holds my attention for about ten seconds. Help me to switch my thinking regarding prayer. Help me to see that even if I don't feel like I'm having a mind-blowing spiritual experience, You are excited just that I'm turning my face toward Yours. This is a little hard for me to believe. Do You honestly love me so much that my attention means that much to You? If I believe what the Bible says, then I have to believe that yes, this is how much You love me. Help me to love You in return with the gift of my time. Amen.

Be Still

JANUARY 6

"But as for me, I am filled with power, with the Spirit of the Lord." (Micah 3:8)

Do you look at the Holy Spirit as someone reserved for the special few, those somehow marked by God for a mission and a purpose that you think must not include you? Does He feel out of reach? If that's the case, listen to these words: "Through his grace, the Holy Spirit is the first to awaken faith in us and to communicate to us the new life, which is to 'know the Father and the one whom he has sent, Jesus Christ'" (CCC 684).

Do you know what this means? It means that if you are seeking God, if you feel faith beginning to awaken in your heart, you can be assured that the Spirit's breath is near. He is wooing you to come closer. He wants you. Can you take a little step nearer to Him by sharing with Him your needs? Ask Him to fill your emptiness with Himself.

The Holy Spirit is meek and humble, and He will not force His way into your heart. Revelation 3:20 says that He "stand[s] at the door and knock[s]; If any one hears [His] voice and opens the door, [He] will enter." He waits to be invited in.

If we do invite Him in, one of the things the Holy Spirit does is search our hearts. One of the reasons He does this is to know how best to pray for us. So often we are blind to what is going on inside us. We're pretty quick to justify our actions, but the Holy Spirit searches us, and intercedes for us based on what we truly need. "And he who searches the hearts of men ... intercedes for the saints according to the will of God" (Romans 8:27).

Will you open the door and invite the Holy Spirit in? Will you ask Him to search your heart and bring to the surface things that you might not recognize within yourself? I promise you, as He reveals them, He'll do so gently. And then He'll be right there, giving you the strength and the courage to ask for forgiveness. And He'll provide all you need for transformation in the very areas of your greatest struggle. Invite Him in.

Dear Holy Spirit,
I invite You in. Please fill me with Your presence and search my heart. Help me to see myself through Your eyes—both the areas of my life that need forgiveness and the parts that are bringing You great joy. Amen.

Be Still

JANUARY 7

"Not by might, nor by power, but by my Spirit, says the Lord of hosts." (Zechariah 4:6)

Is there something you are facing that feels overwhelming? Does the mountain you need to climb look terribly steep? Does it appear impossible to reach its summit with all the burdens you are carrying on your back?

God urges you to keep going, to keep climbing. But He doesn't expect you to do it by relying on your own might and power. He wants you to rely on the power of the Holy Spirit. Lay your concerns at His feet. Spread out the obstacles before Him. Ask the Holy Spirit to search your heart for any way those obstacles are rooted in unconfessed sin. If He reveals something, confess it on the spot. Then ask that the power of the Holy Spirit would fill you. Allow Him to intersect your daily life and transform you.

The Holy Spirit is willing to do so much for us, but He is a gracious guest, and waits to be invited. He leaves it up to you. You can decide to just keep Him in the entryway of your heart, or you can invite Him to come all the way in. It all depends on how much power and transformation you really want to experience. Unfortunately, too many of us are afraid to throw open all the doors of our hearts to Him. We say that certain rooms are off-limits. When we do this, we miss out. The rooms we close off are often ones that contain pain that He is just waiting to heal. Or perhaps they are places where we're stuck in bad patterns of behavior, and He wants to set us free. Take some time to pray about the rooms that you are keeping closed off to the Holy Spirit. Can you open the door a crack and invite Him to enter? I promise you, the breath of His presence will be sweet and gentle.

Dear Lord,
Please come into my heart. I give You permission to open the closets, clean what needs cleaning, and make Your home in me. Amen.

Be Still

 JANUARY 8

"I, brethren, could not address you as spiritual man, but as men of the flesh, as infants in Christ. I fed you with milk, not solid food; for you were not ready for it; and even yet you are not ready, for you are still of the flesh. For while there is jealousy and strife among you, are you not of the flesh, and behaving like ordinary men?" (1 Corinthians 3:1–3)

When Saint Paul wrote this to the Corinthian church, he was longing for them to grow up. It wasn't enough that they had been exposed to truth. They needed to choose to be transformed by it. There was so much "meat" Saint Paul was willing to feed them, but he found he had to keep giving them "milk" over and over.

If we're going to mature, then we need to respond to what we read in the Bible. We can grow as quickly or as slowly as we want to. Some of us have come to Bible study later in life, and we feel like we're late to the party. We think to ourselves, "I've wasted so much time! So many people seem to know more than I do!" We wonder if we're ever going to catch up.

Be assured, it doesn't matter when you start. What matters is how you respond to what God is revealing to you at this point. The rate at which you'll grow is up to you.

Dear Lord,
I want to build my relationship with You on a solid foundation. I don't want to skip over any of the basics that are essential to knowing and following You. At the same time, I don't want to hang out in spiritual diapers any longer than is necessary. I want to move upward in maturity! Give me the strength and the desire to put into practice what You reveal to me in the Bible. Help me to resist laziness. May I make growing more like You the highest priority in my life. Amen.

JANUARY 9

"You have commanded your precepts to be kept diligently. O that my ways may be steadfast in keeping your statutes! Then I shall not be put to shame, having my eyes fixed on all your commandments." (Psalm 119:4–6)

Seeing the world from God's perspective is what leads to an abundant life. Left to our own understanding, we have a darkened intellect—one of the consequences of the fall. We need our intellect to be enlightened, to know better. When our intellect is strengthened, it helps inform our decisions.

We will always struggle with our will. We all, by nature, want what we want, when we want it, how we want it. What we are asked to do is to want what God wants, when He wants it, how He wants it. It's a picture of a surrendered life. Studying Scripture helps us to do the right thing because our intellect can take our will by the hand and say, "This is where we're going, whether you like it or not, because this will ultimately be the better choice." Although this decision is the harder one to make, it's the one that leads to the abundant life God has promised us.

We want our lives to matter. At the end of it all, we'll want to see that our choices were the right ones. So what should we do when we're confused about the right thing to do? We need to go to the source of truth. We need to go to the One who made us, who knows the future, and who knows the hidden pitfalls ahead. It was one of Jesus' greatest heartaches to see people He loved walking down the wrong path. He had this to say to them: "You are wrong, because you know neither the Scriptures nor the power of God" (Matthew 22:29). Interestingly, Jesus didn't hold them accountable just for what they did with what they knew. He held them accountable for the things they were capable of learning. Their choice to not know the Scriptures or the power of God was just that—a choice.

We, too, are held accountable for how we respond to the truth that is available to us. For all our excuses, we have to admit, the Bible is accessible to us all. But we need to pick it up and read it. Good intentions don't mean much if they aren't translated into action.

Dear Lord,
It's embarrassing to think that I can find time to read the newspaper or catch up on Facebook and Pinterest, but I unashamedly say that I don't have time to read the Bible. I realize that I have time for whatever I consider most important. Help me to make the most of my time. Help me to carry a Bible with me so that I can turn to You when little pockets of time appear. Amen.

Be Still

JANUARY 10

"Take the sword of the Spirit, which is the word of God." (Ephesians 6:17)

Memorizing Scripture helps us on multiple levels. For one, the Holy Spirit can bring one of the truths of the Bible to our mind just before we might make a wrong choice. It's like a little whisper reminding us of what we know is true, but there's power in it, because we know they are God's words. For example, in the midst of a conversation in which we aren't listening well, the Holy Spirit can bring to mind Proverbs 18:2: "A fool takes no pleasure in understanding, but only in expressing his opinion." This enables us to make a course correction immediately instead of looking back later with regret.

Memorized Scripture can also be used as a weapon in the spiritual life. When negative thoughts and lies run through our minds, we can take a Bible verse and use it as a weapon to kick out the lie and embrace the truth. Verses that speak of God's unconditional love and forgiveness and our new identity in Christ are especially powerful for this kind of battle. When we feel defeated and like we'll never change, when we falsely assume that God must be ready to give up on us, the Holy Spirit can remind us of 2 Corinthians 5:17: "If any one is in Christ, [she] is a new creation; the old has passed away, behold, the new has come."

Dear Lord,
Please renew my thinking so that I don't get defeated before I even begin, convincing myself that memorizing Scripture is only for the super spiritual. Help me to see myself through Your eyes. You know that I am capable of so much more than I give myself credit for. This isn't because You see all my innate untapped abilities. It's because You know the difference it will make if I depend on You and let You do the work through me. So I come to You, aware of my weaknesses, but assured that "I can do all things in [Christ] who strengthens me" [Philippians 4:13]. Amen.

JANUARY 11

"A thorn was given me in the flesh . . ." (2 Corinthians 12:7)

Even when we are struggling with a thorn in our side, God still asks us to love. He doesn't ask us to scrape the bottom of the barrel of our own resources and just do the best we can. He asks us to drink from His endless supply of grace, poured out on us through the sacraments.

Sometimes all we can do is lift up weary, empty hands and ask for the filling of His grace. I can remember a particularly difficult time of my life when I could barely find the strength to pray. I knew I needed to persevere in loving my family, but the most basic things seemed so very hard. My prayer became little more than the outstretching of my empty hands. My words were few, but the physical action meant a lot. It was my way of telling the Lord that I had nothing to offer, and I needed Him to fill me with His grace. I went to daily Mass and found that simply placing my body where I could receive grace had an enormous impact on my spirit. I believe the Eucharist gave me the strength that I lacked. Bit by bit, I was restored.

God speaks into our weariness. He asks us to let go of the "try hard" life. He offers us His grace, and asks us to offer it to others in turn. But for us to receive His grace, there are some things we need to put down. We need to lay down our self-reliance. Our desire to keep everyone happy, the habit of people-pleasing—that's got to go, too. So does our determination to always be comfortable. Sometimes we have to get uncomfortable for a while in order to experience all God has for us. As Saint Augustine said, "God gives where he finds empty hands."

Spend some time talking to God about what area of your life feels exhausting. Ask Him to help you let go of expectations—those others have of you and those you have of others. Ask Him to replace the expectations with gratitude for the grace He extravagantly pours over you.

Dear Lord,
Our hope lies in You. The renewal and strength that we long for doesn't come from the spa or from perfect circumstances. It shows up when we have nothing to offer, and it fills up our empty hands. Thank You for the grace that strengthens and sustains us. Amen.

Be Still

JANUARY 12

"A soft answer turns away wrath, but a harsh word stirs up anger." (Proverbs 15:1)

Most of us fall into one of two camps. Either we hate conflict and have little difficulty keeping our mouths shut, or we have no trouble standing up for ourselves and often run our mouths more than we should. Both are pitfalls that keep us from dealing with conflict the way God desires.

We might assume that God always wants us to ignore mistreatment, but that would be a misunderstanding of Him. God is truth, God is justice, and God is mercy. He doesn't just pursue those things, He *is* those things. Those qualities are such a part of His nature that He cannot be separated from them.

This means that in any situation we find ourselves in, God wants truth to prevail. He doesn't want us to say it doesn't matter when it does. The conflict-avoidant among us need to grab hold of the courage that the Holy Spirit provides and speak up far more often than we'd like. We are called to speak the truth in love. This requires *speaking*, not just sweeping things under the rug. We can speak truth graciously and softly. Doing so will lessen the likelihood that the response will be aggressive.

God also wants His children to always show mercy. We show mercy when we say, "There is probably more to this situation than meets the eye." Mercy helps us to pause and ask questions to clarify, instead of blurting out the first thing on our mind. Mercy moves slowly. It sees. It notices. It gives the benefit of the doubt. Those of us with a strong inner sense of justice will find it hard to pause when offended. But doing so increases the likelihood that our words will be gentle instead of harsh and therefore received instead of rejected.

When we are offended, we are faced with a choice. We can stir things up and create more of a mess, or we can do what we can to defuse the situation. A gentle answer is defusing. An honest answer helps us not to end up in the same situation later. Speaking the truth in love is the goal, and the Holy Spirit can help us to do it.

Dear Lord,
Help me to have courage to speak honestly when I am afraid of conflict. Help me to pause and be merciful when my injustice alarm has been set off. May my words be Your words. Amen.

JANUARY 13

"Have I not commanded you? Be strong and of good courage; be not frightened, neither be dismayed; for the Lord your God is with you wherever you go." (Joshua 1:9)

On what basis can God command us to be free from fear? He can do this because He promises to be with us wherever we go. His presence makes all the difference.

God dwells within us through the Holy Spirit. In John 14:16 Jesus said, "I will ask the Father, and he will give you another Counselor, to be with you for ever." The Counselor is another name for the Holy Spirit. This means that no matter what we face, we don't face it alone. We may not know what to say, but we can ask the Holy Spirit to speak through us. We may lack the courage to move forward, but we can ask the Holy Spirit within us to embolden us with *His* courage.

God also goes before us. "It is the Lord who goes before you; he will be with you, he will not fail you or forsake you; do not fear or be dismayed" (Deuteronomy 31:8). Whatever fear you may have of the future, God is already there. He is not limited by time. He can be with you right now, and He can go before you into the future. This is exactly what He does, and because of this, we never encounter any circumstance that is a surprise to God. If it has touched us, He touched it first, and made sure that it wasn't too much for us to handle with His grace. It might be too much for us to handle alone, but with Him, we can endure all things.

One of the enemy's favorite tactics is to get us to focus on our imagination—on all the undesirable things that we can picture happening in the future. God's grace is offered to us in the present moment, not in the midst of our imaginings. The more we can discipline ourselves to stay in the present moment with God, the better off we will be. Check your thoughts when you are feeling afraid. What are you thinking about? The future? God is already there. What is going on in the present, in this exact moment? Is God not sustaining you? Are you still here? Yes, you are. You are still standing. There is always sufficient grace available for the present moment.

Dear Lord,
Keep me in the present moment. May I be disciplined in my thoughts so that instead of imagining future catastrophe, I focus on how You are sustaining me right now. Amen.

Be Still

JANUARY 14

"Mercy triumphs over justice." (James 2:13)

God the Father is completely captivated by you. He loves you. When His eyes scan the crowd and catch sight of you, He lights up with pride and says, "There's my girl."

Do you find that hard to believe? Circumstances in your past and present can make it difficult to grasp this truth, but here's the thing: Something can be true even when it doesn't feel true. Because of this, two things need to happen for us to begin understanding the heart of our heavenly Father.

First, we need to take the time to get to know God the Father better, the way He has revealed Himself in Scripture. We get ourselves into trouble when we try to figure things out based simply on what we currently have in our minds and how things appear to be in the moment. The Bible is the best place to start if we are having trouble understanding who God is. It's in His own words. It's His own witness.

 Second, we need to stop judging God by our circumstances, and start judging our circumstances by a bigger view of God. All too often, we look at the things we have that we don't want and the things we want but don't have, and conclude that God is holding out on us or doesn't care. That's what results when we judge God by our circumstances. When we develop a bigger, wider-angled view of God, we see that there is more to our circumstances, sufferings, and limitations than meets the eye. God is at work, even when we don't see evidence of it.

It can be hard to believe that you have a heavenly Father who delights in you, especially if you have been basing whether this is true on how pleasant your current circumstances are. Another thing that can get in the way of opening up to the love of God the Father is awareness of all the ways you have messed up. Perhaps you look at your behavior and wonder if you're beyond the reach of God's mercy. Do you feel you've failed one time too many or that what you've done is just too awful to be forgiven? If this is the case, please hear this truth: There is no sin beyond the reach of God's mercy. Mercy always triumphs over justice.

Dear Lord,
Help me to rest with this truth on my heart: "As far as the east is from the west, so far has God removed our sin from us" [Psalm 103:12]. Amen.

Be Still

JANUARY 15

"I appeal to you therefore, brethren, by the mercies of God, to present your bodies as a living sacrifice, holy and acceptable to God, which is your spiritual worship." (Romans 12:1)

Our culture insists that you are free to do whatever you want with your body. The message is, "It's yours, so as long as you feel comfortable, it's all good." Romans 12:1 presents a different perspective, one rooted in a far deeper respect for your body's beauty and sacredness. God says that what you do with your body matters. It's precious to Him. He created every part of your body for a high and holy purpose. Offering your body as a living sacrifice to God elevates it in importance and infuses everything you do with meaning.

It's been said that one of the problems with a living sacrifice is that it keeps crawling off the altar. Even when we make a decision to give our all—to lay ourselves on the altar before God—discomfort, distraction, and distrust can all cause our bodies to slide off and head in another direction. We might think we're going on our merry way, but where we end up is far from happy. Why? Because God created us to worship Him, and anything other than that leaves us dissatisfied.

When we think of worship, we often assume it means showing up at Mass. It's often limited in our minds to a place we go, rather than an attitude we assume or choices we make. The Catechism of the Catholic Church says, "The moral life is spiritual worship" (CCC 2031). This means that every time we make a moral choice, we are worshipping something. We might be worshipping our comfort, our reputation, pleasure, or accomplishment. Perhaps we're worshipping another person. To say that we don't worship anything is simply not true. We were created to worship. We all worship something or someone.

When God lays out guidelines for the moral life, He isn't trying to spoil our fun. He isn't being a cosmic killjoy. He is actually focused on us experiencing the highest possible level of pleasure. He doesn't want us to content ourselves with mud pies when a heavenly feast is on offer.

What choice is being presented to you today? What's causing you to feel uncomfortable, distracted, or short on trust? Are those feelings tempting you to slide off the altar and pursue something with more short-term pleasure? Hit pause and think about where that road actually leads in the long run.

Dear Lord,
Help me to weigh the long-term benefits of worshipping You with my body over the short-term benefits of pleasure in the moment. Amen.

Be Still

JANUARY 16

"But Ruth said, 'Entreat me not to leave you or to return from following you; for where you go I will go, and where you lodge I will lodge; your people shall be my people, and your God my God.'" (Ruth 1:16)

This was the response of Ruth to her mother-in-law, Naomi, when Naomi encouraged her to go back to her own people in Moab. Naomi had lost both her husband and her two sons while living in a foreign country. Moab was Ruth's home, and it made sense for her to stay there while Naomi returned to her own people. If she went with Naomi to Israel, it was likely an acceptance of perpetual widowhood. Foreigners weren't looked upon kindly. In addition, Ruth had been barren throughout her marriage, so there were no children to comfort her or give her hope for the future.

Yet Ruth chose loyalty. Following Naomi was the harder road, but she did not want Naomi to walk it alone. Both women had endured terrible loss. Perhaps Ruth thought her presence would be a comfort. At least it would debunk the lie that Naomi was all alone.

Could it be that Ruth's infertility made her heart more tender to others' pain? Author Carolyn Custis James writes of what she learned through her own experience of infertility:

> God uses suffering to open our eyes to see more of him than we would under rosier conditions. At some point, we grow weary of tears and our thrashings die down. We are quiet—not because we've gotten answers to our troubling questions, but because we are spent. When we are in pain, we may get the sense that God has vanished from our lives. In truth, the opposite has happened. God meets us in our pain. The death of his son drew [author Nicholas] Wolterstorff limping into a deeper, almost frightening connection with God. "The world has a hole in it now," he sorrowed. "I shall look at the world through tears. Perhaps I shall see things that dry-eyed I could not see."[3]

We choose how we respond to pain, loss, and disappointment. These circumstances offer us many choices. We can choose to go deeper with God, to grow bitter, to let the heart grow numb, or to be overcome with anger, to name a few. What will be your choice?

Dear Lord,
Would You reveal to me the lessons in my hurt that I might miss if I were dry-eyed? Please use every bit of my pain to teach me something I'd otherwise not learn. May nothing be wasted. Amen.

JANUARY 17

"If any of you lacks wisdom, let him ask God, who gives to all men generously and without reproaching, and it will be given him." (James 1:5)

"What am I supposed to do?" How often we experience trials that leave us with no idea of what our next step should be. If only there were instructions for every specific situation we might find ourselves in. Even if we didn't want to do what was recommended, at least we wouldn't feel so confused.

When we are facing a trial, we need more than knowledge. Knowledge is information, but wisdom is the ability to apply knowledge to day-to-day living. Wisdom is what allows us to put the mess of our lives back together.

So what do we do when we don't know what we should do? We ask God for wisdom. God's response is always to give it; it's never to shake His head at us, wondering why we are so slow. He understands that we lack His perspective, and He wants to lead us. Often we turn to every other possible source of knowledge before we turn to Him. He wants us to come to Him first. He often leads us to His wisdom through the advice of other people. But we should start by asking Him.

If you don't know if you should move forward in a certain direction, here are three boxes that you should check off before proceeding. The first is Scripture and Church teaching. If what you are planning/thinking is in agreement with those two sources of wisdom, you can check the first box. The next confirmation you need comes from the advice of holy people you respect. Who you listen to at a time like this is really important. Ask advice from people whose lives reveal their humble dependence on God. When their advice is in agreement with what you've read in Scripture and Church teaching, you can check the second box. The third box is your gut. This is the least reliable of all three, but it still has value. If you feel unrest in your spirit, or by contrast, if you feel peace, that is telling you something. When all three of those boxes are checked, you can proceed, trusting that wisdom has been revealed to you.

Dear Lord,
When I feel confused, may my first step be prayer. Your wisdom surpasses the internet and even the best human advice. May I start with You. Amen.

Be Still

JANUARY 18

"Do you not know that if you present yourselves to someone as obedient slaves, you are slaves of the one whom you obey, either of sin, which leads to death, or of obedience, which leads to righteousness?" (Romans 6:16)

For someone who likes words and lots of them, editing a book can be hard work. After poring over each sentence and getting to the point where she loves them all, no author wants to hear that she has to cut hundreds of words. But that is exactly what a writer is told and tends to be reluctant to do. When I was in the midst of that very process, I received great advice from an editor: "You have to kill your precious." To the writer, every word seems golden. But unless you "kill your precious" and get rid of the parts that are unnecessary, the finished work won't be as impactful.

Following Christ allows us opportunities to kill lots of precious. We all have those sins that we like to justify, the ones that we hide and don't think matter much. It makes me think of Gollum in *The Lord of the Rings* and the way he called the ring he coveted "my precious." This was something that he had possessed that wasn't actually good for him, but he longed for it nevertheless.

What is it that you reach for when you are longing for security or comfort or an escape? Maybe it's attention from someone who doesn't belong to you. Perhaps it's too much wine. Maybe it's shopping and spending money you don't have. It can be porn, or Netflix, or eating food to try to fill a void in the heart . . . anything that distracts or diverts. Maybe it's your ego that needs to die a death. Instead of a hearty dose of accomplishments and accolades, you are actually needing to grow in humility. Even as I write this, it all sounds quite horrible to me. I suppose it does to us all, which is exactly why we reach for these things. They feel so good in the short term.

God is asking us to "kill our precious" not because he is out to spoil our fun, but because He knows that's the very thing that is holding us back from the life that is truly life. Which do I want more, short-term gain or long-term glory?

Dear Lord,
This is the sin I am wanting to play around with: _____ . This is what looks so good to me in the short term. But I want to be a saint, more than I want the quick thrill that sin might bring. And I want to be free. Please kill my precious. Amen.

Be Still

JANUARY 19

"Truly, to see your face is like seeing the face of God." (Genesis 33:10)

A man named Jacob spoke these words to his brother, Esau. You might think a huge compliment like that was born out of a beautiful, loving family relationship. Nothing could be further from the truth. Jacob and Esau were twins who had been rivals even in the womb. Their childhood was marked by favoritism, competition, and deceit. The final straw: Jacob wanted Esau's inheritance, so he deceived his blind father into thinking he was his brother, and stole it. It made Esau so mad that Jacob had to flee for his life.

Decades had passed, and Jacob was returning home. He had no idea how Esau would receive him. He knew he deserved an angry and bitter reception. But Esau surprised his brother and showed grace. He offered undeserved favor and unconditional acceptance. He proved that the bond of family was stronger than sin. That's what caused Jacob to say, "I have seen your face, which is like seeing the face of God."

God gazes at us in that same way, only with greater purity, love, and delight. Because we have been adopted as God's daughters, His divine blood runs through our veins and proves stronger than any sin. "And because you are [daughters], God has sent the Spirit of his Son into [your] hearts, crying, 'Abba! Father!' So you are no longer a slave, but a [daughter], and if a [daughter], then an [heiress] through God" (Galatians 4:6–7). Because we are family, we receive unmerited grace and are accepted just as we are. Soak up that truth. When God looks at you, He says, "Hello, beautiful." He adores you. He delights in you.

And what does He want us to do with all that grace that He's poured over us? He tells us in Ephesians 5:1–2, "Therefore be imitators of God, as beloved children. And walk in love."

If we're going to imitate Him, then we have to ask ourselves: What do our faces communicate to those we encounter? Do people leave your presence feeling like they've seen the face of God? Or does your face tell people that they don't matter much, because you're busy checking out the status update of some old acquaintance? Does your face tell people that they aren't accepted, because their behavior doesn't match your opinion of the right way to do things? What is it like to be on the other side of you?

Dear Lord,
May my face shine with Your love so that everyone I meet catches a glimpse of You in my smile. Amen.

Be Still

JANUARY 20

"Continue steadfastly in prayer." (Colossians 4:2)

A risk we all run when we love others lavishly is neglecting to take care of ourselves. What begins as a passion of the heart—a pure desire to help—can actually place us in a dangerous position in which we find it hard to stay faithful. When we coast on the fumes of a life that lacks spiritual discipline, we can find that we begin to blend in and are no longer offering hope and a better way. We're just like everyone else, no different.

Years ago, I was driving home from my parents' house with my daughter. Barreling down the highway at 70 mph, we noticed smoke billowing from the hood. I pulled over just in time, as our engine blew up. We couldn't believe it. The car had shown no signs of any trouble up to this point. Imagine my mortification when I realized that the engine had blown up simply because I had *never* changed the oil. I guess I just got busy with life and forgot. I didn't take seriously how essential it is to follow the basic directions for taking care of a car.

In that same way, we can be lax about the importance of spiritual discipline. We can coast through life, much as I was in my car, thinking that things that we've done in the past are going to keep us going indefinitely. We can have heart and passion and still lose everything if we ignore these practices.

What does this look like? It's going through life too busy to pray. It's having a schedule that is so full of activities and appointments that there is no time for meaningful relationships and a connection to a faith community. It's getting up and getting going in the morning without taking time to read Scripture. It's having priorities out of order, so that no time is taken to protect and nurture important relationships.

Prayer needs to be the most protected part of our schedules. Morning prayer has the benefit of sending you into the day with a transformed mind-set. If you can't pray first thing in the morning, then look for the first pocket of calm and claim it for Christ, not your phone. Putting Him first in practice and not just in theory will change your life.

Dear Lord,
Help me to consider time with You the most important thing on my calendar. May I write it down and keep my appointment with You with the same diligence I would keep any other commitment. Amen.

Be Still

JANUARY 21

"There is one whose rash words are like sword thrusts, but the tongue of the wise brings healing." (Proverbs 12:18)

Words are so powerful and, unfortunately, easily misunderstood. How often do our imaginations run wild as we try to fill in the blanks and understand? All too often the wrong conclusions are reached. Hurt results, and hearts protectively pull back. We quickly get confused and lose perspective. All that was said or implied is filtered through a cloudy lens of past experiences and assumptions. We're apt to attribute motive without all the facts. And all the while, the devil claps his hands, delighted to see us watering these seeds of discord with mental rehashing of all that was said. He knows that the sadder we feel, the less likely we'll be to enter the spiritual battlefield and focus on what really matters.

What is at stake? A lot. There is a hurting world out there that is just desperate for the women of our generation to band together and do something about it. We often feel defeated as we focus on the culture or pending legislation or the mountain of problems around us. We see these things as obstacles that are getting in the way of needed change. But what really limits the healing movement of God are the things within us that we ignore and justify: Gossip. Lack of forgiveness. Bitterness. Pride. Anger. These are the things that divide us. They weaken us and cause us to quit. They block the flow of the Holy Spirit within us.

This is one of the last things that Jesus focused on before He walked to the Garden of Gethsemane to face the cross. He prayed, "I pray also for those who will believe in me through [the disciples'] message, that all of them [us] may be one, Father, just as you are in me and I am in you" (John 17:20–21). He prayed for our unity.

Are you nursing a hurt? Are you rehashing someone's words that have stabbed your heart? And has it caused you to pull back? Could it be that the devil has you exactly where he wants you because he is afraid of the good you might do if you released the hurt and forgave?

Dear Lord,
Let the change start with me. Help me to identify the problems in my own heart before critiquing the problems around me. Amen.

Be Still

JANUARY 22

"He who sows sparingly will also reap sparingly, and he who sows bountifully will also reap bountifully." (2 Corinthians 9:6)

Imagine a farmer has a finite amount of seeds. He doesn't want to waste them, so he sows only a small amount. The rest he keeps stored away. Fast-forward to harvest time. True, he has more seeds, but if he had planted them, he would have had a far greater harvest.

What is precious to you and as a result hard to share? Is it money? Time? Relationships? Power? Are you holding back any of these things because you're afraid that if you're generous, you'll end up with nothing?

We are promised that because we serve an infinite God, we can never be outdone in generosity. When we sow bountifully—when we give what we have extravagantly—we will reap bountifully. More will come back to us than we gave.

In 2 Corinthians 9:7–8 we read, "God loves a cheerful giver. And God is able to provide you with every blessing in abundance, so that you may always have enough of everything and may provide in abundance for every good work." When we see an opportunity to give of our time, talent, or treasure, we're wise to remember who is the source of all the good we are and have. It's God. When we give, He replenishes the supply. He loves a cheerful giver—one who knows that we serve a God of abundance, not of scarcity.

Sometimes the reward will come to us here on earth. In Matthew 19:29, Jesus said, "Every one who has left houses or brothers or sisters or father or mother or children or lands, for my name's sake, will receive a hundredfold, and inherit eternal life." The richest rewards will be given to us in heaven.

What opportunity to give is in front of you today? Is it something that feels especially sacrificial? Ask God to do the giving through you and to replenish you while you give. God is the ultimate cheerful giver and it brings Him delight to surprise you with His generosity. Try to do the same today. You might be surprised at the joy that results.

Dear Lord,
Help my giving to be cheerful. May I go to You with my needs and serve as a conduit for Your blessings—not grabbing them and holding on to them for my own pleasure, but passing them on to others so we all can share in the pleasure of Your generosity. Amen.

Be Still

JANUARY 23

"Be still and know that I am God. I am exalted among the nations, I am exalted in the earth." (Psalm 46:10)

Do you have an agitated soul? Are anxious thoughts weighing you down? Does your stomach feel unsettled with all you have to do?

God sees all the things that you are carrying. All the people you are concerned about, all the ways you fear you are falling short, all the anxieties about what might happen tomorrow—God is aware of all of it.

He invites you to be still, despite all the thoughts that are clamoring for your attention. He waits for you. Imagine your soul as a home (because it is where God resides in you, through the Holy Spirit). Picture a warm fire in the fireplace and two cozy chairs by the hearth. You are running out the door to solve your problems and get important things done, and God looks at your retreating back, wishing that you would turn around and notice Him gently beckoning you to come and sit down. He knows that if you would let Him in on all that troubles you, He could take care of things far more quickly and thoroughly than you can. He's there every morning and every night before you go to bed. He sits all day, available to you.

Even if you don't take the time to tell Him all that is on your mind, He already knows it. This means it doesn't really matter how perfectly you can explain everything, because God gets it. He understands.

You have a choice. You can carry your burdens and try to solve them on your own, or you can lay them at the feet of God. If you choose the latter, you have given them to the One who is able to figure it all out—better than you can. His love surrounds you and reaches into the future, preparing the way for you. It reaches into the past and brings healing. He is in the present and is always punctual. While God's timing differs from ours, He is never late.

Dear Lord,
My heart is anxious and worried. Please take care of everything. I ask You to unravel these specific knots in my life: _____. Jesus, I trust in in You. Amen.

- reversion of my children
- the healing of their hearts
- courage, faith and hope on the journey
- Savannah to heal from her past and know that she is loved

Be Still

JANUARY 24

"For God so loved the world that he gave his only-begotten Son, that whoever believes in him should not perish but have eternal life." (John 3:16)

This is one of the most beloved verses of the Bible, and for good reason. It summarizes the extent of God's love and reveals who is the recipient of it. Who is the object of God's love, revealed in John 3:16? It's the world. This was a radical thought for the religious people of Jesus' day. They knew that God loved, but assumed that His love was reserved for the Jewish people. To hear that He loved everyone was new and scandalous to many. God loves His own—His people—but His love extends beyond. He loves the world and all who are in it. The arms of God are wide enough to embrace all of mankind.

This is what the Catechism of the Catholic Church says about the intensity of God's love: "God's love for Israel is compared to a father's love for his son. His love for his people is stronger than a mother's for her children. God loves his people more than a bridegroom his beloved; his love will be victorious over even the worst infidelities and will extend to his most precious gift: 'God so loved the world that he gave his only Son'" (CCC 219).

Do you have secret sins that you are certain disqualify you from receiving God's love? This bears repeating: God's "love will be victorious over even the worst infidelities." There is nothing beyond the reach of God's love. His mercy is always enough to cover and cleanse us from every single sin. There is nothing He will not forgive, if we but ask.

God loves the entire world, but the entire world does not receive all that He offers. His offer is dependent upon each person, individually, choosing to receive it. Whether we reject it because we feel unworthy or because we don't think we need it, the end results is the same: We don't receive the gift. And what is the gift? It's Jesus Himself, and the divine life that He brings. It's the promise of eternal life. It's on offer to all, but we must choose to receive it.

If someone gives you a gift but you leave it unopened on the shelf, have you truly received it? No. In that same way, God's gift of love, forgiveness, and eternal life is offered to you, but you need to open your hands and heart and accept it.

Dear Lord,
Please forgive me for underestimating the breadth and depth of Your love. I want to receive the gift of Jesus' presence. Amen.

JANUARY 25

"There is no fear in love, but perfect love casts out fear." (1 John 4:18)

Why is there no fear in love? True love always wants what is best for the other person. What often *claims* to be love can be self-serving, possessive, and objectifying. Love is not so much a feeling as it is a decision. Love should be immovable, sacrificial, pure, steadfast, selfless, patient, gentle, yet fierce when protection is needed.

There are a number of different Greek words for *love* used in the New Testament, but they all are translated as this word. These are different forms of love, and it's helpful to understand the difference if we want to see how God's perfect love is capable of driving out fear.

The different types of love are eros, storge, philia, and agape. Eros is romantic or sexual love. It's a beautiful form of love, but one that God says needs to be protected by the commitment of marriage. Storge is familial love. This is the bond of loyalty and trust that ideally develops within the family unit. Philia is brotherly love. It is the kind of love we are called as Christians to offer one another. When Jesus said, "By this all men will know that you are my disciples, if you have love for one another" (John 13:35), He was talking about philia love. Agape is the highest form of love, and it is divine. This is the love God has for us. It is utterly self-sacrificing, unconditional, perfect, and relentless. When John 13:1 says that Jesus "loved his own who were in the world, he loved them to the end," the word *agape* is used.

Can fear be found in eros love? Most definitely, and especially when it's being experienced without the commitment of the covenant of marriage. The fear of rejection or abandonment will run high with that kind of love. Storge love? Yes, because even the most devoted parents make mistakes, siblings hurt each other purposely and inadvertently, and the hurts suffered in families imprint on us in foundational ways. How about philia love? In the words of Job, "All my intimate friends abhor me, and those whom I loved have turned against me" (Job 19:19).

Only agape love—divine love, love that comes from God Himself—drives out fear. It is God's love that is utterly steadfast and safe. We can count on it, rest in it, and trust it.

Dear Lord,
May I rest in Your love. May I stop defining love by all the ways people have failed me, and may I let You surround me with agape love, driving all fear from my heart. Amen.

Be Still

JANUARY 26

"For everything there is a season, and a time for every matter under heaven." (Ecclesiastes 3:1)

By many measures, our generation is characterized by stress, exhaustion, and anxiety. Yet we have never had more modern conveniences promising to make life simpler and easier. Much of the "improvements" we experience have decreased our need for manual labor, but have also caused us to be more isolated than ever before. Is there a better way?

In Ecclesiastes 3:1, King Solomon advises that we recognize that life has seasons. We don't have to do everything all at once. Whenever we try to do in one season something that is intended for a later one, we end up stressed. Having the patience to wait, to delay gratification, helps reduce the pressure of an overloaded schedule.

He says that there is a time for every matter under heaven. We know that to be true in the sense that things happen whether we want them to or not. Life progresses (and picks up speed as we get older), and this is beyond our control. While Solomon's words are meant to comfort, they can also cause us to feel resignation. Things will happen regardless of what we do, so why bother?

What helps infuse meaning into all the events that intersect our lives is experiencing them in the context of meaningful relationships. This requires slowing down and making time for one another with no screens in reach. When we do this, we can help one another process the passing of time, the events in our current season that we find difficult, and the dreams we have for future seasons.

We often come up with our best ideas and solutions for our problems on our own, when someone offers us a listening ear. The Holy Spirit within us is continuously offering us guidance, but He can be hard to hear. When a friend provides a safe space, we can externally process what is going on in our hearts. When we invite the Holy Spirit to be present in the conversation, we will find that we have often unraveled the knots and life feels a little lighter. Can you offer this safe space to someone you love? Can you refrain from offering advice and just let him or her unravel how this current season is going? Do you have a friend who can offer this to you?

Dear Lord,
Help me to remember that there is always time for the things You have asked me to do. If I am running out of time, could it be that I am doing something You have not asked of me? Amen.

Be Still

JANUARY 27

"But [the older brother] was angry and refused to go in. His father came out and entreated him, but he answered his father . . . 'I never disobeyed your command; yet you never gave me a kid, that I might make merry with my friends. But when this son of yours came, who has devoured your living with harlots, you killed for him the fatted calf!'" (Luke 15:28–29)

The only thing that can limit Christ's forgiveness is our refusal to ask for it. This is why it's so critical that we recognize whether we are more like the prodigal son or his older brother. Typically, the "younger son" knows that what he is doing is wrong. He knows he needs forgiveness. The older son, though, can be easily blinded by self-righteousness.

We don't need forgiveness just for the bad things we've done. We also need it for the good things we've done for the wrong reasons. If we do good things in order to earn our salvation, we have put ourselves in Jesus' place. We have made the decision (consciously or not) to be our own savior. We have gotten so busy trying to save ourselves that we have lost sight of our need for rescue.

Are you trying to control your life through your performance?
Do you feel that obeying God should result in a smoother road ahead?
Do you think you might be trying to earn God's love and salvation?
Is prayer a way to increase the likelihood of getting what you want, or is it a time of intimacy with your friend?

I pray that reflecting on those questions doesn't cause you to feel condemned. I know that's a risk. We want so badly to get it right, and when we realize that we've been doing something good for the wrong reasons, our anger can turn inward. "How could I? Why can't I ever get it right?" That voice of condemnation does not come from Jesus. "There is therefore now no condemnation for those who are in Christ Jesus" (Romans 8:1). The Holy Spirit convicts us (this is different from condemning us) in order to draw us into a healthy relationship with God. God wants to be wanted for Himself, not for the things He gives. He offers you the gift of limitless forgiveness so that anything between your heart and His can be cleared away.

Dear Lord,
I confess that my self-dependence has kept me from depending on You. Please forgive me. Thank You for being my Father, for running to me and blanketing me in forgiveness and mercy. Amen.

Be Still

JANUARY 28

> "Oh Lord, you have searched me and known me! You know when I sit down and when I rise up; you discern my thoughts from afar." (Psalm 139:1–2)

God knows us better than we know ourselves, but our self-perception can get pretty messed up. There are times we go too easy on ourselves, excusing things that God takes seriously. Under other circumstances, we can go to the opposite extreme and hopelessly condemn ourselves. This is why there is enormous benefit in unpacking our sins alongside a priest who can guide us objectively.

In his book *Interior Freedom*, Father Jacques Philippe writes about how important it is for us to have a realistic view of ourselves:

> One of the most essential conditions for God's grace to act in our lives is saying yes to what we are and to the situations in which we find ourselves. That is because God is "realistic." His grace does not operate on our imaginings, ideals, or dreams. It works on reality . . . The person God loves with the tenderness of a Father, the person he wants to touch and to transform with his love, is not the person we'd have liked to be or ought to be. It's the person we are. God doesn't love "ideal persons" or "virtual beings." He loves actual, real people.[4]

What we need in confession is an honest, truthful assessment that brings us back to an awareness of who we are and whose we are. We are beloved, and we belong. This message is at the heart of the sacrament of penance. This is the grace God is whispering to our souls.

Father Paul Farren has this to say about God's message to us in the confessional:

> When we think about the sacrament of Reconciliation our thoughts most often focus on ourselves and our sinfulness. The role of God in some sense might even appear secondary. However, the sacrament of Reconciliation is primarily that sacred place and moment when God confesses. . . . What does God confess? God confesses his love, his forgiveness, his gratitude, his confidence, his trust and his belief in us.[5]

Dear Lord,
Thank You for Your love, Your forgiveness, Your gratitude, Your confidence, Your trust, and Your belief in me. Amen.

Be Still

JANUARY 29

"[May] the eyes of your heart [be] enlightened, that you may know what is the hope to which he has called you." (Ephesians 1:18)

When we experience distance in our relationship with God, it is not because He has moved away from us. It's because we hide in fear, hang our heads in shame, or stick up our noses in pride. We'll do anything to avoid making eye contact with God. It reminds me of times my kids have done something wrong and I'm trying to discipline them. Sometimes they respond with their arms folded, staring at the floor in anger. They are mad that they've been caught. Other times their face is in their hands, and they can't stop crying because they are so upset for messing up. No matter what the heart attitude, what I really want them to do is look me in the eye. I want this for two reasons. One is so they will know that I'm serious about what I'm saying. But I also want them to see the unconditional love in my eyes.

When God invites us to the sacrament of penance, He's asking us to look Him in the eye. He wants to make eye contact with us. In that moment, we can see ourselves from His perspective. Yes, our sin is serious. He isn't saying it doesn't matter. But it doesn't diminish His love for us. In the confessional, we look the Lord in the eye and experience a moment of deep tenderness as He whispers, "It's OK. You're safe here with me. You can stop hiding."

The Lord is inviting you to come and gaze into His eyes of mercy. He's offering you hope for a fresh start. Oh, I pray that the eyes of your heart would be enlightened, and that the darkness of shame would be chased away. Shame keeps your eyes cast down. But God is cupping your face in His hands and calling you to look up.

Dear Lord,
I get so nervous at the thought of looking in Your eyes. I don't know if I'm ready to see myself reflected in them. I feel shame over things I've said and done, and I wonder how You could possibly forgive me. But then I look at the cross, and am reminded that while I was still a sinner, You died for me. Your love for me isn't dependent on what I do. It depends on what You have done for me. So give me the confidence to approach Your throne of grace. I know I am promised that what I will encounter there is mercy—always, without exception. Amen.

Your love for me is not compromised by my sins. ♡

Be Still

JANUARY 30

"For freedom Christ has set us free; stand fast therefore, and do not submit again to a yoke of slavery." (Galatians 5:1)

All too often, we take our freedom and use it to step right back into the bondage of slavery to sin. We get into bad habits that we don't feel able to break. We harbor bitterness and it keeps our hearts in a vise grip. Our words seem to take on a life of their own and are out of our mouths before we can stop them. We feel dominated by sin, and aren't sure how to get free.

This is where the sacrament of penance comes in. We don't go to the confessional just for forgiveness. There is more. The spiritual effects of the sacrament of penance are described in CCC 1496, which says toward the end that the sacrament gives us "an increase of spiritual strength for the Christian battle."

This is it. This is the secret to growing stronger spiritually. When we receive absolution in the sacrament of penance, we receive supernatural grace to help us go back out into our lives fortified in the very areas where we feel the weakest. We get a second wind and find that we are able to keep pursuing the summit. Theologian Scott Hahn describes it this way:

> Through confession, we begin to heal. We begin to get our story straight and stop deceiving ourselves. We come home to resume our place in the family of God. We begin to know peace. None of this comes easily. Confession doesn't make change easy but it does make it possible. It is not a quick fix, but it is a sure cure. We need to go back to the sacrament, and go again, and keep going back, because life is a marathon, not a forty-yard dash. We'll often want to stop, but like a distance runner, we'll need to press on for our second wind, and third, and fourth. In this case, we can count on the wind coming, because it's the "wind" of the Holy Spirit.[6]

He is waiting for you. He is longing to fill you with the peace and freedom that come from hearing that you are beloved, that you belong, that you are forgiven.

"The look in his eyes is the purest, truest, tenderest, most loving, and most hope-filled in this world."[7] —Father Jacques Philippe

Dear Lord,
"Where the Spirit of the Lord is, there is freedom." (2 Corinthians 3:17) Please forgive me and set me free. Amen.

I do feel peaceful Lord when I leave confession Lord — light and sleepy — like all my cares have been taken over. Thank you!

JANUARY 31

"I am the bread of life; he who comes to me shall not hunger." (John 6:35)

When Jesus spoke these words, the people who had been following Him "murmured at him." Who did He think He was, making a claim like that? But instead of backing down because of their critical response to Him, Jesus spoke even more assertively. He went on to say that He was the living bread that came down from heaven, which a man can eat and not die. He said that if they ate that bread, they'd live forever. This made the people even more angry, as they argued among themselves about how impossible this was.

Clearly, Jesus' words weren't winning Him any popularity contests. He could have downplayed what He had previously said or changed the subject. But that's not how He responded. In John 6:53–56 Jesus said, "Unless you eat the flesh of the Son of man and drink his blood, you have no life in you; he who eats my flesh and drinks my blood has eternal life, and I will raise him up at the last day. For my flesh is food indeed and my blood is drink indeed. He who eats my flesh and drinks my blood abides in me, and I in him."

Some of the deeper meaning of the word *eat* gets lost in translation. Two Greek words, *trogein* and *phagein*, are translated as "eat" in English. At the beginning of the discourse, Jesus used the word *phagein*, which describes a human eating. As He continued speaking, He intensified His word choice and used the word *trogein*, which describes the way an animal eats—more of a gnawing. He had opportunity after opportunity to clarify, correct, or back down. Instead, Jesus' words just got more and more intense.

How did the people respond? John 6:66 tells us that many of His followers left and no longer accompanied Him. Make no mistake, Jesus didn't watch with indifference as they walked away. He came to seek and save the lost. His love for each of those retreating souls was so immense that He was soon to die for them. If they had simply misunderstood Him, don't you think He would have chased them down the road to clarify? But if He had meant what He said, simply telling them the truth He had been waiting throughout the Old Testament to reveal, then He would have had to let them respond as they chose. He never has been one to force Himself on anyone.

Dear Lord,
You are the bread of life. You are what I am hungering for. Amen.

February

Charm is deceptive & Beauty is fleeting but A WOMAN who fears the Lord is to be Praised.

PROVERBS 31:30

Be Still

FEBRUARY 1

"Beloved, do not be surprised at the fiery ordeal which comes upon you to prove you, as though something strange were happening to you. But rejoice in so far as you share Christ's sufferings, that you may also rejoice and be glad when his glory is revealed." (1 Peter 4:12–13)

When suffering slams into us from left field, we reel with shock. "Why is this happening to me?" is one of the first things we ask. Saint Peter tells us that we shouldn't be surprised when trials come. There's a lot of wisdom in this because what makes suffering even harder is when it doesn't make any sense to us. While knowing that suffering is inevitable is not the same as knowing why we are going through it, it does help.

This is different than living life waiting for the other shoe to drop. Saint Peter is not suggesting that we live life hopelessly, figuring that something lousy is right around the corner. It's living life victoriously, recognizing that God, in His providence (in His ability to know better than we do because His mind is infinite and ours is not), is doing something important through the suffering.

Our greatest learned lessons do not come from the easy circumstances. Growth in character comes from opportunities to practice virtue when it is hardest to do so. Maturity is won in the battle of trials when we overcome them instead of letting them take us down. There is no easy road to sainthood. It always involves difficulty, and unless we want to remain spiritual infants, we should both expect and welcome trials.

Welcoming trials is not the same as being a masochist. We don't want pain for its own sake; we want to grow, and we recognize this is the way that happens. A mature person recognizes that every trial is presenting an opportunity to know God in a new way, to experience His provision in a deeper way, and to be stretched. When we reach our limit, we cry out to God and tell Him we can't do any more. The smart among us then say, "So please, God, do it in me. Fill me with yourself." Emptied of our own strength, we make room for His.

Dear Lord,
Instead of being surprised by trials, help me to change my attitude and expect that they will come if I am pursuing spiritual growth. May I live in a constant state of preparedness—grateful when life is easy, but planning ahead for the times when it won't be. Amen.

Be Still

FEBRUARY 2

"Therefore you have no excuse, O man, whoever you are, when you judge another; for in passing judgment upon him you condemn yourself, because you, the judge, are doing the very same things." (Romans 2:1)

Saint Paul is talking to the morally upright in this verse. These are words for the people who have their act together and are surrounded by bozos who don't. It's for those of us who take pride in our efficiency and judge the slow checkout clerk at the grocery store. It's for those of us who know the best way to mother and inwardly roll our eyes at the mom who is too lax or too strict (depending on our bias). It's for those of us who smell the alcohol on the homeless man and figure his poor choices got him into that mess. There are countless times when we are the ones Saint Paul is talking to.

Why do we judge? Often it's because without realizing it, we see something of ourselves in those we are judging. This is the part of ourselves that we don't like, that we don't want to look at, and so we focus on the other person's faults instead. Forgiving others—and perhaps more important, forgiving ourselves—is a step toward rooting out judgmental attitudes.

The smaller our circle, the easier it is to be judgmental. Do all your friends believe more or less what you believe? Do you get your news from only one source? Do you live in an echo chamber, where everyone you spend time with agrees with you? This can breed judgmentalism. We are far less likely to offer grace when everyone we are close to is doing just fine in a particular area that we are judging.

Widening our circle can be a game changer if in doing so, we really listen to the people we are getting to know. Our perceptions are so limited. There is more to every story, and if we knew those details, we'd be slow to judge. Pop the bubble and let some new perspectives in.

All of this is not to say that there is no absolute truth. There most certainly is. But God is the one who gets to judge who is following it and who is not.

Dear Lord,
Forgive me for being judgmental. Help me to turn my focus inward first—to put my own house in order before I critique someone else's. Amen.

*Laziness

Be Still

FEBRUARY 3

"Let us press on to know the Lord; his going forth is sure as the dawn; he will come to us as the shower, as the spring rains that water the earth." (Hosea 6:3)

To *know* someone is to recognize and to understand him or her. God invites us to know Him. This is truly incredible. The God of the Universe, the One who created you and everything you see, wants you to get to know Him.

There is something insensitive in responding to this invitation with a satisfaction with superficial knowledge. "I know God well enough," we think. "I know He's good and powerful and saved us. Isn't that good enough?" To gain insight into why this is insensitive, think about one of your closest relationships. Think of how you would feel if your loved one said, "I really think I know enough about you. I've got a general idea of who you are and what you like. I can make some assumptions about what you're going to do and how certain things will make you feel. Sure, there's more than that below the surface, but it would take a lot of effort to get into all that. I think I know you well enough." You'd feel your loved one was being insensitive. You wouldn't feel seen or known, and you'd actually feel a bit cut off.

We all could use a good dose of curiosity about God instead of the disinterest most of us have. God has offered to reveal much more to you about Himself than you are currently seeing. How can I say that with confidence? Because God is infinite, which means you will never figure Him out completely. There is always more to discover.

What we typically do when we want to know God better is lean on our imagination. But this is actually the worst place to turn when we want to grow in this way. This leads us down the path of forming a God that suits our interests and preferences. We need to lean on our intellect to grow in knowledge of God. This is hard work. Our intellect is a muscle that often lies unused. But a little effort pays off when we dig in and get curious.

If we will do this, "He will come to us as the showers, as the spring rains that water the earth" (Hosea 6:3). We'll be refreshed and restored. Deeper knowledge of who He is will make it easier for us to trust Him. This will settle our hearts and decrease our anxiety.

Dear Lord,
May I press on to know You better. May I employ my intellect and not be lazy. Amen.

Be Still

FEBRUARY 4

"Submit yourselves therefore to God. Resist the devil and he will flee from you. Draw near to God and he will draw near to you." (James 4:7–8)

When you have decided that you want to live a life in which you are continuously moving toward God, the enemy will do all he can to discourage you. He'll send people your way who will tell you that you aren't fun anymore, who will encourage you to stay stuck in old patterns of behavior that make them feel comfortable but that you know you need to shed. He'll throw up obstacles—he'll make sure your prayer time gets interrupted and your drive to study the Bible is delayed by a slow driver in front of you. He'll stir up trouble in your life that will tempt you to question God's goodness. He'll pick at you and annoy you and whisper discouraging thoughts. That's his game.

He makes a study of each one of God's children, so he plans his attack on you in a very personal way. Things that might not take me down might drive you crazy. You can count on the things that bother you most being the very things that go wrong. He'll single you out. That's how it works.

So what can we do about this? Do we just have to resign ourselves to being hassled by the enemy all day long? No. Resignation is not the way to beat him at his own game. We need to resist. This means engaging in the battle. The time to do this is right away, at the first sniff of his presence. His shenanigans work like a snowball. At the outset, it's small and can be stopped. But if we let him run his plays without interruption, without resistance, it builds into a huge snowball and can do much more damage.

The minute the enemy starts to mess with you, stand up to him. "He who is in you is greater than he who is in the world" (1 John 4:4). Call him out on his antics. Resolve that the attacks will only make you stronger because they will cause you to lean harder on God. They are actually proof that you are moving in the right direction. If you weren't, the enemy would just leave you alone. Draw near to God. He will strengthen and protect you, taking what the enemy intends for your destruction and turning it to good.

Dear Lord,
Help me to recognize the enemy's attacks right away and meet them head-on with Your strength. May I resist. If I do, I claim Your promise that the cowardly enemy will flee. Amen.

Be Still

FEBRUARY 5

"Behold, I am the Lord, the God of all flesh; is anything too hard for me?" (Jeremiah 32:27)

This is a rhetorical question, my friends, because nothing is too hard for God. He's hoping we've figured that out by now, after looking at all He's done and held together so far. "But wait," you say. "There's a lot in my life that hasn't held together. Things aren't perfect for me." This is worth thinking about a little bit, because it's our crummy circumstances that often cause us to doubt God's care or competence. Regardless of which thing we're doubting, it gets in the way of our trust in God, which gets in the way of Him moving on our behalf.

Let's start by thinking about what He is holding together. That would be the world. God created the world out of nothing; He simply spoke, and it came to be. He didn't pull together various things that already existed and then form them into a new earth. He created *something* out of *nothing*. This is significant, because it means that if God decided He didn't want it to exist anymore, it all would stop existing. Everything we see—our world, ourselves—is held in existence by God's will.

If a carpenter makes a chair and then walks away, the chair continues to exist. Why? The chair is made of something—of parts—and once it is made, it is no longer dependent on its creator. We, by contrast, were made out of nothing. It is God who holds us together. "But we're made up of cells and molecules. We're made of something!" No matter how small we go, whatever we end up with, that is what God made—out of nothing. God holds everything together and we owe Him every breath.

So why do parts of our lives not hold together? Because of sin, and often it's our own that is to blame. Self-reliance plays a big part in the trouble. We try to do God's job and then blame Him when things go wrong. We need to get out of His way, invite Him into the mess, and ask Him how He would like to order it all. If we set our priorities without consulting Him first, things aren't going to run smoothly. If we make our own comfort our highest goal, things aren't going to run according to plan. Letting God be God in our lives is the most sane thing we can possibly do, because there is nothing too hard for Him to handle.

Dear Lord,
Help me to get out of the way—to allow You to be in charge. Amen.

Be Still

FEBRUARY 6

"The boat by this time was . . . beaten by the waves; for the wind was against them. And in the fourth watch of the night [Jesus] came to them, walking on the sea. But when the disciples saw him walking on the sea, they were terrified, saying, 'It is a ghost!' And they cried out for fear. But immediately He spoke to them, saying, 'Take heart, it is I; have no fear.'" (Matthew 14:24–27)

The emotion of fear is a gift insofar as it alerts us to danger. Our senses become heightened, and we look for a way out. Fear lets us know the storm is coming or has hit, but it's not enough to get us through the storm. We need something more than that.

A spirit of fear will alert us to danger and sharpen our senses, but it will never provide us with what we need to navigate the storms of life. To make it through those circumstances, we need supernatural power, God's unconditional love, and the self-control that helps us choose to dwell on certain things and not others. The good news is, this is exactly what the indwelling Holy Spirit provides. If we replace our spirit of fear with the spirit of power, love, and self-control, we can conquer our fears.

Fear is unavoidable, but what we choose to do with it is up to us. In the very moment that we feel afraid, we can remind ourselves, "God did not give us a spirit of timidity but a spirit of power and love and self-control" (2 Timothy 1:7). That is what is inside us.

When panic hits, grab hold of Jesus' hand. Lock your eyes on the truth that you are not alone, that He is present, and that His presence makes all the difference. Ask Him to dispel your fear.

"He who dwells in the shelter of the Most High, who abides in the shadow of the Almighty, will say to the Lord, 'My refuge and my fortress; my God, in whom I trust'" (Psalm 91:1–2).

"I learned that courage was not the absence of fear but the triumph over it. The brave man is not he that doesn't feel afraid, but he who conquers that fear."
—Nelson Mandela

Dear Lord,
Help me to turn to You when I am in the grip of fear. Jesus, I trust in You. Take care of everything. Amen.

FEBRUARY 7

"The Lord is my light and my salvation; whom shall I fear? The Lord is the stronghold of my life; of whom shall I be afraid?" (Psalm 27:1)

A survey conducted by Chapman University, in California, discovered that one of Americans' greatest fears is walking alone at night.[8] When people answered the survey, they were probably thinking of the dark alley, the dimly lit parking lot, that sort of thing. I understand this fear. Once the sun goes down, I imagine someone is hiding under my car in the mall parking lot, just waiting to slash my ankles. I start to regret that my hair is always in a ponytail because that's easy for some ne'er-do-well to grab. I walk with my finger over the alarm button on my key fob because you just never know. So I get being freaked out at night.

Night can mean all that—or it can be a metaphor for a general darkness in our circumstances or a darkness in our souls. And we are very afraid of walking through those times alone. That's when walking with your hair down and the key fob in hand just doesn't offer much comfort.

Saint John of the Cross wrote, "God has to work in the soul in secret and in darkness because if we fully knew what was happening and what Mystery, transformation, God and Grace will eventually ask of us, we would either try to take charge or stop the whole process."

The deepest soul work is done in the darkness, and it isn't a group exercise. There are times when God allows us to go to places that we wouldn't choose to go, because it is only there that we will be transformed in the most beautiful of ways. But we shouldn't be afraid of this, because God accompanies us there. We never walk in darkness alone. True, we may feel alone. But our feelings don't define reality; God does. And He promises never to leave us. He is there in the secret places in a way that our minds don't really comprehend.

Dear Lord,
Thank You for making it so that I do not need to be afraid, because You are with me. I don't need to be anxious, because You are my God. Thank You for strengthening me. Thank You for helping me. Thank You for upholding me with Your victorious right hand. Thank You for grasping hold of me and never letting me go. Amen.

Be Still

FEBRUARY 8

"The fear of man lays a snare, but he who trusts in the Lord is safe." (Proverbs 29:25)

We don't always recognize fear of rejection as a personal struggle because we don't connect this fear with its fruits. This fear manifests itself as people-pleasing, approval-seeking, a heightened sensitivity to criticism, feelings of worthlessness, and a rejection of others so that we turn away before they can reject us. We need to get to the root of this fear if we want to walk in freedom.

A snare is a trap that typically has a noose of wire or a cord. Caring too much what others think is a snare that strangles our freedom. It causes us to crave approval and fear rejection, and it puts people in a place meant for God alone.

We all experience rejection at some point in our lives; it's unavoidable. But being afraid of it or totally train-wrecked by it is actually optional. It all boils down to what our identity is based on. If the way our worth is defined is through people's acceptance of us, then fear of rejection will always be a noose around our necks. But if we can fully embrace the truth that people's opinions do not determine our worth or identity, that our worth is determined by God and our identity is rooted in being His beloved daughters, then freedom can be ours.

God's approval is the only one that ultimately matters, and He *adores* you. Yes, *you*. You are not an exception to the rule, no matter what you've done or what you're struggling with today.

Do you want to see God show up in your life in a powerful way? Are you tired of the status quo and ready for more? Would you like to see God, in all His glory, intersect your circumstances?

God wants us to experience His glory. He wants to pour out His power on us and to see us living freed, transformed lives. This has always been His desire. When Jesus walked the earth, there was nothing He wanted more than for the people to see His glory and to be changed as a result. But so many of them missed it. Why? The reason is found in the Gospel of John: "for they loved the praise of men more than the praise of God" (John 12:43). They wanted something more than God's power and glory. They wanted human praise. Jesus is turning to you now and asking, "What do you want?" How will you answer Him?

Dear Lord,
Help me to care more about what You think of me than what anyone else thinks. Amen.

Be Still

FEBRUARY 9

"I came that they may have life, and have it abundantly." (John 10:10)

"What if I fall?
Oh, my darling, what if you fly?"⁹

Have you ever realized that your life is going pretty well, and instead of resting in the joy of that moment and thanking God for all He's given, you think, "Oh no! The other shoe is about to drop"? In her vulnerability research, Dr. Brené Brown has found that the most terrifying, difficult emotion we experience is joy. We're afraid to lean in to joy, because the thought of it being taken away is so scary. She describes our mental response as "dress-rehearsing tragedy": imagining something bad is going to happen when in reality, nothing is wrong. "How many of you have ever stood over your child while they're sleeping and thought, 'Oh . . . I love you'—and then pictured something horrific happening?"¹⁰

This isn't how God wants us to live. He wants us to lean in to joy and soar! So how can we break free of our tendency to pull back in fear and miss our lives because we are living in the gray? Underneath our reluctance to really embrace joy is the fear that we will fall. And consciously or not, we figure that the higher the place we're falling from, the more it will hurt. So we climb down from the peak of joy and sit in the middle ground of low expectations because it feels safer. And life passes us by. Have you whispered these questions? "What if I fall?" "What if I fall because of disappointment?" "What if I fall because of tragedy?" "What if I fall because I'm just not good enough?"

I can't promise that you will never fall or that life will never bring you pain. But God makes us promises in Scripture that should make an enormous difference in the way we live. In Deuteronomy 33:27, He promises, "The eternal God is your dwelling place, and underneath are the everlasting arms."

If you fall, God will catch you. It's as simple as that. He promises that beneath you, no matter what height you are falling from, He will catch you in His everlasting arms. What do we find at the end of our resources, the end of our dreams, the end of our hopes? We find God's mercy. We find God's graciousness. We find shelter from the storm.

Dear Lord,
I claim this promise: "He will shelter you with his pinions, and under his wings you may take refuge." (Psalm 91:4) May I come under Your wings and rest. Amen.

Be Still

FEBRUARY 10

"Say to those who are of a fearful heart, 'Be strong, fear not!'" (Isaiah 35:4)

So how do we conquer our fears? It's a journey. Sometimes it feels like two steps forward and one step back. But even then, progress is being made. When fear starts to get the better of me, I go back to these lessons to readjust my thinking *and* my feelings:

Develop a mature view of suffering.
Because I live in a fallen world, I am quickly influenced by the world's view of the relationship between suffering and joy. We're told that they are polar opposites, but the truth is, there can be joy in suffering. When we meet God in the dark places and He gets us through, we can feel the joy of His presence. We can also feel joy when we realize that we are progressing spiritually as we face our fears, even when doing so is hard. A mature woman realizes that suffering can't be avoided, and that if we never encountered it, there would be a lot of life lessons missed.

Grow in faith and trust.
Faith and trust are the antidotes to fear. I'm so glad that we can ask God to give us more faith when we feel we are lacking. When we stay close to the Lord and exercise the little faith we do have, He waters that seed of faith and makes it grow. When I focus on how God has been faithful to me in the past, I grow in trust. It's been helpful for me to keep a prayer journal so that I can go back and see the ways God has rescued me and given me what I have needed countless times. When I read the Bible, I get to know God better, which helps me see that He is worthy of my trust. I won't trust someone I don't know. If we want to grow in trust, we have to take the time to get to know God personally.

Remember that I am never alone.
This comforts me most of all. Jesus has suffered more than I ever will, so He knows how I am feeling. The Bible promises that no matter what happens to me, God has made sure I can endure it (1 Corinthians 10:13). But He doesn't say I'll be able to handle anything in my own strength. I will have to cling to Him in order to receive the strength I need, just as a small branch clings to the main vine.

Dear Lord,
I affirm my trust in Your goodness and Your control over all things. Thank You for Your wise plan for my life. Amen.

[Handwritten at top: "This really speaks to me Lord — do I wear my suffering as a badge? Be Still"]

FEBRUARY 11

"[God] disciplines us for our good, that we may share his holiness. For the moment all discipline seems painful rather than pleasant; later it yields the peaceful fruit of righteousness to those who have been trained by it." (Hebrews 12:10–11)

What happens when we expect God's love to always feel good? God's discipline, which was meant to help us and teach us something, ends up making us bitter. That root of bitterness goes down deep into our hearts, and we start to question God's character. That's not all. We get stuck there. Instead of growing up in our faith, we become perpetual spiritual teenagers.

We don't all experience "the peaceful fruit of righteousness"; it doesn't automatically accompany discipline. Some women who've been through a lot wear their suffering as a badge. We notice it, and there is always a certain amount of respect we give to someone who has endured something terribly difficult. But the holiness we're after isn't the same thing as wearing a badge of suffering. We need to be refined by what we experience. It's not *that* you've suffered that really matters; it's *how* you've suffered.

In his book *The Problem of Pain*, C. S. Lewis discusses how hard it is for us to turn our thoughts to God when everything is going well. This means He is going to have to allow some things to intersect our lives that are temporarily difficult so that we stop settling for false sources of happiness. Lewis writes:

> Thus the terrible necessity of tribulation is only too clear. God has had me for but forty-eight hours and then only by dint of taking everything else away from me. Let Him but sheathe that sword for a moment and I behave like a puppy when the hated bath is over—I shake myself as dry as I can and race off to reacquire my comfortable dirtiness, if not in the nearest manure heap, at least in the nearest flower bed. And that is why tribulations cannot cease until God either sees us remade or sees that our remaking is now hopeless.[11]

God desires that we resemble our older brother, Jesus, because He knows that the more we are like Him the more happy we will be. Have you resisted the discipline of your heavenly Father? Let today be the start of a new attitude toward the difficulties He allows to come your way.

Dear Lord,
Instead of responding to my difficulties with the words "Why me?" I am changing my response to, "Father, what are You trying to teach me?" Amen.

Be Still

FEBRUARY 12

"The Lord is not slow about his promise as some count slowness, but is forbearing toward you, not wishing that any should perish, but that all should reach repentance." (2 Peter 3:9)

Suffering comes into our lives uninvited. What has God promised to us during those times when we desperately want relief? He promises that He is present even when we feel that He isn't. He promises that we are known and we are precious to Him. He promises that prayer makes a difference. He promises that His timing is perfect. It often feels slow, but He is never late.

God also promises that our suffering always has a purpose. Whether or not that purpose is fulfilled depends on how we decide to be shaped by it. Will it form us into bitter, unforgiving, hardened women? Or will we be refined and come out the other side stronger, wiser, and more like Christ? The choice is ours. Even in the most horrific circumstances, the choice is still ours. No one says it better than WWII concentration camp survivor Viktor Frankl: "Everything can be taken from a man but one thing: the last of human freedoms—to choose one's attitude in any given set of circumstances, to choose one's own way."

There is always a purpose in suffering. That purpose is directly tied to God's greatest desire: to spend eternity with each person He lovingly created. Our life on earth is simply our journey toward that destination. And along the way, suffering is unquestionably one of the ways we are prepared to meet Him face-to-face. In the words of author Philip Yancey:

> The Bible consistently changes the questions we bring to the problem of pain. It rarely, or ambiguously, answers the backward-looking question "Why?" Instead, it raises the very different, forward-looking question, "To what end?" We are not put on earth merely to satisfy our desires, to pursue life, liberty, and happiness. We are here to be changed, to be made more like God in order to prepare us for a lifetime with Him. And that process may be served by the mysterious pattern of all creation: Pleasure sometimes emerges against a background of pain, evil may be transformed into good, and suffering may produce something of value.[12]

Let's live with our eyes fixed on eternity and filter our thoughts about suffering through that perspective.

Dear Lord,
Help me check my expectations. Am I expecting life to be on earth what God promised me only in heaven? Amen.

Be Still

FEBRUARY 13

"Do you not know that you are God's temple and that God's Spirit dwells in you?"
(1 Corinthians 3:16)

While it's true that God loves us unconditionally, He loves us too much to leave us as we are. He knows that the sins that disfigure us are keeping us from the abundant life He created us for. We are promised in 2 Corinthians 5:17, "If any one is in Christ, he is a new creation; the old has passed away, behold, the new has come." A *new creation* is a picture of freedom—a beautiful butterfly that has emerged from a cocoon after metamorphosis. This means that the Holy Spirit *in you* wants to bring new life to places you have long felt were dead. He wants to radically change you from the inside out.

The first step to move you toward becoming the woman you long to be is admitting that the area where you want to change is actually a problem. It's not a "thorn in the flesh" that you're expected to live with forever, and it's not a quirky part of your personality. This is something that God wants you to be free of.

What is an area of your life where you would like to see transformation? Is this something friends and family believe you have a problem with? Is it impacting your relationships with others? Do you try to hide it from people? Can you go without engaging in this behavior for a week? Do you arrange parts of your life (your schedule, your spending) around it?

I believe it's easier to face our problems—to call them what they really are: sins, addictions, idols—when we believe that freedom from them is possible. So lean in close and listen: God does not want you to stay in this place. He is just waiting to help you experience freedom and victory. But it has to start with you. It has to begin with you acknowledging that your behavior is hurting you—and probably people close to you. It has to begin with you admitting that this ingrained habit isn't something that you can control in your own strength. You are at a crossroads. You can choose to face the need to change or you can ignore it. But hasn't it been heavy to carry this load? Aren't you tired of the price you pay? God wants to lift this burden from you. He lovingly waits to be invited into the struggle.

Dear Lord,
I want to be free. I am naming the problem:_____. I am asking You for Your help. Amen.

Be Still

FEBRUARY 14

"To this end I labor, struggling with all his energy, which so powerfully works in me."
(Colossians 1:29)

Really coming to terms with our need to change—naming a problem that requires a solution—is the first step toward freedom. The next is to invite God into the process. As good as this sounds in theory, it isn't our typical response. Most of us begin to address a problem by getting to work and searching for solutions. This is trying to change in our own strength, and all too often, we'll fail to see real transformation. We are promised in Mark 10:27 that "with man it is impossible, but not with God; for all things are possible with God." We aren't promised that all things are possible in *our own* strength. In fact, in John 15:5, we are told, "apart from [God] we can do nothing." There's a big difference between saying we're going to pray about something and then actually doing it.

As we battle toward freedom from sin, God gives us weapons to help us fight. According to 2 Corinthians 10:4, these weapons "have divine power to destroy strongholds." In the original Greek, the word *stronghold* describes the place a person goes to seek shelter (a safe place) or to escape reality. When we think of battling to break free of habits and sins that have a grip on us, it's helpful to consider them strongholds that need to be destroyed. Why do we continue to do these things that we know ultimately harm us and those we love? Sometimes we're trying to escape reality. Sometimes we fool ourselves into thinking that these behaviors or coping mechanisms are helping us to be more in control of things. Whatever our reason, the very things we think will bring us greater control end up controlling us. On our own, we can't get out from under them. But with the weapons God gives us, freedom can be won.

We have to get rid of the illusion that we have it within us to break down the strongholds that keep us from freedom. We have to let go of our pride, which says it's all up to us. When we're talking about deep-seated issues, long-held patterns of behavior, and addiction, we must have weapons that are powerful enough for the battle. The weapons God gives us allow us to fight in the spiritual dimension. They add supernatural power to our resolve, self-discipline, and determination.

Dear Lord,
I invite You into my struggle. Please break through any barriers that are keeping me away from a life of freedom. Amen.

FEBRUARY 15

"Be strong in the Lord and in the strength of his might." (Ephesians 6:10)

In Ephesians 6, we read about the armor and weapons God provides:

The Belt of Truth: When God's truth surrounds us, we are protected from lies that keep us from living as beloved daughters of God. The lies say, "I can't. I'll never change." The truth says, "All things are possible with God" (Mark 10:27).

The Breastplate of Righteousness: Greek historian Polybius described the breastplate that covered the soldier from the neck to the thigh as "the heart protector." A holy life protects the most vital part of us: the soul. Self-discipline is like a muscle—the more it gets exercised, the stronger it becomes. There is protection in obedience.

Feet Fitted with the Gospel: A soldier's shoes had nails or spikes in the sole to help him stand firmly and keep his balance. In that same way, the gospel gives us something solid to stand on. We don't stand on the foundation of our own perfection. We stand on the truth of Christ's perfect sacrifice having paid the price for our sins. He makes up for where we are lacking.

The Shield of Faith: We put up the shield of faith to protect ourselves from the fiery darts of doubt, fear, discouragement, and condemnation. Our prayer becomes "I believe; help my unbelief!" (Mark 9:24). God faithfully strengthens our faith when we ask Him to.

The Helmet of Salvation: The helmet protects the brain. When we focus on the gift of salvation, our minds are protected from thoughts of worthlessness and hopelessness.

The Sword of the Spirit: The sword of the Spirit is an offensive weapon. This is Scripture, and the more we know it, the more we can use it to gain ground spiritually instead of just staying in the same place. When we memorize Scripture, the Holy Spirit can bring God's truth to our minds just when we need to fight temptation or negative thoughts.

Dear Lord,
Buckle the belt of truth around my waist. Help me to dwell on what is true. I take the breastplate of righteousness from Your hand. May I be protected by Your grace by making the right choices today. Place the helmet of salvation on my head and protect my mind. May my feet be shod by the gospel. Everywhere I go today, may I spread that message. Oil my shield of faith with the Holy Spirit so that all the fiery darts flung at me will be extinguished. I take up the sword of the Spirit. Let me be ready to fight back any lies with the truth found in Scripture. Amen.

Be Still

FEBRUARY 16

"Do not be deceived, bad company ruins good morals." (1 Corinthians 15:33)

There's no question that God gives us everything we need to resist temptation. While He certainly equips us for battle, there are some battles He wants us to just walk away from. These are the battles on top of quicksand, and the only way to win is to avoid the area completely. This is essentially the message of Romans 6: You are free from the grip of sin, so *walk away from it.*

Reflect on your choice of friends. Do some of your friends encourage you to live the way God wants you to? Do others consistently draw you into behavior that you later regret? Is God asking you to change where you are spending your time?

We are wise to be discerning in choosing our friends, because as it says in Proverbs 13:20, "He who walks with the wise becomes wise, but the companion of fools suffers harm." No matter how strong our personality or how well we know ourselves, we are always influenced by our friends. Even Jesus gave careful thought to choosing His friends. He spent all night in prayer before selecting His twelve disciples, asking God to help Him discern whom He should surround Himself with.

There's no growth in holiness without battling temptation and walking away from people and situations that are sure to take us down. It involves a thousand little deaths. It's hard, and it requires grit and sacrifice. Through it all, we're called to persevere. As Saint Gregory of Nyssa said, "He who climbs never stops going."

Dear Lord,
This is where the rubber meets the road. As long as I don't feel equipped to change, I feel like I don't have to. I have an excuse. In John 5:6, You asked the man lying by the pool in Bethesda, "Do you want to be healed?" The man replied with an excuse. He was so used to being crippled that all he could think of were the reasons he'd never get better. And there You stood, with all the power imaginable at Your disposal, ready to help. You looked at the man and said, "Rise, take up your mat, and walk."

I know that You ask me the same question. "Do you really want to be well?" It's time for me to stop making excuses and to grasp hold of Your promise from Philippians 4:13: "I can do all things in him who strengthens me." It's time for me to pick up my mat and walk—toward freedom. No more excuses. I want to be well. Amen.

Be Still

"His divine power has granted to us all things that pertain to life and godliness." (2 Peter 1:3)

Author Adrian Warnock wisely observed, "When Christians stop being different from the world and instead fall back into their old habits, it is as tragic as finding a royal prince sleeping out on the streets in a gutter, having forgotten he belongs in the palace."[13]

You are God's beloved daughter, a child of the King of kings. He doesn't want you lying on a mat, crippled by sin. He offers you His hand, invites you to get up and walk with Him toward the freedom of holiness.

Holiness is within reach; it isn't beyond you. This isn't a call to live in a constant state of fear, afraid of disappointing God or making Him angry. It's an invitation from your heavenly Father, who is *good*, who is *for you*, and who gives you the power of the Holy Spirit. This power breaks the chains of addiction, destructive habits, and behaviors that hurt us.

As it says in The Message version of Matthew 5:3, "You're blessed when you're at the end of your rope. With less of you there is more of God." You can't change in your own power. If you feel overwhelmed at the thought of breaking free of sins that have long held you in their grasp, then turn to the One who is bigger than all things. He will be strong in your weakness.

God has given you everything you need in order to live your life the way He desires. He's given you His very presence in your soul. The Holy Spirit fills you with love, joy, peace, patience, kindness, goodness, faithfulness, gentleness, and self-control. If those are the things you need, you can't say you don't have them. It's just that we often fail to tap into the power that is within us. God has given us the sacraments to fill us with His grace, which is exactly what we need for whatever we face.

"Do not be afraid to be holy! Have the courage and humility to present yourselves to the world determined to be holy, since full, true freedom is born from holiness." — Saint John Paul II

Dear Lord,
Help me to see that You have placed everything within me that I need in order to live a life of victory and freedom. May I walk away from the trap of self-reliance and instead draw on the limitless resources of Your power at work within me. Amen.

Be Still

FEBRUARY 18

"I will sprinkle clean water upon you, and you shall be clean from all your uncleannesses, and from all your idols I will cleanse you." (Ezekiel 36:25)

When we mess up, what is it that God wants from us? Is He most interested in us cleaning up our outward behavior? Is His primary objective getting His kids to behave in public so they don't embarrass Him? CCC 1430 reveals that God wants us to go deeper than just behavior modification: "Jesus' call to conversion and penance, like that of the prophets before him, does not aim first at outward works, 'sackcloth and ashes,' fasting and mortification, but at the conversion of the heart, interior conversion. Without this, such penances remain sterile and false; however interior conversion urges expression in visible signs, gestures, and works of penance."

What God is looking for is a conversion of our hearts. Conversion means turning—turning away from something that has been hurting us and toward the One who only wants what is best for us. Our hearts are created to worship. We either worship God or we set up idols in our hearts and worship them instead. We place an idol on the throne and it controls us, whether we realize it or not. Our idol can be our reputation, our appearance, money, power, comfort, a person . . . the possibilities are endless. When we move God off the throne and replace Him with an idol, we fall into sin; our idols lead us in the wrong direction.

Pastor Tim Keller has this to say about idols: "When people say, 'I know God forgives me, but I can't forgive myself,' they mean that they have failed an idol, whose approval is more important than God's."[14] This is a profound statement, and one that should give many of us pause.

When we sin, God wants us to turn to Him and ask Him to cleanse and forgive us. We aren't strong enough to dispose of our idols, but He is. That being said, He waits for us to ask Him to intervene. But an idol that isn't replaced crawls back on the throne. We must choose to replace the idol with God. This means asking Him to sit on the throne of our hearts (which is conversion of heart). How many times do we need to do this? As many as it takes. Sometimes it's multiple times a day.

Giving God the right place in our hearts comes first. The outward behavior will follow.

Dear Lord,
Please remove this idol from my heart:_____. I invite You to sit on the throne. Amen.

FEBRUARY 19

Be Still

"A new heart I will give you, and a new spirit I will put within you; and I will take out of your flesh the heart of stone and give you a heart of flesh." (Ezekiel 36:26)

Why do we need a new heart? Jeremiah 17:9 says that "the heart is deceitful above all things, and desperately corrupt." Our hearts are often poor guides, because they convince us that receiving what they desire is the key to happiness. So we convince ourselves that if only we could graduate with a certain degree, then we'd be happy. Then the goalpost changes, and we are sure that the perfect job will make all the difference. When that fails to deliver, we pin our hopes on finding our true love. But that relationship brings its own set of challenges. The truth is, God knows far better than we do what will truly bring us fulfillment. What we currently want can be very different from what we actually need. "Following your heart" can lead you where you ultimately won't want to be.

The heart of stone is unchanging in its pursuit of its desires. The heart of flesh is malleable, open to God changing its desires to better match His. Ultimately, the only thing that will fulfill us is God Himself. We were made for Him. Unless we live our lives in proper relationship with Him, the deepest fulfillment will remain elusive; something will be missing.

CCC 1432 tells us, "The human heart is heavy and hardened. God must give man a new heart. Conversion is first of all a work of the grace of God who makes our hearts return to him: 'Restore us to thyself, O Lord, that we may be restored!' God gives us the strength to begin anew." This means we can always start again. Each day, God offers us the chance to turn over a new leaf. When our hearts become hardened through sin, confession softens them again.

Do you want to discover what will fulfill your deepest desires? Read the Beatitudes (Matthew 5:1–12). This is Jesus' explanation of what will truly satisfy your desire for happiness. The new heart that God gives you is what makes this kind of living possible.

Dear Lord,
Please give me a heart of flesh—one that is able to be molded by You. Amen.

Be Still

FEBRUARY 20

"And I will put my spirit within you, and cause you to walk in my statutes and be careful to observe my ordinances." (Ezekiel 36:27)

How is the human heart changed from a heart of stone to one of flesh? God puts His own Spirit, the Holy Spirit, within us. The Holy Spirit, the third person of the Trinity, is the love between God the Father and Jesus, the Son.

There are so many times in our lives when we whisper, "I can't." *I can't be more patient with my kids. I can't forgive him. I can't keep going. I can't bear this loss. I can't give any more.*

The Holy Spirit comes to us in those moments and whispers: I know you can't. I see. I see your limitations. I see your hurts. I see what's been done to you. But even though you can't, *I can*. I have come to break all the chains that keep you from living the life of freedom that you were meant to live. You were made for more, daughter of God. I am here for you. I am for you. My love for you is relentless.

I am your **Comforter** (one who relieves another of distress).
I am your **Counselor** (one whose profession it is to give advice and manage causes).
I am your **Helper** (one who furnishes another with relief or support).
I am your **Intercessor** (one who acts between parties to reconcile differences).
I am your **Strengthener** (one who causes you to grow, become stronger, endure, and resist attacks).

Is there a place in your life where you are not living in freedom? Do you feel chained to old habits of behavior and powerless to change? Do you feel bound by lies about your identity—lies that say you are worthless, or ugly, or stupid? Do you feel stuck in the rat race, unable to slow down, unable to breathe? These are the very places where you need to invite me to come and set you free. Don't treat me as an interesting character in a book. Ask me to jump off the pages of the Bible and into your heart.

Dear Lord,
Breathe on me, breath of God. Come, Holy Spirit. Come. Amen.

FEBRUARY 21

"God opposes the proud but gives grace to the humble." (James 4:6)

What is the right posture for prayer? Is it kneeling, lying prostrate, standing with arms lifted to heaven? What we do with our bodies can reflect what is going on within our hearts. The outward expression can vary from person to person, but at its depth, what God is looking for is helplessness. This is found in the heart of a person who knows that the answer does not lie in him or her. The solution is found in God.

We fight against this. Our preference is to figure things out on our own and then invite God along to help us execute our plan. When we take this approach, God lets us run with it. And when we come to the end of our rope, He is there. He patiently waits until we are ready to hand things over, but He knows that we'll save ourselves a lot of heartache if we surrender before we become desperate.

In his book *Prayer*, author Philip Yancey writes, "In the presence of the Great Physician, my most appropriate contribution may be my wounds."[15] God alone knows how deep the wound goes. He remembers when it occurred and all the things that trigger the pain again. He is tender with us. We are promised in Isaiah 42:3 that "a bruised reed he will not break and a dimly burning wick he will not quench; he will faithfully bring forth justice."

May we uncross our arms and give God access to our wounds. He sees them all and then sets out to restore and heal us completely. When we are willing to lay down our weapons and leave the fighting to Him, He executes justice perfectly. As it says in Exodus 14:14, "The Lord will fight for you. You have only to be still."

Can you come and rest in His arms? You have permission to lie there helplessly. This is the posture of a child who is utterly confident in his or her Father's ability to make all things right. Crawl into His lap and allow Him to take care of everything.

Dear Lord,
You are love. You don't just do loving things; Your nature is perfect, infinite, all-encompassing love. May I rest in You as You heal my wounds and fight on my behalf. Amen.

Be Still

FEBRUARY 22

"If any man would come after me, let him deny himself and take up his cross daily and follow me." (Luke 9:23)

Jesus isn't interested in us giving Him a nod of approval, or just attending His weekly get-togethers, or wearing a label that has no bearing on our hearts. He wants us to be *all in*. He wants a wholehearted commitment from us. He wants to be the game changer that turns our world upside down. Because of this, following Christ can be hard. It's always costly. It involves challenges that aren't for the fainthearted.

The alternative to denying yourself and following Christ is saying, "I'll follow Jesus when it's comfortable. But this area of my life is off-limits. When it comes to [blank], I'm doing it my way." Is there an area of your life where what Jesus is asking of you just seems too much? Where are you feeling tempted to take the easy way out?

Picking up a cross and carrying it is always painful. It involves accepting a load that God has asked you to carry and *walking forward*. This is different from sitting down with the weight of a cross on your back, a pool of pity and tears at your feet. Picking up a cross is accepting circumstances that you are powerless to change and determining to allow them to refine you, to sharpen you, to make you more spiritually fit.

We are called to take up our cross daily—as in day after day. It's one thing to gear up for one really tough challenge and to give it all you've got. But the self-sacrifice that Jesus asks of us is the kind that feels especially hard because there is no guarantee that the end is in sight.

But Jesus' next words in the Gospel of Luke are critical motivators: "whoever would save his life will lose it; and whoever loses his life for my sake, he will save it" (Luke 9:24). Let's never forget the second part of that verse. The end of the story is not misery. The end of the story is life—a life well lived, a life with meaning, a life with depth. A life with empathy because you know; you understand. A life in which you have loved Jesus for who He is, not what He gives you. A life in which the message of Calvary has become your story: After death comes the promised resurrection.

Dear Lord,
Please give me the strength to pick up my cross daily and follow You. Amen.

FEBRUARY 23

"Let no evil talk come out of your mouths, but only such as is good for edifying, as fits the occasion, that it may impart grace to those who hear." (Ephesians 4:29)

We are called to be committed to our families and to love them as Christ loves us. But when we have to make a choice between pleasing God and pleasing the people in our lives (even those who are closest to us), we are to choose God. While Jesus did say, "blessed are the peacemakers" (Matthew 5:9), He never advocated the kind of peace that ignores or avoids hard discussions just for the sake of artificial harmony.

When we have chosen to follow Christ and people close to us are following a different path, conflict inevitably arises. Most people respond in one of two ways. They either avoid uncomfortable discussions or situations, and if that involves compromise at times, so be it. Or they are always willing to engage, but feedback from others would suggest that they are coming off as judgmental. So what exactly are we supposed to do?

As Christians, we are called to be "imitators of God" (Ephesians 5:1). As we seek to reflect Him to a world that finds Him repugnant and divisive, there will be times when conflict arises. When it does, we aren't to shrink back and compromise. We aren't to deny what we know to be true. But as we communicate, we should be doing it in a way that makes it clear it's all about Him, not all about us. And perhaps that's where a lot of our difficulties lie. We take things personally. We get our feelings hurt. We feel devalued, alone, dismissed. These are genuine hurts, and the Lord does not take lightly the fact that you are suffering for Him. But He asks that you bring that hurt back to Him instead of responding in bitterness, rage, and anger. Those feelings have got to go somewhere. We can bury them, we can hurl them back at the people we disagree with, or we can take them to Jesus and ask Him to absorb them in His limitless love. Have you been hurt by people who don't respect or embrace your decision to follow Christ? Go to God with your pain. He listens and cares. He is waiting to bind up your wounds and kiss your tears.

Dear Lord,
May my words reflect You—your truthfulness, gentleness, and graciousness. Amen.

Be Still

FEBRUARY 24

"Be watchful, stand firm in your faith, be courageous, be strong." (1 Corinthians 16:13)

As we face specific challenges, being watchful means being aware of times when the devil is at work stirring up trouble and making things worse. We are wise to always remain aware of who the real enemy is. As we face these challenges, we need to stand firm. The devil wants to take us out at the knees, to see us give up. God calls us to stand firm in the face of this. He calls us to remain courageous and strong—not because we have confidence in our own strength, but because of our confidence in *Him*.

To stand firm in your faith, you need to pay attention to your conscience. Ignoring the prick of the conscience leads us to sin, which weakens us in battle. We live, grow, and persevere in our faith by nourishing it with the Word of God and begging the Lord to increase our faith.

As we strive to stand firm, may we never forget that "He who is in you is greater than he who is in the world" (1 John 4:4). Do you know how terrified the enemy of your soul is of you? You may think of him and the evil in the world as being powerful and pervasive, and you're right. He is powerful, and it is pervasive. But authority trumps power. What do I mean by that?

Think of a policeman directing traffic. An enormous Mack truck could be driving down that road, but if a policeman stepped into the road and held up his hand, that Mack truck would stop. Obviously, the truck driver wouldn't want to run over the policeman. But there is more at play here. It is also the authority of the policeman that causes the driver to stop. And you have access to the greatest authority in the universe because He is your daddy. And He loves you. And He steps out and fights for you.

If you can recognize who you are as a child of the King, if you know the truth of Scripture and have it at your fingertips, you can step into the spiritual battle with authority, and Satan will be terrified of you every waking moment. Men and women who know who they are in Christ are his worst nightmare.

Dear Lord,
Help me to focus more on Your authority and power than I do on the obstacles facing me. Amen.

FEBRUARY 25

Be Still

"And calling to him a child, [Jesus] put him in the midst of them, and said, 'Truly, I say to you, unless you turn and become like children, you will never enter the kingdom of heaven. Whoever humbles himself like this child, he is the greatest in the kingdom of heaven.'" (Matthew 18:2–4)

What is the opposite of childlike faith? It's faith in our own abilities rather than in what God can do. It's self-sufficiency coupled with a desire or need for control.

Childlike faith isn't naive; it's trusting in God. It isn't about being innocent; it's about being dependent. It's a steady acknowledgment that it isn't all up to us. What we can't do ourselves, Jesus will do. It's an acknowledgment that we aren't perfect super-saints, but are spiritual children who desperately need God. For people who like to be strong and self-sufficient, this is a challenge.

It's a challenge to make sure our confidence is rooted in God and not in our own abilities and strength. I often find myself white-knuckling it—doing something in a state of fear and tension. What does this look like? I'm clenching something so tightly that my knuckles have turned white. I'm trying so hard to be perfect that I'm worn out. When this is where I am at, I have forgotten the secret of the Christian life.

What's that secret? God dwells within us through the Holy Spirit, and He wants to do the work in and through us. He wants us to live a life of constant dependence on His care and guidance. God knows that on our own, we are no match for the intensity of the spiritual battle. Anytime we fool ourselves into thinking that we're doing OK without Him, we are setting ourselves up for defeat. Our prayer life indicates just how much we are relying on Him.

As we set out to follow Christ, we need to be sure to meet the challenges in God's strength, not in our own. "Not by might, not by power, but by my spirit, says the lord of hosts" (Zechariah 4:6).

Dear Lord,
I come empty and ask You to fill me. This is the area of my life where I find it most difficult to exhibit childlike faith: _____. Forgive me for the times when I rely on myself instead of on You. I affirm my faith in Your strength and power. Amen.

Be Still

FEBRUARY 26

"The Lord will cause your enemies who rise against you to be defeated before you." (Deuteronomy 28:7)

Most things that are really worthwhile involve some hard work, and the Christian life is no exception. If we choose to live above the level of mediocrity, then we will soon see that the Christian life is a battle, and in this battle, we have an enemy.

Satan is the tempter, and he tries to keep us from following Jesus in many ways. Like no other time in history, women now have the capability to really make a difference in the world. Yet we can be quickly distracted by things that don't matter. These things seem very important in the moment, but if we were to take a step back and think about whether they matter eternally, we might choose to spend our time in different places. Satan tempts us—not to join him, but simply to do nothing, to watch from the sidelines.

When we sit on the sidelines, he's not nearly as interested in us. Why? We aren't getting in his way! We're not having a real effect on the battle. But when we step in and decide that we want to be women who bring change, who make this world a better place for our children and grandchildren—this gets him annoyed. He knows the power of one person's holiness. So he gets out his weapons and makes it challenging to follow Christ and really make a difference in this world.

This reality may make you want to head over to the sidelines, where it seems safer. But if we do that, what will happen to our culture? What will happen to the many hearts that won't be touched by the love of Christ? What will our children be left with?

Jump into the battle. You'll never regret it, because it is there that you will experience God's great power. In this battle, there are no vacations. But this life of adventure is the only one truly worth living.

"Evil can only exist if good men do nothing." —Edmund Burke

Dear Lord,
I commit this week to living out my baptism to the utmost. When I feel discouragement or self-pity, I won't give in to it. Instead, I'll refocus on what I can do: love. Alone, I can do nothing. But with God, all things are possible. Amen.

FEBRUARY 27

"Let us hold fast the confession of our hope without wavering, for he who promised is faithful; and let us consider how to stir up one another to love and good works, not neglecting to meet together, as is the habit of some, but encouraging one another." (Hebrews 10:23–25)

In this very moment, Catholics in other parts of the world are literally putting their lives at risk in order to come together and worship. It's similar to the time of the early Church when Christians were fed to lions, beheaded, and imprisoned because they followed Christ. And what was the result of followers of Christ being persecuted in this way? They turned the world upside down. In the words of Jon Tyson, author of *Sacred Roots: Why Church Still Matters in a Post-Religious Era*:

> The growth of the early church is arguably the most remarkable sociological movement in history. The numbers are staggering. In AD 40 there were roughly one thousand Christians in the Roman Empire, but by AD 350 there were almost 30 million. Remarkably, 53% of the population had converted to the Christian faith. What on earth could have compelled half an empire to convert? How could a Jewish political rebel, crucified on a Roman cross, become the Savior of the empire that killed him? The early church leaders didn't have the things we now consider essential for our faith to foster church growth. They didn't have fancy buildings and social media, no celebrity pastors or vision statements. Yet they loved and they served and they prayed and they blessed, and slowly, over hundreds of years, they brought the empire to its knees.[16]

Could it be that it is time for us to overcome our deeply ingrained consumer mentality? Instead of abandoning the Church when it frustrates us, are we being called by God to dig in deeper with our commitment to the local parish?

True, we have high standards for where we share our most precious resource: time. But what if we stopped complaining about what we don't like and decided to be a part of the solution?

Dear Lord,
Forgive me for the times when I complain about the Church but then do nothing to help make things better. Help me to see how the small difference I can make, added to the small differences others can make, can actually transform a culture. Amen.

Be Still

FEBRUARY 28

"The Lord passed before him, and proclaimed, 'The Lord, the Lord, a God merciful and gracious, slow to anger, and abounding in steadfast love and faithfulness.'" (Exodus 34:6)

Moses had asked God to show him His glory. We must never forget that God longs to be known. If He didn't, He wouldn't bother revealing anything about Himself to us. While we will never understand Him (He is infinite, we are finite, so we are incapable of fully grasping who He is), we can grow in our understanding.

There is something insensitive about not bothering to even try to know God better. True, who He is is complex. The fact that God is three persons in one Divine nature (the Trinity) is a mystery that we can't fully comprehend. But we can grow in our understanding of it, and when we don't even try, that communicates something to God. Imagine your spouse knowing you on a surface level and saying, "I know you well enough. There's more to you, but it seems pretty complicated. It would cost me a lot of effort to get to know you more. This is enough." Could you still function within the relationship? Yes, but your heart would grieve the fact that your spouse doesn't want to go deeper and know you more.

When Moses asked God to reveal Himself to him in a deeper way—to show him His glory—God hid him in the cleft of a rock. He explained that no one could see His face and live, but that He would cover Moses with His hand until He passed by, and would let him see His back. He explained that He would make all His goodness pass before Moses.

This is what God did, and as He passed by Moses, He proclaimed His name, saying, "The Lord, the Lord, a God merciful and gracious, slow to anger, and abounding in steadfast love and faithfulness" (Exodus 34:6). God is compassion in action. He doesn't just feel for us; He steps in and helps. He doesn't have a short temper with us; He is slow to anger and quick to show mercy. He doesn't just have a little bit of steadfast love and a bit of faithfulness to offer us; He abounds in both. He has a limitless supply of all these things because they embody who He is. God is changeless, so He cannot be other than who He is revealed to be here.

Dear Lord,
Whatever touches me has gone through Your hands. This means that even if it feels cruel and hard, it is an act of compassion and mercy. Help me to filter my circumstances through that perspective. Amen.

FEBRUARY 29

"Mary took a pound of costly ointment of pure nard and anointed the feet of Jesus and wiped his feet with her hair; and the house was filled with the fragrance of the ointment." (John 12:3)

If we want an example of a gift that means a great deal to God, we need look no further. Mary's gift was sacrificial. The ointment she poured over Jesus was expensive and rare. In biblical times, ointments and spices were used as investments because they were small and easy to sell. The value of her ointment was likely equivalent to a year's wages. She poured out what was precious and considered Jesus worth the sacrifice.

Her gift was humble. While it wasn't unusual to wash a guest's feet when they arrived at one's home, anointing was typically done over the head. Mary knelt before Jesus humbly, letting down her hair, and recognizing that the humblest service to Jesus had great honor. She was ridiculed for her gift by Judas, but she kept her eyes on Christ, knowing that the only thing that mattered was what He thought of her sacrifice.

When Jesus affirmed the value of Mary's gift, He drew attention to the fact that there wasn't a lot of time left—they would not always have Him with them. The same is true for us. Our time on earth is fleeting, and it's only here that we can sacrifice for Christ. Saint Albert the Great said, "An egg given during life for love of God is more profitable for eternity than a cathedral full of gold given after death."

What is most precious to you? In what do you invest your time or money? Are you willing to offer it to Jesus? Can you pour out your life in service to Him? Others will likely say that you are wasting what's precious. But can you live for an audience of one, caring more than anything about what the Lord thinks of you?

Dear Lord,
May I hold nothing back from You. May I offer You my time, my abilities, my resources, my reputation, my possessions. You held nothing back from me, sacrificing Your very life for my sake. How can I be stingy in response? Amen.

March

I am the VINE
You are the BRANCHES
WHOEVER REMAINS in
Me & i in Him will
Bear MUCH Fruit
because Apart from
Me You can do
NOTHING.
JOHN 15:5

MARCH 1

"God is not man, that he should lie, or a son of man, that he should repent. Has he said, and will he not do it? Or has he spoken, and will he not fulfil it?" (Numbers 23:19)

These words were spoken by Balaam, a prophet hired by the King of Moab to curse God's people. The king was afraid of the Israelites' power and wanted to call in some spiritual protection. Balaam was unable to say anything other than what God wanted him to say. What came out of his mouth was not a curse over God's people; instead, it was a blessing.

Balaam also revealed something about God's character, stating that God isn't like man. He can't lie. If He says something, He will do it. If He speaks a promise, it will be fulfilled. We do not need to worry that God's promises expire. They do not. He is steadfast and faithful and always follows through.

We become discouraged when we expect God to operate on our timetable. Even when we believe that He will provide relief and rescue, the long wait can feel interminable. If we only knew when the waiting would end, we would have it within us to endure. *We would have it within us.* We would be able to dig deep, rely on our own strength, and power through. But is this God's ultimate goal for His children? Or is He more interested in our dependence on Him?

When the waiting is endless, when the relief is long in coming, when we can't see the why behind what we are suffering, we must have faith. Faith is believing in what we cannot see. It is tested during times of trial, but it can be strengthened, too. When we hold on to hope because we trust that God will come through for us, this builds our faith in the same way that exercise builds a muscle. The next time difficulties arrive, we'll face them differently.

This is one of the reasons it's beneficial to keep a prayer journal. Record the dates—how long you waited, the depth of your desire for rescue, when the consolation came, and how it felt. Going back and revisiting your journal will remind you of God's faithfulness. When you are going through a trial, the enemy will tempt you to forget all the times God has come through for you. It is your job to remember.

Dear Lord,
I bring to mind this particular time when You came through for me and fulfilled Your promise: _____. You do not change. You will come through for me again.
Amen.

Be Still **MARCH 2**

"Therefore I tell you, her sins, which are many, are forgiven, for she loved much; but he who is forgiven little, loves little." (Luke 7:47)

These words were spoken by Jesus about a woman who had a bad reputation in town. She had apparently invited herself to a dinner that Jesus was attending and humbled herself in front of everyone there, anointing His feet, crying over them, and then covering them with her kisses. The host of the dinner, Simon, was scandalized and wondered why Jesus would allow someone so sinful to draw so close.

Jesus responded by telling a story about a creditor with two men in his debt. One owed a great deal; the other, much less. The creditor forgave both debts, and Jesus asked Simon which of the two he figured had more love for the creditor. "The one, I suppose, to whom he forgave more," said Simon. This was the right answer.

Have you ever looked at the sacrament of confession as a way that we can increase our love for God? When we humble ourselves and speak our sins out loud to the priest, we are always forgiven. The more we bring, the more honest we are, the more the mercy and love we receive will mean to us.

What gets in the way of this? We think we don't need God's forgiveness. We'd never say that out loud, but our actions reveal what's truly going on inside our heads. We think that we can stay on track on our own if we just set the right goals and reward ourselves along the way. We justify how serious our failings are, elevating the seriousness of other people's sins and minimizing our own.

Regular confession is a sure way to increase our love of Christ because it draws our attention to our need for Him. When we go to confession rarely, we find it hard to even come up with anything to say. We've perfected the habit of justifying our sins. But when we go regularly, we are able to go deeper, grow in our self-knowledge, and start getting to the root of our sin. We also receive grace to break habits. We're spiritually strengthened.

Has your spiritual life reached a plateau? Go to confession more often. This is sure to bring you to a new level of maturity.

Dear Lord,
Help me to see myself as You see me—the good and the bad. May I be faithful to confess my sins, and honest about what I am truly struggling with. I need Your grace in order to be the person You call me to be. Amen.

MARCH 3

"The name of the Lord is a strong tower; the righteous man runs into it and is safe." (Proverbs 18:10)

Knowing God's name signifies knowing something about who He is. A name has great significance in the Bible; it goes beyond being something that sounds nice or has sentimental value. In the Bible, a name represents the worth, character, and authority of a person. When someone knows God's name, it means that he or she has taken the time to know Him intimately. When we know Him, we can base our trust on His character, instead of on our ability to understand our suffering.

The essence of who God is can be grasped in a small yet faith-building way by studying His names. As you read these Hebrew names, focus on God's character and ask the Lord to help your trust in Him grow.

El Shaddai (The All-Sufficient One)
This name reminds us that God alone has everything we need.
El Elyon (The Most High God)
This name emphasizes God's strength and might. He is able to handle all our problems.
Jehovah-Raah (The Lord My Shepherd)
This name reminds us that the Lord will seek and save us when we are lost.
Jehovah-Rapha (The Lord That Heals)
This name reminds us that God is the Great Physician.
Jehovah Shammah (The Lord Is There)
This name reminds us that we are never alone.
Jehovah Mekoddishkem (The Lord Who Makes You Holy)
This name reminds us to call on the Holy Spirit—the Sanctifier—to ask Him to make us holy.
Jehovah Jireh (The Lord Will Provide)
This name reminds us that it isn't all up to us.
Jehovah Shalom (The Lord Is Peace)
This name reminds us that we can experience peace despite our circumstances, because God who is peace dwells within us.

God doesn't promise us an answer to our whys, but He promises something better: His presence.

"And he shall stand and feed his flock in the strength of the Lord,
in the majesty of the name of the LORD his God.
And they shall dwell secure, for now he shall be great
to the ends of the earth.
And this shall be peace." (Micah 5:4–5)

Dear Lord,
I call on Your name [say the one that means the most to you] and run to You for refuge. Amen.

Be Still

 MARCH 4

"I have said this to you, that in me you may have peace. In the world you have tribulation; but be of good cheer, I have overcome the world." (John 16:33)

When you are in the midst of suffering, it can seem as if it is never going to end. But take heart—this is not the end of your story. Things will not remain as they are in this moment. But moving forward might require you to emotionally go to places you'd rather avoid.

Crisis brings all sorts of emotions to the surface that have likely been present for a long time. Many of us are experts at sweeping things under the rug. What has been ignored now demands attention. Our emotions are moving us toward healing, but we need to be willing to journey in that direction.

God wants us to do more than just cope. He wants us to overcome, to be victorious, to grow stronger in the midst of our trials. There are many ways we're helped to experience this: the sacraments, the Bible, doctors, medication, therapy. Taking advantage of it requires that we surrender our self-reliance and admit that we need help.

This is a call to make friends with our weaknesses, to stop ignoring them, and to acknowledge that they are a critical part of who we are. Our weaknesses are gifts to us because they remind us of our need for God. It may *appear* that we are giving up, but it is actually the process of gaining spiritual strength.

Our hope does not lie in pulling ourselves up by our bootstraps. It lies in God. Lamentations 3:22–24 offers encouragement: "But this I call to mind and therefore I have hope: The steadfast love of the LORD never ceases, his mercies never come to an end; they are new every morning; great is your faithfulness. 'The LORD is my portion,' says my soul, 'therefore I will hope in him.'"

Dear Lord,
Help me to be kind to myself and take advantage of the help that is offered to me. Forgive me for the countless times I grit my teeth and try to persevere when You are asking me to admit that I can't do it alone. Please come to my aid in this area of need: _____.
Amen.

MARCH 5

"If my people who are called by my name humble themselves, and pray and seek my face, and turn from their wicked ways, then I will hear from heaven, and will forgive their sin, and heal their land." (2 Chronicles 7:14)

When God addresses the issue of a land that needs healing (and I think we all agree that ours does), whom does He begin talking to? Is it the group of people who are far from Him? No. He begins by talking to *His own people*—the ones who are called by His name. He starts with family talk.

And what's the first thing He asks us to do? Go out and convince people to look at things the way we do? No. The first thing He asks is that we'd humble ourselves. That we'd seek His face. That we'd turn from our wicked ways.

This isn't where we want to start. Our desire for justice all too often causes us to look outside ourselves. *That's* where we want God to start making things right. But He insists that the place to begin is within each of our hearts.

We don't need to limit ourselves to confessing sins that we have personally committed, although that is a good starting point. We can confess on behalf of our Church, in the same spirit that the prophet Daniel did when he confessed on behalf of the Israelite people in Daniel 9. Daniel was known for his holiness, but perhaps he was able to confess in this way because his humility reminded him that there was nothing the Israelites were capable of doing that he wasn't also capable of doing, and that the sin of one affected all. We are in this together.

We can also pray that all people, ourselves included, would experience conversion of heart. There is nothing more critical than this. All too often, what we begin with is a focus on outward behavior. We jump right away into discussions about how we are supposed to act as Christians. If this is as far as we go, then we have done an enormous disservice to the gospel. The heart of the gospel message does not begin with us cleaning ourselves up and behaving in the right way. The critical starting point is an acknowledgment that we cannot save ourselves. We need a savior. We do not start with behavior. That leads to self-righteousness and moralism. We start with confession and the gospel. That leads to Jesus.

Dear Lord,
I confess the following: _____. I ask You to forgive my sins, heal my family, and heal my country. We all desperately need a savior. Amen.

Be Still

 MARCH 6

"If you then, who are evil, know how to give good gifts to your children, how much more will your Father who is in heaven give good things to those who ask him!" (Matthew 7:11)

One of the consequences of sin entering the world is our tendency to distort God's image in our minds. We filter our experience of Him through our experience with people here on earth, and attribute to our Creator attributes that don't belong to Him. CCC 239 tells us "that human parents are fallible and can disfigure the face of fatherhood and motherhood." But we can take great comfort from this truth: "no one is father as God is Father."

We need to keep this truth in the forefront of our minds because when we are hurt, which inevitably happens, we become hesitant to trust. Trust is a critical part of our relationship with God, so we need to do all we can to separate how we see God from how we see other people.

God's goodness to us is perfect. There is no selfish motive, no expectation of payback, no bitterness over sacrifice involved. Because our heavenly Father has a limitless supply of all we need, it overflows to us continuously without measure. We do not need to be suspicious of God.

Because God desires a true relationship with us, He never forces us to accept His gifts. He wants friendship, not robotic compliance. He allows us to attempt to satisfy our desires in all sorts of places that don't deliver, but He longs for us to turn to Him in trust. God is offering good gifts to us each day, but we often don't like the packaging. Could it be that there's a good gift of encouragement on offer to us but it's packaged as the daily discipline of Bible study? Could it be that there's a good gift of refreshment on offer to us but it's packaged as slowing down and ignoring some things we'd like to get done? Could it be that there's a good gift of teaching on offer to us but it's packaged as listening to a podcast when we'd rather watch Netflix?

Keep an eye out for God's good gifts. They are there and are on offer daily. Press in and look for them, be willing to open the ones whose packaging requires a little effort, and the goodness you long for will flow into your life.

Dear Lord,
Open my eyes to the packages I have ignored and not bothered to open. Please give me a new experience of Your goodness. Amen.

MARCH 7

"Everyone who is of the truth hears my voice." (John 18:37)

The following commentary from Father John Bartunek sheds light on what being led by truth requires of us:

> Whoever lets himself be led by what is true will be drawn into communion with Christ and will hear and heed God's ceaseless invitations to follow Him more closely. But being led by truth requires humility. It requires recognizing a higher authority than oneself: if I am obliged to discover, accept, and conform to what is objectively true (morally, physically, historically), then I am not autonomous; I am not the master of my universe; I am not God.
>
> That act of humility, which frees us from the enervating bonds of selfishness, is hard to make. Our fallen human nature tends toward pride, self-sufficiency, control, and dominance. To resist that tendency requires courage. It takes courage to obey the truth and expose oneself to the burning love of God.[17]

In Romans 1, Saint Paul described what resulted when people suppressed the truth instead of embracing it. Instead of honoring God and giving thanks to Him for all the goodness received, they "became futile in their thinking and their senseless minds were darkened" (Romans 1:21). "Claiming to be wise, they became fools" (Romans 12:22). "They exchanged the truth about God for a lie and worshiped and served the creature rather than the Creator" (Romans 1:25). This isn't just something that went on during Saint Paul's time on earth. It's the way most people respond to truth today.

This exchanging of truth for a lie is so very subtle. It's a slippery slope, a gradual acceptance of what the world says matters most. We don't worship creatures in the form of carved stone idols, but we worship comfort, money, beauty, and prestige. And when we worship them by allowing them a place in our hearts that was meant for God alone, we start to believe all sorts of lies.

It takes a lot of humility and courage to ask, "God, where have I exchanged Your truth for a lie? Where am I defining truth for myself instead of humbly accepting what You have said is right and wrong?" If there is a teaching of the Church that you find hard to accept, take some time to pray about it with a humble heart.

Dear Lord,
Please reveal to me if pride, self-sufficiency, or a desire for control is getting in the way of me obeying the truth. Amen.

Be Still

MARCH 8

"By this all men will know that you are my disciples, if you have love for one another." (John 13:35)

The early Christians loved in a way that was truly radical. It captured the attention and the hearts of an empire, and the world was changed. Jesus said His followers would be known by their fruits (Matthew 7:16), and they have been. That revolutionary kind of love has continued to be at the core of the Church's activities as the centuries have passed.

The Catholic Church started hospitals and orphanages, and is the largest charitable organization in the world.[18] More children have been educated by the Catholic school system than by any other scholarly or religious institution.[19] The Catholic Church has made significant contributions to science: Catholics developed the scientific method[20] and laws of evidence.[21] The Catholic Church created the university system.[22] She continues to defend the dignity of all human life and the importance of the family. Her extraordinary contributions to art and architecture have brought inspiration, beauty, and hope to the world for centuries.

Yet today, so many of us feel ashamed of our story. We don't know how to articulate the beauty of what the Church has contributed and continues to contribute to the world. Yes, the sexual scandals and corruption within the Church are a part of who we are. But it isn't our whole story.

What made the early Christians stand out was their radical love. And that type of love is as needed today as it ever has been. The outpouring of love, mercy, and practical help that the Church became known for is still active and strong today. What is missing, however, is an experience of that revolutionary love on a personal level. Is this what people feel when they walk through the doors on an average Sunday at Mass? Think about the deep sense of community and belonging that the early Christians experienced. Think about their strong sense of family. Then think about this: That is our heritage. That is what we should be experiencing today. But far too many people walk through the doors to Mass and walk out again at the end feeling unknown, unloved, unimportant. Will anyone notice whether or not they come next week? What difference can you make in this regard?

Dear Lord,
Help me to see the difference I can make in my parish. Amen.

MARCH 9

"Arise, for it is your task, and we are with you; be strong and do it." (Ezra 10:4)

Are you frustrated by your circumstances and don't know what to do about it? Or perhaps you just feel a spirit of heaviness over everything. Maybe you are at a crossroads and feel paralyzed by the need to make a decision. We all have times when we feel stuck. So what do we do to get moving?

1. Arise.
   Literally, stand up. Take a walk. Get your body moving. Don't lie in bed or on the couch watching Netflix. That will not help.

2. For it is your task.
   Identify what is your responsibility and what is not in your control. Do you need to do some research to understand next steps? Google and YouTube can teach you an insane amount of things. Is there a task you don't feel like doing but you know you should? Do it now. Do it first. Start with what is hard and then move on to what is more appealing. Do your duty, do your job, and then pray over the list of things that are not in your control.

3. We are with you.
   Take a look around and notice who is on the home team. Who are your supporters? They may not be saying the perfect thing at the moment, but look for the people who are *for you*, and thank God for them. Spend time listening to what they are saying and zero time listening to the people critiquing you from the cheap seats. Remember the communion of the saints. Which saint has a special devotion to what you are dealing with? Ask for his or her intercession. And most important, don't forget that God is always with you and has even given you the Holy Spirit to dwell in you so you are never alone.

4. Be strong and do it.
   Be strong by putting on your spiritual armor (Ephesians 6) and asking God to help you. Tell Him you want to do your task through the strength of the Holy Spirit, not your own abilities. Entrust the results to God. Then step out and just do it. You might fail. That's OK. If you do, it's because God decided there was some bit of gold to be mined in that experience. And if it succeeds the first time around (how amazing is that?), then be sure to give God the credit.

Dear Lord,
Help me to live in this way and not give up. Help me to press on. Amen.

Be Still

MARCH 10

"As your days, so shall your strength be." (Deuteronomy 33:25)

God is in control. There is nothing that touches His children—no event, no person, no heartache—that He has not first weighed in His hands. He then measures it against our strength, plus His. Only the things that can be handled by *us plus Him* are allowed to intersect our lives.

When we say, "I just can't take it.... I can't handle this anymore.... It is too much," we are speaking honestly about the limits of our own strength. It's OK to recognize when we come to the end of our resources. That's authentic and being realistic. But in the next moment, we need to remember the difference God makes. When He steps in, we can take it. We can handle it. It isn't too much.

So why don't we automatically do that—invite Him into the struggle—each and every time? For a couple of reasons. We forget. When circumstances are wearing us out, we naturally focus on them. Thinking about our trials instead of disciplining ourselves to note what we are grateful for keeps us sleepy and forgetful.

Also, we want to do it ourselves. We aren't all that different from the ten-month-old baby who wants to hold the spoon herself, even though that means none of the food is reaching her mouth. Stubbornly wanting to be enough, we keep trying. We like to stand on our own two feet and owe nothing to anyone. Even to God.

We fall into the pit of self-pity. Often the solution is available, but it isn't what we want it to look like. We start behaving like martyrs without even realizing it. Imagine a ferocious dog, bound by a chain but able to do great damage within a certain circumference. We stand within that circle and are getting beaten to a pulp. But we could choose to step out. That is in our power. But self-pity causes us to sit down and feel sorry for ourselves instead. We can do something to move ourselves out of the pit, but there's something about that solution that we don't like, so we wait for the perfect one. And we get more beaten down every minute we refuse the help on offer.

Ask for help. It's as simple as that. God will provide the strength you need. It may not come in exactly the way you'd prefer, but it will be enough to get you through.

Dear Lord,
Please come. Help me. Infuse me with strength so I can move out of the pit of self-pity. Amen.

MARCH 11

"For out of the abundance of the heart the mouth speaks." (Matthew 12:34)

It's been said that what comes up in the bucket was down in the well. Whatever is in our hearts ends up surfacing, no matter how much we might try to keep it all tucked away. Those words matter. They can cause tremendous damage, and once they are out, we can't get them back.

When our hearts are full of resentment or anger, we may manage to keep the emotions in check when we are dealing with the person who has caused it. This is true of those of us who have become experts at stuffing our emotions. But the feelings are still in there, and they will surface another time, often directed toward a person who didn't cause the original problem but has inadvertently triggered us.

Our emotions seep out. They don't stay safely locked away—that is, unless we choose to numb them, in which case we end up numbing everything, including joy.

The battle is won or lost in the heart. God needs to reign there, helping us make the right decisions and ordering and healing our emotions. He is to be the king of our hearts, and also the great physician. If we give Him authority in our lives and obey Him, we'll likely get our outward behaviors right. But eventually, the unresolved emotions will rise up and come out, often in not very pretty ways. We need to allow Him free reign to be our heart healer.

Dear Lord,
I invite You into the depths of my heart. There are so many emotions there, countless things that I want to hide from You. But instead, I ask You to come in and order them. Distill Your peace and perspective. Bring me healing and hope. Bind up my wounds and bring blessing. Amen.

Be Still

 MARCH 12

"Go your way, eat the fat and drink sweet wine and send portions to him for whom nothing is prepared; for this day is holy to our Lord; and do not be grieved, for the joy of the Lord is your strength." (Nehemiah 8:10)

These words were spoken to the Israelites after years of exile. They had lost everything and were now back home, beginning the long journey of rebuilding. Ezra (the priest) and Nehemiah (the governor) had taken out the book of the law and read it to them. As the people listened to him read, they wept and mourned as they realized how far they had fallen from what God had asked of them.

Ezra and Nehemiah's response to their grief and repentance was interesting. They told the people to feast and celebrate. Why? Because "there will be more joy in heaven over one sinner who repents than over ninety-nine righteous persons who need no repentance" (Luke 15:7). When we are sorry for our sin, there is rejoicing in heaven because we are now on the path to a renewed relationship with God. God is now able to do amazing things in and through us. When we remain stuck in our sin, justifying ourselves, the Holy Spirit is quenched. His power is put on hold. But when we repent, it is released.

After confession, we would do well to shout, "The joy of the Lord is my strength!" Heartbreak over sin ushers in a fresh start in which there is no limit to what God can do. Once you have confessed your sin, don't wallow in despair. Grab hold of God's mercy and radiate that grace to others. You now have a blank page of paper and only you will limit the life adventure that can be written on it. Give God the pen, do it with joy, and stand back to watch Him create a masterpiece.

May your life be a feast that makes others want to join the party.

Dear Lord,
May Your joy fill me and be my source of strength. May confession usher in a reboot that kicks old habits to the curb and releases an outpouring of the Holy Spirit within me. Amen.

MARCH 13

"And in the morning, a great while before day, he rose and went out to a lonely place, and there he prayed." (Mark 1:35)

If Jesus felt the need to get up early and pray, why do I think I can get away with skipping it? Do I really think my plans, goals, and hustle are what makes all the difference? My actions speak louder than words. If I am skipping morning prayer, then that is exactly what I believe.

Inevitably, when I start my day with great intentions and grit but skip prayer, something nose-dives. I might do OK for a little while, but it doesn't last. I hit roadblocks, my patience fails, and frustration sets in. But when I do begin with prayer, more often than not I find my hours have somehow multiplied. I have accomplished more in less time. The Holy Spirit has been a wind within me and behind me, propelling me forward in His strength and grace.

Morning prayer begins the night before. If my house is a mess, I'll wake up and start putting things in order. But if I have taken fifteen minutes the night before to clean the kitchen and tidy the room where I want to pray, I am far less distracted. If I have thought ahead to what my family will need when they wake up and prep it the night before, that buys me some more time. Getting to sleep at a reasonable hour is critical because we need rest.

The game changer for me has been rising one hour before anyone else in my house. You might not need to get up so early, you may not need this much time, but this is what works for me. I'm able to make my tea, settle into my chair, pray and read Scripture, and commit my day's schedule to the Lord.

Having a dedicated place to pray is also a huge help. Choose a spot in your house where you can be alone, and make sure all the things you need to pray are there: your Bible, prayer journal, pen, rosary, and anything else you might need.

Make yourself a promise that you won't skip this divine appointment. It will truly change your life.

Dear Lord,
I commit to getting up in the morning and starting my day with prayer. I will do this for thirty days. If I keep this promise, I will reward myself with: _____. Amen.

Be Still **MARCH 14**

"He brought me to the banqueting house, and his banner over me was love."
(Song of Solomon 2:4)

What is the purpose of a banner? It's a flag or a standard raised during a battle, to indicate the rallying point. This is where the eye is supposed to go, and the symbol on the banner is to remind the warriors of what they are fighting for. Picture exhausted soldiers in a grueling battle, and then a white stallion breaking through the ranks, one brave mounted soldier waving their country's flag, calling them to be brave and fight for what they love. It lifts eyes to the purpose of the battle and offers hope.

The banner God raises above us is one of love. It was for love of you that Jesus sacrificed His life for you. It was for love of you that God brought you into the world. It was for love of you that God created beautiful sunsets, majestic mountains, and the raging sea. It was for love of you that God allows both the hard things and the delightful ones to intersect your life. He looks at you and the overwhelming emotion felt is love. Raise your eyes to the banner of love.

The banqueting table He invites you to is both now and later. One day, you'll be invited to the heavenly banquet, where the feasting will be beyond compare. That will occur later, but now, He invites you to the banquet table of this life—this one wild, unpredictable life that, while containing heartache, also brings moments of pure joy, surprise, and beauty.

A battle rages every day between you and that banquet table. The enemy wants to keep you from sitting down and enjoying the life God has prepared for you. He wants your focus to remain on all the things you don't like and to prevent you from practicing gratitude. Gratitude clears a path straight to the banquet table. The enemy wants to keep your focus down, not up—because if you look up, you'll see the banner of love waving above your head and it will change your perspective. It'll rally you to move forward toward the banquet table.

Keep your eye on the banner. Remember that everything that happens to you has been filtered through the Father's love. It can all be worked to good in His capable and tender hands. Look for the blessings. Keep an eye out for the surprises God has placed in your path today—the little consolations, the small things that can deliver great joy if you slow down and really see them.

Dear Lord,
Thank You for inviting me to the banquet of my unique, hand-picked-by-You life. I raise my eyes to the banner of Your love and pray that they remain there throughout my day. Amen.

MARCH 15

"The Holy Spirit will come upon you." (Luke 1:35)

What kind of help does the Holy Spirit offer? The Holy Spirit confirms that you are God's child. Perhaps sometimes you question who you are. The Holy Spirit lives in your heart and reminds you from within that you are God's child, His beloved daughter. If you live your life from that identity, you're more likely to make wise choice- instead of people pleasing.

The Holy Spirit makes you holy. When the Holy Spirit took up residence inside you, He brought along love, joy, peace, patience, kindness, goodness, faithfulness, gentleness, and self-control. This means that you always have these qualities at your disposal. If you're not feeling patient, you can ask the Holy Spirit to be patient *in you*, to replace your impatience with His presence—with His patience.

The Holy Spirit helps you to pray. You don't have to pray perfectly. You can just talk to God as you would a friend, and ask the Holy Spirit to intercede for you, communicating within the Trinity in a way that you don't understand but that asks perfectly for what you truly need.

The Holy Spirit helps you to speak. When you are heading into a conversation and you're not sure what to say, the Holy Spirit is willing to *speak through you*. I can pray, "Give me the right words. Please speak through me. Please keep me from saying the wrong thing," and He will do it.

The Holy Spirit remains with you. You are never alone. If you need to be comforted, encouraged, or strengthened, the Holy Spirit is always there, just waiting to be asked for help. He's the quiet guest of your heart.

The Holy Spirit is willing to do so much for you, but He is a gracious guest, and waits to be invited. You can decide to just keep Him in the entryway of your heart, or you can invite Him to come all the way in. It all depends on how much power and transformation you really want to experience. Unfortunately, too many of us say that certain rooms are off-limits. When we do this, we miss out. The rooms we close off are often ones that contain pain that He is just waiting to heal. Or perhaps they are places where we're stuck in bad patterns of behavior, and He wants to set us free. Take some time to pray about the rooms that you are keeping closed off to the Holy Spirit.

Dear Lord,
I open the door and invite You to enter. Come in with the breath of Your sweet and gentle presence. Amen.

Be Still **MARCH 16**

"Now you are the body of Christ and individually members of it." (1 Corinthians 12:27)

We need one another. Just as the head needs the neck, the leg needs the hip, and the fingers need the hand, we do not do well cut off from the body. To live as a family—as the body of Christ—will take a conscious choice. We live in a highly individualistic society that encourages us to stand on our own two feet, to rely on no one, to be confident in our own strength. To participate in a faith community—"doing life" together, as opposed to merely attending a religious service together—takes time and sacrifice. When we draw close to one another, we receive the comfort of another's presence, but we also see each other's faults a little more clearly. But that's what it means to be in a family.

Our family spans the globe and includes every race, the rich and the poor, the educated and the simple. We are diverse. We are full of complex differences. But what draws us together is a love for Jesus and for His body—the Church.

Spend some time talking to the Lord about how it feels to walk into your parish. Ask Him to open your eyes to ways in which you can be His hands and feet, bringing His warmth, His grace, His provision, and His love to the aching souls that come to Mass week after week. Ask Him to help you see people as He sees them. And ask for the courage to step out of your comfort zone to radically love those God has called to be your Church family.

> If the Church was a body composed of different members, it couldn't lack the noblest of all; it must have a Heart, and a Heart burning with love. And I realized that this love alone was the true motive force which enabled the other members of the Church to act; if it ceased to function, the Apostles would forget to preach the gospel, the Martyrs would refuse to shed their blood. Love, in fact, is the vocation which includes all others; it's a universe of its own, comprising all time and space—it's eternal![23] —Saint Thérèse of Lisieux

Dear Lord,
Help me to notice the furthest person out at Mass. May I step out of my comfort zone and be a conduit of Your love to that person. May I be moved to action, not just inward compassion. Amen.

MARCH 17

The Feast of Saint Patrick

"We know that in everything God works for good with those who love him, who are called according to his purpose." (Romans 8:28)

While many details of Saint Patrick's life remain unknown, one thing is certain: He was courageous and faithful. When Saint Patrick was sixteen, he and a large number of his father's vassals and slaves were captured and sold into slavery in Ireland. Working as a shepherd, he learned to persevere in the cold, with hunger a steady reality.

Years later, he escaped to France. He entered religious studies and became a bishop by the age of forty-three. While being enslaved was miserable and certainly not his preferred path, it's what led to his spiritual conversion. Being enslaved brought him to ultimate freedom. God worked for Saint Patrick's good in the midst of miserable circumstances. Patrick would have agreed with C. S. Lewis, who wrote, "Pain insists upon being attended to. God whispers to us in our pleasures, speaks in our consciences, but shouts in our pains. It is his megaphone to rouse a deaf world."[24]

One would expect Saint Patrick to never again set foot on Irish soil after his escape, but he felt called by God to return. Ireland was a pagan nation, and Saint Patrick wanted the people there to know Christ. Because of him, Ireland was not only Christianized, it sent out countless missionaries who spread the gospel in Europe. He's a great saint for us to turn to when we need just a little more courage than fear. Ask for his intercession so that you can step out boldly, filled with God's strength.

Saint Patrick's breastplate is a powerful prayer:

I arise today, through
God's strength to pilot me,
God's might to uphold me,
God's wisdom to guide me,
God's eye to look before me,
God's ear to hear me,
God's word to speak for me,
God's hand to guard me,
God's shield to protect me,
God's host to save me
From snares of devils,
From temptation of vices,
From everyone who shall wish me ill,
afar and near . . .

Christ with me,
Christ before me,
Christ behind me,
Christ in me,
Christ beneath me,
Christ above me,
Christ on my right,
Christ on my left,
Christ when I lie down,
Christ when I sit down,
Christ when I arise,
Christ in the heart of every man who thinks of me,
Christ in the mouth of everyone who speaks of me,
Christ in every eye that sees me,
Christ in every ear that hears me. Amen.

Be Still

 MARCH 18

"And let us not grow weary in well-doing, for in due season we shall reap, if we do not lose heart. So then, as we have opportunity, let us do good to all men, and especially to those who are of the household of faith." (Galatians 6:9–10)

When we look at church as a destination—a place that we *go*—we inadvertently develop the mind-set of a consumer. We go there to have our needs met. We go there to be filled. We go there to receive. That is *part* of what the Church does for us, but it is only a portion of the whole picture. The way in which needs are met in the Church is not only through receiving the sacraments. Needs are also met through the hands and hearts of God's people—through the ways in which we minister to one another. This means that each one of us has a part to play. When we do not step up and do our part, the body of Christ suffers.

We're busy. But what if our schedules are filled up with things that aren't really going to matter in the long run? And by long run, I mean eternity. What if when we stand before God and explain to Him what we've done with the time and talent He's given us, we realize that we used it selfishly or for superficial pursuits?

God isn't so concerned with how skilled we are, but He's very concerned with how obedient we are. As has been wisely said, "God doesn't call the equipped. He equips the called." And make no mistake—He is calling you.

God has been pouring His Spirit and His grace into you. You are now faced with a choice. You can turn your focus inward. You can become a spiritual consumer who is always looking for the next thing you need to feel spiritually high. Or you can embrace the power of the word *and*. You can keep doing the things that help you grow spiritually *and* you can turn your focus outward. We aren't here to form a spiritual club, to be a part of a holy huddle. It's time to step out.

Where is God calling you? Start small. Just be obedient and respond to the need that He places in front of you. What is driving you crazy in your parish? Can you step in and be a part of the change that you want to see?

Dear Lord,
I offer you my hands and feet. I commit to stop focusing on my limitations. I will fix my eyes instead on You and on Your immeasurable power. Amen.

MARCH 19

Feast of Saint Joseph

"An angel of the Lord appeared to [Joseph] in a dream, saying, 'Joseph, son of David, do not fear to take Mary your wife, for that which is conceived in her is of the Holy Spirit; she will bear a son, and you shall call his name Jesus, for he will save his people from their sins.'"
(Matthew 1:20–21)

God's plan to save His people from their sins was unconventional. It certainly wasn't what Joseph would have expected or initially hoped for. His life was planned out, and Mary being pregnant by someone other than him was not a part of that plan. Joseph could have opted out. God didn't force him to take part in the redemptive mission. But once Joseph was convinced that God was behind it all, he went all in. He became the protector, father, guide, and teacher that Jesus needed as He grew.

What is your response when God upsets your plans? Surrendering our agendas is very difficult, especially for those of us who like to be in control. One way I have been helped in this area of personal weakness is to spend some prayer time in the morning with my calendar in my lap. I read through what I want to get done in the day and discuss it with the Lord. "This is what I think is most important," I say. Then I've learned to follow that statement with these words: "But you may have other plans. In fact, you probably do have other plans. So help me to see interruptions in my day as divine appointments, set up by you."

Does this mean that it's easy to have my plans upended? No, but I save time with this attitude. Instead of getting frustrated and derailed, I am far more likely to just accept things as they are and get on with it. If items on my agenda didn't get done because of one of those divine interruptions, I can't say that I like it, but I can say that I don't beat myself up over it. If God allowed the interruption, He knew that with limited hours in the day, something else would not get done. And in His providence, He has decided that's OK. If it's OK with Him, it should be OK with me, too.

Dear Lord,
I give You my day to order as You will. Amen.

Be Still **MARCH 20**

"God has reconciled us to himself through Christ and given us the ministry of reconciliation."
(2 Corinthians 5:18)

God has brought a beautiful woman into my life who is willing to let me borrow her glasses—to see life from her perspective. It's different than mine in so many ways—she is African American and I am white—yet we are very much alike at the heart level. We met at a dinner and cut to the chase, immediately going deep and talking about the racial divide in our country. I asked her if she would be willing to keep the dialogue going and send me articles and concerns that are intersecting her life that I might be missing. She has been faithful in doing that, giving me things to think about that have softened my heart and challenged me.

She challenges me to not tell her how to feel, to not make assumptions about what it is like to walk in her shoes. Instead, she invites me to lean in and listen, to make room in my heart for her perspective, and to allow what she teaches me to open my eyes.

Lent is a time when we focus on fasting. I've heard it said that we fast in order to make more room in ourselves for God. Following that thought, how can we fast to make more room in our hearts to welcome someone whose perspective on life is different than ours?

What if we fasted from speaking and listened instead?
What if we fasted from the holy huddle and made sure we took time every day to talk to someone unlike us?
What if we fasted from comfort in order to build a bridge of unity across the divide?

Thought leader Howard Ross suggests using the following questions to engage in dialogue with someone whose point of view is different than yours:

1. Why do you feel the way you do?
2. What is it about the other point of view that frightens you?
3. What are some questions you have about the other person that you want to ask?
4. Is there anything you need to say to be complete?

God has given us the ministry of reconciliation. The message He has entrusted to us is helping to reestablish a close relationship between two parties that are experiencing a divide. I believe it is time to stop fasting from ignoring this mission and instead take it up.

Dear Lord,
Help me to trade lenses with someone this Lent, fasting from my own point of view and feasting on what life feels like in someone else's shoes. Amen.

MARCH 21

"Those who are well have no need of a physician, but those who are sick; I came not to call the righteous, but sinners." (Mark 2:17)

What is the diagnosis? Man, apart from Christ, has a terminal disease. He will die; it won't end pretty. But there is a remedy, a guaranteed cure. The problem is, it requires that we give up control. We have to surrender. We have to obey. Our remedy cost Jesus everything, and He asks for everything from us in return. But "what does it profit a man if he gains the whole world and loses or forfeits himself?" (Luke 9:25)

People who consider themselves righteous don't believe they need a savior. Until we get to a place where we recognize our helplessness, there's not a lot God can do to help us. Our hands need to be emptied in order to be filled by His grace.

When we think we need to first clean ourselves up before we can be acceptable to God, we are completely missing who He is and how He wants to be approached. Nothing delights God more than when a person recognizes his or her need for a physician for the soul. When we acknowledge that we need the healing touch of a savior, God is free to move. But if we insist on taking care of ourselves, God will respect that choice.

Come dirty, come sick, come messy, come broken. Come as you are. Let Jesus meet you in that place. Encounter Him as the divine physician and you will discover that He has the most accurate diagnosis, a surefire cure, and He will pay the bill with His own blood.

Dear Lord,
I am done trying to clean myself up. I am done trying to save myself. I stand before You and ask You to do for me what I am unable to do for myself. Please save me. Amen.

Be Still **MARCH 22**

"Rejoice not over me, O my enemy; when I fall, I shall rise; when I sit in darkness, the Lord will be a light to me." (Micah 7:8)

Something that steals our hope and keeps us in darkness is the myriad of lies that swirl around us. Not every thought that crosses your mind comes from you. The enemy of your soul loves to whisper distortions of truth, to sow seeds of confusion and despair. For the next five days, we'll focus on four lies that are keeping us in darkness. War is upon us, whether we wish it or not, but the truth is a powerful weapon and Jesus promises it will set us free.

Lie: The world is going to hell in a handbasket.
The truth: We are a part of an epic tale, a story that God has been writing since the beginning of time, and the ending is *good*.

When the postmodern culture tells us that there is no grand narrative, something in us should pause and say, "No. That's not right. There *is* a narrative that actually makes sense out of all the crazy things that go on in our world. There *is* a story; there *is* an eternal plan. The problem: So many of us have forgotten our story.

Saint John Paul II proposed that the Holy Spirit came into the world to remind us of our story. "The world does not know where it came from, what sustains it, or where its destiny lies, although it assumes that it knows all these things."[25] This is why the Church is so important. In the words of George Weigel, who wrote Pope John Paul II's biography, the Church is "a sanctuary of truth telling in a world dominated by lies."[26] And if so many of us have forgotten our story, then we need good storytellers to help us to remember it.

The truth is, we are a part of a glorious story that ends in victory. We are a part of a grand narrative that He conceived of and planned out and has been bringing to reality and fruition since the very beginning of time. And He is 100 percent in control of what we're experiencing. He is working all things to the good. He is not asleep on the job. The evil in the world is never going to extinguish the power of the good. The end of the story is glorious.

Dear Lord,
I commit to learning where the world came from, what sustains it, and where its destiny lies. Help me to become a great storyteller. Amen.

MARCH 23

"The people who walked in darkness have seen a great light; those who dwelt in a land of deep darkness, on them has light shined." (Isaiah 9:2)

Let's continue to unpack the lies that keep us in darkness.

Lie: There's nothing we can do about the droves of people who are leaving the Church.
The truth: People are still searching for truth, hungering for happiness, and desiring lasting peace. Christ is the answer to that search.

People are asking big questions, and Christ is the answer. They are asking: Who am I? How can I find real love? What does it mean to be happy and live a good life? How do I focus on what matters and live up to my potential? How can I experience lasting peace?

The goal is for people to seek the truth. We are assured in Jeremiah 29:13 that those who seek God wholeheartedly will find Him. This journey may be direct or have a lot of detours. Let's not freak out and lose hope over the detours. What is to be avoided is stubborn self-assurance, which rejects the need to keep learning.

Once people are discussing their questions, we can start to explore the ways we all search for answers. When we do this, we'll discover the points when our Christian faith answers the question in one way and the secular world answers in another. We can then start to unpack the faulty logic that leads many people to head away from Christ as the answer and toward what the world says is going to satisfy—a path that we know ultimately does not bring the light, joy, and abundance that our culture promises.

If the Lord has placed someone specific on your heart, I encourage you to not give up. Keep storming heaven. No method of discussion or engagement will ever replace the impact of prayer. Keep asking God to bring people into your loved one's life who can tell him or her about Jesus and who are good examples of a follower of Christ. Keep asking God to break down the barriers that are getting in the way. Keep interceding and asking the Lord to heal any hurts that are making it hard to see His irresistible and unconditional love. And renew your commitment to not play around with sin in your own life. Be passionately committed to your own holiness so that nothing gets in the way of the light of Christ shining out of you. Your loved one is watching you to see if Christ is answering *your* questions.

Dear Lord,
Shine Your light in the heart of my loved one. Amen.

Be Still

MARCH 24

"For once you were darkness, but now you are light in the Lord." (Ephesians 5:8)

Lie: The past can stay in the past. I've moved on and I'm fine.
The truth: Not dealing with our brokenness keeps us in darkness.

We may think we're fine, but our wounds don't really stay put away in a box. Even though we put the boxes up in the attic, what's inside leaks out. Our hurts leak into our lives and we end up in a place where we can give in to despair because we are stuck. We become trapped in unhealthy patterns of sin and unhealthy responses to things that trigger us.

We have to take a step back into the darkness of past hurts to step forward into the light of healing. We all have memories that we'd rather not revisit. They are painful to remember. But if we are smart, we'll go back and check whether in that moment a lie was spoken to our hearts. In that moment of pain, did you hear the lie "I am unwanted"? "I am ugly"? "I am alone"? "I am out of control"? "I am powerless"? "If I trust, I will be destroyed"? "Nothing ever changes"?

This litany of lies (or just one potent lie that is tailor made to our wounds) is whispered to us by the enemy. Not every thought we have is ours. The problem comes not when the lie is whispered—we can't really do anything about that—but when we *agree* with it. And when we agree with the lie, we panic at the thought that it is possible to feel this way again, to be hurt this way again. So we make a vow. We say things like "I will never," or "I will always," and we develop unhealthy coping mechanisms rooted in ungodly self-reliance. What this does is keep us bound and in darkness because we are not really living with the light being shone on why we are reacting in certain ways when we're triggered. Not dealing with our brokenness keeps us in darkness. But bringing it all into the light is the first step toward healing.

Dear Lord,
I give myself permission to come a little undone—to revisit what has hurt me—so that You can shine a light into the darkness and guide me to freedom. Help me to find the right people to accompany me on this journey who will speak truth and wisdom into my heart. Amen.

MARCH 25

"He has delivered us from the dominion of darkness and transferred us to the kingdom of his beloved Son." (Colossians 1:13)

Lie: Refusing to forgive won't hurt me.
The truth: Unforgiveness keeps us locked in darkness.

It's said that refusing to forgive is like drinking poison and expecting the other person to die. Unforgiveness keeps us locked in darkness and destroys us from within. Something that gets in the way of our willingness and ability to forgive is unconsciously defined ourselves by what has hurt us. The hurt becomes who we are. A woman defined by her hurt is often filled with a determinism that says, "I can't help how I react! Because I'm a victim, I'm allowed certain escapisms. Because of _____, I deserve _____." These "deserved escapes" reveal an inner attitude that says, "I am not responsible. I am not responsible for the problem or what has resulted from it. I'm entitled to all these things. I know it's not good, but the world should make up for my hurt." There is no personal responsibility.

What's the alternative? We can choose to define ourselves as God's beloved daughters, to look at our good qualities and all the gifts we've been given. The result is being filled not with self-pity, but with gratitude. It is only as our hearts are filled with gratitude that we are able to forgive. We are enabled to forgive as we focus on how God has forgiven us. This truth is addressed in the book *From Anger to Intimacy*. The authors write:

> No matter what has happened, you are invited to forgive just as God has wholly and fully forgiven you. Where do you find that kind of forgiveness? Through the person of Jesus Christ. Matthew 10:8 says, "Freely you have received, freely give" ... If you are not a forgiving person, if you have unresolved anger, bitterness or resentment in your heart—and you do nothing to get rid of it, then you have not yet experienced or realized the forgiveness you have received.[27]

Do we truly appreciate the forgiveness that Christ purchased for us? Or have we become callous to what it cost Him? What might change in your life and the lives of your loved ones if you offered forgiveness?

Dear Lord,
Please give me the strength to endure the temporary pain of working through forgiveness, so that I can experience healing on the other side. Amen.

Be Still

 MARCH 26

"He saved us, not because of deeds done by us in righteousness, but in virtue of his own mercy, by the washing of regeneration and renewal in the Holy Spirit, which he poured out upon us richly through Jesus Christ our Savior." (Titus 3:5–6)

So many of us head into each day hoping that our performance will earn us the verdict *good enough*. Every morning we are, in essence, getting ready for the trial we think we're going to face. In this tribunal, we have to prove that we are enough—young enough, smart enough, good-looking enough, successful enough, holy enough, thin enough. Some days we feel we nail it. Other days we don't. A new day dawns and the proving just starts all over again. We never quite get to that place where we can say, *done*. The result of this yo-yo life? Insecurity and exhaustion.

But a game-changing event took place more than two thousand years ago, and it changed everything about this tribunal. When we forget this, when we relegate this fact to a part of our lives just reserved for Sunday, we miss out on the peace we are promised.

What happened when Jesus died on the cross all those years ago? He entered the courtroom on our behalf. He stood trial for all our sins and shortcomings. When the guilty verdict came in for what we have done, Jesus took the punishment in our place. What did He say on the cross just before He died? *It is finished.*

So when we choose to go into the courtroom each morning, ready to be on trial for our worthiness, God waits for us to turn and notice that He is there, with something to say to us. Sometimes we rush by Him. We're so busy with so much to prove. But when we take the time to pause, when we turn our face to His, He tells us, "You don't have to go in there. The trial is over. The punishment has already been meted out and was paid for by me. You are free to go and live differently."

There is nothing to prove when we know that we are forgiven.
There is nothing to prove when we know that we are unconditionally loved.
There is nothing to prove when we know that we are accepted by God, not because of anything we have done, but because of what Jesus has done.

It's already been decided. The jury is in. You have been declared enough, not because of any righteous things you have done, but because of Jesus and what He did.

Dear Lord,
May I pass by that courtroom door each day and instead come into Your presence. Amen.

MARCH 27

"Forgetting what lies behind and straining forward to what lies ahead, I press on toward the goal for the prize of the upward call of God in Christ Jesus." (Philippians 3:13)

Are you dragging unnecessary baggage along life's journey?

Some of us are carrying the good girl's suitcase. We figured out early on what the expectations were, and we set out to meet them. We've been being good girls for so long, it's second nature. Reputation is important, so we work to keep ours impeccable. We hide behind masks, because being weak, being afraid, and being a mess affects what people think of us. We follow the rules. We serve where needed. We hear that the Christian life is supposed to be about freedom, but to us, it just feels like hard work. Sometimes we get a little frustrated with a God who expects so much. We look at pursuing lasting purpose according to God's design and wonder if this means we'll just have a whole new area where we need to perform. That's a heavy suitcase to drag around.

Some of us are dragging the suitcase of guilt. It's filled with past sins—some confessed, some unconfessed. All put together, they weigh a ton. When Christ invites us to seek forgiveness, we peek inside and conclude that this garbage is just too much. It's too wretched to bring to the surface. Even if God might forgive it, we say that we can't forgive ourselves. We ignore the pride implicit in setting ourselves up as higher judges than God and keep lugging this junk on the journey.

Some of us are holding tight to the suitcase of bitterness. Too many dreams have been dashed. We've believed in the promises in the past, but their fulfillment was too long in coming. We've resigned ourselves to just getting through life. Why hope if we're just going to be disappointed? This suitcase is sitting on our hearts and weighing us down. We feel the continual heaviness and there seems to be no relief.

Jesus wants us to drag all these suitcases to the foot of the cross and leave them there. He wants to take our burden of past mistakes and exchange them for His forgiveness. He invites to take our burden of perfectionism and attempts to earn God's favor and exchange them for His unconditional love. He longs for us to bring our bitterness to the cross and look up to see our champion, who will fight for us and right every wrong.

Dear Lord,
I want to answer the call to forget what lies behind and strain forward to what lies ahead. Eyes up, forward focus! Amen.

Be Still

MARCH 28

"Pilate said to him, 'What is truth?'" (John 18:38)

Most people believe that truth does not exist apart from what they personally determine is truth. Postmodernism is the prevailing mode of thought influencing our culture. This is a worldview that asserts that external, absolute truth cannot be known through reason (this was the focus during the Age of Enlightenment), or science (the focus of Modernism), because absolute truth is either nonexistent or unknowable. Postmodernism asserts that experience is more reliable than reason. Truth is *created* rather than *discovered*. I *feel* has replaced I *know*.

Postmodernists say, "If it's true for you, then it's as true as it needs to be. And no one has the right to question what you have chosen as truth for yourself." But does the phrase "what is truth" or "what's true for you" really mean anything? Can truth exist as a reality solely for the people who believe it?

Say you and your friend find an apple. Your friend believes that the apple is full of worms. You believe that it is fresh and worm-free. Can your differing views about the apple create two truths that you both can experience as a reality? The way to find out is to slice open the apple. Then you'll discover that either the apple has worms or it doesn't. The moment you slice into it, either your "truth" or that of your friend will be exposed as an error.

In the quest for truth, people check if something works. So if your faith helps you to have a nice life with morals and peace, then great. It works. Your faith is true for you. But if a priest is accused of child abuse, then the truth he taught is proven to not be true because it didn't work. That's how many people discern what is true.

God says that truth itself will stand up to scrutiny, and when put into principle and action, it will result in a life that works. It's not "If it works, it's true"; instead, it's "If it's true, it will work." There *is* absolute truth, and whether that truth is true does not depend on whether anyone chooses to believe it.

Instead of sitting contentedly and looking at the apple, one of us thinking it's full of worms and the other thinking it's fresh, we need to investigate. We need to dig deeper so that we learn not just what we believe, but why we believe it.

Dear Lord,
I commit to digging deeper and studying so that I can understand why I believe what I believe. Please guide me on that path to the best things to read and wise people to learn from. Amen.

MARCH 29

"Jesus said to him, 'I am the way, and the truth, and the life.'" (John 14:6)

Truth matters. How we handle truth matters. When Jesus described Himself as the way, the truth, and the life, He was letting us know that truth is found by following Him. That's what Pilate hadn't figured out when he flippantly asked Jesus, "What is truth?"

When we hear the name Pontius Pilate, we immediately think of his weakness—his unwillingness to do what was right if it meant personal sacrifice or risk. Little did Pilate know how all ages of history would judge him for his choice of actions during his once-in-a-lifetime encounter with Jesus of Nazareth.

How do you want to be remembered? Note that Pilate thought his actions in Jesus' trial were just events in a day, but they ended up shaping who he was for all of history. In the same way, the legacy that we leave behind stems from seemingly insignificant decisions we make each day. Every day, we encounter the same decision Pilate faced: Will I do what I know is right regardless of what it costs me, or will I choose to ensure my comfort and protect my reputation?

We don't need to travel to the other side of the world or do full-time religious work to make a difference and leave a legacy. We can meet needs right where we are, and do it with authenticity, grace, and love. Author Gabe Lyons gives a beautiful description of the kind of people that can change the world: "As a Christian, when you restore where you are, people take notice. You become the model of a person who pursues deep relationships, lives with purpose and meaning, commits to the service of others, and reconciles injustices wherever they exist. If you strive to be faithful to Christ, your life will paint a picture of what every human soul is longing for."[28]

Dear Lord,
People are starving for something that works—a life-changing, authentic faith that fills the emptiness inside. They are also waiting to see authentic faith that focuses outward to meet the needs of the world—the physical hunger, poverty, and mistreatment of the weak. May both aspects of true faith be seen in my life, through Your grace at work in me. Amen.

MARCH 30

"Take heart, it is I; have no fear." (Matthew 14:27)

God desires that we live free of fear. But what do we do with our anxieties and worries? Do we just ignore them? Do we spend all our energy trying to control every situation to ensure a better outcome? Should we just distract ourselves so that we don't have to think deeply about what we're afraid of?

No. This isn't what Jesus is talking about when He tells us not to be afraid. What Jesus is speaking about is the opposite of fear—it's peace of soul. This peace of soul is not dependent on our circumstances. In John 14:27, Jesus said, "Peace I leave with you, my peace I give to you; not as the world gives do I give to you. Let not your hearts be troubled, neither let them be afraid." A heart filled with this kind of peace sounds like the person described in Psalm 112:7: "He is not afraid of evil tidings; his heart is firm, trusting in the Lord." Peace of soul comes from trusting God.

Author Linda Dillow identifies two possible meanings of the question "Do you trust God?" She writes, "The first is 'Can you trust *God*?' Is He dependable in times of adversity? But the second meaning is also critical: 'Can *you* trust God?' Do you have such a relationship with God and such a confidence in Him that you believe He is with you in your anxiety, even though you don't see any evidence of His presence and His power?"[29]

Suffering is wanting what we don't have or having what we don't want, and it is unavoidable. Without faith, we'd have great difficulty dealing with suffering. But faith allows us to say, "Even though this circumstance is not what I want, I can see that God is giving me what I need in the midst of it." God promises to always give us what we need. But we have to recognize the difference between our wants and our needs. What do we need most? Him. And He promises that He will never leave us or forsake us.

His presence is enough. We see this best in hindsight. As we walk through the storm, we are often worried that it's going to get worse and we won't make it. Afterward, we see that we were stronger than we thought, could endure more than we'd imagined, and that God made all the difference.

Dear Lord,
I want to invest in my relationship with You so that my confidence in You grows greater every day. Jesus, I trust in You. Amen.

MARCH 31

"Let the peace of Christ rule in your hearts." (Colossians 3:15)

We don't grow in peace and trust in God through academic proofs or someone explaining things to us perfectly from a theological perspective. That's never enough when we are in the moment of heart-gripping fear or debilitating sadness. We grow in peace and trust by holding a contemplative gaze on Jesus. We meditate on Christ and His love for us. "No one has greater love than this, to lay down one's life for one's friends" (John 15:13).

Why was it necessary for Jesus to lay down His life for us? What was the purpose? Our redemption required that someone be punished. It was going to be either us or a substitute. But our substitute couldn't be just anyone; the person needed to be a perfect, unblemished sacrifice—sinless. It had to be Jesus. His death purchased our freedom, our redemption, our forgiveness, our right to be called children of God.

What was the purpose of His suffering? Couldn't He have died a quicker, less agonizing death? His suffering proved to us that His love is something we can trust. As He suffered through the mocking, the scourging, the beatings, the agony of the nails going through His hands, the horror of death by suffocation, He proved to us that He is in it for the long haul. There is nothing He wouldn't endure for you and me. What do we have to fear from a God who is willing to do *anything* for us?

We are so fortunate to be able to contemplate, to gaze on Christ, and to be in His presence in adoration. When we stop and take an hour to reflect on Christ's love for us and the way He has suffered for us, the circumstances don't change, but our hearts do.

This is where the Holy Spirit can do His secret work inside us. When we take the time to prayerfully contemplate—not just reciting a rote prayer—then our perspective is changed, and we are filled with strength. This is different from sitting down and listing our requests to God, and then hurrying on with our next activity. What we see on the cross is perfect love, and focusing on it transforms us.

Dear Lord,
It says in 1 John 4:18, "There is no fear in love, but perfect love casts out all fear." I pray that as I contemplate You on the cross, evidence of Your perfect love would drive the fear from my heart. Amen.

April

For God so loved the world that He gave His only Son so that everyone who believes in Him might not perish but might have Eternal Life.

John 3:16

APRIL 1

"The Lord is good, a stronghold in the day of trouble; he knows those who take refuge in him." (Nahum 1:7)

The first victory the enemy of our soul achieved was to convince Adam and Eve that God was *not* good—that He was holding out on them. It's the oldest trick in the book, and he continues to use it when we go through times of difficulty. Because our minds can rarely figure out how a loving God would allow our current pain, the enemy's lie seems to make sense.

When we agree with the lie "God is not good," we don't run to God as our stronghold and instead rely on ourselves. We think, "God is not going to do anything about this. It is all up to me. I need to control whatever I can to minimize the damage." This determination to create control and protect ourselves does not give us the strength and support we need, and our suffering actually intensifies.

One of the hardest aspects of suffering is a sense that no one really understands what we are going through. Even when parents grieve the loss of a child, the way each experiences the grief is profoundly different. The sense of aloneness intensifies the pain. The enemy exploits this by whispering, "You are all alone. No one understands you. It's better to withdraw and try to find a solution within yourself. Don't speak. Stay silent. Isolate."

When we are suffering, it's important for us to remember that God cares. He is paying attention. When the prophet writes, "[God] knows those who take refuge in him," it means that He knows everything about us. He knows when we cry, when we pray, and when despair is overpowering our hearts. He knows our deepest desires. He knows who we want to be, and how aware we are of falling short. There isn't a groan we make, a secret longing we hold deep in our hearts, a self-deprecating thought we dwell on, a dream about to die that He does not see and understand.

He knows all about you. He has been with you in the depths of despair and on the mountaintops of joy. He knows you better than you know yourself. He can see the parts of your heart where the emotions you can't figure out dwell. You are not too complicated for Him. You make sense to Him. He asks that you run to Him for strength, comfort, safety, and protection. He offers to be your refuge and will never close the door on you.

Dear Lord,
May I see You as my stronghold, my refuge, my safe place. Amen.

Be Still

APRIL 2

"But the woman, knowing what had been done to her, came in fear and trembling and fell down before him, and told him the whole truth." (Mark 5:33)

In a pressing crowd, there was a woman who had been hemorrhaging for years. She believed that if she could just touch Jesus' cloak, she would be healed. She moved forward, reached out and <u>touched His garment</u>, and Jesus felt it. He felt the touch of her faith. Immediately He began to look for her, asking, "Who touched me?" The disciples must have thought He was crazy. All sorts of people were touching Him—that was the nature of being in a close crowd of people. But Jesus didn't see the crowd; He was looking for one specific woman who needed to tell the truth.

The woman's bleeding had stopped when she touched Jesus, but there was a deeper healing He wanted to give her. This would require her telling Him the whole truth. She did and was fully healed as a result.

Jesus asks the same of us. If we are afraid to tell the whole truth and instead hide, our healing will remain out of reach. When we develop a pattern of insisting that everything in our lives is fine when it isn't, of avoiding conflict, of smiling when our hearts are breaking, we can become such good liars that we don't even realize we aren't telling the truth. When we ignore huge parts of our stories, we are betraying ourselves. We are living a lie, which keeps us in bondage and far from freedom.

Your truth needs to be spoken. Burying it under coping mechanisms and peace-keeping compromises weakens the muscle you need to rely on during those times in life when your *yes* or your *no* really matters. If you are able to say no to your spouse or your parent or your boss in the little things, then one day when your no has far bigger consequences, you'll be able to do it.

Telling the whole truth builds our character. Stuffing our emotions, lying about how we really feel, weakens it. When crisis hits, our true character will be revealed. If our character is strong, we will be likely to learn something through suffering. If our character is weak, we'll be apt to blame others and think the world (or God) is unfair.

Telling the whole truth is critical if we want to be well and strong. Bring it all to God. Hold nothing back. He can handle it.

Dear Lord,
I am grateful that nothing shocks You. Help me to speak my truth to You and others that I may be healed. Amen.

APRIL 3

"Though the fig tree does not blossom, nor fruit be on the vines, the produce of the olive fail and the fields yield no food, the flock be cut off from the fold and there be no herd in the stalls, yet I will rejoice in the Lord, I will joy in the God of my salvation. God, the Lord, is my strength; he makes my feet like deer's feet, he makes me tread upon my high places." (Habakkuk 3:17–19)

Habakkuk the prophet prayed this prayer after dialoguing with God. He was discouraged because it seemed to him that evil was triumphing and God wasn't doing anything about it. God replied to his complaints by saying, "Write the vision . . . for still the vision awaits its time; it hastens to the end—it will not lie. If it seems slow, wait for it; it will surely come, it will not delay" (Habakkuk 2:2–3).

God always has a vision that goes beyond our own. He has a plan, and it is not just good, it is phenomenal. So often, the fulfillment of it seems slow, but God encourages us to wait. When it appears that evil is triumphing, the virtue we need is patience.

Time with the Lord gave Habakkuk the perspective he needed to say, "No matter what happens, I will still rejoice." He recognized that his strength didn't lie in his productivity or wealth. Its source was God, and praising Him strengthened Habakkuk deep within. It's been said that what we praise becomes our strength. If it's our own accomplishments we praise, then those accomplishments will be the source of our strength. But if it's the Lord we praise, He will be our source, and the strength within us will be divine.

These verses describe our feet being like deer's feet. Picture a deer leaping gracefully from one rock to another. Its tiny feet, placed in just the right spot, can carry a deer to great heights. A deer's movement is an illustration of skipping through life with joy rather than just plodding along. God can make our feet like the deer's by showing us the next step to take, but it's up to us to take it. If we keep our eyes up and fixed on Him, we can leap to spiritual heights that give us fresh perspective on His power and glory. We can grow in leaps and bounds if we will keep our eyes on Him and just keep moving.

Dear Lord,
I raise my eyes to You and ask You to just show me the next step. As I take that one, and the next, and the next, may I reach the heights and catch a new vision of You. Amen.

Be Still  **APRIL 4**

"I am sure that he who began a good work in you will bring it to completion at the day of Jesus Christ." (Philippians 1:6)

God began a good work in you when His supernatural life was given to you in baptism. There was nothing you did to deserve that gift; it was given simply because God is good and wants to share His life with you. It is up to you to receive that gift and protect it—to live in such a way that you continue to nourish the spiritual growth that God made possible. He's given you the Holy Spirit to help you do that. It would be an act of cruelty to demand something of you that you are unable to complete. The Holy Spirit within you makes it possible for you to do what God requires. Whenever you say, "I can't," to God, the Holy Spirit says, "But I can. And if you ask me, I will."

God not only asks you to live in a way that will lead you to heaven and help you flourish on earth, He gives you everything you need to do it. He is at work within you, bringing to completion what He began. But what is He working on? He is forming you in such a way that you resemble Jesus more and more.

When trials and hardships intersect your life, God is giving you an opportunity to become more like Jesus. When your patience is tried, God is giving you an opportunity to respond like Jesus. When you feel hemmed in on every side, God is giving you an opportunity to see like Jesus—to see past the fences to a greater purpose that lies beyond.

God doesn't start a job and then abandon it. He did not part the Red Sea and then leave the Israelites stuck in the middle. He didn't get Mary, Joseph, and Jesus halfway to Egypt and then leave them there. God doesn't give up. He has a limitless supply of perseverance and patience. He has not given up on you, and He never will.

God asks you to "work out your own salvation with fear and trembling; for [He] is at work in you, both to will and to work for his good pleasure" (Philippians 2:12–13). God has given you everything you need to run your race all the way to the finish line. He will not abandon you and will faithfully supply what you lack.

Dear Lord,
This is what I am lacking right now: _____. Please supply what I need and the will to keep running my race. Amen.

APRIL 5

"Return to me, says the Lord of hosts." (Zechariah 1:3)

We all have periods of life when our joy has vanished and our hearts are heavy. We bemoan our current circumstances as we remember times when things were lighter and our spirits were lifted. Our focus turns inward, and we can quickly spiral to a dark place where we can't see the point of it all and assume that God is either disinterested or out to make our lives miserable. When we find ourselves in this state, the worst thing we can do is sit still. The last thing we feel like doing is moving, but it's critical that we lift up our eyes and get going.

Where do we go? This verse says that we return to God. We might argue that we haven't gone anywhere, but it is worth at least asking ourselves, "Is there something I was doing spiritually when things felt better that I have stopped doing now?" A common response to discouragement and desolation is to stop doing the spiritual disciplines that we have previously done. The logic is that we aren't seeming to get anything out of them, so why bother? Crisis hits and all too often we start praying less. We stop going to Bible study because we don't feel like it and doubt it will be a magic bullet that fixes everything. The next thing we know, we're watching more Netflix than before, eating garbage, and feeling sorry for ourselves.

Walking away in frustration when God isn't answering our prayers as we'd like reveals something about the true motive for our relationship with Him. God is not a genie in a bottle or a cosmic personal assistant. He longs to be wanted for who He is, not just what He gives. We return to God for His presence more than His presents. When we are in a season in which relief is not being provided and God's good gifts aren't apparent, we have an opportunity to show what we truly love about Him.

We return to God when we recommit to the spiritual disciplines that keep us strong and connected to Him. We also return to God when we intentionally spend time with people who draw our focus to His goodness and provision. Do the right thing and ask God to take care of your emotions. Whether you feel like it or not, get moving, and move in God's direction.

Dear Lord,
May I return to You with all my heart. Help me to move my body into a posture of worship. May my feelings follow as I commit to obeying You. Amen.

APRIL 6

"I will betroth you to me forever; I will betroth you in righteousness and justice, in love and compassion." (Hosea 2:19)

In his book *I Believe in Love*, Father Jean D'Elbée writes, "Religion is not something; it is Someone."[30] That Someone, God, created you. Have you ever wondered why He created you? Why He created people? Did He create us so that He'd get a little fan club, a remnant of people who could praise Him for all eternity? Did He need us? No. God doesn't need anything. He was never lonely. So why did He make us?

We begin to answer that question by looking at CCC 221: "God has revealed his innermost secret: God himself is an eternal exchange of love, Father, Son and Holy Spirit, and he has destined us to share in that exchange." For all eternity, there has been an exchange of love going on between God the Father, Jesus, and the Holy Spirit. Why did He create us, especially when He knew it would cost Him His only Son? In the words of author and speaker Christopher West, "Because love wants to share itself. True love wants to expand its communion. All the hungers we have for love, for union, for happiness are given by God to lead us to Him. The difference between a saint and the greatest sinner is where they go to satisfy that hunger."[31]

Throughout Scripture, we see many images that God uses to describe His relationship to the people He created. The image of God as the bridegroom and us as the bride is seen in Hosea 2:19: "I will betroth you to me forever; I will betroth you in righteousness and justice, in love and compassion." God shows His love for us by holding nothing back—by giving up what was most precious to Him, His Son. D'Elbée writes, "As if that were not enough, He invented the Eucharist; a God who makes Himself into bread, a little host, in order to descend onto our lips and into our hearts, to bridge all distance between Himself and us."[32]

How does God want us to respond to His love? He wants us to love Him in return.

Dear Lord,
May I respond to Your love with my own love. I choose You. I prefer You. I want You. Amen.

APRIL 7

"Greater love has no man than this, that a man lay down his life for his friends." (John 15:13)

We question a person's faithfulness to us when we sense that his or her motive in the relationship is self-seeking. When we recognize that someone is really out for him- or herself, we know that a time may come when we end up hurt or betrayed. This is why it's so important for us to recognize that God's desire for us is utterly pure. He is not self-seeking. He has proven on the cross that His love for us is selfless. "For God so loved the world that he gave his only-begotten Son, that whoever believes in him should not perish but have eternal life" (John 3:16).

Father John Bartunek reflects on this in *The Better Part*:

> No hidden agenda, no selfish undertones—pure generosity. This is the heart of God, of the Lord who longs for our friendship. Only when a Christian internalizes this fundamental and overarching motive of God does Christian discipleship really begin to mature. This is Christ's revolution. That disinterested, self-forgetful love has the power to overcome all evil and renew every human heart and the human race as a whole.[33]

Something you can count on: God is *for you*. When important people in our lives fail to love us well, we often allow those experiences to cloud our impression of who God is and how He loves us. The truth is, God's love is perfect, never failing, and ever enduring. Oh that we would have grace-healed eyes that can see Him as He is.

Dear Lord,
You have proven Your faithfulness to me on the cross. Thank You for resisting the urge to call down legions of angels to rescue You. Thank You for staying there until my freedom was won. Amen.

APRIL 8

"[Jesus] is the image of the invisible God, the first-born of all creation." (Colossians 1:15)

Oftentimes, we think of God as a harsh father—one who judges and condemns—while we see Jesus as the tender one, the merciful one, the approachable one. But the truth is that every gentle quality we see and experience in Jesus is true of God the Father as well. "He is the reflection of God's glory and the exact imprint of God's very being" (Hebrews 1:3).

In the encyclical *Veritatis Splendor*, Saint John Paul II writes, "The light of God's face shines in all its beauty on the countenance of Jesus Christ, 'the image of the invisible God' (*Col* 1:15)."[34] God the Father's heart is revealed in Jesus. But things can get in the way of us experiencing an intimate relationship with Him. We learn from CCC 29 as well as our own experience that ignorance of truth, attachment to possessions, and scandal caused by other believers and fear all can break the bond of intimacy that God wants with us.

We need to be reconciled to God. But how is this made possible? Colossians 1:21–22 tells us: "And you, who once were estranged and hostile in mind, doing evil deeds, [Jesus] has now reconciled in his body of flesh by his death, in order to present you holy and blameless and irreproachable before him." Jesus makes forgiveness and reconciliation possible. On the cross, He received the punishment for sin that we deserved so that we could draw near to God and be healed.

We imagine that God's disapproval of us brings separation, but in reality, whenever there is a chasm between God the Father and us, it is because we have rejected Him. We do not trust Him, and we act apart from His loving guidance. Yet God waits for us, and He thirsts for our friendship. Spend some time contemplating any distance you might be experiencing in your relationship with God. Have you been too distracted by worries and busyness to open your heart to Him? Is there a sin you need to confess? Have you been confused and wrongly assumed that God didn't want to draw close to you? Be assured, He loves you and waits for you.

Dear Lord,
Thank You, Jesus, for making a way for me to go straight to the heart of God. May nothing hold me back from intimacy with You. Amen.

APRIL 9

"Let us cleanse ourselves from every defilement of body and spirit." (2 Corinthians 7:1)

Imagine you have a little girl who is the love of your life, and one day she disappears. You go to great lengths to find her. You search for days, frantic with despair that you might never see her again. You agonize over the loss of your precious daughter.

When you finally find her, she is dirty and covered with cuts and sores. What will you do? You will wrap your arms around her, carry her safely home, bathe her carefully and lovingly, treat her wounds, and then take her to the doctor. If medication is prescribed, you will purchase it and give it to her exactly as the doctor instructs, because you want her restored to full and vibrant health. It's not that you don't love her the way she is—you want her to be healthy and whole *because* you love her.

Now try to imagine that when you find your baby girl hurt, infected, and sick, you see a hungry lion stalking her little body, ready to pounce. If you can get the lion to come after you, perhaps she can escape. What will you do? What does God do?

This filth and sickness is a picture of the sin that infects us. The lion is Satan, and sin is his invitation to approach us. God loves us in the same way we would love a precious daughter. He loves us just as we are, and *because He loves us*, He demands that we be removed from the things that hurt us and can even kill us. He makes a way for us to be clean, healthy, and safe. We can be restored in this way because Jesus got the lion, Satan, to come after *Him* instead of us. Jesus suffered and died in our place, in order to offer us a way to escape.

God does not reject us because of sin. He rejects sin because of us. It is true that God hates sin. He hates disobedience because it threatens us, it hurts us, it covers us in filth, and it invites the enemy to draw near. God wants you to run to Him when sin has entangled you. He wants you to ask Him to wash you clean, to heal your wounds, to give you a fresh start. Your experience of freedom is directly proportional to the degree to which you take confession seriously. What is holding you back?

Dear Lord,
I am dirty and in need of rescue. Thank You for meeting me with outstretched arms of mercy. Amen.

Be Still

APRIL 10

"For you did not receive the spirit of slavery to fall back into fear, but you have received the spirit of sonship. When we cry, 'Abba! Father!' it is the Spirit himself bearing witness with our spirit that we are children of God." (Romans 8:15–16)

Sometimes we look at Christianity as the way to make sure that we are forgiven. We're covering our bases so that we are "safe" (as in the baseball kind of safe). But when we stop there and go no further, we totally miss out on what God (and Christianity) really offers. What God is truly after is so much more than just forgiving us. He *wants* us. He longs for us to come home to Him, our heavenly Father. Christianity is all about relationship.

When we read the story of the prodigal son, we can mistakenly think it's all about the son finally coming to his senses and asking for forgiveness. But the real focus of the story is the father's heart. It's the picture of the father running to his son the minute he sees him on the horizon. It's about the compassion and joy and mercy that the father is completely thrilled to pour all over his child. And that is exactly how God the Father feels about you.

You are the daughter of a strong, faithful, totally engaged Father, a Father who loves you too much to ignore self-destructive sin in your life, a Father who made sure you had a safe way to get home to Him even before you were born, through Christ's death and resurrection.

Your Father is going to go the distance with you. He knows that you need Him for the long haul. You need to be able to count on Him to stay when everyone else leaves. You'll never stop needing His direction and guidance and parenting. And that's OK, because His love for you is never ending. His arms are always open. You are His beloved. You are safe with Him.

Dear Lord,
I don't want to run anymore. I want to come home and rest. Thank You for always keeping the door open. Here I am, Lord. Here's my heart. Amen.

APRIL 11

"The Lord, your God, is in your midst, a warrior who gives victory; he will rejoice over you with gladness, he will renew you in his love; he will exult over you with loud singing." (Zephaniah 3:17)

You are delightful to God. Everything about you—the quirky things, your talents, your weaknesses, your physical features, your emotions—He loves it all. He is drawn to you with the purest of love and motive. Each morning, He is there, wanting you to turn to Him for a pep talk. He knows what you're going to face today and exactly what you need to go forward with strength and grace. When you rush out the door, too busy to spend time with Him, He waits. You are always on His mind. He sings over you throughout the day because you are such a source of joy in His life, and because He hopes that you'll hear a strain of the music and turn your face to His.

God is a warrior who is always fighting on your behalf. He is aware of the enemy's schemes. Before they even occur, God has ordered it all to your good. He is stealthy, tireless, strong, strategic, courageous, and decisive. Nothing surprises Him.

When you are weary, God knows what will deeply satisfy and replenish you. You often turn to other things when you are worn out, and while there's nothing wrong with watching Netflix, it doesn't ever renew you deep down, and it's deep within that you are weary. God can go there, and do unseen work that rebuilds and strengthens you on the soul level.

What might really refresh you is honest confession. Cleaning out the junk in your heart will leave you feeling free and light. People resist what is best for them, so it's critical to build confession into your life as a habit, something done without even thinking about it. When you are weary, you are usually far more aware of what others are doing to frustrate you than what you are doing to make things worse than they need to be. Owning your part of the problem, searching for ill motive, or recognizing when you have fallen into pride, just to name a few pitfalls to overcome, can set you on the road to consolation.

Dear Lord,
Thank You for seeing the obstacles in my life—every single one of them—and fighting for me. May I listen for the faint strains of Your singing in my day; it comes in the moments that delight me. All those fragments of joy—may I recognize they were sent to me by You. Amen.

Be Still

APRIL 12

"But you, O Lord, are a shield about me, my glory, and the lifter of my head." (Psalm 3:3–4)

What has been flying at you lately? Harsh words? Too many tasks? Financial demands? Heartache? Disappointment? Perhaps what has come your way has been good but too many opportunities have left you unsure of what you should do next. When you feel as if things are coming at you and you are reacting instead of responding, you need something to shield you from it all.

God is your shield. He stands between you and the tasks, needs, heartache, disappointments, and opportunities and says, "Slow down. Hit pause. Breathe." He holds it all back and asks you to look Him in the eye. He reminds you that He has got everything under control. Knowing how overwhelming it can be, He helps you to see what the next right thing is. The whole plan won't be handed to you; He wants you to come to Him continually. But He'll shine light on the next step.

When it's words that have hurt you, He stands between you and the opinions of others as a shield, reminding you that His opinion is the only one that ultimately matters. He is a balm on the wounds of your heart. He is your defender and guardian.

But God offers more than protection. He lifts your head and offers you hope. Hope comes when you gain a perspective that is higher than your circumstances. There may be nothing glorious about what is going on in your life, but there is glory in God. When you focus on Him—when you live for an audience of one— you can let other things fade into the background.

We can find glory in a lot of things—power, reputation, achievements, possessions—but none of those things give us lasting satisfaction. In fact, the more we have of each of these things, the more we want. True contentment never comes from getting the next thing on the list, because each thing is continually replaced with a new longing. Our desire for just a little bit more will never be satisfied if we are seeking glory in the wrong things.

Needs around us will be never-ending. The only way we will avoid this is by isolating ourselves from others, and that is a poor solution, as we need connection and community to be happy. But God shields us from all of it and allows us space to think, prioritize, fix our eyes on Him, and go forward.

Dear Lord,
Thank You for being my shield. Please lift my head so my eyes remain on You. Amen.

APRIL 13

"Many are the plans in the mind of a man, but it is the purpose of the Lord that will be established." (Proverbs 19:21)

I've always tended toward saying yes to too many things and overcommitting myself. There are times this has made me feel a little overwhelmed. There have also been times when staying busy has kept me from asking the deeper questions and noticing my inner emptiness. A swirl of activity can delude you into thinking that you're really living, when you're actually just running in the gerbil wheel.

I barreled through high school and college, keeping up my pattern of lots of activities and pursuits. Then I got married, moved to Germany, and everything slowed down. My husband traveled Monday through Friday, I didn't have a work permit, didn't have classes to attend, and, horror of horrors, didn't have the internet or Netflix. And it got very, very quiet. And the questions started coming. Why am I here? What's the point of my life? Is this all there is?

We can ask these questions when we're wiping noses and making peanut butter and jelly sandwiches. We can ask them from the corner office in a prestigious law firm. We can ask them when we lie in bed with disease or retreat to our rooms with depression.

Feeling lost and purposeless, feeling bland and too busy for passion, feeling stuck in a rut . . . Is this the life God created us for?

No—an emphatic *no. We were created for more.*

Can you sense a restlessness in your soul? A desire for more? A hunger for purpose? Do you feel that somewhere along the way, you lost yourself?

God is pursuing you, and He wants to reveal your part in His story. I say *His* story because ultimately it is all about Him. When we make it about us, we miss the point. We end up motivated by ego or people's opinions, and in the end, we're dissatisfied. But if we make *His* story, *His* plan, *His* glory the focus, there's no limit to the good He can do through us. And that means a life of fulfillment and deep satisfaction for us. When our ultimate goal is for Jesus to shine brightly into our world, we are free to dream. We can be bold in our hopes. We can put out into the deep, take risks, and really start living.

Dear Lord,
May I pursue Your purpose for my life, seeking how I can fit into Your story instead of squeezing You into a corner of mine. Amen.

Be Still  APRIL 14

"Whatever gain I had, I counted as loss for the sake of Christ. Indeed I count everything as loss because of the surpassing worth of knowing Christ Jesus my Lord. For his sake I have suffered the loss of all things, and count them as refuse, in order that I may gain Christ and be found in him." (Philippians 3:7–9)

Saint Paul wrote this after describing all the worldly accolades that belonged to him. He considered them all worthless ("I count everything as loss") compared to the good of knowing Jesus. This is the first and most important purpose of our lives—to know Christ.

Nothing was more important to Saint Paul than this. His determined purpose was to continually become more deeply acquainted with Jesus. Every day, he wanted to better know Christ's power and personhood. As he grew in understanding of Jesus, he made it his goal to reflect Jesus to the world. This is God's purpose for us as well.

In 2 Corinthians 5:18–20, we read, "All this is from God, who through Christ reconciled us to himself and gave us the ministry of reconciliation; that is, in Christ God was reconciling the world to himself, not counting their trespasses against them, and entrusting to us the message of reconciliation. So we are ambassadors for Christ, God making his appeal through us." Reconciliation is the act of reestablishing a close relationship between parties. This is exactly what Jesus did for us—He opened the way for us to have a close relationship with our heavenly Father. He now asks us to help reconcile others with Him and with each other. This is one of our core purposes in life. He asks that we be peacemakers.

To pursue this purpose requires a choice. Worldly accolades satisfy us on some level, but we can't pursue them and also wholeheartedly pursue knowing and reflecting Jesus to the world. We can't do a thousand things well. We have to focus. We have to choose what matters most. These are strong words, but they are true: If we fail to make knowing Christ and becoming more like Him our highest priority, we will have settled for a lesser, shallow existence.

Take some time to prayerfully identify the things that tempt you to take your eyes off your primary purpose of knowing and becoming more like Christ. Is it your reputation? Your desire for comfort? Other goals?

Dear Lord,
Please give me the grace to put knowing You and becoming more like You ahead of all other pursuits. Amen.

APRIL 15

"For you formed my inward parts, you knitted me together in my mother's womb. I praise you for I am wondrously made. Wonderful are your works! You know me right well; my frame was not hidden from you when I was being made in secret, intricately wrought in the depths of the earth. Your eyes beheld my unformed substance; in your book were written, every one of them, the days that were formed for me, when as yet there was none of them." (Psalm 139:13–16)

Have you ever questioned whether God has a specific plan for your life or if He is too busy with weightier matters to have time for that level of detail concerning you? Be assured, God knows how He wants your life to turn out. His love for you is personal. Your heavenly Father doesn't just look on mankind in general; He sees *you*. He wants you to determinedly pursue the purpose of knowing and becoming more like Jesus, and He wants you to discover the unique contribution He is calling you to make in the world. When He gave out callings and life purposes, *He did not skip you.*

God's specific plan for your life was put together before you were born, and His plan is *good*. "For I know well the plans I have in mind for you, says the lord, plans for your welfare, not for woe! Plans to give you a future full of hope!" (Jeremiah 29:11)

"For we are His handiwork, created in Christ Jesus for the good works that God has prepared in advance, that we should live in them" (Ephesians 2:10). What a difference it would make if we got that verse into our heads and hearts and really believed it. We could be world changers in our own little corners instead of spending all the live-long day dwelling on who we are not and what we don't have. It's time to step out and live in the truth that we are God's masterpieces— His handiwork—and He has created us to make a difference. He's placed unique gifts into each one of us, and He wants us to use those gifts to help those around us.

What is holding you back? Are you waiting for the approval of those around you before you live the life God is holding out to you? You don't need it. God offers you courage and strength. He has got your back. Step out. You don't have to be anyone other than the woman God created you to be.

Dear Lord,
I pray that I would go forward bravely, trusting that You are calling me to something greater. Amen.

Be Still

APRIL 16

"God saved us and called us with a holy calling." (2 Timothy 1:9)

Many of us feel so consumed by day-to-day life that we can't imagine adding some enormous *life mission* on top of everything else. It's important to remember that God doesn't want us to live stressed out, overwhelmed, and overcommitted. But He doesn't want us living bored, numb, and empty, either. Somehow we've got to wrestle through the tension that exists when we add to our plates in order to add to the meaning of our lives. It can get a little messy. The alternative—playing it safe and not venturing out into the deep—is the easier option. Living a life that says yes to God and His purposes requires bravery. But one day, we'll be standing before God, and we'll have to explain to Him what we've done with the time, spiritual gifts, and other resources He has entrusted to us. I don't know about you, but I don't want to tell Him, "I stayed as comfortable as I could. I avoided stress as much as possible. I kept things under control." I want to tell Him that I went *all out*. I want to tell Him I gave it all I had, that sometimes it made me really tired, but that He was worth every bit of it. How about you? Are you ready to start living the life you were created for?

We hear a lot of voices and opinions every day. Because most of us hate to disappoint the people we love, we can spend our whole lives pursuing someone else's dream for us. But living the life that someone else wants you to live (as opposed to the life God is calling you to) will never lead you to your true purpose and calling. Which voices or opinions are pulling you in a certain life direction? Saint Paul drives home this point: "Am I now trying to win the approval of human beings, or of God? Or am I trying to please people? If I were still trying to please people, I would not be a servant of Christ" (Galatians 1:10).

What suffering in the world really wrecks you? What gets you upset enough that you inwardly say, "Something has got to be done about this"? There isn't a simple formula to discover your unique calling. It's birthed out of time spent in prayerful reflection on your life. Bring before God your holy discontent, your passions, your experiences, your successes, your seasons of pain. Ask Him to reveal His plan to you.

Dear Lord,
Help me to pay attention to the places where my pain, my compassion, and the need of others come together. Amen.

APRIL 17

"Unless a grain of wheat falls into the earth and dies, it remains alone; but if it dies it bears much fruit." (John 12:24)

If we're going to fulfill our callings while reflecting Jesus to the world, we need to have the attitude of a servant. In Matthew 20:26–28, Jesus said, "Whoever would be great among you must be your servant, and whoever would be first among you must be your slave; even as the Son of man came not to be served but to serve, and to give his life as a ransom for many." We've been given gifts for the benefit of others. We're called to start at the bottom and serve humbly.

That's what we're supposed to do, but few of us actually do it. Why? We find the answer in John 12:24. Saying yes to God—serving for His sake instead of for our own gain—requires a little death. Do you like feeling in control? You have to let that expectation die, because going where God calls you means life gets messy. Do you like it when everyone approves of you? You have to let that die, because I promise you that doing what God asks of you will mean someone in your life will disapprove of your choice. But my sweet friend, if you will let those things die (and allow all sorts of other little deaths that will come along), you will start to truly *live*.

Dear Lord,

If I start to feel that what I offer this world is insignificant and pales in comparison to the great things that other people do, help me to remember that I am significant in Your eyes. You see the smallest act of love and it matters. Help me to remember that I'm not valued because of my gifts and talents. That is simply what You pour into me so that I can get out in the world and love people the way You love them. I'm valued because You made me; I'm Your beloved daughter, and You don't create mistakes.

On the other hand, if I start to get a little impressed with all that I'm doing and the difference I'm making and the way people around me are thinking I'm pretty fabulous, help me to remember that any good in me comes from You. Help me to never step out in the name of Christian service in my own strength. May everything I do be done through the inner work of Your Holy Spirit with the purpose of bringing attention to You, not me. Amen.

Be Still

APRIL 18

"Now I know in part; then I shall understand fully, even as I have been fully understood." (1 Corinthians 13:12)

In every circumstance in your life, you are given the opportunity to get to know God a little better. When you take the time to look for Him in every situation, you'll start to gain a greater understanding of His heart. Knowing God is a lifelong pursuit. One day you'll stand before Him, and all those fragments of understanding will come together, and you will "see Him as He is" (1 John 3:2).

But that's not all. Although God wants us to live with our focus on the day we'll meet Him, He wants us to use our time here on earth purposefully. He created you for a reason, and He doesn't want you to miss it. He has work that needs to be done in the world—suffering that needs to be relieved, comfort that needs to be given, teaching that needs to be heard, beauty that needs to be created—and He wants to use you to fulfill His plan. Another reason this is so important to Him is that He adores you, and He wants you to experience the fulfillment and joy that comes from being a part of His story and running the race He created you for. This is *your* race—not your sister's, or your mother's, or your friend's. *Yours.*

Figuring out which race is meant for you is a messy process. It's a matter of always growing in knowledge of who God is, and at the same time growing in knowledge of who you are. This is different from self-absorbed navel gazing. It's getting to know how you are wired for the purpose of bringing attention to God.

So reflect on the things in life that have been painful. It could be that in the midst of that pain, the seeds of your purpose were planted. Take some time to think about the moments when you have never felt so satisfied. Perhaps your passion was ignited then. Think about the people who are suffering who make you ache. Could it be that God placed that love and concern in your heart because He wants to work through you to help them?

Please don't give up on this journey and just settle for comfort. Rise up and take your place within God's story. Run your race—the race you were created for. Run your race with your eyes fixed on the finish line, when you'll crash into God's arms, fully known and fully loved.

Dear Lord,
I want to rise up and take my place within Your story. Amen.

APRIL 19

"Forgive and you will be forgiven." (Luke 6:37)

When the Allied soldiers found the Nazi concentration camp at Ravensbrück, where about ninety-two thousand women and children had died, they found a note tied to a rock that had been placed next to a dead woman and child. It was a prayer written by one of the women:

> O Lord, when I shall come with glory into your Kingdom, remember not only the men and women of good will; remember also those of ill will. But do not only remember the suffering they have inflicted on us. Remember the fruits we bought thanks to this suffering; our comradeship, our loyalty, our humility, the courage, the generosity, the greatness of heart which have become part of our lives because of our suffering here. May the memory of us not be a nightmare to them when they stand in judgment. When they come to judgment, let all the fruits that we have borne be their forgiveness. Amen. Amen. Amen.[35]

These words render us speechless. In the face of unthinkable brutality, cruelty, and evil, a hand of mercy was extended. Those who needed this forgiveness probably never realized it had been offered. But that wasn't what mattered. The writer of these words was behind barbed wire, but in her soul, in the most valuable part of her, she was free.

Forgiving what feels unforgivable—we simply cannot do it in our own strength. But with God, all things are possible. Jesus, who was able to forgive those crucifying Him even as He experienced indescribable pain, offers His own merciful heart to us. Once we make the decision to forgive, when we take the first step, when we say the words or write the letter or lift the hand, He gives us what we need to make it genuine. He then is free to heal us, to bring us the freedom we long for. Truly, divine love is stronger than sin. And it is ours for the asking. Can you ask the Lord for it? Can you ask Him for what you lack? He will give you the courage you need to take the first step.

Dear Lord,
I come to You with my empty, hurting, angry heart. Please give me what I need so I can forgive. Amen.

Be Still

APRIL 20

"So if the Son makes you free you will be free indeed." (John 8:36)

The poet Maya Angelou wrote, "You are only free when you realize you belong no place—you belong every place—no place at all. The price is high. The reward is great."[36]

At first glance, this might make you think that if she's right, freedom is impossible to experience, because who can get rid of the deep desire to belong?

I am in no way suggesting that the desire to belong is wrong. I believe it is hardwired within us. The ache to belong is so familiar to me. It makes me think of a memory of all my friends making me walk home on the other side of the street because I had danced with the wrong boy during PE in sixth grade. Then countless memories of betrayal by a high school boyfriend whom I had trusted with my heart come to mind, and it still stings. I remember a social event where everything was riding on my winning the approval of the women there. I gave it my best shot, but backs literally turned after I was looked at with disapproval. After decades of being Catholic I still feel like there is an "inner club" that I will never belong to because I grew up Protestant and am a woman. I have spent decades of my life in pursuit of the holy grail of belonging, and the price I've paid for compromise is too high to count.

I think it's worth exploring what Maya Angelou was describing. It has everything to do with learning how to live for an audience of one. I know how easy it would be for us to think, "OK, so God's opinion is the one that really matters, so I need to perform well for Him." To that, I say an emphatic *no*. We do *not* perform for God.

A quote from Scottish Olympic athlete Eric Liddell comes to mind. His words were made famous by the film about his life, *Chariots of Fire*. In one of the scenes Eric says, "God made me fast. And when I run, I feel His pleasure." As God watches you, it gives Him enormous pleasure when you run *your* race, remaining true to who you really are. If you allow His pleasure to be your deepest motivator, you'll begin to experience a sense of deep belonging when you are being your true self, the woman God created you to be.

Dear Lord,
May I fix my eyes on You and focus on who You designed me to be—Your daughter, full of the greatness and glory of my Father. Amen.

APRIL 21

"Am I now seeking the favor of men, or of God? Or am I trying to please men? If I were still pleasing men, I should not be a servant of Christ." (Galatians 1:10)

If we want to grow closer to God, then it's worth pausing to take a look at what motivates our behavior. Ideally, we're motivated by a pure love for God. But in the lives of most women, the opinion of others is a primary motivator. Instead of seeking security and value in God, we look for other people to measure our worth. As a result, our actions are driven by our desire for affirmation, to be noticed, and to be praised: "I'll do, so I can be loved." There is a difference between liking to be appreciated and doing something in order to be appreciated. In the latter case, our value is determined by the opinions of others. We become people-pleasers, motivated more by what those around us want than by what God is calling us to do and be.

The greatest need of a woman who is driven by others' opinions of her is to be loved. Out of a fear of rejection, we define ourselves by how other people perceive us. God calls us to define ourselves by His unconditional love for us. When we settle for the fickle love of other people, it's harder for us to soak up God's love. Ideally, we'll be so filled up by His love that it can spill over into the lives of those around us, helping us to love as Christ loves. But when we're obsessed with what others think of us, we often struggle to have intimate relationships. Our greatest concern is to be affirmed and validated, and so the temptation is enormous to wear a mask and be whoever we think those around us want us to be.

Oftentimes, when we recognize that we are motivated by others' opinions of us, we find that some of this has come from our relationships with our earthly fathers. If our earthly fathers don't love us unconditionally and communicate that effectively, as young girls we often seek that affirmation from friends. Later, we'll seek it in a boyfriend and then in a husband. In these relationships, we are seeking security. We are seeking affirmation that we are worthy. When this is what drives us, we desperately need God's unconditional love to fill us.

Dear Lord,
May I turn to You, first thing in the morning, and soak up Your love. May I sit in Your presence until I accept that there is nothing I can do to make You love me any more or less. Amen.

Be Still

APRIL 22

"Therefore do not be anxious, saying, 'What shall we eat?' Or 'What shall we drink?' or What shall we wear?'" (Matthew 6:31)

This verse reminds us that the problem isn't whether our outfits are fashionable. Wearing something ugly or outdated doesn't make us holy, and wearing something cute doesn't make us sinful. What Jesus is pointing out is our tendency to get preoccupied and worried about superficial things. First things first: He asks that our main focus be God's kingdom and our righteousness.

In his book *Making All Things New*, Henri Nouwen comments on the way Jesus responds to our worried way of living. Jesus isn't saying that nothing matters and we should just withdraw in solitude. Nouwen writes:

> Jesus' response to our worry-filled lives is quite different. He asks us to shift the point of gravity, to relocate the center of our attentions, to change our priorities. Jesus wants us to move from the "many things" to the "one necessary thing." It is important for us to realize that Jesus in no way wants us to leave our many-faceted world. Rather, he wants us to live in it, but firmly rooted in the center of all things. Jesus does not speak about a change in activities, a change in contacts or even a change of pace. He speaks about a change of heart. This change of heart makes everything different, even while everything appears to remain the same. This is the meaning of "set your hearts on his kingdom first . . . and all these other things will be given you as well." What counts is where our hearts are. When we worry, we have our hearts in the wrong place.[37]

In Matthew 6:21, Jesus said, "Where your treasure is, there will your heart be also." Where is your heart? In other words, what is at the center of your attention?

Dear Lord,
Help me to focus primarily on You. May You be my first thought in the morning. I want to offer You my day, and affirm that I am Your child, and You are in charge. I ask You to help me love what You love and value what You value. Please purify my heart so that my superficial worries fade away. Amen.

APRIL 23

"A cheerful heart is a good medicine, but a downcast spirit dries up the bones."
(Proverbs 17:22)

Hardwired into our souls are "longings for the infinite and for happiness" (CCC 33). The Catechism goes on to say that this "desire [for happiness] is of divine origin: God has placed it in the human heart in order to draw man to the One who alone can fulfill it: We all want to live happily; in the whole human race there is no one who does not assent to this proposition, even before it is fully articulated" (CCC 1718). This is a holy and God-given desire. But we get ourselves in trouble when we seek to have that desire satisfied in superficial ways.

Sometimes we gain just enough pleasure that we stop seeking deeper fulfillment and satisfaction. Our focus turns inward, and our perspective can quickly darken. It's as our focus turns outward that light rushes into our souls, filling us with the perspective we need to remain grateful at all times and suffer well when that is required.

When we make our self-worth our main focus, we will not experience the fullness of life we were created for. The abundant life is found in self-giving.

In the words of Saint John Paul II:

> It is Jesus that you seek when you dream of happiness; He is waiting for you when nothing else you find satisfies you; He is the beauty to which you are so attracted; it is He who provoked you with that thirst for fullness that will not let you settle for compromise; it is He who urges you to shed the masks of a false life; it is He who reads in your heart your most genuine choices, the choices that others try to stifle.
>
> It is Jesus who stirs in you the desire to do something great with your lives, the will to follow an ideal, the refusal to allow yourselves to be ground down by mediocrity, the courage to commit yourselves humbly and patiently to improving yourselves and society, making the world more human and more fraternal.[38]

Dear Lord,
Are You asking me to shed a mask? To let go of something that is preoccupying me and taking up too much of my time? Please give me the courage to overcome my fears. Amen.

Be Still

APRIL 24

"So teach us to number our days that we may get a heart of wisdom." (Psalm 90:12)

This verse is a prayer, asking God for help to live well—to know what to do and when to do it. Jesus reiterates the importance of this in Matthew 6:33 with the words "Seek first his kingdom and his righteousness, and all these things shall be yours as well."

What does it mean to seek something *first*? What might look different in our lives if we rearranged our priorities regarding where we spend our time and put God's kingdom and our righteousness first?

One practical way to look at the word *first* is to think about the way we start the day.

What do we grab first? The phone or the Bible?
Whom do we talk to first? Our friend or God?
Where do we look for the day's schedule? The calendar or the guidance of the Holy Spirit?

I'm not suggesting that we ignore a schedule or never make a to-do list. But I do think it helps us set our priorities when we look at our calendars *while* talking to the Lord, letting Him know that these events and commitments are what we think matter most, but we recognize that maybe He has a different plan. Starting the day with this attitude can help us view inevitable interruptions as divine appointments.

Jesus points us to a life of self-giving. Many of the interruptions we experience are opportunities for us to give. Sometimes what discourages us from responding graciously is feeling that the little we do doesn't make much of a difference. But love doesn't need to be extraordinary. It just needs to be consistent. Faithfully loving in the hidden places changes hearts, one at a time.

Dear Lord,
Help me to look for opportunities in my day to practice quiet acts of kindness. Instead of thinking that it doesn't make much of a difference, may I focus on the person in front of me, recognizing that for him or her, it can be a significant day brightener, offering much needed hope. Amen.

APRIL 25

"How great is the love the Father has lavished on us that we should be called children of God!"
(1 John 3:1)

You are the daughter of a generous, protective, and engaged Father, a Father who will never leave you or abandon you.

And for many of us, this is one of the hardest things in the world to truly believe.

In Matthew 7:9–10, Jesus asked, "Which one of you would hand his son a stone when he asks for a loaf of bread, or a snake when he asks for a fish? If you then, who are wicked, know how to give good gifts to your children, how much more will your heavenly Father give good things to those who ask him." If imperfect earthly fathers (at least ones who aren't cruel or somehow unable) give their children what they need, we can count on our heavenly Father to give us good things—as opposed to holding out on us—if we ask Him.

The seed of doubt regarding the Father's goodness was planted in the Garden of Eden. God had surrounded Adam and Eve with beauty, abundance, and provision. Only one thing was withheld, the fruit from the tree of the knowledge of good and evil. The serpent slithered up to Eve and asked her, "Did God really say, you shall not eat from any of the trees in the garden?" Look at him, making God's restriction sound even harder. See how the liar exaggerated in order to make his point? And Eve paused and engaged with the enemy. She leaned in and listened to the father of lies (John 8:44) and added to God's words. Instead of just saying that they weren't to eat the fruit, she said that they weren't to touch it either. The truth about God's words became fuzzy, and the slide toward compromise and slavery to sin began.

Are you done listening to lies? Are you ready to take a leap of faith, a step toward believing that God the Father loves you and is treating you as a good Father should?

Dear Lord,
I'm done with listening to lies. I may not understand why You have allowed certain things into my life and withheld others, but one thing I do know: I want my mind to be filled with truth. So I ask You, Jesus, what is the lie that I am believing about the Father? I will pause and pay attention to what comes to mind. Then I will take the first lie that comes into my mind and say: Jesus, will You take that lie from me forever? Father, what's the truth? Show me who You really are. Amen.

Be Still

APRIL 26

"He found them in a wilderness, a wasteland of howling desert. He shielded them, cared for them, guarded them as the apple of his eye." (Deuteronomy 32:10)

It's dark and frightening in the wilderness. The wasteland makes everything seem pointless and can cause us to feel ruined. When we're in the howling desert, searching for an oasis, our desperation can reach a fever pitch.

This is where our Father meets us. We are lost and wandering, and He comes for us. Instead of waiting for us to clean up and make our way back to Him, He goes on a rescue mission, enters into the confusion and the mess, and grabs hold of His daughters. As we're promised in Matthew 18:14, "Your Father in heaven is not willing that any one of these little ones should be lost." That includes you. He has come to rescue you, the apple of His eye.

When we feel like God is slow to bring the relief we desire, it's tempting to assume that He is asleep on the job. But nothing could be further from the truth. According to Psalm 121, God never slumbers. He is your guardian. He's the shade at your right hand, making sure that you're not burned. Your relief finds its source in Him. He holds on to you so that your foot doesn't slip. He is guarding your soul at this very minute and forever.

Our limited perspective means that the struggle we are in the midst of isn't always what it appears to be on the surface. God has the big picture, seeing things invisible to us. Ephesians 6:12 reminds us that we aren't just wrestling with flesh and blood, but against spiritual forces. There's a spiritual battle raging around us. God defends us in this battle. Although the battlefield can be invisible to the naked eye, it's no less perilous. God defends us in places where we can't even see what is truly going on.

We have an enemy who is behind all the hits we take on the spiritual battlefield. In CCC 2851, he is described as "a person, Satan, the Evil One, the angel who opposes God." When we pray, "Deliver us from evil," in the Our Father, we are not talking about evil as an abstraction. Satan is also known as the devil, and he throws himself across God's plan.

But he is no match for God. And God is within you through the indwelling Holy Spirit. Never forget that "He who is in you is greater than he who is in the world" (1 John 4:4).

Dear Lord,
Please protect me in the wilderness. Be my shield. Amen.

APRIL 27

"No weapon that is fashioned against you shall prosper." (Isaiah 54:17)

God promises that the enemy's plans for His beloved daughters will fail. If we turn to God for protection, no weapon that the enemy fashions and forms to take us out will succeed. God will make sure that we are not defeated. He promises victory.

The enemy may think he has come up with the perfect weapon to take you out at the knees. We know from Saint Ignatius' *The Discernment of Spirits* that the enemy makes a study of our souls and attacks where we are weakest. But an amazing thing happens when he pulls out his weapon to strike the apple of God's eye: God takes that very weapon and turns it back on the enemy. How does He do this? By allowing the attack to alert His beloved daughter to an area of weakness or woundedness that God wants to strengthen and heal. Suffering brings all sorts of long-buried things to the surface. Sometimes it's the only way God can get to those deep places in our hearts to set us free. What Satan intends to use to destroy us, God uses to transform us in beautiful ways—if we cooperate with the process.

In 2 Corinthians 4:8–9 we learn the perspective we should strive for when we feel we are being devasted by the battles in life: "We are afflicted in every way, but not crushed; perplexed, but not driven to despair; persecuted, but not forsaken; struck down, but not destroyed."

You may feel like God isn't defending you the way you'd like, but you have *not* been destroyed. You are still here. You are still standing. You may be pressed on every side, but you are not crushed. You may be perplexed, but God can hold you back from despair. You may feel the heat of persecution, but you are never forsaken. You may be struck down, flat on the mat, but you are not destroyed.

Dear Lord,
Thank You for defending me both when I'm desperate for Your help and when I'm being attacked and don't even know it. I am so grateful that Your eyes are always on me, that there is no detail of my life, not even the smallest circumstance that You are not aware of. You care about it all, and are always at work, bringing good out of everything that comes my way. Give me eyes of faith to trust You are there even when Your work is hidden. Amen.

Be Still

APRIL 28

"My son, do not regard lightly the discipline of the Lord, nor lose courage when you are punished by him. For the Lord disciplines him whom he loves, and chastises every son whom he receives." (Hebrews 12:5–6)

What is the first thing most of us do when we get on a roller coaster ride? We usually test the safety bar to make sure it truly is working. What's going through our minds when we test it? Do we want to find that it gives and isn't a firm barrier? Absolutely not. We push on it in hopes that it'll hold fast because we want assurance that we're not going to fall out when we're hanging upside down.

Living life without boundaries and guidelines from God would be a bit like careening through an amusement park ride without the safety barrier in place. We need to know what is safe and what isn't, and because of our tendency to test the boundaries, we need discipline to help us to stay within the lanes. Whether we like it or not, consequences help us to learn.

Sometimes God's discipline is obviously the consequence of our poor choices. We mess up and later pay the price. We may not like it, but at least we know what's going on. But when His discipline comes in the form of trials, more often than not we feel confused. We want God to give an explanation for what He is allowing, and more often than not He seems silent. So we begin to wrestle.

We wrestle with whether or not God really is in control. Because if He is, and if He loves us, then why wouldn't He make the painful trial end? Seasons of suffering can leave us with all sorts of questions, and we run the risk of losing heart.

What this passage is telling us is that the very things that people intend to use to hurt us, God wants to use to discipline us—to teach, correct, transform, and heal us. There is not an ounce of suffering that is not without meaning or purpose, if we will allow God to work on our hearts through it.

When we are going through trials, God is not a passive observer. Nor is He unable to intervene, only bringing good from the situation later, as a way to redeem at least some aspect of it. God is all-powerful and in control, and at work. But our cooperation is required.

Dear Lord,
I want to learn all that I can from my trials. Help me to suffer well. Amen.

APRIL 29

"For the moment all discipline seems painful rather than pleasant; later it yields the peaceful fruit of righteousness to those who have been trained by it." (Hebrews 12:11)

God's discipline bears fruit in the lives of women who are teachable. These are women who are asking the right question. Instead of saying, "Why is this happening to me?" these women ask, "What can I learn from this?"

In no way is this easy. Those who ask this question often do so through tears and brokenness. But the one truth they will not let go of is that somehow, in the midst of this pain and agony, God is still good. Instead of judging God by their circumstances, they assess their circumstances through lenses that focus on His steadfast love.

The Old Testament is filled with examples of God disciplining His children out of love for them, while teaching them how to behave like beloved sons and daughters. During a significant episode of discipline after the Israelites had worshipped the golden calf, God revealed His character to Moses in Exodus 24:6-7. He revealed Himself as gracious and merciful, slow to anger, abounding in love and fidelity, continuing His love for a thousand generations, and forgiving wickedness, rebellion, and sin. Yet He doesn't declare the guilty guiltless; He brings punishment for their parents' wickedness on children and children's children to the third and fourth generation.

What a passage. The first part brings us comfort. We love to read about God's graciousness and mercy. We're grateful that He's slow to anger and abounding in love, and lavishes forgiveness. But then we read of punishment being passed down to the children to the fourth generation and we cry foul. What is going on here? What we might see as God cursing an unborn and unsuspecting generation is better understood as the way that natural consequences are felt. When a parent makes destructive choices—say with alcoholism or any kind of abuse—the consequences continue to be felt for subsequent generations. Patterns of behavior are established. Behaviors are modeled, protected, and all too often passed down and emulated.

But those sinful patterns of behavior do not have the last word among people who choose to be transformed by their trials. There are brave women who stop saying, "This isn't fair." Instead, they say, "This pattern stops now and healing begins here." When God is invited into the process, everything can change. We do not need to end as we have begun.

Dear Lord,
May dysfunctional patterns of behavior stop with me. Give me the strength and wisdom to chart a new course, following a healthier path. Amen.

Be Still

APRIL 30

"I consider that the sufferings of this present time are not worth comparing with the glory that is to be revealed to us." (Romans 8:18)

God keeps His eyes on the big picture. We tend to see life through a close-up lens, while He looks at it through a wide angle. He knows who we are capable of becoming and the deep satisfaction it will bring us as we become more like Jesus. All the things that worry us today can be put in their place. A new perspective can be ours. We can consistently experience peace of heart. This is what He wants for us, and He knows what it will take to get us there.

His discipline is always for a purpose. In 1 Corinthians 4:17–18, Saint Paul writes, "For momentary, light affliction is producing for us an eternal weight of glory far beyond all comparison, while we look not at the things which are seen, but at the things which are not seen; for the things which are seen are temporal, but the things which are not seen are eternal." It may be temporarily painful. But to those who are willing to learn the lessons and be transformed by the pain, there is something better, richer, more satisfying on the other side.

What we must never lose sight of is God's motivation. He disciplines us because He loves us, not because He hates us. His discipline is not His anger; it is His fatherly protection and instruction. It will be rare that we understand His ways and methods. More often than not, His timetable will take longer than ours. But for those who wait, for those who are humble enough to be taught, for those who cling to His steadfast love, something glorious and beyond our imaginings will come. "Wait for the Lord; be strong, and take heart" (Psalm 27:14).

Dear Lord,
I want to be humble, but more often than not, my desire to understand overrides everything. I know this robs me of peace, because I am not capable of understanding You. My mind is finite; Yours is infinite. So what I need is trust. I know that trust is like a muscle. It's built through being exercised. That means that when I ask You to help me to trust You, I am going to be given opportunities to work on it. When they come, please bring to my mind the purpose behind them. You are giving me an opportunity to grow. May I grasp it, learn from it, and be transformed. Amen.

May

There is NO FEAR in love
BUT
Perfect love
DRIVES out fear.
1 JOHN 4:18

MAY 1

"I will not leave you as orphans." (John 14:18)

God has given us a spiritual family—a heavenly Father, a heavenly mother, and the best older brother imaginable. We are children of God, adopted into a family. We belong. This is where we are cherished and protected. We discover a safe haven in the context of these relationships.

May is the month we honor all mothers, especially Mary. The Catholic Church has always believed that when Jesus hung on the cross in John 19, His final words to the apostle John and His mother, Mary, had meaning for the entire Church. When Jesus said to Mary, "Woman, behold, your son," and to John, "Behold your mother," Mary was being given the role of mother of all Christians. "Mary had only one Son, Jesus, but in him her spiritual motherhood extends to all whom he came to save" (*Compendium of the Catechism of the Catholic Church* 100).[39]

In his book *Hail, Holy Queen*, Scott Hahn writes:

> Every family needs a mother; only Christ could choose His own, and He chose providentially for His entire covenant family . . . For a family is incomplete without a loving mother. The breakaway Christian churches that diminish Mary's role inevitably end up feeling like a bachelor's apartment: masculine to a fault; orderly but not homey; functional and productive—but with little sense of beauty and poetry.[40]

What does Mary have to do with our relationship with Christ? As our heavenly mother, she wants what is best for us. She knows that so many of our attempts to connect and be known by people around us will fill the hours but never the heart. Because of this, she never stops pointing us toward the only One who will truly satisfy our inner longing for belonging, safety, and love. She always leads us home to her Son. We don't just want to have a friendship with Christ; we want to grow more and more like Him. We want to be changed. In our efforts to follow Christ and more closely resemble Him, no greater example exists than the Blessed Mother.

Draw close to Jesus through Mary.

Dear Mary,
I want to love and follow the Lord the way you did. Please intercede on my behalf. While I do all I can to remain like putty in the Lord's hands, please ask your Son to give me the grace I need to obey Him. Amen.

Be Still

 MAY 2

"Then Moses answered, 'But behold, they will not believe me or listen to my voice, for they will say, "The Lord did not appear to you."' The Lord said to him, 'What is that in your hand?' He said, 'A rod.' And he said, 'Cast it on the ground.' So he cast it on the ground, and it became a serpent; and Moses fled from it. But the Lord said to Moses, 'Put out your hand, and take it by the tail'—so he put out his hand and caught it, and it became a rod in his hand." (Exodus 4:1–5)

Earlier, God had asked Moses to go before Pharaoh and demand that he free the enslaved Israelite people. It was an incredible ask, and one that Pharaoh would surely refuse. Why would he let an entire low-cost workforce go? No wonder Moses doubted his ability to convince Pharaoh to comply.

Of course, God had a plan all along to work *through* Moses. At no point was this operation about Moses' abilities—it was God who would orchestrate it all. Nevertheless, God required his cooperation. If Moses was unwilling to trust God and step out, the rescue mission would be stalled.

In order to build Moses' trust, God had him throw down his rod, which He changed into a snake. What was Moses' response? He fled, like any wise person would—snakes can kill. God's next command deserves a moment's pause. He told Moses to go back and take the snake by the tail. What would you have done in the same situation? Would you have trusted that God would protect you? Could you find within yourself just a little more courage than fear to step forward?

There are many moments in our lives when God asks us to put out our hand and "take the snake by the tail." Perhaps He has asked you to have a hard conversation when you would prefer artificial peace. Maybe He is asking you to stay in a difficult marriage, taking hold of the very thing that is causing you pain. Taking hold of the tail might mean letting go of something you want to try to control. It could be that it's the first step toward freedom from addiction by admitting to someone you trust that you need help. In all cases, there is a risk, and fear is rife. But if you will take the snake by the tail, God will transform it into a rod of support and strength.

Dear Lord,
Fill me with divine courage so I can take the next step, no matter how scary. Amen.

MAY 3

> "But Moses said to the Lord, 'Oh, my Lord, I am not eloquent, either heretofore or since you have spoken to your servant; but I am slow of speech and of tongue.' Then the Lord said to him, 'Who has made man's mouth? Who makes him mute, or deaf, or seeing, or blind? Is it not I, the Lord? Now therefore go, and I will be with your mouth and teach you what you shall speak.'" (Exodus 4:10–12)

God already knew Moses' weaknesses. He chose which strengths Moses would receive at birth, and which areas would require that he rely on Him. An important thing to remember about God is that He doesn't need anything. When He sets out to do something in the world and chooses one of us to be a part of that mission, He doesn't need our giftedness. He wants our willingness.

When God calls you to go on mission with Him, you will feel that you are incapable of doing what He has asked of you. And you'll be right, if you only look at your own abilities. But if you expand your mind to the possibility of God working *through* you, giving you what you lack, then anything is possible.

Having a fixed or a growth mind-set will affect how you approach God's call. A fixed mind-set operates from the belief that whatever intelligence or giftedness you have, you got at birth. You either have it or you don't. When a person has this mind-set and encounters a challenge or anything that is going to require significant effort, he or she will say, "I'm just not good at this. I'm not smart at this. So I'm not going to do it." By contrast, a person with a growth mind-set believes that we can always learn what we don't yet know. When he or she encounters a challenge that requires real effort and involves failure, it causes the person to think, "I'm really learning something here. And at the other end of this, I'll be better than I was at first."

Having a growth mind-set is critical if you are going to answer the call of God on your life. His call will always go beyond what you can do in your natural abilities, and He will fill in the gaps. But as you step out of your comfort zone, you will also find that you are learning and growing. You will not finish as you've started.

Dear Lord,
Help me to have a growth mind-set and the humility to recognize that answering Your call does not depend on my abilities, but on my dependence on You. Amen.

Be Still

MAY 4

"Do nothing from selfishness or conceit, but in humility, count others better than yourselves. Let each of you look not only to his own interests, but also to the interests of others."
(Philippians 2:3–4)

Nestled within your soul is the potential to change the world. You have gifts that the world desperately needs, a voice that matters, a beauty to reveal. All the things you see in the world that make you cry out for grace and justice? God the Father watches your heart enflame and waits to see if you will answer His call. As it turns out, He cares about those deep, wild, impossible dreams, and He's calling you forth to explore them with Him.

You were not created for some stale, safe, generic existence. You were created to reflect God's love to a world that desperately needs to see that He is real, He is good, and He cares for them. This brings Him glory and is why we are here. There is nothing more thrilling than letting God weave your soul, your story, your dreams, and His desires into a tapestry of His design.

It would all be so amazing if it wasn't for the waiting. Waiting to see exactly what that tapestry is going to look like can just about do you in. We want answers. We want it all laid out. And God cups our faces in His loving hands and whispers, "Trust me."

So how do we remain dreamers and trusters at the same time? Matthew 6:33 reminds us that we are to seek God's kingdom and glory before our own. If we are seeking to build up the kingdom of God, that means we aren't trying to build up our own at the same time. It means that we take a look at the motives behind our dreams. Am I seeking a platform? Will I mind if others get the glory and I don't? In Philippians 2:3–4, Saint Paul teaches us that we're not to do anything out of selfish ambition or vain conceit. We're to consider others better than ourselves.

We need to circle back to these checkpoints often. Self-centeredness and ambition can slip into a dream that was once pure in motive. When the waters get muddied by our self-focus, that doesn't mean we have to quit. But it does mean we need to purify our hearts and get back on track. Another good question to ask ourselves is if our dream is for "the interests of others." Who benefits if the dream comes true? Me or others?

Dear Lord,
Please purify my motives and alert me to anything self-serving within them. Amen.

MAY 5

"He who trusts in his own mind is a fool; but he who walks in wisdom will be delivered."
(Proverbs 28:26)

Walking in wisdom isn't something that just automatically happens. Wisdom is the ability to take the things you know to be true and apply them to real-life situations. It means taking the time to learn what God says, and then relying on those truths in day-to-day life. The alternative is assuming that we know better—that we already know enough.

I can remember a time in my early twenties when I felt completely stuck and sidelined. Living in Germany without a work permit, I was only allowed to babysit or teach English, and neither option sounded good to me. I remember calling my dad and telling him that it all felt like such a waste. I had dreams of speaking or writing, but there weren't any open doors in front of me. My dad challenged me to take that time as a gift—as a chance to grow in wisdom, to dig deep into Scripture and study so that when an opportunity came, I would actually have something to say. Those words were game changing for me. Some of my richest studying of the Bible and memorization of Scripture came out of those years that felt wasted. I still go back to old notes and know without a doubt that a foundation of God's wisdom was laid in my heart during that time.

The truth is, you can achieve things beyond your wildest dreams. I pray you would dream big and bold. But I also pray that while you are waiting and trusting, you would find someone, *serve* him or her, and give it your all. I pray you would give to him or her out of the abundant gifts that God has placed in you, while relying utterly on the Holy Spirit. And I pray that instead of quitting when it isn't fun anymore, you would push through. That you would show grit. I pray you would give everything you have and make the most of where you are today. Be faithful where you are, and God will see to the results.

Dear Lord,
I don't want to settle for playing it safe. I know there are things in the world that break Your heart. Some of them break mine, too. So I am grabbing hold of Your hand, and setting out to do what I can to make a difference. I will start small and trust You for the results. One act of selfless love matters in Your kingdom. Thank You for being the wind behind me, urging me to go for it. Amen.

Be Still

 MAY 6

"I believe that I will see the goodness of the Lord." (Psalm 27:13)

When asked how to evangelize in a culture that is indifferent to God and religion, Bishop Robert Barron has said that we should begin with the beautiful, which leads you to the good, which points you to the truth. We need to show that Christianity is attractive. As Blaise Pascal famously said, we are to make good men wish it was true.

So how do we do this? One way is to increase exposure to beautiful and good literature, art, and music. The imagination can offer a spiritual opening as we consider the possibility that there is something of deeper meaning that moves us more than the superficial things surrounding us. But nothing beats the beauty of a life well lived. This is especially true of someone who is able to find beauty and meaning while suffering. When we see this, we lean in, wondering how it is possible. When a person of faith faces adversity with grace and grit, a watching world wonders if perhaps her beliefs are true.

While beauty can be found in the ashes, that's not the only place we find it. There's something incredibly attractive about a woman who knows who she is and what she is here for. Our world is disarmed by genuine transparency, and people know how to spot a hypocrite. This means that the way we live is critical. Who we are is intricately tied to what we do; we can't separate the two. The choices we make are forming who we are. Our actions and our choices are not disconnected from the person we are becoming.

Your current actions and choices are forming who you are, right now. You are becoming a certain kind of person, and this plays out especially in the little things.

I've heard it said that there's no treading water in the spiritual life—you are either moving forward or going backward. Each and every action is reinforcing a habit, and all the habits together are forming who you are becoming, what kind of a person you truly are.

As Coco Chanel said, "Beauty begins the moment you decide to be yourself." When your true self is a beloved, chosen, forgiven daughter of God, you have an irresistible beauty to share with the world.

Dear Lord,
May I bring beauty, goodness, and truth to a world aching for all three, whether it realizes it or not. In doing so, I will be pointing them to Christ. Amen.

Be Still

 MAY 7

"The Lord is a stronghold for the oppressed, a stronghold in times of trouble." (Psalm 9:9)

Bible teacher Beth Moore has written in her study *Breaking Free* about a stronghold she saw in the city of Corinth, Greece. The Greek guide explained that "virtually every ancient Greek city had a stronghold or a fortress on the top of its highest peak in the vicinity. In times of war, it was considered practically impenetrable and unapproachable. It was the place of hiding for the governors of the cities in times of insecurity."[41] That's where they ran for security and safety when they felt threatened.

How does this apply to us? We construct strongholds in our lives, places we go to find our security and safety when we feel threatened. We go to those places instead of going to God. In that moment, we choose to rely on ourselves rather than on Him.

When we experience a hurt, all too often, instead of dealing with that hurt, we judge the other person and barricade our hearts. At the same time, we internalize a belief about ourselves, such as "I am alone," or "I am unlovable." These are lies, but in the moment of pain, they *feel* true. When we agree with the lies, they take root in our minds and hearts.

The resulting sense of isolation and rejection feels awful, and we vow to save ourselves from ever feeling this way again. Author Dr. Bob Schuchts describes inner vows as decisions we make to save ourselves from further hurt. They are promises we make to ourselves regarding how we are going to save ourselves from now on. When we make these vows, we start to construct a fortress—a stronghold—that shuts out others and God.[42] We think they will keep us safe, but they actually keep us in bondage.

To destroy a stronghold, we need immense strength—more strength than we possess. The good news is that the weapons we are given by God have divine power. What are these weapons? Prayer, the sacraments, Scripture. The divine weapons we are given are strong enough to demolish those strongholds.

The only stronghold that will truly shelter and protect us is God. He invites us to run to Him instead. His arms are always open wide.

Dear Lord,
I pray that You would destroy the stronghold of _____ in my life. May I run to You instead. Amen.

Be Still

 MAY 8

"Cast all your anxieties on him, for he cares about you." (1 Peter 5:7)

It's been said that worry is a misuse of the imagination. This resonates with me, probably because of my award-worthy ability to come up with worst-case scenarios and potential catastrophes. God asks us to cast our anxieties on Him, but sometimes we struggle to know exactly how to do that. I have found that there is something incredibly powerful about praying God's words back to Him out loud.

Why? The enemy can hear us. When we speak our self-defeating thoughts and worries, he hears them. He stores them away for later use. He uses them against us, and they ring true to us on some level because they were our thoughts and words to begin with.

So instead of speaking defeat, fear, and worry, we can choose to speak truth. I call this the "I Declares." I wrote them for various sources of struggle, including fear of the future, pain from the past, suffering, and marriage. These are the "I Declares" I speak the most often, the ones I battle with for the hearts of my children.

I declare that You who began a good work in my child will bring it to completion. (Philippians 1:6)
I declare that You can reach down from on high and take hold of my child, drawing him out of deep waters. (2 Samuel 22:17)
I declare that my work as a mother will be rewarded and that my child will come back from the land of the enemy. (Jeremiah 31:16)
I declare that there is hope in my future and in my child's future, and that my child will come back to her own border. (Jeremiah 31:17)
I declare that all Your promises are yes in Jesus, and that not one word of Your promises has ever failed. (2 Corinthians 1:20 and 1 Kings 8:56)
I declare that You are able to accomplish abundantly more than all I could ask or imagine. (Ephesians 3:20)

If we want to mature as Christians, if we are tired of being tossed by waves and swept along by lies and worries, then we need to grab hold of our Bibles, to anchor ourselves with the truths found in its pages.

Dear Lord,
May I go to Scripture with the passion of a lover who longs to hear the voice of her beloved. I know You are called faithful and true, and You will always meet me in the pages of the Bible. As I pray Your words back to You, please intervene in my circumstances and calm my heart. Amen.

"A time to keep silence and a time to speak . . ." (Ecclesiastes 3:7)

The best gift I have ever received is a pair of noise-canceling headphones. At the same time, I love my family and am interested in the details of their lives. For years, I felt that those two statements were paradoxical—that for one to be accepted, the other would need to be rejected. That was before I learned the importance of solitude.

I have spent the majority of my life wanting *more*—more conversation, more interaction, more excitement, more activity. But lately, I have found that I long for more quiet—sacred space where the cacophony of voices and opinions that swirl in my head are hushed, a place where I can hear God's whisper. This often has caused me to feel guilty, as if somehow this longing is a rejection of people around me. As I've processed this change in me, I have been comforted by the words of C. S. Lewis in *The Weight of Glory*: "We live, in fact, in a world starved for solitude, silence, and privacy and therefore starved for meditation and true friendship."[43] What an interesting thought—that without solitude and silence, we'll have trouble experiencing true friendship with people and deep communion with God. What happens in solitude that is beneficial to our relationships?

It takes time alone to get to the bottom of what we are feeling and why we do what we do. When we just keep going and allow distractions to shield us from what is stirring within, we live disconnected from our hearts. This greatly increases the likelihood that we will just go through the motions in our relationships, that we will react instead of respond, and that we will make assumptions about others' motives instead of digging deeper and asking clarifying questions.

For some of us, it takes being alone to even recognize what we need. We all know the airplane rule: Put on your own oxygen mask before helping someone else. Some of us need to take a few moments to be quiet and alone, to be able to identify what we need. Unless I am by myself, I am distracted by what I think the other person might need. Someone might think that makes me selfless, a constant helper, but the truth is, when I cannot figure out and ask for what I need before I am desperate, I am prone to acting like a martyr. This has harmed my close relationships more times than I can count, and the only one who can bring change here is me.

Dear Lord,
Teach me to keep silence and use it well. Amen.

Be Still

 MAY 10

"Thou art a hiding place for me, thou preservest me from trouble; thou dost encompass me with deliverance." (Psalm 32:7)

Solitude is the place where God meets me. He is my hiding place, my refuge, and my shield. He holds me in a sacred space and invites me to reflect on the thoughts running through my head. I write the emotions down and allow it all to pour out on paper, an uninterrupted stream of consciousness. When it's all out of my system, the Holy Spirit leads me into truth (John 16:13), helping me to identify any hopelessness, lies, or exaggerations that have infiltrated my thinking.

So what gets in the way of my solitude? I could claim busyness is the culprit, and it certainly doesn't help matters. But the truth is, solitude can be painful. In his book *Making All Things New and Other Classics*, Henri Nouwen writes:

> As soon as we are alone . . . inner chaos opens up in us. This chaos can be so disturbing and so confusing that we can hardly wait to get busy again. Entering a private room and shutting the door, therefore, does not mean that we immediately shut out all our inner doubts, anxieties, fears, bad memories, unresolved conflicts, angry feelings and impulsive desires. On the contrary, when we have removed our outer distraction, we often find that our inner distractions manifest themselves to us in full force. We often use the outer distractions to shield ourselves from the interior noises. This makes the discipline of solitude all the more important.[44]

So that is the divine invitation—to seek out solitude and then fill it with self-reflection in God's presence. This is the place where we will experience real spiritual growth. No one can accompany you in those hidden moments—you must be alone—but those closest to you will benefit from it.

We cannot create more time; the hours in the day are limited. But we can use the time we have far more wisely. I am challenged by Ralph Waldo Emerson's words, "Guard well your spare moments. They are like uncut diamonds. Discard them and their value will never be known. Improve them and they will become the brightest gems in a useful life."

Dear Lord,
May I use my time well. Help me to slow down and allow my mind and heart to become quiet. May I listen for Your voice—the one calling me beloved, the one guiding me to deep and lasting peace. Amen.

"If we have died with him we shall also live with him." (2 Timothy 2:11)

What seems logical to me in terms of how a problem should be solved or a prayer answered is usually different from God's plan. But this I know: God does not ignore the pleadings of His children. He is entirely tuned in and aware of every heartache. Psalm 56:8 reveals that God keeps each one of our tears in a bottle. I am comforted by this and need to continually remind myself that when He seems slow to intervene, He is actually working out a much better plan than mine.

Is there something that God is asking you to surrender today? What do you desperately want to control? Does letting it go feel as if it will mean sure loss or deprivation? Could you open your heart to the possibility that surrendering will ultimately mean that you win what matters most? With God, what *appears* to be us being conquered is often the defeat of the things that are hurting us most.

There is no limit to the miracles that God can do in our lives. But we hamper His efforts and put the miracle on hold when we are clinging to our own plan, our desires, our dreams, and our worries. God works best when our hands are open, vulnerable, and ready to receive.

Each surrender feels like death. Letting go costs us something and makes us feel out of control. God understands this, so for Him, our letting go is the greatest gift we can offer. The time to give these gifts to God is now, because in heaven, we'll no longer have the opportunity. Our immediate trials, the very things we most want to change, are the perfect opportunity for us to let go and surrender to God's will. Yes, this is costly. I know it's easier said than done. But God is never outdone in generosity. As we are promised in 2 Timothy 2:11, "If we have died with him we shall also live with him." Real life, true freedom, and joy are not found in perfect circumstances. They're found in the release of control, the unclenched fist, the surrender, the fiat.

Dear Lord,
I am throwing off the weight of trying to keep it all under control, and I release it to You, because You are the only One who has the power to bring the miracle, raise the dead, and usher in hope. Amen.

Be Still **MAY 12**

"A broken and contrite heart, O God, you will not despise." (Psalm 51:17)

One lesson that I've learned over the past decade is that what we offer to the Lord does not need to be perfect in order to be good. In fact, when we are weak and imperfect, that is when He shows up most powerfully.

In hindsight, it has been during times of brokenness that I have most fully seen God's goodness and blessing being extended to me. But in the midst of it, I don't. When we're stuck in the middle, we are susceptible to lies about the heart of the Father. We question His love, His goodness, His power, and His interest in us.

In his book *Life of the Beloved*, Henri Nouwen writes about the importance of putting our brokenness under the blessing. All too often, what we do instead is put our brokenness under the curse. We do this when we allow our difficult circumstances to confirm lies that have been swirling in our heads. We filter our current experience through the lie, and it feels true.

We are called to resist this train of thought, to see it for what it is: a road to hopelessness. Instead, we bring our brokenness and stand under the blessing of God's grace. We are honest with Him in terms of how we feel, but we speak truth about what we know of His character.

God's desire is that we accept ourselves as His beloved in the very moments when we feel least deserving of it. I'm moved by John Steinbeck's words, "And now that you don't have to be perfect, you can be good." When we can rest in God's grace, when our belovedness doesn't feel like it is perpetually on the line, we are free to love. Recognizing that God loves us in our brokenness frees us from the chains of perfectionism and allows us to extend that same grace to others. We can invite our loved ones to exhale and drop the mask. We can become soft places for others' hearts to land because we aren't so busy trying to prove ourselves. The unconditional love we have received is passed on to people who are desperate for a place to belong and call home.

Dear Lord,
Thank You for welcoming me as I am. Not the cleaned-up version of me, but the real me. In my weakness, in my brokenness, You still call me beloved. Thank You for loving me in this way. Amen.

MAY 13

Be Still

"Therefore, since we are surrounded by such a great cloud of witnesses, let us throw off everything that hinders and the sin that so easily entangles. And let us run with perseverance the race marked out for us . . . fixing our eyes on Jesus." (Hebrews 12:1–2)

These verses were written to people who felt beaten down and discouraged. They were ready to give up and were likely asking, "If God loves me so much, why is following Him so insanely hard?" The author asks them to picture a race within an arena, with a track for the athletes to compete on and spectators to witness it all.

The word *race* comes from the Greek word *agon* (a-gōn'). We get the word *agony* from this root word, and the word *race* could also be translated "conflict," "struggle," or "fight." What the author of Hebrews wants us to get is that life is a race, and the race is one of agonizing struggle. It isn't a short sprint; it's a marathon.

We need patience, endurance, and the willingness to persevere in order to run this race. I love what N. T. Wright has to say about the race:

> This race is a long haul, and you need patience. There are always some runners who really prefer a short sprint; some of them, faced with a ten-mile run, will go far too fast at the start and then be exhausted after two or three miles. Sadly, many of us will know Christians like that too: keen and eager in their early days, they run out of steam by the time they reach mature adulthood . . . Give me the person, any day, who starts a bit more slowly but who is still there, patiently running the next mile and the next and the next, all those years later.[45]

I think it's great news that this race isn't only for sprinters. There is an honored place for plodders, for those who are steady at the wheel when the race is exciting, and when it's boring, and when it's sucking the breath out of them. This is the woman who is less concerned about her personal passions, gifts, and platform than she is about the fact that in the Christian life, someone has to be willing to take out the garbage.

This woman's Instagram feed might look insignificant, but don't let that fool you. She's too busy running her race to photograph it all beautifully.

Dear Lord,
So much of what I do goes unseen and uncelebrated. I am grateful that You see everything and value the hidden service I offer. May the way I run my race bring You joy. Amen.

Be Still

 MAY 14

"The glory of the Lord was like a devouring fire on the top of the mountain . . . Moses entered the cloud . . . Moses was on the mountain for forty days and forty nights." (Exodus 24:17–18)

Picture how terrifying this must have been for Moses. It makes me think of my heroic husband's journey, which began with a prayer. He asked God, quietly and without fuss, to grow him in humility and closeness to Him. A short time later, stress in his life increased, catapulting him into a season that felt like a devouring fire. Was the suffering an answer to his prayer for spiritual growth? I don't know. Perhaps. But it lasted exactly forty days. For forty days, we had no idea what things would look like on the other side. My husband's suffering was acute and isolating. The days and nights were filled with unrelenting waves of anxiety. Debilitating fear made his heart and mind pound constantly. A dark night of the soul filled him with spiritual doubts, which made everything even harder. The combination of very little sleep, no diagnosis, and no clear end date was overwhelming.

The thought occurred to me that as Moses walked through this experience on the mountain, he hoped the Israelites would remain faithful in his absence. As he stood in the firestorm, he was counting on them to keep their focus on God. He needed them to wait well—to not give in to the temptation to take matters into their own hands.

Maybe they could have done it for six days. But forty? That proved too much. The people created and worshipped a golden calf instead. They took matters into their own hands because it felt like God was not going to come through.

How long are we willing to wait?

God always shows up. And not just at some remote time in the future. He is at work now—right in this very moment that feels hopeless—in this current set of circumstances that seems without end. During the waiting, our job is to remember. When has He come through for you in the past? Dwell on this.

Hold steady and rebuke the lie that says, "It's all up to me." The truth is, we have an all-powerful rescuer who never leaves our side. Reject the lie that says, "Things will never change." The darkest hour is the one before dawn. Wait faithfully.

The very thing that we think will destroy us can be what strengthens and heals us. Suffering brings all sorts of long-buried things to the surface. Sometimes it's the only way God can get to those deep places in our hearts to set us free.

Dear Lord,
May I not lose heart, and may I hold on to hope that I will see Your goodness unfold. Amen.

MAY 15

"For He is our peace." (Ephesians 2:14)

Are you feeling the hassle of the hustle while you long for a little rest? Are you ready to step off the treadmill and live in the present moment? Are you searching for inner peace? We're told where we can find the true source of peace in Ephesians 2:14, which says that Jesus is "our peace, he who made us both one and has broken down the dividing wall of hostility." The passage goes on in verse 17 to say that Jesus "came and preached peace to you who were far off and peace to those who were near."

Maybe you are feeling like you're in the camp of those who are far off. You can point out all sorts of people who you figure are near to God. You wonder if the promises about Jesus apply only to them. They don't. Jesus came for those who are far away and those who are near.

Jesus is the true source of peace. If we look for it anywhere else—in our relationships, our bank account, our yoga class, or our own achievements—we will come up empty. Only He can go to the places deep within that need His presence and truly satisfy.

As you seek peace, I encourage you to show Jesus where it hurts. Instead of masking your emotions, stuffing them, or numbing your feelings, show Jesus where it hurts. Take some time, ideally in the morning, to recognize what you are feeling. Bring the myriad emotions to Jesus in prayer and ask Him to order them—to redeem them. Listen to your body—it doesn't lie. Is it telling you that something is wrong? Don't ignore it.

Don't worry about shocking God with your doubts, fears, depression, or anger. None of it takes Him by surprise; He's seen it all. He even made sure loads of emotion was recorded in the book of Psalms so that we would know it's OK to be honest with God. God wants the real you.

Some people do this out loud; others like to journal this type of prayer. There isn't one "right way" to express yourself to God. But the choice to stuff, mask, or numb your emotions is never the best choice.

The hustling never delivers on its promises. But Christ always does. Go to Him for peace and you will never be disappointed.

Dear Lord,
Please help me to peel back the layers of self-protection and come to You with my deepest needs.
Amen.

Be Still

 MAY 16

"Surely the Lord God does nothing, without revealing his secret to his servants the prophets." (Amos 3:7)

While it is true that much about God remains a mystery, there is a great deal that He has revealed. It's interesting to look at the conversation Jesus had with the high priest after He was arrested. The high priest asked Jesus about His disciples and His teaching. Jesus replied, "I have always spoken openly to the world; I have always taught in synagogues and in the temple, where all Jews come together; I have said nothing secretly. Why do you ask me? Ask those who have heard me, what I said to them; they know what I said" (John 18:20–21).

Jesus was making the point that the high priest had been given plenty of opportunities to learn about Jesus and His teachings. He just hadn't bothered, and Jesus wasn't going to offer it all now. What relevance does this have for us? We are going to be held responsible—not just for what we know, but for what we had the opportunity to know but chose not to learn about.

Yes, much about God is a mystery. But there is a great deal that He has revealed, and it's on us to learn all we can about it. What a tragedy it will be if we come to the end of our lives and have never taken the time to understand what it is that God has expected of us during our time on earth. It simply will not hold up if we shrug our shoulders and say we didn't know. If we've had time to stay up-to-date on our friends' social media feeds, if we've been able to keep track of current events, we have had time to learn about God. We make time for what is most important to us.

As it says in Deuteronomy 29:29, "The secret things belong to the Lord our God; but the things that are revealed belong to us and to our children for ever, that we may do all the words of this law." We need to pay attention to what has been revealed, and pass it on to the next generation. We ignore this at our own peril. One day, ignorance will certainly not be bliss.

Dear Lord,
I commit to learning something new about You and Your Word each week, and recording it in my prayer journal. May I know You better in a year than I do today. Amen.

"Why then did you not obey the voice of the Lord?" (1 Samuel 15:19)

I'm often asked about the best way to pass a living faith on to the next generation. It would be so simple if the solution were found in a book or a program. But that's not what I've seen to be the most effective. I believe the game changer is *women who are radically obedient to God*.

In 1 Samuel, we find Saul, a man who stood head and shoulders above all the Israelites. God chose him as Israel's first king, but even with all his accolades, good looks, and brawn, Saul had self-esteem issues. We know this from the prophet Samuel, Israel's spiritual leader. In 1 Samuel 15, the prophet was calling Saul out for not obeying the Lord. Saul was supposed to wait for Samuel to come and offer a sacrifice before a battle, but his patience wore thin, and Saul took matters into his own hands and did it himself.

When Samuel saw Saul, he said, "Though you are little in your own eyes, are you not the head of the tribes of Israel? The Lord anointed you king over Israel" (1 Samuel 15:17). He then went on to ask Saul why he didn't obey the voice of the Lord after being given clear instructions.

Samuel was basically saying, "Saul, even though you don't think you are adequate or amount to much, God has chosen you for a really important task. He anointed you to *lead*. He told you to obey. So what were you thinking?!"

Saul responded by saying, "I have obeyed the Lord. I went on the mission He sent me on. These are all the things I *did* do. Why the obsessive attention to minute details? I obeyed in the big things. Isn't that good enough?"

And Samuel's answer brought down the hammer: "Has the Lord as great delight in burnt offerings and sacrifices, as in obedience to the voice of the Lord? Surely, to obey is better than sacrifice, and to heed than the fat of rams" (1 Samuel 15:22). Then the news was delivered that God had rejected Saul as king. Obedience didn't matter just in the big stuff; God was concerned with the details.

The same is true in our lives. Nothing will have a greater effect on others than our own radical obedience, not just in the big things, but in the little, day-to-day decisions that most people in our lives don't see—but our children do.

Dear Lord,
May I never forget that people watch what I do more than they listen to what I say. Amen.

Be Still **MAY 18**

"But be doers of the word and not hearers only, deceiving yourselves." (James 1:22)

What does it mean to be a doer of the Word? It's living out Romans 12:1, which says we are to offer "[our] bodies as a living sacrifice, holy and acceptable to God, which is [our] spiritual worship." We offer everything we have on an altar to God. It's a declaration that we are willing to take our hands off our lives and let Him be utterly in charge. It's giving Him the right to call the shots on the big things and the little things. It's committing to a life of prayer in which we are in touch with God throughout the day so that we recognize the small ways He's asking us to obey, not just the big, obvious ones. It's committing to radical obedience in which we do what He has asked *all the way, right away*.

This is what our family and friends notice. *This* is what impacts them deeply. They are wondering, "Is this faith thing for real? Does Jesus really make that big a difference?" And they look to our lives more than our words for the answer.

We hear that call to offer our lives as living sacrifices—to be doers of the Word, to obey radically—and all too often we say, "God, I'll obey you if . . ."

Make no mistake. Whatever is on the other side of that word *if* is what we want and worship most. That is what we are willing to sacrifice for. And our family and friends know it; they see it. We all worship something. Whether it's comfort, a career, a relationship, status—there is something that we will give anything to have and hold on to. God asks that it be *Him*. He asks that our obedience not be tied to conditions.

The only way we will ever be able to obey Him in this way is if we see Him as infinitely wise and infinitely kind. We need to know Him in order to trust Him. This is why we delve into Scripture—so that we can know Him better; so that we can see evidence of His wisdom and can therefore trust in His plan for our lives; so that we can hear of His kindness and remember He is utterly *for us*.

Where is God asking you to obey right now? What choice is in front of you? Whom will you worship in this moment?

Being up-to-date on our social media feeds, having perfectly organized homes, nailing it with deliverables at work—all of that feels great. But the simple acts of obedience *change the world*.

Dear Lord,
May my trust in You translate into brave obedience. Amen.

"First cleanse the inside of the cup and of the plate, that the outside also may be clean." (Matthew 23:26)

We all dread the phone call that comes unexpectedly and causes life to feel like one big before-and-after. With seven children, I've gotten my fair share of these calls. There is nothing worse than a call that involves your child.

Someone asked me if I would be worried about my reputation if my worst-case scenarios regarding my kids came true and became known. Without a moment's hesitation, I said, "Absolutely not." The reason I responded in this way has everything to do with the way I define success and failure. I believe it's worth sharing, because I think there are a lot of moms out there who are dealing with their own set of disappointments that involve their families, and there's a lot of hiding going on. This hiding doesn't help anyone or anything, and it's actually the devil's playground. He loves the shadows. So many mothers feel like failures, and I believe they are using the wrong measure to determine how well they are mothering.

We live in a world that measures success by the outward appearance. Physical beauty, athletic ability, academic accolades, and a charismatic personality are considered the highest prizes. As long as outward appearance looks good, all too often mothers are willing to hide or ignore sins and deficits of their child's character. We don't want our children to suffer, but perhaps just as much, we don't want their *reputations* to suffer. As a result, we step in the way of natural consequences that God wants to use to teach our children lasting lessons. We make excuses, cast blame, and bail them out so that their spirits aren't crushed. And in doing so, we warp their understanding of choices and consequences. We leave them ill-equipped for a world that will not continue to soften the blows or buffer them from discomfort. The result? They will never grow up.

Why do we do this? Because we are caught up in the things the world values. We gain an extra ten pounds and feel less valuable. We measure our worth against our accomplishments. Striving and hustling to be considered good enough, we focus on the tip of the iceberg and ignore the enormity of what lies beneath. "Man looks at the outward appearance, but the Lord looks at the heart" (1 Samuel 16:7). God cares about what's going on beneath the surface.

Dear Lord,
I want to trade the world's definition of success for Yours, focusing on the inner life instead of outward appearance. Please help me to do this. Amen.

Be Still

 MAY 20

"For the weapons of our warfare are not worldly but have divine power to destroy strongholds."
(2 Corinthians 10:4)

Even when we recognize that life is a battle, too many of us are fighting with the wrong weapons. The true battle isn't what we see with our eyes. Ephesians 6:12 tells us that "our struggle is not against flesh and blood, but against the rulers, against the authorities, against the power of this dark world and against the spiritual forces of evil in the heavenly realms." The battle is in the spiritual realm, and only one kind of weapon can meet the battle in the air.

The weapons of the world are reputation, money, influence, power, and a shiny outward appearance, which can take us only so far. And from the Lord's perspective, these things are affecting only the tip of the iceberg, the part that is evident to all. But the weapons that have an impact below the surface are far more powerful than the worldly weapons.

The sword of the Spirit is the Word of God (Ephesians 6:17). This is an offensive spiritual weapon. Prayer is tremendously powerful because it literally moves the hand of God and calls down angels to battle on our behalf. The Eucharist has been used in physical battle, and the Rosary's power has been seen for hundreds of years.

It's what's going on below the surface that makes all the difference and is the true measure of success. And that's where we employ the weapons discussed in 2 Corinthians 10:4. It's a hidden battle, waged in the quiet of our homes and adoration chapels. It's fought on our knees and pushes back the darkness.

The worldly weapons are less powerful because they have nothing to do with the release of the Holy Spirit. If we seem to win a battle by using the world's weapons, from God's perspective we have lost. By contrast, if we seem to lose a battle but we have relied on the Lord, trusting in Him and the weapons of prayer and His Word, we have won. We have *won*, regardless of what it looks like to the rest of the world. This means that what others might consider a failure can actually be an enormous victory.

Dear Lord,
May I spend more time battling on my knees than I do worrying about problems and trying to solve them in my own strength. Amen.

MAY 21

"Come to me, all who labor and are heavy laden, and I will give you rest." (Matthew 11:28)

How do we release the weight of the world onto the shoulders of the One who carried it to the cross on Calvary? Something has already happened that needs to be put into effect in our day-to-day lives. We are told in Isaiah 53:4, "Surely he has borne our griefs and carried our sorrows." All the hurt and sin that is found everywhere was heaped on Jesus as He hung on the cross. Rejected, abandoned, shamed, He appeared powerless. But nothing could be further from the truth. Jesus chose to relinquish His power to His Father—to trust—and to let nothing deter Him from walking toward His calling. If Jesus has absorbed all the suffering of the world, why are we still trying to carry it?

He suffered *redemptively*. He experienced all the wounds that accompany suffering, yet He didn't allow it to mess with the truth that He was God's beloved Son. Knowing who He was gave Him the strength and courage to continue loving in the face of pain and fear. We are asked to do the same. Even when everything seems hopeless, when we feel powerless, when it seems that evil has the upper hand, God asks us to remember whose we are and keep walking forward in our calling.

He asks us to continue to love, right where we are. We don't continue to love because we trust the people who have betrayed us. We continue to love because we trust in our heavenly Father and His plan.

He asks us to keep walking toward our calling even when we feel hopeless, because we know hope doesn't depend on us; it depends on God. Powerlessness is true power when we relinquish our control to the Lord.

As my local priest said on Sunday, "It's time to reacquaint our knees with the floor." That is where the true battle is waged. Part of the battle is confessing our sin of self-reliance and handing the weight of carrying it all to Jesus. The next part of the battle occurs when the grace of the Holy Spirit starts to pour through us. It's water running through the pipe, bringing refreshment and healing to our aching world.

Dear Lord,
May I enter the brokenness of the world as a balm, bringing Jesus to people longing for redemption. Amen.

Be Still **MAY 22**

"A bruised reed he will not break, and a faintly burning wick he will not quench."
(Isaiah 42:3)

So many of us have an image of God as one who sets a high standard, who gets disappointed and perhaps angry when we don't meet it. Is this really who God is? I don't believe so. God knows our limitations. He is very familiar with our weaknesses. While people in our lives may have unrealistic expectations of us, God sees the whole picture and the degree to which we are trying. And when we're weary, He comes to us with arms of comfort, eyes of understanding, and lips that speak encouragement. When we are weakest, He asks that we rest in His lap and lay our head on His strong shoulder. He doesn't want to break us; He came to restore us.

This is the heart of the Gospel. God saw the chasm that sin created between us and Him. He knew that no matter how hard we tried, we'd never be able to achieve the perfection required to be in His presence. Instead of telling us to jump higher or try harder, He stooped down and said, "I'll do for you what you can't do for yourself." Jesus, who had never sinned, allowed all the sins ever committed to be placed on His shoulders. He paid the price of sin so that we wouldn't have to.

Jesus's sacrifice cleared the way so we could have a personal relationship with God. This is a privilege offered to everyone, but it's enjoyed by relatively few people. Do you know *about* Jesus, or do you *know* Him personally? I don't ask this question as a rebuke, but rather as an invitation. He's inviting you to draw closer.

Once we know Jesus personally, we never need to be lonely again. We no longer have to worry about being perceived as too emotional when we pour out our hearts. We don't have to worry that our private concerns will be gossiped about if we share them with Him. He is the most intimate, true friend, connecting with us body, soul, and spirit.

Because of Jesus, we can let go of the "try-hard" life. We can rest in His all-sufficiency. We can ask the Holy Spirit to run through us like sap in a tree, nourishing us and doing in and through us what we can't do for ourselves.

Dear Lord,
What I have the least of is _____ [patience? love? empathy? strength?]. I am storming heaven with my prayer, asking You to give me what I lack. Help me today, Lord. Amen.

MAY 23

"Though he falls, he will not be overwhelmed, because the Lord God holds his hand." (Psalm 37:24)

It had started out perfectly. Charlotte was a new baby, and Bobby was a bright-eyed five-year-old. Our trusty dog, Bailey, needed a little exercise, so we decided to take a walk. Bobby wanted to hold the leash, insisting that he was big enough, and since Bailey was walking so calmly by our side, I handed it over. All was well until we got to the top of a hill. Bailey saw a squirrel and took off at breakneck speed. It happened so quickly: Bobby's little legs couldn't keep up, he waited too long to let go of the leash, and he took a fall that threw me into a total panic.

I raced to him as quickly as I could and gathered him up in my arms. Between gulps and tears, Bobby looked into my face with fear in his eyes and asked, "Am I *dead*?" I assured him that he was not dead, that he would be OK. And he was. Scraped up? Oh yes. Many Band-Aids and kisses were applied. But he would fully recover.

We are right to want to protect our children, but we also want to raise children who are resilient. This will happen only if we take some risks, and risk-taking means they will fall sometimes. When they do, what they need to know is that emotionally, they are safe. The core part of who they are is untouched by physical distress. They can take risks—they can step out and try new things, and falling is not the end of the world. Falling and failure doesn't spell death—it is something we recover from.

Bobby looked into my face for reassurance that everything was OK. Whenever possible, I want to be there for my kids when they fall. I want them to be able to look into my eyes and see my calm confidence that they can and will stand back up again. That this is not the end of the road. A fall is always an opportunity to learn.

At the heart of Bobby's question were ones that we all ask—children and adults alike. "Am I safe?" "Am I secure?" "Is everything going to be OK?" When this is what we feel, we can turn to the face of our heavenly Father for reassurance. He will acknowledge the pain involved in the fall, but He will quickly assure us that it is well with our souls. No matter what obstacles we face, regardless of the depth of the disappointment—even when everything seems to be bottoming out—our souls can rest secure. *Who* we are remains unaltered because of *whose* we are.

Dear Lord,
Help me to keep my eyes on Your face. Amen.

Be Still **MAY 24**

"God, who is rich in mercy . . . even when we were dead through our trespasses, made us alive together with Christ." (Ephesians 2:4–5)

What profound truth is found in Saint Irenaeus' words: "The glory of God is man fully alive." This statement is pregnant with hope. Isn't it incredible to think that as we come fully alive, it gives God glory? He so longs to see us flourishing, thriving, *truly living*, that His own glory is connected to it. His fatherly heart is so tender toward us.

We are His beloved children, and so when we trudge through life weighed down by negative thoughts, or race through our days with stress as our main fuel, or simply exist because we don't know what more is available to us, God grieves.

When He sent Jesus to offer the ultimate sacrifice to purchase our freedom, He didn't want us to simply replace slavery to sin with slavery to performance. Nor did He intend for us to spend our lives trying to clean ourselves up so we'd be worthy of love. Scripture tells us, "if anyone is in Christ, he is a new creation: the old has gone, the new has come!" (2 Corinthians 5:17). Do you see yourself through that lens? Or are you consumed with thoughts of your inadequacies, limitations, and faults? That mind-set train-wrecks the heart and stands in the way of experiencing the life that Jesus died to give us.

It makes me think of Moses' words to the Israelites just before he died. He begged and pleaded with these words: "Today I have given you the choice between life and death, between blessings and curses. Now I call on heaven and earth to witness the choice you make. Oh, that you would choose life" (Deuteronomy 30:19).

Oh, that you would choose life. This is the plea. This is the offer of Christianity: to fully live.

Dear Lord,
May I choose life, becoming fully alive as I embrace Your mercy and my true identity as Your beloved child. Amen.

"God is able to provide you with every blessing in abundance, so that you may always have enough of everything and may provide in abundance for every good work." (2 Corinthians 9:8)

Why do so few of God's children really experience the abundant life promised in Scripture? I don't have all the answers, but I have learned that sometimes we first need to allow God to let some of our wounds come to the surface, to acknowledge that they need tending and that the healing is going to take time. It means saying some hard nos so that we can say yes to the journey toward wholeness.

Sometimes it means believing that God places dreams into the hearts of His children, and He wants us to taste the rush of being used by Him. It's scary to step out of the comfort zone, and messy, and full of imperfections. But ignoring what we were made for means we become sterile, abbreviated versions of who we were created to be.

I know that being fully alive requires hands to hold. We weren't created to walk this journey alone. Sometimes we need the hands to pull us a little higher, to support us while challenging us to stretch and grow. Sometimes we need those hands to hold us back when our pace has become unhealthy. Sometimes we need those hands on our cheeks along with the words "You are never alone." We need each other.

The whisper of shame will always try to lure us back into covering up our wounds (*What would people think if they knew?*). It will cause us to be self-conscious of our dreams (*Who do you think you are?*). Shame tells us to stay silent and not reach out for help (*You can talk about anything, but not this. If you speak these words, you will be misunderstood. It will be unbearable.*).

Jesus wants to restore us to what man once had in the Garden of Eden: nakedness—vulnerability—without shame (Genesis 2:25). He longs to break those chains that tether us to a life of existence instead of a life of abundance.

He does this *for* us, but it isn't just *about* us. Jesus doesn't free us from the grip of shame just for our own benefit. His hope is that as we are transformed, others will see the change, and they will be drawn to Him.

Dear Lord,
I want to experience the abundance that You have for me. Make clear what is blocking that, and clear the way to Your blessings. Amen.

Be Still

 MAY 26

"In your anger, do not sin." (Ephesians 4:26)

Scrolling through Facebook and other social media sites makes it clear that people feel free to express rage, disgust, and disappointment however they choose. Differing opinions are nothing new. But the way in which we are *discussing* those differences has changed in recent years.

It seems we have lost our ability to listen first and to only post something we would be willing to say to someone's face. Distance demonizes, and the social isolation that results from communicating screen-to-screen, instead of face-to-face, is hurting us.

We are relegating character and integrity to the backseat as our emotions are unleashed, and sadly, Christians are not the exceptions to this rule. All the while, a watching world observes us becoming unhinged by our hatred and disgust.

In Colossians 4:6, Saint Paul writes, "Let your speech always be gracious, seasoned with salt, so that you may know how you ought to answer each person." Salt enhances flavor—it makes food more appealing. In the past, it was used to preserve meat. When Saint Paul compares our words to salt, he's encouraging us to communicate in a way that is winsome, drawing someone closer, preserving unity whenever possible. Being behind a screen or in the midst of an angry group does not give us permission to let graciousness go by the wayside.

We might look to politicians to fix the problems we see. But the truth is, it begins with us. The hard work of reaching your hand across the aisle, of being an agent of reconciliation—that begins in our communities, our churches, our neighborhoods, and our homes.

Nowhere in Scripture will you find Jesus exhorting us to defend our rights. But there are countless times when He implores us to lay down our rights for another. We are able to do this because we have our eyes fixed on heaven. We have a sure hope as an anchor for the soul (Hebrews 6:19), and because of this, we don't need to be afraid. God is in control—His purposes and plan will not be thwarted.

Dear Lord,
May my fear be replaced with courage and hope. May my rage be ruled by self-control. May my judgment be overpowered by mercy. Amen.

"Would that even today you knew the things that make for peace! But now they are hidden from your eyes." (Luke 19:42)

There are so many things that promise us peace but don't deliver on that promise. We think that financial freedom will bring us peace because we'll no longer be anxious about money. A perfect body promises peace because we're certain that we'll finally look in the mirror and like what we see. Our relationship woes, so irritating and often heartbreaking, leave us certain that if only we were loved well, our hearts would be full of peace and joy. To be clear, none of those things are bad in and of themselves. But we end up deeply disappointed when we think they'll bring us peace. They just don't deliver. The bar is constantly raised. We receive one thing, and in no time we are longing for something else, and peace remains out of reach.

Why are the things that make for peace hidden from so many people? It's because God reveals the pathway to peace only to those who turn to Him and ask for it. Unfortunately, most of us want to figure things out for ourselves. We read in Jeremiah 29:13, "You will seek me and find me; when you seek me with all your heart." This verse is connected to our quest for peace. We first need to seek God with all our hearts, then He will reveal Himself to us. As we come to know Him, we come to know peace. The two quests are entwined. "For [Jesus] is our peace" (Ephesians 2:14).

We desperately need spiritual curiosity, a hunger to know God better and to more deeply understand what He has said about what will bring us peace. This requires humility. If we think we already know it all, or if we're just too lazy to dig a little deeper, we will never find peace.

Dear Lord,
Please give me a heart that is curious, humble, and aware that You know so much more than I do. Grant me a hunger to search for truth, a willingness to do the hard things required, and a teachable spirit that wants to learn. Instead of stubbornly insisting on figuring things out for myself, help me to turn to You for guidance and to ask advice from people who are following You faithfully and humbly. Amen

Be Still

 MAY 28

"The God of all comfort . . . comforts us in all our troubles, so that we can comfort those in any trouble with the comfort we ourselves have received from God." (2 Corinthians 1:4)

Affliction comes in many forms. In the midst of a sin-saturated world, people need to know that they matter, that their pain matters, that they are seen. What a difference the presence of a comforter can make. We can't answer all the questions about the suffering, but we can say, "I see it. And most important, I see you. I won't let this pain swallow you or overwhelm you."

Isn't this the message of the Incarnation? Bridging all distance between God and man, Jesus moved into the neighborhood. He reached out and touched the leper, looked into and healed the eyes of the blind man, and restored Peter when his heart was overwhelmed with his own failure. He rushed in when there was pain instead of recoiling or standing back where it felt safe. This is how we are asked to live.

Nothing makes us more effective ministers of comfort than having suffered ourselves. Not one of your tears of pain will be wasted, if you allow them to be redeemed in the life of another. God can use every ounce of what you have been through to make this world a better, kinder place. We are told in 2 Corinthians 1:4, "The God of all comfort . . . comforts us in all our troubles, so that we can comfort those in any trouble with the comfort we ourselves have received from God."

If you have experienced miscarriage, divorce, grief, abuse, financial crisis . . . could it be that God is calling you to step out and encourage others who are going through those very things today? You are uniquely equipped to offer comfort because you have been there. You understand. You are proof that life does go on. You are a carrier of hope.

This is the call to the body of Christ. We are to surround one another, to press into one another's pain, to offer the gift of our presence. Sometimes sitting silently alongside someone is the best gift we can give. Sometimes it's making a meal. Sometimes advice is truly helpful. The important thing is that *we show up*. That we slow down enough to notice the pain in someone's eyes. That we ask questions, and then wait for the answers. You might be surprised at the life-changing impact your comforting presence provides.

Dear Lord,
Open my eyes to see the invisible wounds people carry. Help me to look through grace-healed eyes that search deeper, that pause, that step closer when an aching heart is near. Amen.

MAY 29

"I will turn the darkness before them into light, the rough places into level ground." (Isaiah 42:16)

God invites you to step out and trust Him in the scary places. He may be inviting you to stop trying to control someone in your life and instead to trust Him to intervene. Perhaps it's a hard conversation He wants you to have. Maybe it's finally working up the courage to say out loud, "I am drinking to numb the pain and I don't know how to stop." It could be that He's asking you to admit that you are experiencing despair, and that you need professional help. It's a stepping out into the unknown, and even as He extends His hand, the pretend places of safety look preferable to the free fall of trust.

And that's where God meets us. When we quit pretending, when we stop burying the things that need attention, He stands right in front of us, cups our face in His hands, and whispers, "You are so brave."

He cheers when we take that first scary step. He knows that's the hardest step to take. He calls to our hearts, "Fear not, for I have redeemed you; I have summoned you by name; you are mine!" (Isaiah 43:1). He grabs hold of our hands and does not let go for one second. His strength is infused into us, and we find that we can take another step, and then the next. Every single moment of the free fall, He goes before us, turning the darkness into light and making the rough places smooth. He coaxes us forward and promises, "When you pass through the waters, I will be with you. When you pass through the rivers, they will not sweep over you. When you walk through the fire, you will not be burned; the flames will not set you ablaze" (Isaiah 43:2).

Ask the One who loves you to give you just a little more courage than fear. That's all you need to take the first step. You don't need to have it all scripted out. You don't need to have the whole plan in place. You just need a little more courage than fear, and the knowledge of where the free fall ends. Oh, my sweet friend, it doesn't end with you in a heap on the floor. It ends with you cradled in His arms. You can rest there. And when the time is right, He'll set your feet back on the ground and say, "See, I am doing a new thing! Now it springs up; do you not perceive it? I am making a way in the desert and streams in the wasteland" (Isaiah 43:18–19).

Dear Lord,
I am grateful for Your mercy that never fails. Amen.

Be Still

 MAY 30

"What has happened to all your joy?" (Galatians 4:15)

Can you remember a time in your life when you felt joy? Has it been a while? Do you wonder if your joy is buried under circumstances that you wish would change?

When life is out of kilter, our "fake fine" and ability to hold it all in goes out the window. We end up being real and authentic whether we intend to or not. I really like being in control, and my go-to preference has always been for people to see the best side of me at all times. But lately, I've been trying out saying what I really think. I've been quicker to admit that I don't know what I'm doing. I've been slower with dispensing advice. I've been doing more sitting in the disappointment with people than trying to fix their problems.

This is what I've found: Being real and authentic is messy but it wakes up your soul and lets you feel alive and present. This doesn't feel like tidy living, but with each authentic conversation, with each time that I venture out past what feels safe and into what feels more honest, my soul wakes up a little bit more.

I am feeling more alive and more present than I ever have. Instead of trying to rush to a solution that brings everything under control, I'm pausing and thinking about the fact that my fix might not be the right one—that I should listen for a little longer before jumping in with my words. And like I said, this doesn't feel nice. But I'm letting myself *feel* and sit there for a little bit.

While this waking up of my heart is causing me to feel the hard stuff a little longer and more acutely, it is also waking me up to joy. I feel joy more than I ever have, and I'm sitting *there* a little longer, too. Instead of rushing past it, I'm grabbing hold of it and remembering that this is why we are here. This is what it means to really live.

In Galatians 4:15, Paul asks, "What has happened to all your joy?" I've found it and embraced it, right in the middle of the crazy. It was hidden underneath all sorts of feelings and emotions, and I had to take the time to feel each one in order to get to it.

Dear Lord,
Help me to be real and authentic, even when it feels messy. May I rediscover joy, right where I am. Amen.

MAY 31

"To everyone who has, more will be given." (Luke 19:25)

The best day can be instantly derailed when we encounter someone who has exactly what we want but don't have. Do I compare my best to your worst? No. I compare me at my worst to you at your best. My low points are compared to your highlight reel. God cares about what all this comparison and competition is doing to our hearts.

He cares because He knows that it holds us back from practicing gratitude, and being grateful is a key component of happiness. God wants us to be happy, and He knows that what we *think* will make us happy often only brings short-term satisfaction. He also cares because it impacts the important work that needs to be done in His kingdom. That's what Luke 19:25 is talking about. This verse is taken from a parable in which Jesus describes a nobleman entrusting his servants with a sum of money. One invested his and made more, while another was afraid of failure and just stored his. In the end, the one who doubled his money was entrusted with even more. The one who had hidden his money away lost the little that he had; it was given to the wiser servant.

What does this have to do with us? God has entrusted each of us with gifts and abilities. No one was passed over; no one was skipped. He handpicked particular gifts for each one of us, hoping that we would use them to further His kingdom (not our own). Some of us have taken what we've been given and stepped out to serve. But many of us are looking at what God has given someone else and are leaving what He has given us stored away. Then we look at the blessings that continually seem to fall upon this "golden person" and wonder why we are so shortchanged. What we are missing is the fact that God is waiting for us to take what we've got and run with it. He waits to bless us until we stop complaining about what we don't have and start thanking Him for what we do.

Lord,
I want You to be able to say to me, "Well done, good and faithful servant." Help me to be grateful for what You have given me and how You have made me. Help me to stop looking to the left or the right. Help me to stop comparing myself to others. May I see myself as Your unique design. May I remember that You want to use me to display Your glory. Amen.

June

My God will fully supply whatever you need, in accord with His glorious riches in Christ Jesus.

Philippians 4:19

JUNE 1

"My soul finds rest in God." (Psalm 62:1)

While many of the voices around us are trying to convince us that the quality of our summer has to do with how we look in a swimsuit, I propose that there is something we can drop that's far weightier than pounds. What would be different this summer if we decided to drop striving and comparing ourselves to others?

Striving goes beyond working hard. It's white-knuckling and ignoring the inkling that maybe it's OK for things not to be perfect. It's looking at what I need to get done and being intolerant of the thought of not finishing well. Writer and research professor Brené Brown describes it as pushing the dig-deep button, forcing ourselves to continue when secretly we are exhausted and overwhelmed. This unhealthy pressing forward has been my norm for far too long.

Comparing myself to others is looking in someone else's garden and thinking they have it better or easier. It's thinking their spiritual gifts are better than mine. It's thinking my obstacles are higher, my limitations are greater, and their teeth are whiter.

Step one for those of us who struggle in this area: Stop trying so hard. Here's the deal—sometimes we need to overcorrect in order to get back to a place of balance. So when we feel like we're really trying hard and are hitting the dig-deep button, we need to stop. We need to ask God if it's OK to just let Him run with the task for a bit. Trying hard can be a signal to us that we need to assess what's really going on. We'll often do the task at hand, but we might take a fifteen-minute break to refresh ourselves and let the delivery of the task be late. This is not the end of the world.

When life feels out of control and like less than what I'd hoped for, I'm going to sing, "It is well with my soul." Because it is. Because the most important things are being taken care of by God. Because it isn't up to me. Because He is in charge.

Because not one thing, not one pain, not one inconvenience, not one obstacle intersects my life without God having measured *me + Him* against the hardship. And if the suffering has been allowed, that means He concluded that apart from Him, I can do nothing, but with Him, this can be endured and overcome.

Dear Lord,
In a world full of demands and impossibly high standards, may I listen to Your voice encouraging me to pursue freedom instead. Amen.

Be Still **JUNE 2**

"This poor widow has put in more than all of them; for they all contributed out of their abundance, but she out of her poverty put in all the living that she had." (Luke 21:4)

Jesus saw wealthy people making big donations as He sat opposite the treasury at the temple. While He noticed those gifts, it was the sacrificial gift of a widow that grabbed His heart. What she gave, most would say would make little difference. It was just two copper coins. Yet Jesus saw what it cost her. It was proof of her sold-out surrender. Her willingness to give everything she had revealed her trust in Him as her provider.

Living in the age of social media can lead us to the faulty conclusion that if our lives aren't extraordinary and worthy of a great photo, then we don't matter very much. We mindlessly reach for our phones and encounter countless examples of people doing incredible things (and looking good while doing them). This deflates us and causes our own lives to look insignificant. It tempts us to buy into the lie that only the epic accomplishments have value.

What is the truth? There is no sacrifice you make that goes unnoticed by God. Hidden acts of heroic love that are personally costly, the choice that won't earn you an accolade or even a thank-you, the secret surrenders—God sees it all. Not only does He see it, He values it and measures it as greater than the flashy achievements.

But perhaps you are at a point in life where you feel so weak that hidden acts of service are beyond your ability. Is your emptiness the only thing that you can offer God? If you will turn to Him in times like these and say, "Jesus, I trust in You," God sees this as a tremendous offering.

If all you can do right now is not quit, if all the faith you can muster is a gesture of surrender, know this: In God's eyes, that is like the widow's mite. Some might say it's not much. But God sees that it is your everything; it is all that you have. God sees it for what it is—your *all*—and He says, "Well done, good and faithful one."

Dear Lord,
I offer You my emptiness and ask You to fill me. I lift my weak and shaking hand and ask You to grasp it. I offer You my fear and ask You to give me Your calming presence. Amen.

JUNE 3

"Simon, behold, Satan demanded to have you, that he might sift you like wheat, but I have prayed for you that your faith may not fail." (Luke 22:31–32)

We have an enemy, and he wants nothing more than to destroy us. Sometimes his work in the world makes it appear that he has limitless strength. But this verse from Luke teaches us something interesting: The enemy is limited by God. He and God are not equal in power—the enemy's counterpart is Saint Michael the archangel, not God. God determines just how far evil goes, and it has a limit.

God allows temptation and trials in our lives only when He is certain that they can be used for our benefit. His desire is that they cause us to stop relying on ourselves and instead rely on Him. He also allows trials to strengthen us. Faith is like a muscle: If we never really have to exercise it, it won't get stronger. We can always learn something during trials, either about ourselves or about God. Both have tremendous value. God never allows difficulties to come our way that will simply destroy us. But whether His good purposes become our reality is actually up to us. It's all about how we decide to respond to the trial. The ball is in our court.

But God doesn't leave us to battle alone. Jesus sits at the right hand of God, interceding for us, asking Him to give us strength so that our "faith may not fail" (Luke 11:32). He has sent us the Holy Spirit, who will make up for all the places where we are lacking. One of the negatives of living in a culture that is very focused on feelings (more than any other culture has been in the past) is that if we feel something is true, we believe it is true. One of the areas where this gets us in trouble is when we face trials. We feel like we can't endure it, and so we assume that this must be true. The real truth? We are far more resilient than we think, not because we're so amazing, but because the Holy Spirit in us does what is needed. But He's a gentleman, and waits to be asked.

Dear Lord,
Please forgive me for all the times I rely on myself, trying out every human solution before turning to You. Holy Spirit, please release Your power within me. I surrender to You. Please take care of all that I am facing today. Thank You for going before me, staying within me, and guarding me from behind. Amen.

Be Still

 JUNE 4

"Father, if you are willing, remove this chalice from me; nevertheless not my will, but yours, be done." (Luke 22:42)

It has been said that suffering is wanting what you haven't got and having what you don't want. No one gets through life without suffering, and there isn't an aspect of suffering that Jesus can't relate to. He, like us, dreaded suffering. When He prayed those words in the Garden of Gethsemane, He gave us an example to follow of how we should battle when we are in the midst of suffering.

First of all, Jesus was honest. He let His Father know that what He really wanted was for the chalice of suffering to be removed from Him. God desires the same honesty from us. He wants to hear our hearts. He is not a disinterested bystander. What worries are weighing you down? What circumstances do you want to avoid? What dreams do you wish would become reality? He wants to hear it all.

But Jesus didn't stop there. Immediately after being honest, He said that what He wanted more than anything was for God's will to be done. These weren't just empty words. His prayer of surrender ended with His sweat becoming "like great drops of blood falling down upon the ground" (Luke 22:44). He wrestled in prayer.

The Christian life requires surrender. And that can be the hardest thing in the world to offer to God, especially for strong and capable people. We want to be able to save ourselves, to figure it all out, to come up with the solution. Lifting hands in surrender to God doesn't come naturally. But if we don't do it, we'll unwittingly place our trust in ourselves, and at some point, we'll come up short.

We can wait to surrender until we have no other choice, until every other option has been exhausted. But this isn't the ideal. Far better is to wrestle daily in prayer, taking the time to identify which areas of life we most want to control. Once we've identified them, we hand them over to God. Sometimes we have to do this several times a day, or even multiple times in an hour. However long it takes, we are to wrestle it out of our hands and place it in God's.

Dear Lord,
These are the things that I desperately want: _____. These are the aspects of my life that I wish would go away _____. I am tired of trying to fix it all. I offer You each of these things and ask You to take care of everything. Amen.

JUNE 5

"Father, forgive them; for they know not what they do." (Luke 23:34)

If we want to break out of the cycle that unforgiveness produces, then we will very often have to forgive even if the other person never apologizes.

Choosing to forgive is a matter of the will. It is choosing to no longer bring up the offense, play around with it in your mind, or throw it in the person's face. It is refusing to rehearse or rehash the hurt. It is no longer wanting to hurt the person because he or she hurt you. Forgiveness is not a onetime thing. As we learn new things about how the hurt is affecting us, we have to re-forgive. As more consequences develop, we have to forgive each time.

It's important to remember that forgiving someone doesn't mean that you continue in a relationship that is unhealthy. Forgiving does not mean enabling. If the hurt has been caused by destructive behavior, it is essential that you set boundaries for the future that will protect you. You get to the root of anything that was unhealthy in the relationship and fix it. You make new rules. You have new parameters. You can forgive and demand that it never happen again.

Forgiveness does not let the other person off the hook with God. He is a God of justice, and He will deal with the person who has hurt you. Choosing to forgive means that you are no longer the enforcer—God is. If a punishment needs to be doled out, God will do it. Each time I'm triggered and can feel the anger returning, I need to say, "This no longer belongs to me. It belongs to God." Give it to Him again.

We can't control what happens to us, but we can decide what we're going to dwell on. If we want to be free from bitterness and resentment, which eat at our own hearts, then we need to refuse to rehearse or replay whatever happened in our minds. Each time a memory of the hurt comes back to you, use that as an opportunity to be reminded of your own sin and God's constant, gracious forgiveness.

Dear Lord,
I have resentment, anger, and unforgiveness in my heart toward [name]. I recognize that forgiving someone is not a matter of what I am feeling, but a matter of exercising my will. Because of this, I will say the words "I forgive [name]." And now I ask You to take care of the feelings in my heart. Help me to hand this over to You in trust. Amen.

Be Still

 JUNE 6

"Forgive us our trespasses as we forgive those who trespass against us." (Matthew 6:12)

We agree that rules are good and should be enforced when someone else breaks them, but it gets tough when we look at ourselves. If we're honest, we know that we've broken God's rules. Maybe we try to make ourselves feel better by assuming God will go easy on us. It's almost as if we're back in high school, hoping that our teacher is going to grade the test on a curve. We look around, and figure we'll come out ahead. We think of the most wicked people we can, and compare ourselves to them, and then we feel better.

The problem? God's not going to grade us on a curve. God's judgment is about him holding us up to his law, and seeing how we measure up. When we imagine ourselves held up to God's perfect law, it doesn't take us long to realize that we are guilty. God created us, gave us laws for living, and we have broken those laws. At the end of our lives, He has every right to punish us as severely as he sees fit. He's the Creator. That would be perfectly fair.

The most amazing truth is that in spite of everything that we have done, God still loves us. He loves us so much that He had His son take our place. If no one had been punished, then God wouldn't have been fair. There was a crime. Someone needed to be punished. But why Jesus instead of us? Because He loves us.

Can you think of anyone that you love enough that you'd die for them? Perhaps you can. But can you think of anyone you love enough that you would allow your child to be tortured and killed, in his or her place? We can't even begin to comprehend the depth of God's love for us. We may not be able to fathom it, but we can be overwhelmingly grateful for it.

How has God asked us to show our gratitude? We find the answer in Colossians 3:13, "You must make allowance for each other's faults and forgive the person who offended you. Remember the Lord forgave you, so you must forgive others."

Dear Lord,
I'm sorry that I'm far more aware of people who have hurt me than I am of the ways I have hurt you. Please replace my disgruntled spirit with a heart of gratitude. I pray that the overflow of the gratitude in my heart would be a readiness to forgive, regardless of how much I have been hurt. Amen.

JUNE 7

Be Still

"We are Christ's workmanship, created in Christ Jesus for good works which God prepared beforehand, that we should walk in them." (Ephesians 2:10)

You were created for a purpose. There are good works that God has put your name on. Do you question whether you have anything to offer? Here's the good news: it isn't about you— your platform, your abilities, your ability to be articulate— it's about Him.

Questioning our worth and our call can keep us on the sidelines of the life we were created for. So can looking at other women and figuring they are the ones God has really called. This really trips us up and holds us back.

I had the opportunity to speak at a large conference for Catholic college students. You might think that I was so honored to be asked to speak that I walked around the conference center feeling pleased with my situation. What I spent far too much time doing was comparing myself to the other speakers. I'd hear that not very many people showed up to a breakout session, but people lined up an hour ahead for another speaker's talk. It totally unglued me. When I was heading to Adoration an hour before I was to speak, lines were already starting to form outside certain rooms—but not mine, so I started to compare myself. Then I got a text from a friend that read, "Don't look to the left or the right. Do not compare yourself to others. You are a unique design and God wants to use you to display HIS glory." I wonder if those are words you need to hear today. Don't look to the left or the right. Do not compare yourself to others. You are a unique design and God wants to use you to display *His* glory.

Your life is too short and your calling too great to waste time comparing yourself to others.

Dear Lord,
When You created me, You placed certain passions and gifts within my heart. 1 Corinthians 12:7 tells me that "to each one the manifestation of the Spirit is given for the common good." This means that certain gifts were placed in me that You want me to use for Your glory. I was not skipped over. Help me to stop comparing what You've given me with what You've given others. If my gifts have been lying dormant within me, help me to discover them. And may I use all that You have placed inside me to benefit others and bring focus to You, the giver of all good gifts. Amen.

Be Still **JUNE 8**

"To all who received him, who believed in his name, he gave power to become children of God."
(John 1:12)

If I ask you, "Who are you?" and you say you're a mother, a student, an actress, a lawyer, so-and-so's spouse, an artist . . . I propose that you have just described a false identity. Why? Because any of those things could be taken away. They can't be counted on.

If I ask, "Who are you?" and you say you are ugly, you are unwanted, you are stupid, you are boring, you are untalented, you can't do anything right, you are too fat, you are too loud, you are too quiet . . . then I would say that is not who you are. Those are self-defeating thoughts. That is a litany of lies running through your head.

God wants you to focus on who you *are*.
The enemy wants you to focus on who you *were*.

Before you were rescued by Jesus, you were helpless, hopeless, stuck. There were powers at work in your life, and they were stronger than you. But then you were rescued. When did this happen? When Jesus was on the cross. The devil will want you to see yourself as you were, and he is trying each and every day to enslave you again. There is a battlefield out there and there is a battlefield in your heart and mind. And this is key: **If you do not know who you *were* and now who you *are*, you are at great risk of being enslaved again.**

Who are you? Why not ask the One who made you? He will tell you.

You are chosen. You belong. You are His beloved child. You are a daughter. You were created to be happy. And God knows what will make you happy. God says that your true identity is something that can never be taken away.

Dear Lord,
Who am I? How do You see me? Help me to replace the litany of lies that run through my head with the truth of how You define my worth and identity. Help me to spend more time listening to Your voice than I do to all the voices that tell me I'm not enough. The voice I listen to will end up defining who I am. May I listen first and foremost to You. Amen.

JUNE 9

"As far as the east is from the west, so far does he remove our transgressions from us."
(Psalm 103:12)

You are not the exception to the rule. Your sin, your failings, your shortcomings, they are not beyond the reach of God's mercy. Do you find this hard to believe? Are you, in this very moment, closing your heart off to the possibility that God's mercy is on offer to the likes of you? I beg you, stop. Will you just hold on to hope for one moment, and consider the possibility that you have been lied to?

Have you been told that you need to earn God's love? Have you been left with the impression that God is hard to please, and that certain sins are unforgivable? Have you believed the lie that you are damaged goods, beyond repair? How this grieves the heart of the Father. People put words in God's mouth that He never said. He is poorly represented constantly. Can we give God the floor and allow Him to speak for Himself?

Satan whispers the lie that you aren't good enough, that God could never love that part of you. But the truth is found in Romans 8:38–39: "Neither death nor life, neither angels nor demons, neither the present nor the future, nor any power, neither height nor depth, nor anything else in all creation, will be able to separate us from the love of God that is in Christ Jesus our Lord."

Satan whispers that the sin you are struggling with is beyond the reach of God's forgiveness. But the truth is found in 1 John 1:9: "If we confess our sins, he is faithful and just and will forgive us our sins and purify us from all unrighteousness."

Satan whispers that we'll never change, that we're damaged goods. He whispers that we'll never get away from that past sin; it's a part of us, stuck to us like tar. But the truth is found in 2 Corinthians 5:17: "If anyone is in Christ, he is a new creation, the old has gone, the new has come."

We are not who we used to be. We are no longer defined by how we've been treated or the choices we've made. We get a fresh start. When we are forgiven, we are washed clean, no exceptions.

Dear Lord,
Your mercy seems too good to be true. I'm so afraid to open my heart to the possibility that Your love is unconditional and Your forgiveness is without measure. So help me to trust. Help me to have just a little more courage than fear to open my heart to You and Your mercy. Amen.

Be Still

JUNE 10

"For our struggle is not with flesh and blood but with the principalities, with the powers, with the world rulers of this present darkness, with the evil spirits in the heavens." (Ephesians 6:12)

We are on a battlefield. It is the earth, and there's no opting out. The war is between two kingdoms—the kingdom of God and the kingdom of darkness. They are two powerful kingdoms, but they are not equal. One is stronger.

When the devil went to war against us, he had a significant victory early on. This victory occurred when man believed the devil's lie that God isn't good. As a result, two things happened: Sin entered the world, and humankind sold itself into slavery. Apart from Christ, we are enslaved to powers and dominions that we can't fight against. We are helpless. We aren't strong enough to rescue ourselves.

You may think my language is a little melodramatic. But let me ask you—have you ever experienced knowing something is wrong and that you shouldn't do it, yet you find yourself doing it anyway? Have you ever struggled to master your own impulses but felt that they are somehow stronger than you?

So what did God do about this? Jesus came to fight and to rescue you. This is what He was doing on the cross. He was going to war against all the demonic forces, against the powers and dominions we can't fight against. Jesus invaded enemy territory—the world that the enemy thought was under his control—and He took it back.

What looked like defeat—crucifixion, the most degrading, humiliating, stripping, agonizing death imaginable—was actually Jesus going to war for you and me. And He *won*.

What He won for us was our freedom. We were previously enslaved to sin. We have now been rescued. But God didn't just rescue us and then tell us to go fend for ourselves. He invites us to come and be a part of His family. He adopts us, and places His own Spirit, the Holy Spirit, inside us. This Spirit gives us everything we need to continue to persevere on the battlefield.

Dear Lord,
Romans 8:15 says, "you did not receive the spirit of slavery to fall back into fear, but you have received the spirit of sonship." May I live out of my true identity as Your child and not act like a slave. You have set me free so I can be fearless. Help me rely on the Holy Spirit within me so I can be brave no matter what I face. Amen.

JUNE 11

"Jesus turned, and saw them following, and said to them, 'What do you seek?'" (John 1:38)

Jesus asks you the same question. What are you longing for? What are you pursuing? What are you searching for? Is it peace? A sense of significance? Happiness? Worth? Security? Purpose? Truth? Guidance? Identity? All of the above?

We search for those good things in all sorts of places, but all too often we remain dissatisfied. A healthy bank balance doesn't bring the security we expected. The ideal job doesn't deliver the deep sense of purpose we thought it would. Losing weight doesn't provide the feeling of worth that we hoped for. Finding true love still leaves emptiness inside. The world tells us who we are or who we're supposed to be, and we end up feeling lost inside.

It's up to us how much time we are going to spend running down every possible road in search of what we long for. Many people do it for an entire lifetime, and then at the end are filled with regret.

Jesus patiently waits as we try out all the other options. He won't ever force us to turn to Him. He respects our free will. Yet His heart aches, because He knows none of those other pursuits ever deliver on their promises.

True soul satisfaction only comes from a relationship with Jesus—not from knowledge about Him, or a Church membership, or the fact that you were baptized. It requires a turning of the heart to Him. He issues each one of us an invitation and says, "Come and see. Allow me to satisfy all your deepest longings. Come to me with your questions and see that I have the answers. Stop running in the other direction. Turn, and come back to my open arms."

To do so requires trust that He is *for us*. He wants only what is best for us. He knows what will truly make us happy. How can He make this claim? He made you. And if you want your life to work, if you want to find happiness, then you need to figure out what God says you were made for, what your true purpose is, and what things you need to have put inside you so that you can function well. You can find in Him everything you are searching for.

Dear Lord,
I have run down so many paths in search of purpose, worth, and happiness. The world has not delivered on its promises. I am turning to You. I am coming to You with my questions and longings. Please fill my emptiness with Your presence. Amen.

Be Still **JUNE 12**

"This is my commandment, that you love one another as I have loved you." (John 15:12)

Nothing kills a good friendship like comparison. When we feel we don't measure up, we often fall into gossip. The Hebrew word for *gossip* in the Old Testament means "traveling with a confidence." Proverbs 18:8 tells us, "The words of a gossip are like choice morsels; they go down to a man's inmost parts." How often do we forget gossip that we've heard? Not very often—it was interesting. Whether we wanted them to or not, those words traveled deep within us; they lodged in our inmost parts. Just as it's hard to resist a dessert once we've had one taste of the choice morsel, it's hard to shut the door on gossip once we've taken the first bite.

Women struggle to be authentic with one another. We want to be liked; rejection hurts. Many of us have been hurt enough in the past that we are afraid of intimacy and afraid of revealing who we truly are. What if this friend proves untrustworthy? Or what if she doesn't like what she sees when she sees the real me? We fear not being accepted. So we put the mask on, and go out with our best foot forward. We think, "So what if it isn't the real me? I don't want to be rejected!" But is a friendship between two women who are wearing masks particularly satisfying? No.

What is the real problem here? It's that we measure our worth by the wrong things. If I base my worth on the quality of my accomplishments, if my worth is based on my appearance, if my security lies in what people think of me, then I am not free to love. Instead, I'm scoping out the competition.

But when you define yourself as God's beloved daughter, everything changes. It means that you enter any relationship coming from a place of being loved—of knowing you are precious to God, full of grace, and a new creation. These truths give us the confidence to be vulnerable. We see that if we are made in the image of God, then we are likable. We have something to offer. We have something to give.

Dear Lord,
Help me to define myself as Your daughter, and to receive my sense of worth from You—not from what I do, have, or look like. May this allow me to be a better friend, who sets out to love others as You have loved me. Amen.

JUNE 13

"The Spirit of the Lord God is upon me . . . to give them a garland instead of ashes, the oil of gladness instead of mourning, the mantle of praise instead of a faint spirit." (Isaiah 61:1, 3)

The spiritual battle can be brutal at times. As we follow Christ, all is not sunshine and rainbows. We feel a spirit of heaviness, carry worries in our hearts, grieve our losses, and experience the grip of anxiety. What difference does the Spirit of the Lord God make when this is our reality?

Tucked into Isaiah 61:3 is a weapon that we can wield when we feel the weight of discouragement. It does not change our circumstances, but it does change us. What is this secret weapon? It's the mantle of praise. When we lift our voices in praise in those times when the enemy expects us to give up, it delivers a kick in the teeth to the demons who seek our ruin.

When we are struggling with heaviness of heart, it is critical that we pay close attention to which spiritual disciplines we are tempted to quit. The more discouraged and depressed we become, the more we are tempted to pray less, watch mindless videos, and seek comfort in food and drink. We assume that because we feel horrible, we deserve these little consolations. But when we do this, we leave ourselves wide open to further attack.

Instead of giving in to this temptation, we can put on the garment of praise. What music do you listen to when you're discouraged? Switching over to edifying music does more good than we realize. Raising our voices in song makes a huge difference. It causes a spiritual shift to occur that offers us protection and helps us to resist the enemy. In that same way, keeping an eye on the programs we are watching is especially important during discouraging times. All these things are delivering messages to our heads and hearts. When we are discouraged, we need voices of hope to surround us. We need to choose to listen to those voices. No one will make us do this, and no one can prevent us from doing it. This is something entirely in our control, and it can be a game changer.

Dear Lord,
Help me to battle better. Help me to fight back instead of giving in to discouragement. Give me the strength to resist the enemy's temptations and instead to take a step forward, doing a little bit more to grow in holiness. May I trade a garment of praise for the spirit of heaviness. Amen.

Be Still **JUNE 14**

"The angel of the Lord encamps around those who fear him, and delivers them." (Psalm 34:7)

There are times when we feel surrounded by enemies on all sides. "I'm all alone," we whisper. "It's all up to me." Fear takes over.

Psalm 34:7 reminds us that how things appear is not always how they actually are. The truth? Our God is called the "God of hosts," which means "God of angel armies." He deploys angels to come to our aid, and they encamp around us and offer us protection.

"I'm all alone" and "It's all up to me" are lies straight from the pit of hell. They are words whispered by the enemy with the intent of isolating us. The minute we agree with those lies, we take a step away from depending on God and a step toward relying on ourselves. We determine to get control of the situation and to direct events. This gets in the way of the work that God is doing on our behalf. It blocks us from surrendering to Him and simply asking Him to take care of everything.

If we accept the truth that we are never alone, that God is always present with us, we are better equipped to refute the lie that it's all up to us. It's actually all up to God, and He has all the resources needed to deliver us, protect us, and orchestrate the circumstances of our lives.

There is a battle that wages in your mind each and every day. There are two sides, two perspectives, and they both want to win. The enemy whispers lies to you, and God and the angels whisper truth. It's up to you to decide whom you will listen to, which voice will win. One voice comes from the heart of the One who only wants what is best for you. The other is bent on your destruction.

Just as the enemy attacks each and every day, the angels guard us. That's one of their primary responsibilities, and they do it without fail. We don't see the battle being waged around us, but it is there. How fortunate we are that an army of angels fights on our side. You are not alone. You are guarded, protected, and cared for. You have not been left to fend for yourself.

Saint Michael the Archangel, defend us in battle. Be our defense against the wickedness and snares of the devil. May God rebuke him, we humbly pray, and do thou, O prince of the heavenly hosts, by the power of God, thrust into hell Satan and all evil spirits who wander through the world seeking the ruin of souls. Amen.

JUNE 15

"His mother said to the servants, 'Do whatever he tells you.'" (John 2:5)

This is a simple explanation of what it means to follow Christ. But doing whatever Jesus tells us to do messes with our desire to be in control. We want to be the captains of our souls, the writers of our stories, the ones in charge. Jesus knows this, but He also knows that we don't do well with that level of responsibility.

He asks for our obedience because He knows the future and what is needed for us to achieve what we truly desire. All our circumstances are woven together by God into the perfect setup for our fulfillment. But when we insist on doing things our own way, we delay and sometimes forfeit our happiness.

We often set out to live in such a way that we are glorified. We don't use words like *glorified*, but the truth is, we want the credit, the attention, the raise, the coveted position. But God created us in such a way that we will be happiest when *He* is glorified. When this is our goal, the pressure rolls off. The need to achieve is put in its place.

Do you want to live a life of purpose and meaning? Do whatever Jesus tells you. The way He does this is by helping us to identify the next right thing that our duty in life requires. We ask the Lord, "What is the next right thing that You would like me to do?" It might be unloading the dishwasher or calling a friend and apologizing. The next step is to do that next thing for God's glory, not our own. And this changes everything.

If the next right thing feels insignificant, say to the Lord, "I am going to fold this load of laundry for Your glory. I entrust the results to you." Suddenly this simple activity has become an opportunity for you to encounter God. He is present there with you, delighting in the fact that you are doing the next right thing with a good attitude.

If the next right thing is something that feels overwhelming, say to the Lord, "I am going to step out and do what feels difficult for your glory. I entrust the results to you." If it goes well, the glory goes to God. If it doesn't go well, the results of it rest with God. Neither the success nor the failure rests on you.

Dear Lord,
Help me to do whatever Jesus tells me to do. Help me to see what is the next right thing, and to do it right away. Amen.

Be Still **JUNE 16**

"Behold, I stand at the door and knock; if anyone hears my voice and opens the door, I will come in to him." (Revelation 3:20)

Pope Emeritus Benedict XVI has explained that the "door of faith" is opened at one's baptism, but we are called to open it again, walk through it, and rediscover and renew our relationship with Christ and His Church.[46] We do this through conversion.

The word *conversion* means "the act of turning." It's a turning away from one thing and a turning toward another. When you haven't experienced conversion of heart, you are turned *toward* your own desires. You are the one in charge, and you do what you feel is right and best at any given moment. You may choose to do things that are very good for other people, but the distinction is that *you are choosing*. You are deciding. You are the one in control.

Imagine driving a car. You are sitting in the driver's seat, and your hands are on the steering wheel. You've welcomed Jesus into the passenger's seat, and have listened to His comments. But whether or not you follow His directions is really up to you. You may follow them or you may not, depending on what seems right to you.

When you experience interior conversion, you decide to get out of the driver's seat, move into the passenger's seat, and invite God to be the driver. Instead of seeing Him as an advice giver or someone nice to have around for the holidays, you give Him control of every aspect of your life.

God will never demand that you do this. As Revelation 3:20 says, He stands at the door and knocks. It's up to us to choose to open the door. He won't force His way in.

How does it go when you insist on doing things your own way? Have you discovered that relying on yourself has resulted in pressure, expectations, and disappointments? Are you ready to allow God to be in the driver's seat of your life? Just turn to Him, and invite Him in. He isn't waiting for you to clean yourself up. He waits to be invited into your mess. Once He is there, He'll do the reorganizing and cleaning, and the order will bring you a deep relief that only comes from relying on Him.

Dear Lord,
I want You to be in the driver's seat. But at the same time, I am afraid of where You might take me. Lord, I believe, but help my disbelief. Amen.

JUNE 17

"The wages of sin is death, but the free gift of God is eternal life in Christ Jesus our Lord."
(Romans 6:23)

Conversion of heart isn't possible without humility. The first step of conversion is to recognize your desperate need of a savior. When you hear Romans 6:23, you might be tempted to justify your behavior, or compare yourself with others. You might think to yourself, "I'm not a murderer. I'm not as bad as this or that person. If someone were to put my good deeds and bad deeds on a scale, my good ones would outweigh the bad. So surely I am good enough? Surely I don't deserve death!" When this is your line of thought, you are missing a very important truth: Just one sin is enough to separate you from a holy God. Just one sin is enough for you to deserve death. Even your best efforts to do good fall short of what God has required in order for you to spend eternity with Him. Isaiah 64:6 says, "All our righteous deeds are like a polluted garment." If you come to God thinking that you are going to be accepted by Him based on your "good conduct," He will point out that your righteousness is nothing compared to His infinite holiness.

Saint Thérèse of Lisieux understood this well, and wrote, "In the evening of my life I shall appear before You with empty hands, for I do not ask You to count my works. All our justices are stained in Your eyes. I want therefore to clothe myself in Your own justice and receive from Your love the eternal possession of Yourself."[47]

She recognized that her works, her best efforts, wouldn't be enough to earn salvation. Salvation cannot be earned. It's a free gift. Saint Thérèse accepted this gift, and said that if her justices or righteous deeds were stained, then she wanted to clothe herself in Christ's own justice.

He offers the same robe of righteousness to you. This is the divine exchange— we offer Christ our mess, and He gives us His merits in exchange. It's the greatest deal going, yet so many of us walk right by, determined to just figure things out for ourselves. Which brings us back to the first point. Conversion of heart isn't possible without humility.

Dear Lord,
Please forgive me for the pride in my heart that thinks it can earn Your love. Coming to You with empty hands, coming to You in my mess, feels so vulnerable. Please give me the grace to lift empty hands to You, asking that You fill them with Your graces. Amen.

Be Still **JUNE 18**

"For our sake he made him to be sin who knew no sin, so that in him we might become the righteousness of God." (2 Corinthians 5:21)

How did God make Him who had no sin to be sin for you? This was foretold by the prophet Isaiah: "But he was wounded for our transgressions, he was bruised for our iniquities; upon him was the chastisement that made us whole, and with his strips we are healed" (Isaiah 53:5).

Jesus accomplished this on the cross. Every sin committed, past, present, and future, was placed on Him. Now, *all the merits of Jesus can be yours.* He wants to fill your empty hands with His own virtues.

But first, you need to recognize, just as Saint Thérèse of Lisieux did, that you are little. You are weak. You fail. You need forgiveness. You need a savior. When you come before God in prayer and acknowledge these truths, He looks at your heart. He sees your desire to trust Him, to please Him, to obey Him. He says to you, "My precious child, you don't have to pay for your sins. My Son, Jesus, has already done that for you. He suffered, so that you wouldn't have to. I want to experience a relationship of intimacy with you. I forgive you. Jesus came to set you free. When you open your heart to me, you become a new creation! The old you has gone. The new you is here. If you will stay close to me, and journey by my side, you will begin to experience a transformation that brings joy and freedom. I've been waiting to pour my gifts into your soul. Beloved daughter of mine, remain confident in me. I am your loving Father. Crawl into my lap. Trust me. Love me. I will take care of everything."

This is conversion of heart. This act of faith lifts the veil from your eyes and launches you into the richest and most satisfying life. You don't have to be sitting in church to do this. Don't let a minute pass before opening your heart to God and inviting Him to come dwell within you. Let Him sit in the driver's seat. Give Him the keys to your heart. Your life will never be the same again.

Dear Lord,
I need a savior. I've tried to do it all on my own, and that hasn't gone so well. I want to invite You to be the One in charge. I give You my heart. I offer You the keys and invite You to come in and fill me. Amen.

JUNE 19

"They who wait for the Lord shall renew their strength, they shall mount up with wings like eagles, they shall run and not be weary, they shall walk and not faint." (Isaiah 40:31)

When we are weary and fainthearted, we are desperate for something to fix what's broken. Our exhaustion reaches a limit and we are certain that we need a break, immediately. Often, we take matters into our own hands and aren't happy with the results. Maybe we turn to other people and they end up disappointing us. Whether we turn to God right away or after exhausting all other options, we usually lay out our requests with the postscript ASAP. We may not use those words, but that's the sentiment behind our fervor. We have explained to God that we can't take any more. We need relief to come *now*. And when it doesn't come on our timeline, we think that Isaiah 40:31 must be some kind of cruel joke.

But have we missed the beginning of the verse in our desire to jump to the end? Have we forgotten to whom this promise is given? It's given to those "who wait for the Lord." Those who *wait* have their strength renewed. They are the ones who run without weariness and walk without fainting.

Patience is the virtue we need when we are weary and fainthearted. Patience says, "Although I am feeling desperate, I trust that relief is going to come. This is a time of desolation, but consolation is around the corner. The darkest hour is the hour before dawn. Just hold on."

Patience coupled with humility acknowledges that something is happening in the waiting. God is present there, and *He is at work*. Dwelling on this truth allows us to hold on to hope. God will not fail us. He is not asleep on the job. He may be hidden, but He is always actively working for our good.

The spiritual life is like a marathon, not a sprint, and the prize goes to the one who perseveres until the end. Can you stay faithful to the task at hand? Don't focus on the uphill climb, just ask the Lord to show you the next right thing. Then do it. Consolation and relief are coming, you can be assured of that. Patiently wait, and it will be yours.

Dear Lord,
Thank You for placing the fruit of the Spirit within me through the presence of the Holy Spirit. Release the fruit of patience so that I can wait on Your timing. I don't want You to conform to my timetable, I want the grace to trust Yours. Help me to be patient. Amen.

Be Still   **JUNE 20**

"For it is not by measure that he gives the Spirit." (John 3:34)

We serve a God of abundance, not of scarcity. We serve a God of limitless supply. Whatever we truly need, He has, and He has more than enough. How often we look at what God gives to others and make the faulty assumption that this means there is less for us. There is not only room at the table for us all, there is an all you can eat buffet of goodness that is filled to overflow.

Could it be that we "do not have because we do not ask?" (James 4:2) Or could it be that we are asking God for the wrong things or with the wrong motives?

God does not measure out His goodness with a spirit of stinginess. It is impossible to give more than God— He will never be outdone in generosity. He is a loving Father who longs to pour out blessings on us, but often we sit with clenched fists, jealous of what's been given to another. God can't put His gifts into clenched fists.

Or perhaps the things we are asking for are not really going to satisfy us and God knows it. So He waits for our hearts to be purified so we ask for the right things.

Sometimes the issue is our motives, because we want these things for the sake of our own glory. We wouldn't put it that way, we just want our house to look a little better, or our clothes to be a little prettier, or our reputation to be a little more stellar, or for our opinions to be a little more respected. We don't think we are seeking our own glory, but that's just because we're dressing it up with different words. When this is the case, God waits until our motives are purified so that He can give us things without them destroying us with pride.

There is no greater gift than the Holy Spirit. The Holy Spirit comforts us, enlightens our minds, gives us strength beyond our own, reminds us of things we've learned, convicts us when we're going down the wrong path, and supercharges our natural abilities with divine power. God does not give the Holy Spirit in a measured way— He gives the Spirit superabundantly to all who ask.

Dear Lord,
I pray for an outpouring of Your Holy Spirit within me. May Your Holy Spirit be released to do in and through me, more than I can ask or imagine. Amen.

JUNE 21

"Every one who drinks of this water will thirst again, but whoever drinks of the water that I shall give him will never thirst; the water that I shall give him will become in him a spring of water welling up to eternal life." (John 4:13-14)

Jesus spoke those words to a woman whose heart was filled with longings. The Samaritan woman at the well had gone from man to man in search of fulfillment and happiness. Inside, her heart was broken and in need of healing. She had a thirst for true love that wasn't being quenched.

Can you relate to the Samaritan woman? We may hold it together on the outside, but so many of us are walking around with deep hurts and hungers within. The woman who gives away her virginity in hope that it will guarantee love; the woman who hates herself so much that she eats to fill the void; the woman who throws up what she eats in order to find control and the "right" body; the divorced woman who wonders if she'll ever be loved again; the married woman whose marriage is not what she hoped it would be; the woman who whispers, "Is this all there is?"...

There are a lot of aching hearts looking for healing.

Take a moment to contemplate a specific hurt or insecurity within you. Could you open that part of your heart to God, and ask Him to bring healing and freedom there? That's why Jesus came. He came to bind up the broken hearted, and to proclaim freedom to the captives. He came for you. Can you thank Him for loving you that much and for caring about the little hurts and the enormous pains that you have experienced and are experiencing? Let Him wrap His arms around you. Rest there.

The Samaritan woman's search ended with an offer of living water, coming from an unexpected source. It was an offer of refreshing healing and restoration, and it's available to you and me today. The Holy Spirit is the source of that living water "welling up to eternal life." It wells up in the heart that prays.

"Oh God, you are my God, I seek you, my soul thirsts for you; my flesh faints for you, as in a dry and weary land where no water is. So I have looked upon you in the sanctuary, beholding your power and glory. Because your merciful love is better than life, my lips will praise you. So I will bless you as long as I live; I will lift up my hands and call on your name." (Psalm 63:1-4)

Be Still

 JUNE 22

"The Lord passed by, and a great and strong wind tore the mountains, and broke in pieces the rocks before the Lord, but the Lord was not in the wind; and after the wind an earthquake, but the Lord was not in the earthquake; and after the earthquake a fire, but the Lord was not in the fire; and after the fire a still, small voice." (1 Kings 19:11-12)

This passage is a part of the story of Elijah, one of God's faithful prophets. Elijah was deeply discouraged to the point of despair. Holiness had been very costly for him. He was desperate for relief.

It is interesting to note how God's voice came to Elijah. It wasn't in the strong violent wind. It wasn't in the earthquake. It wasn't in the fire. All those things were loud and attention grabbing. God's voice was a still, small voice. If Elijah hadn't been listening, he would have easily missed it.

The voices around us sometimes feel as loud as a violent wind. Unless we get quiet— turning down the noise— we're going to have a hard time hearing God's still, small voice, calling us to a better place. Calling us to freedom. Calling us to trade the slavery of defining success the way most people do, and instead defining it as God does.

How does God define success? From God's perspective, success has everything to do with how we love. It's summarized by Jesus in Matthew 22:37-39, "You shall love the Lord, your God, with all your heart, with all your soul, and with all your mind. This is the greatest and the first commandment. The second is like it: You shall love your neighbor as yourself."

First of all, He wants us to love Him. Then He wants us to love others. God wants us to pursue holiness. Holiness, not perfection. The measure of holiness is how we love. God wants all our decisions to be filtered through this lens. Which choice is going to help me love God better? Which one will help me to love others as Christ loved?

When we do this, when we decide to listen to His still small voice, we flourish. We experience the freedom of simplicity. We find that his yoke is easy, and his burden is light. He'll give us the strength to love as he wants us to love. Things that kept us up at night will become less important. The pressure will come off. Pursuing success as God defines it: holiness— which is measured by how we love, will bring deep lasting joy.

Dear Lord,
Please help me to quiet down so that I can hear Your still, small voice calling me to a place of simplicity. May I trade the world's definition of success for Yours. May I pursue holiness— loving well— more than anything else. Amen.

JUNE 23

"Moses did not know that the skin of his face shone because he had been talking with God."
(Exodus 34:29)

When Moses went up Mount Sinai, he spent forty days with the Lord and received the Ten Commandments. Coming down from the mountain, he didn't realize that his appearance had so radically changed. Moses was radiating the glory of God after spending time with Him.

When we spend time with God, the same should be true of us. Granted, we won't have rays of light streaming from our faces, but there should be something different about us. Our time with God is meant to be transformative. It's our souls that should shine and radiate His glory after we pray.

What has gotten in the way of the radiance of God shining out of your heart? For me, it often results from discontentment. God hasn't changed my circumstances. Because I find this disappointing, all too often I walk away from prayer with a focus on what I *don't have* instead of what I *do*.

The way I see it, there are things that need to change *so that I can love better*. So how could God not want to answer a prayer with such a lovely motivation?

God has been working on my heart recently in this very area. As I sat in Mass, asking Him to remove a particularly stressful and heartbreaking circumstance in my life, I reminded Him that it was getting in the way of my ability to love others. I listened for His response and felt Him impress a truth on my heart. This was the message:

Only you can place a limit on how much you can love.

It isn't my circumstances that are limiting my ability to love, it's my decision that I will only go so far. It's the boundary line I have placed between love willing offered and love that feels too costly. I have placed the boundary there; I have chosen where to put it. The truth is that God wants me to love with divine love—He wants to do the loving *through* me. This in no way requires me to conjure up feelings that I lack. But it does require that I remain steadfast and continue to love, even when I am weary.

Dear Lord,
The love required of me today feels especially costly. I ask You to love through me. Forgive me for the times that I decide to limit my ability to love because I am relying only on my strength and not Yours. Amen.

Be Still

 JUNE 24

"It is no longer because of your words that we believe, for we have heard for ourselves, and we know that this is indeed the Savior of the world." (John 4:42)

These words were spoken by the Samaritan people after they had heard the testimony of the Samaritan woman at the well. She had convinced them to come and listen to Jesus, and their belief resulted from that personal encounter with Him.

Many of us believe because of other people's words. We hear the priest talk about Jesus on Sunday, we've heard Christian authors talk about their relationships with Christ, we've listened to some good podcasts and have gained spiritual insights. All these things are good, but they are nothing compared to hearing for ourselves. By this, I mean having a direct encounter with Jesus Christ.

"That's not for me," you may be thinking. "That's something reserved for a special group of people." If these are your thoughts, I want to gently protest. Because nothing could be further from the truth.

Jesus wants to encounter you personally. If you were the only person on earth, He still would have come and died on the cross for you. He doesn't look at mankind as a group of indistinguishable people. He is able to see each person, individually. In Luke 12:7, Jesus said, "even the hairs of your head are all numbered." He knows you, better than you know yourself. He can see into the depth of your soul.

This truth can make some of us want to cover up the parts of us that we think must be repugnant to Him. When we do, His heart is grieved. What Jesus longs for us is for us to invite Him into the mess, and ask Him to clean it up. He doesn't find our weakness revolting. He finds it inviting.

How do we encounter Jesus? We do this through prayer. You can go to a Church, spend time in Adoration, or stay home. God will meet you wherever you are. The words don't need to be fancy, just heartfelt. You might want to place your hands on your thighs, palms up, hands open, as a gesture of surrender.

Dear Lord,
I want to encounter You personally. I open my heart to You and ask You to come in. Please reveal Yourself to me. Amen.

JUNE 25

"Whatever you have said in the dark shall be heard in the light, and what you have whispered in private rooms shall be proclaimed upon the housetops." (Luke 12:3)

Words matter. How often do we speak carelessly because the person we are talking about isn't within earshot? God desires that we be vigilant about what comes out of our mouths. While we might get away with gossip, slander and lying in the moment, a day will come when every word we have spoken will be laid out.

When I tried to teach this principle to my son, I gave him a paper plate and a tube of toothpaste. I asked him to squeeze all the toothpaste out on the plate, which he did with relish. When it was empty, I asked him to put the toothpaste back in the tube. This proved to be an impossible challenge.

This is how it works with our words. They come out so easily but are very hard to retract. Once they are out, they are free and cannot be controlled. Unless we are comfortable with all parties involved hearing what we said, we would be best to edit our words.

Proverbs 15:28 says, "the mind of the righteous ponders how to answer, but the mouth of the wicked pours out evil things." What would change if we slowed down and started to think before we speak? And how might our words change if we also paid attention to what we were thinking? St. Paul issues that challenge in Philippians 4:8, "Whatever is true, whatever is honorable, whatever is just whatever is pure, whatever is lovely whatever is gracious, if there is any excellence, if there is anything worthy of praise, think about those things."

That's our litmus test. If our thoughts about a person are not honorable, pure, lovely or gracious, we'd be wise to pause before we speak about them. This kind of thinking doesn't necessarily come naturally and will be greatly impacted by the company we keep. Is there a friend that always tempts you to gossip? You might want to consider how much time you are spending with her. We come to reflect the people we spend time with. Whether we choose to or not, we begin to resemble them.

A person of integrity is the same person when no one is looking. She doesn't have to edit her story depending on who is around, because she is a gracious truth teller wherever she goes.

Dear Lord,
"Set a guard over my mouth, O Lord, keep watch over the door of my lips!" (Psalm 141:3)
Amen.

Be Still

JUNE 26

"Let me hear in the morning of your merciful love, for in you I put my trust. Teach me the way I should go, for to you I lift up my soul." (Psalms 143:8)

What are your first thoughts when you wake up? Does the to-do list start to run in your head before your feet hit the floor? Does regret weigh your heart before you've had your coffee? Does anxiety have you in its grip before you can pray?

We can't help the thoughts and emotions we wake with, but we can decide what we are going to focus on as we move forward. Instead of letting what we feel take charge, we can choose to focus on truth.

Do you know that God sings over you? Zephaniah 3:17 says, "The Lord, your God, is in your midst, a warrior who gives victory; he will rejoice over you with gladness, he will renew you in his love; he will exult over you with loud singing." Each morning that you wake up to a life that feels like a battle, God wants to remind you that He is a warrior who gives victory. He sees all that you face and promises to find alongside you, in front of you, within you, and behind you. Victory is guaranteed because He is a mighty warrior.

As He fights by your side, He rejoices over you with gladness and sings. Why? Because you bring Him so much joy. He does not look at you with eyes of disappointment. He is not there telling you to pull yourself up by the bootstraps (an impossible task, at any rate). He is there, delighting in you.

His delight is not based on what you accomplish, what you look like, or on what others think of you. He delights in you simply because you belong to Him. You are His child.

He waits every morning to see if you will turn to Him in trust, and lift up your soul. Is your soul weary? He will fill you with strength. Is your soul battered? He will heal your wounds. Is your soul feeling abandoned? He will embrace you.

There is no one more worthy of your trust than the Lord. He will never leave you or forsake you. He truly understands what you face. He knows what will get you through the trials. Ask Him to teach you in the way that you should go, and He will faithfully lead you.

Dear Lord,
May I turn my face to Your merciful love before I do anything else in my day. I trust You. I lift my soul to You. Teach me the way I should go. Amen.

JUNE 27

"I will save the lame and gather the outcast, and I will change their shame into praise." (Zephaniah 3:19)

It has been said that guilt causes us to say, "I've done something bad," while shame causes us to say, "I am bad." Shame can result from something that has been done to us that we had no power to prevent, and it can come from our own free choices. Regardless of what has caused us to feel shame, shame tempts us to hide. This began in the Garden of Eden. When Adam and Eve sinned, they immediately wanted to hide from God. Pride and shame together can keep us hiding indefinitely.

When we don't want to be exposed, we try to cover up with all sorts of disguises. We say we're fine when we're not, we say we don't care when we do, we allow walls to be built around our hearts so no one can see inside. This might protect us on some level, but at the same time, leaves us in bondage. A heart that is self-protecting is unable to love. It's closed off, not open.

When we feel paralyzed by regret, God says, "I will save the lame."
When we feel we don't belong, God says, "I will gather the outcast."
When we feel covered in shame, God says, "I want to replace that with praise."

God is the only one who can remove our shame. He absorbed it all on the cross, and broke free of it on our behalf. He offers to not cover our shame but cleanse us from it. But pride will hold you back from experiencing this freedom. It requires humility.

Are you ready to stop hiding? Are you ready to put the washcloth down and stop trying to clean yourself up? The only one who can remove the stain is Jesus, and that is exactly what He offers to do.

Dear Lord,
I want to come out of hiding. Please change my shame into praise. May I praise You not just for the gifts You give me but for who You are— merciful, tender, steadfast and faithful. I ask for Your forgiveness. I hand over the spirit of heaviness and ask You for the garment of praise. Amen.

Be Still **JUNE 28**

"I glorified you on earth, having accomplished the work which you gave me to do." (John 17:4)

Jesus glorified God the Father by accomplishing the work that He gave Him to do. There was much that Jesus left unfinished; not everyone was healed, not everyone had the chance to hear Him preach, many needs were unmet. But Jesus was able to end His life at peace with what He had accomplished, because He knew that nothing mattered more than what God the Father said had priority. And those things He had done.

So many of us are busy and frazzled and although we don't *want* to live this way, everything looks important. We can't imagine working any harder or faster, yet we never seem to get caught up. Who is giving us our marching orders? Who is deciding which things have the greatest priority?

We are only called to do the works which *God* has asked us to do. God has promised us that His yoke is easy and His burden is light. This means that if what we are carrying feels destructively hard, it is possible that we have chosen to pick some things up that God has not asked of us.

This is not to say that every day feels simple and happy. Trials come our way, and there are times when our duties are very demanding. But when there is never a break, something is wrong. It is highly possible that we are doing work that God has not asked us to do, which He has, in fact, asked someone else to do. But if we are sitting in that seat in that particular role, it won't be filled by the right person. Sometimes we need to vacate a spot and let it sit empty for a while for the person whom God is calling to hear His voice, loud and clear.

For many of us, the most important work we will ever do will be within the walls of our own home. This work doesn't earn us many accolades and can easily move down the list of our priorities. But it could be that the greatest contribution you are going to make in the world isn't a goal you'll reach, rather the person you're raising and the change he or she will bring.

Dear Lord,
Help me to go to You each morning, asking You what priorities You have for my day. May I look at all I want to accomplish, and have the humility to ask if this is consistent with what You think is most important. May I look at any interruptions as potential divine appointments. Amen.

JUNE 29

"If any one is in Christ, he is a new creation; the old has passed away, behold, the new has come." (2 Corinthians 5:17)

This passage begins with the words "if any one", letting us know right out of the gate that there are no exceptions to this rule. "Any one" means that this promise is on offer to us all, regardless of all the categories we throw up to disqualify ourselves and others. But it isn't a blanket statement either; there is a disclaimer. This promise is offered to those who are "in Christ." It's a way of describing a person who has decided to trust in Christ instead of in his or her own abilities, credentials, or good works.

What is promised? The gift of becoming a new creation. It's the guarantee of a fresh start— a do-over button. This reminds us that God doesn't just forgive us— He remakes us— He transforms us. He doesn't just patch us up and set us on our way. He makes us new.

This spiritual rebirth is a bigger deal than the work He did at creation. Why? Because creation did not resist coming into existence. God spoke, and each aspect of the world came to be. But the human heart *does* resist. We aren't passive. We have to choose to cooperate with God.

The process of us becoming new is both God's work and our own. It is certainly not all up to us. As Charles Spurgeon said, "Beloved, if you have no more religion than you have worked out in yourself, and no more grace than you have found in your nature, you have none at all. A supernatural work of the Holy Ghost must be wrought in every one of us, if we would see the face of God with acceptance."[48] At the same time, the choices we make are critical. This is our part of the deal; we "work out [our] salvation with fear and trembling" (Philippians 2:12), recognizing that the way we live matters. Each and every day we are presented with countless opportunities to either resist the call of God to live as He desires, or to do things our own way. One leads to transformation and freedom, the other to slavery to sin. The choice is ours.

Dear Lord,
As Your child, I am a new creation. Help me to act like who I really am. I pray today for a supernatural working of the Holy Spirit within me. I know I'll face challenges today where I will want to take the easy way out. Help me instead to do the right thing, and to do it in Your strength. Amen.

Be Still **JUNE 30**

"But I, O Lord, cry to you; in the morning my prayer comes before you." (Psalm 88:13)

In Revelation 2:2-4, Jesus said, "I know your works, your toil and your patient endurance. . . . but I have this against you, that you have abandoned the love you had at first." He was talking about their love for him.

God whispers that same message to us in our busy, nonstop world. God doesn't say this to us because He just doesn't understand all that we have to do. Who more than Jesus understands what it feels like to be so busy and inundated with people's needs? God tells us that we need to go back to our first love, to Him, so that He can begin to make sense and order out of the madness that is our lives. If we are willing to make Him the first priority of our day, then He promises to come down in the midst of the craziness and start ordering things for us.

Our prayer life is a direct measure of how well we are placing God first in our lives. If we are not praying, we are not making Him a priority. It's as simple as that. Service *for* God is not a substitute for spending time *with* Him. It is only through spending time in prayer that we will begin to see what things in our day are most important to God, and which things we can let go of.

If you want to put God first and live a life of purpose, then finding time to pray is not an option. It must be the most protected part of your daily schedule. There's really nothing better than morning prayer time, as it sets the tone for the day. I know this is hard to do, and that there are seasons in life when giving God the first part of the day is especially difficult. During those times, I encourage you to look for the first pocket of quiet in your day. Ask God to provide it for you. And when it comes, reserve it for God. Resist the temptation to throw in another load of laundry or answer just a few e-mails.

You may not need to get up terribly early. The time on the clock is not what matters. What matters is that prayer is the highest of priorities in your life.

Dear Lord,
Help me develop the discipline of giving You the first moments of my day. "Satisfy [me] in the morning with Your mercy." (Psalm 90:14) Amen.

July

It is the Lord who MARCHES Before you; HE will be with you AND will NEVER Fail you OR FORSAKE you, so do not fear or be dismayed.

DEUTERONOMY 31:8

JULY 1

"But wisdom from above is first pure, then peaceable, gentle, open to reason, full of mercy and good fruits, without uncertainty or insincerity." (James 3:17)

The wisdom of the world has all sorts of advice for how you can get ahead. But if that isn't your goal— if your desire is to live in the way that God says is best, then you're going to need to listen to a different kind of wisdom. That wisdom is described in James 3:17. It's a great litmus test to help us check if the advice we're receiving is the sort of advice God would give.

Wisdom from above is first of all pure. When the word pure is used here, it's not talking about sexual purity. It's describing a purity of motive and a lack of a sinful attitude. Does the person who is giving you advice truly want what is best for you? Is he or she speaking with a spirit of humility or of pride?

Wisdom from above is also peaceable and gentle. This is a description of the kind of King that God is. He is gentle and kind even though He has the right to be stern and domineering. How is the tone of the person giving you advice? Is it gentle or aggressive?

Wisdom from above is open to reason. This means that it's not stubborn and is able to listen to the other side. There is an ability to yield, and to admit when one is wrong.

This wisdom is full of mercy and good fruits. Is this person quick to judge or is he or she able to give grace and the benefit of the doubt? Do they ask questions to clarify or do they just make statements?

Wisdom from above is also without uncertainty or insincerity. This doesn't mean being dogmatic, but there's got to be some strength— a belief system— a backbone. You don't need advice from someone who is wishy washy or morally relativistic. If their conclusion is "you do you," then it's likely that their wisdom may be based purely on their own experiences rather than on an understanding of what is true, good and beautiful.

When we come to a moment of crisis or a critical decision, the people we listen to are going to have an enormous impact on which direction we go. If we're smart, we'll listen to people with wisdom from above, and do our best to draw on that wisdom when others turn to us.

Dear Lord,
May we pay attention to who we listen to, and may our advice to others reflect the wisdom from above. Amen.

Be Still **JULY 2**

"No temptation has overtaken you that is not common to man. God is faithful, and he will not let you be tempted beyond your strength, but with the temptation will also provide the way of escape, that you may be able to endure it." (1 Corinthians 10:13)

We are prone to excuse our failings because of our unique set of circumstances. Our tendency to self-deceive is extremely high; we can usually justify our mistakes. This verse reminds us that our circumstances aren't nearly as unique as we'd like to think. The truth is, we have a similar set of struggles that many people do. The saints didn't have an easier road than our own; they just chose to doggedly follow God when most people had quit. They also didn't have natural abilities terribly different from our own. They simply chose to call on God for help while most of us choose self-reliance.

The next part of this passage is one of the most comforting to be found in Scripture. It says that God supervises our temptation. He does not allow one thing that is beyond our capacity to resist to touch us. Just as a mother might choose to completely avoid the candy aisle at the grocery store because her toddler just can't handle it, God steers us down the path that we can handle with His grace. The trials and temptations that fly at us have a limit, and God is the one doing that limiting. This means that if He has allowed something to tempt us, we do have the strength to stand firm. God will always provide a way of escape.

The need for a way of escape presupposes that there's another route that, while dangerous, is more open and direct. That's the path well traveled. There's sure to be company on that road. We're often so busy telling each other, "You're OK," and "We're all just doing the best we can," that we don't even notice the way of escape that's available. We have to look for it. We have to slow down and think about the choices we have in the face of temptation.

The way of escape is not an easier path. It's usually the harder one. But if we don't take it, then we're actually emboldening and strengthening our enemy. When we resist temptation, we see his weakness. The enemy is actually quite a coward. When he is faced down, he cowers and flees.

Dear Lord,
Help me to slow down and to look for the escapes You provide. May I stop making excuses for myself, face the enemy squarely, and stand my ground through Your strength. Amen.

JULY 3

"It is the Lord who goes before you; he will be with you, he will not fail you or forsake you; do not fear or be dismayed." (Deuteronomy 31:8)

Do you feel you are stepping into the unknown? Are you in the midst of suffering and unable to find anyone else facing the same difficulty? Is insecurity messing with your heart? This is a time when you are especially susceptible to the enemy's lies.

The reason the enemy's lies make sense is that he is clever enough to mix them with truth. But he paints a picture of our circumstances *without* God's grace and presence. When we feel insecure, unsettled, and anxious, the enemy loves to whisper, "You are all alone." You see some truth in what he is whispering, because the people around you aren't saying quite the right thing, and you figure they don't really understand what you are going through. But are you truly alone? No. It's a lie. If people are there, they may not be saying the perfect thing, but they are showing up out of love for you. If people aren't there, God is. This is not a consolation prize. God's presence is what we most need.

Not only is He there with you in the present moment, He has gone before you. He is also in the future. This means He has made sure that whatever you are going through right now can be used for your good. The enemy loves to play with our imagination, tempting us to imagine a future where everything is worse. Resist this temptation and stay in the present moment. God is timeless, which means He is in the past, present, and future, but He is distilling grace *in the present moment*.

The enemy cannot get inside your soul because it is filled with the Holy Spirit. He cannot get in your mind because, according to 1 Corinthians 2:16, you have the mind of Christ. But he can wreak havoc in your imagination. So pay attention to where your thoughts go when you are anxious. You'll tend to focus on either the past or the future, but rarely the present moment. The enemy wants you to stay in the land of your imagination, picturing how awful the future is going to be, or how doomed you are because of your past. Resist him.

Dear Lord,
Thank You for going before me and staying with me. Thank You for never failing me or forsaking me. Because of this, may I not fear or be dismayed. Amen.

Be Still JULY 4

Independence Day

". . . what is the immeasurable greatness of his power in us who believe, according to the working of his great might which he accomplished in Christ when he raised him from the dead . . ." (Ephesians 1:19–20)

President Harry S. Truman once said, "America was not built on fear. America was built on courage, on imagination, and on an unbeatable determination to do the job at hand." To live this way, we need the Holy Spirit. He fills us with the exact same power that raised Jesus from the dead.

This is an absolute game changer and courage builder—if we choose to tap into it. But too many of God's children are living in defeat because they are trying to do all that God asks *in their own strength*. This is like trying to vacuum a room with the vacuum cleaner unplugged. It's frustrating and nothing ever changes. What's the solution? We need to plug into the power source, the Holy Spirit, and we need to do this every day. The best way to check if you're trying to do this on your own or if you are plugging into the power source is to take a look at your prayer life. No prayer? No power.

President Truman also said that we need an "unbeatable determination to do the job at hand." I believe that the job at hand for many of us is to finally take a look at the state of our hearts and deal with our wounds. To own our stories. To invite God into the mess and allow Him to begin the process of healing. But to embark on this journey requires "an unbeatable determination."

Why should we bother? What is at stake? I believe that if we ignore God's call to enter into the process of healing, we will continue to live in fear. This will cause us to live our lives in self-protective mode, which is the opposite of the way Jesus lived.

Pope Francis invites us to build bridges, not walls. Where does this begin? It begins in our hearts. If we don't deal with our own fears, we'll forfeit the freedom God offers us. We'll also ignore the call of Christ, which asks us to go out and rescue others. There is a whole world out there that desperately needs strong women and men who aren't just taking care of themselves. "It's all up to me" is a lie. But so is "I can't do anything about this."

Dear Lord,
Please help me to do the job at hand courageously and imaginatively through the power of the Holy Spirit. Amen.

JULY 5

"You have said, 'Seek my face.' My heart says to you, 'Your face, Lord, do I seek.'"
(Psalm 27:8)

According to the Talmud (the recorded Jewish oral traditions), there was a beautiful tradition that happened three times a year. During that time, the bread of offering was taken outside the temple, allowing the Israelite people to see it. The priests "used to lift it up and exhibit the Bread of the Presence on it to those who came up for the festivals, saying to them, 'Behold, God's love for you!'"[49]

This brings Eucharistic adoration to mind. For Catholics, the Eucharist is the face of Christ. According to 2 Corinthians 3:18, when we gaze on Christ's face in adoration, "we all, with unveiled face, beholding the glory of the Lord, are being changed into his likeness."

Do you want to become more like Jesus? Spend time in His presence, beholding His Glory. Ask Him to change you. This is the secret of the Christian life—God actually does for us what we are unable to do for ourselves. But He never forces Himself in. He waits to be invited. We cooperate and do our part, but He does the heavy lifting.

The Jesuit priest Anthony de Mello said, "Behold God beholding you . . . and smiling."[50] This is the perspective we should bring to adoration. God wants to spend time with you. Longing for an intimate encounter, He hopes you will draw near to be reminded of His love for you. The "bread of the face" willingly waits to bless you.

Dear Lord,
I pray that You would transform me as I sit in Your presence. Help me to want what You want, when You want it, how You want it. Please give me the desire to be more like You. When I rest in Your presence, I pray that I would feel Your love for me, that I would believe that there is nothing I can do to make You love me more or less. I do believe, Lord; help my disbelief. Amen.

Be Still

 JULY 6

"Do not throw away your confidence, which has a great reward. For you have need of endurance, so that you may do the will of God and receive what is promised. For yet a little while, and the coming one shall come and shall not tarry; but my righteous one shall live by faith, and if he shrinks back, my soul has no pleasure in him. But we are not of those who shrink back and are destroyed, but of those who have faith and keep their souls." (Hebrews 10:35–39)

When our suffering feels too great, we are tempted to throw away our confidence in God. We begin to think, "Where is He? Is He cruel? Why doesn't He stop this pain?" When this is our pattern of thought, it's critical that we remember the kind of Father we have. He is not barbaric. He is, in fact, tender and kind. He's also attentive to what we truly need and doesn't give us candy when we need medicine. There is nothing that touches us that God cannot work for our good. He is gentle, compassionate, and merciful.

Letting our thoughts run in the opposite direction will lead us into deep discouragement exactly when we are needing endurance. The promised consolation will come; it is just around the corner. Faith is believing in God's goodness even when our circumstances cause it to appear otherwise.

There are times when shrinking back from serving God might *appear* to be a good idea. If serving God makes us a target for the enemy's attacks, wouldn't it be better to shrink back and stop serving? But shrinking back does not rescue or protect us; it actually is destructive. It's destructive to our faith, and it's destructive to our purposes on earth.

But how can we resist the temptation to shrink back when we are discouraged and suffering? We rely on the power of God within us. We take advantage of the graces given through the sacraments. We keep showing up to God, with empty hands, and asking Him to fill us, guide us, and get us through.

He will come through for you. This present trial is not the exception. He will sustain you. Has He not given you what you need for this present moment? Don't look ahead. Stay in the now. He is there. He is carrying you. He is enough.

Dear Lord,
Give me the strength to not shrink back. Help me to remain steadfast and faithful because You are within me. Amen.

JULY 7

"God did not give us a spirit of timidity but a spirit of power and love and self-control." (2 Timothy 1:7)

We all encounter situations in which we experience fear. We might be afraid of heights, rejection, public speaking, confrontation, failure, or the future. Regardless of the cause, fear can be paralyzing. A good first step for dealing with it is to recognize that it doesn't come from God. We are assured in 2 Timothy 1:7 that God hasn't given us a spirit of fear, but a spirit of power. The power God has placed in us is enough to face down our fears.

It has been said that fear is false evidence appearing real. The truth is, most of what we fear never occurs. Fear is rooted in our imagination. We picture a future catastrophe and assume we will not be able to handle it. But we are stronger than we think. The power that God has placed in us is the same power that raised Jesus from the dead. We can endure far more than we give ourselves credit for.

This same spirit also fills us with love and self-control (or a sound mind, in some translations). We can get a grip on our thoughts. Fear runs through our minds and is connected to specific thoughts. When you are in the grip of fear, write those thoughts out. Then see which of them are consistent with what God says about your situation, and which sound more like the enemy's voice. Which thoughts are rooted in hope, and which are rooted in despair? God's voice always contains hope because with God, anything is possible.

When we realize that a fear-based thought is not from God, we should reject it. Cross it out on the paper. Say out loud, "I reject this." Then take that same statement and infuse it with hope. If you wrote, "Things will never change," say out loud, "God can change anything." Do this over and over again, with every fear-filled thought. This is tiring and hard work, but your mind can handle it. This is how we practice self-control in our thinking.

Dear Lord,
Help me to remember that I can be brave because You placed Your Holy Spirit within me. This is a Spirit of power, love, and self-control. Fear is not from You. I reject thoughts that are fear-based and filled with despair. Give me Your hope and help me to do the work of cleaning the garbage out of my mind. Amen.

Be Still

JULY 8

"The Lord has sought after a man after his own heart." (1 Samuel 16:7)

Do you long to be a woman after God's own heart? Do you sometimes get discouraged when you see the chasm between how you behave and how you would like to be? Can you relate to what Saint Thérèse of Lisieux said about there being such a difference between her level of holiness and the holiness of the saints that she could compare it to "a mountain whose summit is lost in the heavens and an obscure grain of sand, trampled under the feet of passersby"?

Don't be discouraged. God recognizes our weakness and realizes that perfection is a lofty goal for little children. "The eyes of the Lord roam over the whole earth, to encourage those who are devoted to him wholeheartedly" (2 Chronicles 16:9). What is God searching for? He is looking for a devoted heart.

Take some time to talk to God about your desire to have a heart like His. Admit your weakness and ask Him to fulfill in your life the promise He made in 2 Corinthians 12:9: "My grace is sufficient for you, for my power is made perfect in weakness." Jesus will do for us what we cannot. What is lacking in our hearts is present in His. He will take our sin and give us His righteousness. He will fill our hearts with His own virtues. When we ask Him, He will come into our lives and fill in the gap. Yes, we are weak. Yes, we will fail and fall short. But if we ask Him, Jesus will make up for what we do badly and leave undone. His heart is fully devoted to us, and it knows us intimately. Don't try to go through life in your own strength when Jesus is just waiting to give you His.

Dear Lord,
I come to You full of failings and weakness. Thank You for loving me in such a way that You invite me to come, just as I am. Please change me. I don't have the strength to change myself. But I do trust in You and Your ability to do anything—even to mold my heart in such a way that I desire what You desire. I am sorry for the ways that I have disappointed You and not loved well. Please forgive me. Fill me with Your divine love. I promise to share it with those I encounter. Amen.

JULY 9   *Be Still*

"The Lord is my shepherd, I shall not want." (Psalm 23:1)

Ahhh . . . contentment. That seemingly elusive quality so connected to inner peace. Without it, we are on a fast track to misery. With it, we have abiding joy that can't be taken from us. What do you feel is blocking your personal contentment? Can you name it? So often, we assume contentment comes from the lifting of difficulty, or the receipt of something longed for. But that's not how it works. True contentment comes when we quit acting like discontented sheep, standing at the gate and noticing how green the grass is on the other side. It comes when we look up at our shepherd and trust that He can see farther than we can, and He is giving us everything we need in this moment. It comes when we accept our life as is, as what His hands have provided. We may not like our circumstances. Our life may be filled with grief, hurt, disappointment, and pain. When this is the case, our good shepherd asks us to come to Him, so He can offer comfort and hope.

Make no mistake, God is deeply concerned about you and what you are longing for. He can see when your motive is pure—when your desire is a good one. But He asks that you trust Him and His timing. The bigger your view of God, the easier this will be. The more you grow in awareness of His majesty, the complexity and faithfulness of His plans, and His limitless love, the more you'll accept and believe that He is a God worthy of your trust.

Take some time to talk to God about what stands in the way of your contentment. Explain to the One who knows and loves you like no other why this matters so much to you. Then place it at His feet. Tell Him that you trust Him with this, your greatest desire. Ask Him to fill your heart with contentment. Ask Him to help you grow so that more and more, you desire what He wants. Every time your heart aches in longing, go back to Him, and give it to Him again. The desire will be safe with Him. He will not forget. He is your good shepherd, and He promises to provide all that you need.

Dear Lord,
You never forsake me. You provide for all that I need. Help me to not focus on my wants and instead to focus on the provision You have provided. Help me to trust Your timing and release control. Amen.

Be Still **JULY 10**

"Even my bosom friend in whom I trusted, who ate of my bread, has lifted his heel against me."
(Psalm 41:9)

When you've experienced the sting of betrayal, it's important to remember who the real enemy is: Satan. It isn't the friend who gossiped about you. It isn't the spouse who was unfaithful. It isn't the person who damaged your career path. Regardless of how much you may feel God has let you down, it isn't Him, either.

Satan, your real enemy, despises you. Why? Because you are God's delight, His treasure. Satan knows he's no match for God, so he goes after His children instead. The enemy of your soul knows that "he who touches you touches the apple of [God's] eye" (Zechariah 2:8).

Satan does all he can to spread division. You can be assured that the discord you experience in relationships has been stoked and stirred by him. When you give in to bitterness, when you refuse to forgive, when you allow your hurt to drive a wedge between you and God, then you are handing Satan the victory.

Perhaps the enemy has been playing around with a relationship in your life. Are you the one who has been betrayed? Where should you begin in order to get out of Satan's messy web? You begin in the same way the psalmist did in Psalm 41. In verse 4, he wrote, "O Lord, be gracious to me; heal me, for I have sinned against you!" He turned to God with his hurt instead of away from Him. He asked God to take note of him—to see him and his situation—and to respond with mercy and compassion. This is a request God always loves to answer with a resounding "Yes, of course!"

This is an essential starting point if we're going be set free from the bitterness of unforgiveness. We must begin with an awareness of our own propensity to mess up and our history of falling short. We may not have failed so terribly in terms of our relationship with the person who has hurt us, but we can certainly find evidence of times when we have been less than faithful to God. Yet how does He respond to us? With mercy, compassion, and forgiveness.

Is there a betrayal that you need to let go of? Are you feeling a tug on your heart to release this to God? Don't be afraid. Give it over to the One who loves you and wants to defend you. Let Him fight your battle.

Dear Lord,
I unclench my fists and offer You my hurt. Please cover me with the balm of Your love. Amen.

JULY 11

"As for me, I am poor and needy; but the Lord takes thought for me. You are my help and my deliverer; do not delay, O my God!" (Psalm 40:17)

The starting point for all of us is recognizing that we have a need. It's to admit that on our own, we aren't doing so well. Do any of the following thoughts ring true for you?

"I'm afraid of not being liked."
"I hate to look in the mirror. I'm just reminded of the weight I need to lose."
"I sometimes wonder if this is all there is. This is what life is supposed to be about?"
"I'm so sick of falling into the same bad habits time and time again. I never seem to progress."
"I'm afraid of getting cancer. I'm afraid to die."
"I wonder if my teenagers love me. I've given them all I've got, but the way they treat me makes me feel worthless."
"I'm afraid that my husband will leave me."
"I feel like I can't both be a good mom and do all I need to do at work."

We all have fears. We all have needs. We can cover them up by pretending that they aren't there. We can get busy to distract ourselves. We can do whatever it takes to be liked, even if it means compromise. We can slap on a happy face and try to convince ourselves it isn't so bad. We can turn to alcohol to take off the edge. But the underlying issues will remain and rob us of sleep and peace.

Jesus cares deeply about all these things that are going on within our hearts. He came to point us to a better way. His way doesn't cover things up—it exposes them to the warmth of His merciful love. Take some time in His soothing presence to tell Him all the ways in which you need Him.

Dear Lord,
Thank You for being the safe place for me to hide. There is nothing within me—no thought, memory, or fear—that is hidden from You. How grateful I am that my secrets that I hate do not repulse You. You draw close in order to cleanse me and free me from what hurts me. I give You access to my heart and ask You to heal my hurts. Amen.

Be Still

 JULY 12

"The Lord is my light and my salvation; whom shall I fear? The Lord is the stronghold of my life; of whom shall I be afraid?" (Psalm 27:1)

Whenever we face a circumstance that seems daunting, overwhelming, or even frightening, we can be strengthened by meditating on Jesus, the Lord of Hosts. He goes before us, stands behind us, and is always at our side. There is no one stronger, no one more faithful, no one more valiant, no one more in control. He commands angel armies who fight on our behalf.

Think about that: We are surrounded on all sides by God, who can command legions of angels to come to our aid. He reigns forever on earth and in heaven, yet offers us personal friendship. No matter how much darkness surrounds us on the battlefield of life, Christ is our light.

In the words of professor of philosophy Peter Kreeft:

> The devil is not like a dragon but like Dracula: he flees from the light. He is actually afraid of you insofar as you have Christ in your soul. The devil is also afraid of your guardian angel, who is a "being of light." Darkness fears light. Pray to the angel God has appointed to guard you when you are tempted. Only important people in the world get bodyguards, but each of us is so important to God that He has given each of us a Heavenly soul-guard.[51]

Dear Lord,
When darkness surrounds me, may Your light shine brighter. Thank You for being my stronghold, my safe place. You are my refuge and surround me with angelic beings who fight on my behalf. May this reality (which is no less real because I can't see it with my eyes) chase the fear from my heart. Amen.

JULY 13

"Every good endowment and every perfect gift is from above, coming down from the Father of lights." (James 1:17)

The landscape of our mind will determine the quality of our day. If our mind-set is one of gratitude, contentment will follow. In the words of Christian author Elisabeth Elliot, "It is always possible to be thankful for what is given rather than resentful over what is withheld. One attitude or the other becomes a way of life." This requires a refusal to fall into the pit of self-pity.

Self-pity causes our focus to turn inward, and things get very dark very quickly. When we allow a litany of our woes to run through our minds, self-defeating thoughts begin to build up and cloud our ability to see anything good. Lies such aa "Things will never change" start to make sense, and we head down the path to despair.

The antidote is cultivating an attitude of gratitude. Even the most miserable circumstances contain an opportunity for growth. We can thank God for this. I have found that this is critical when I feel stuck in a situation I hate. Instead of asking God, "Why is this happening to me?" I ask Him, "What are You trying to teach me?"

I have begun asking God this question in the midst of chaos, and then telling Him that I want to learn every single bit of the lesson this time around so that I don't have to return to the same set of miserable circumstances to try to learn better later. This is one of the reasons why giving in to escapism gets in the way of our maturity and does not ultimately result in happiness.

If those hard circumstances return, it's tempting to assume that the original lesson must never have been learned and to become discouraged as a result. But this isn't necessarily the case. If you did learn the lesson—if the trial resulted in spiritual growth and maturity—then coming up against those same circumstances again means that God is doing a deeper healing. It's the peeling of an onion; the growth is going to be more profound.

Every good and perfect gift in your life comes from God. Those gifts may come in packaging that you don't like, but if you are willing to open them up anyway, the lessons you will learn will be life-changing. They will be the difference maker between you becoming an immature and superficial person and becoming a person of depth, wisdom, and maturity.

Dear Lord,
What are You trying to teach me right now? Help me to learn everything You have for me in my current circumstances. Amen.

Be Still JULY 14

"Wisdom is with the aged, and understanding in length of days." (Job 12:12)

Living in a world of moral relativism (which we do) means a tremendous amount of common sense has gone out the window. We are suffering as a result. Basic wisdom that used to be passed from one generation to the next—the truths that explain how to make life work—is not being conveyed. In the past, unchanging principles helped guide decisions. Now tolerance is the highest value, and holding to unchanging principles can appear judgmental. What results is an inability to make decisions; we don't know what is right or best to do. It's a veritable mess, and it is destroying our happiness.

Without rules and moral judgments, chaos results. When we don't have a firm footing, we expend tremendous amounts of energy trying to figure things out that were crystal clear in the past. This hinders our ability to be creative, to experience interior peace, and to build a good life that lasts.

A word that you rarely hear today is *duty*. In times past, this was one of the highest values. People had to do their duty. This is what helped society function. Our culture now focuses on feelings to a heightened degree. Feelings get in the way of doing one's duty because often, one does not *feel like* doing it. We've been taught that doing things that make us feel worse are to be avoided at all costs. As a result, relationships are abandoned, homes are neglected, and employees do half-hearted work.

What is the next right thing that needs to be done in your life? What duty does your state in life require? Just do that next right thing. Do your duty. Will you enjoy every minute of it? Probably not, but what you will enjoy in the evening is a job well done. You'll get busy doing what you're supposed to be doing, and you might be too tired at the end of the day to analyze how much fun it was. As you move along, just doing the next right thing, you will find you have actually been building a life of meaning. You'll have been contributing to the common good in a way that matters.

Take some time to listen to the older generation. Ask them what they believe is critical for living a good life. You might discover some age-old wisdom that can be a game changer today.

Dear Lord,
Help me to have the humility to learn from those who have gone before me—to ask questions and listen intently to their answers. Amen.

JULY 15

"The heart is deceitful above all things, and desperately corrupt; who can understand it?" (Jeremiah 7:9)

"Just follow your heart." You can't get far in our culture without receiving that message. But just because a voice is loud and persistent doesn't mean it's pointing us in the right direction. Will following our hearts lead us where we want to go? According to the prophet Jeremiah, it's a pretty lousy guide.

The heart is the seat of our emotions. While our emotions are incredibly important, they should not drive our decisions. Prayerfully journaling about our emotions is a very fruitful exercise if the point of it is to get it all out and then ask God to make sense of it. He cares deeply about what we feel, longs for us to be honest with Him, and then, if we are willing, redeems our emotions. He helps us to get to a stronger, healthier place emotionally.

Our hearts are made to worship, and we all worship something. If it isn't God, we'll substitute something (or someone) else. Often we worship ourselves—our comfort, our reputation, our advancement. Each of our hearts houses a throne. Whoever or whatever we worship sits on that throne, but there is only one who deserves it and rules wisely. What we love most sits on the throne.

When we love anything more than God, our hearts will be led in a direction that runs counter to the selfless love He asks of us. We can follow our hearts when our hearts are sold out with love for God. When what we desire more than anything is what He wants, then our hearts are far more trustworthy. But because our ability to deceive ourselves is so high, we should be slow to assume that our motives are pure.

The good news is that God gives us a new heart. "A new heart I will give you, and a new spirit I will put within you; and I will take out of your flesh the heart of stone and give you a heart of flesh. And I will put my Spirit within you" (Ezekiel 36:26–27). The Holy Spirit within us is the One who reorders our lives and settles our emotions. This new heart still bends toward evil, but we now have the strength to resist it.

Dear Lord,
Help me to check each day who is sitting on the throne of my heart. If it's anyone or anything but You, help me to have the strength to make the shift, inviting You back into that place of authority in my life. Amen.

Be Still

JULY 16

"Before I formed you in the womb I knew you." (Jeremiah 1:5)

The philosopher Aristotle was obsessed with the questions "Who am I?" and "What does it take to be happy—to live a good life?" What he was trying to figure out was what it means to be a flourishing human being. Aristotle started by asking, "What is man's proper function?" In other words, what is our purpose? He reasoned that if you were to think about an object such as a watch, you'd know what a good watch is based on its basic purpose or function. A good watch tells time accurately. For Aristotle, the same was true of a person.

He said that *who we are* is intricately tied to *what we do*. We can't separate the two. The choices we make form who we are. So he challenges us to think about our choices, instead of just letting life happen to us.

This means that your actions, your choices, are not disconnected from the person you are becoming. The person you are going to be five years from now is connected to the choices you are making today. Have you ever said, "I'm a good person deep down, despite what I did last weekend"? That kind of a statement would have seemed ridiculous to Aristotle. In large measure, you are what you do.

If I were to say, "I'm a good soccer player; I just never make a goal and I don't know how to dribble the ball," you would say, "I'm sorry, but you're actually not a good soccer player." Your desire, your good intentions, don't translate into that actually being who you are. So once you determine who you are at the core—a beloved, precious, chosen daughter of God—you then need to decide what kind of a person you want to be.

When we feel lost, like we can't figure out who we are, it's often because we have never answered the question for ourselves, "Who do I *want* to be?" Your current actions and choices are forming who you are, right now. You are becoming a certain kind of person, and this plays out especially in the little things. In the words of author Brittany Rust, "The definition of who you are belongs to the Creator of the Universe and is left to you to decide who to become."

Dear Lord,
I commit to taking time and thinking about what kind of a person I want to become. Then I promise to start making choices that are consistent with that goal, through Your strength and power. Amen.

JULY 17

Be Still

"[She] who conquers shall have this heritage, and I will be [her] God, and [she] shall be my [daughter]." (Revelation 21:7)

You are a victorious daughter, and your Father is the King of kings. You belong to Him. His love for you flows from the depths of eternity. There is nothing you face alone. Your Father stands behind you. He infuses you with strength so that you can bear and overcome all that you face, achieving victories in the spiritual life you never imagined possible.

"It is the Spirit himself bearing witness with our spirit that we are children of God, and if children, then heirs, heirs of God and fellow heirs with Christ" (Romans 8:16). The Holy Spirit assures us that we belong to God, and that He is going to shower us with a heavenly inheritance. There are also gifts we receive on earth. One of the most beautiful of those gifts is "God's love [being] poured into our hearts through the Holy Spirit who has been given to us" (Romans 5:5).

This means that we have a limitless supply of love at our disposal. Our heritage, our legacy, is one of self-sacrificing, world-changing love. Is that how you are known by others? "She always goes the extra mile. I don't know how she does it, but she never holds a grudge. Just when most people want to quit, she shows up and serves. No matter how tired she is, she still manages to keep her tone of voice kind." Do people look at you and say these things? Maybe it seems like an impossible standard. It would be, if God expected us to do it in our own strength. We get discouraged when we rely on our own supply of human love; it always falls short. But if we take the time to fill up on God's divine love (infused into us through prayer, the sacraments, and Scripture reading), then we can do the impossible.

"We are more than conquerors through him who loved us." (Romans 8:37)

We can conquer fear.
We can conquer bad habits.
We can conquer lack of love.
We can conquer unforgiveness.
We can conquer ungodly self-reliance.
We can conquer toxic relationships.
We can conquer self-deprecating thoughts.

God is our Father, and He has passed to us a legacy of love and victory. Warrior, it's time to arise.

Dear Lord,
May I be an overcomer, through Your strength and power. Amen.

Be Still

 JULY 18

"There is laid up for me the crown of righteousness, which the Lord, the righteous judge, will reward to me on that Day, and not only to me but also to all who have loved his appearing." (2 Timothy 4:8)

You're going to receive a beautiful crown in heaven. When this happens, all that you are experiencing right now for His sake, every bit of it, will feel worth that priceless crown.

What will you do with that crown when you receive it? Perhaps you'll respond the same way the twenty-four elders did in Revelation 4:10–11, because of your wholehearted love for the Lord:

> ... the twenty-four elders fall down before him who is seated on the throne and worship him who lives for ever and ever; they cast their crowns before the throne, singing:
>
> "Worthy are you, our Lord and God,
> to receive glory and honor and power,
> for you created all things,
> and by your will they existed and were created."

He is worthy.
He is worth it.

Persevere, precious daughter of God. In this world, you will have trouble. There will be more expected of you than you feel able to handle. There will be times of pain and pressure. But never forget, God is upholding you. "The eternal God is your dwelling place, and underneath are the everlasting arms" (Deuteronomy 33:27).

Dear Lord,
Help me to keep my eyes on heaven. When I expect everything on earth to satisfy my deepest longings, I always end up disappointed. The true fulfillment of all I desire, the justice that makes everything right, the peace that knows no end . . . it is coming. Help me to be willing to sacrifice short-term pleasure for long-term gain. Amen.

JULY 19

"You know that you were ransomed from the futile ways inherited from your fathers, not with perishable things such as silver or gold, but with the precious blood of Christ, like that of a lamb without blemish or spot." (1 Peter 1:18–19)

The word *ransomed* is used in reference to slavery. A slave was considered ransomed when someone paid money to purchase that slave's freedom. This applies to us because when we were slaves, Jesus ransomed us. "Wait a minute," you might be thinking. "I'm free! I've never been a slave." Not so fast. We *all* have been enslaved. We have to go back to the beginning to understand how that happened.

When the enemy convinced our first parents to believe his lie (God isn't good—He's holding out on you), two significant things happened. First of all, sin entered the world. In addition, our race, humankind, sold itself into slavery. Apart from Christ, we are enslaved to powers and dominions that we can't fight against. We are helpless. We aren't strong enough to rescue ourselves.

Without Jesus, we're slaves to the worst parts of ourselves, utterly lacking the ability to experience inner transformation. We may mistakenly think that doing whatever we feel like doing is freedom, but the truth is, it's the worst kind of slavery.

When Jesus ransomed us through His blood—something far more precious than writing a check—He purchased our freedom. Now we are "set free from sin, [and] have become slaves of righteousness" (Romans 6:18).

In certain skilled crafts, an apprentice works under a master, who trains, shapes, and molds his apprentice in the finer points of his craft. All people choose a master and pattern themselves after him. Without Jesus, we would have no choice—we would have to apprentice ourselves to sin, and the results would be guilt, suffering, and separation from God. Thanks to Jesus, however, we can now choose God as our master. Following Him, we can enjoy new life and learn how to work for Him. Are you still serving your first master, sin? Or have you apprenticed yourself to God?[52]

Dear Lord,
I recognize that I was bought with a price, and that price was Your life. I want to apprentice myself to You, out of gratitude for all You've done, and also because that is the only way I can truly be free. Help me to notice the times when I am serving my old master, sin. Help me to follow You alone. Amen.

Be Still **JULY 20**

"You shall receive power when the Holy Spirit has come upon you." (Acts 1:8)

What would you give to be able to go to Jesus directly with your problems? How would you like to hear one of His parables from His own mouth? What difference would it make to look into Jesus' eyes of love and hear Him say, "You did not choose me, but I chose you" (John 15:16)?

This was the experience of the disciples. So imagine how shocking it was for them to hear Jesus say in John 16:7, "I tell you the truth, it is better for you that I go. For if I do not go, the Advocate will not come to you. But if I go, I will send him to you." It's better if He *goes*? It must have seemed unbelievable to them. What could be better than having Jesus, in the flesh, at their fingertips?

Little did they know that when Jesus ascended to heaven, the Advocate (the Holy Spirit) was going to come to live in them, giving them new hearts. These hearts would be so utterly transformed that they would go on to change the world. The Holy Spirit made the seemingly impossible possible.

What in your life requires strength beyond your own? Are you facing something for which an evaluation of your resources reveals that you don't have what it takes? Be assured, the indwelling Holy Spirit makes all the difference.

As author L.B. Cowman writes in *Streams in the Desert*: "The sight of seemingly impossible tasks ... are not sent to discourage us. They come to motivate us to attempt spiritual feats that would be impossible except for the great strength God has placed within us through His indwelling Holy Spirit. Difficulties are sent in order to reveal what God can do in answer to faith that prays and works."[53]

Dear Lord,
Please quiet my heart. Help me to see that it's not all up to me. I am the glove, but You are the hand. Do in and through me what I am unable to do in my own strength. Amen.

JULY 21

"It is no longer I who live, but Christ who lives in me." (Galatians 2:20)

Because of Jesus, you have a new heart and a new identity. As it says in 2 Corinthians 5:17, "Therefore, if any one is in Christ, he is a new creation; the old has passed away, behold, the new has come!" You are now the adopted daughter of your Father. How does He see you? He sees you as His precious daughter. Nothing more, nothing less. You might say, "But I don't feel it!" But that is who you are. We don't achieve this through effort. It isn't something that we have to obtain. The work is in recognition and awareness. We need to recognize what is already there. You are God's beloved daughter. You already have this dignity. You just need to begin to let go of your blindness, the faulty way you see yourself, and start acting like God's beloved daughter.

The starting point for this change is prayer. As you pray, the Holy Spirit is released to transform you from the inside out. Your heavenly Father loves you too much to leave you as you are. God wants to mold you into a woman who serves as a beacon of hope to a broken world. Our world is desperate to see something that works. People want to see a faith that makes a difference. A friend's example and testimony carries far more weight than historical authority and tradition. People are asking, "Does it work?" and then are looking at us to find the answer. They are observing.

Dear Lord,
Please, may our hearts not get in the way! Help us to choose the things that will draw us closer to You, and may we literally run from the choices that distance us from You. Amen.

Be Still

JULY 22

"But God shows his love for us in that while we were yet sinners Christ died for us." (Romans 5:8)

Jesus proved that His love for you has no limit when He "poured out his soul to death" (Isaiah 53:12) in your place. Take a moment to let that truth journey from your head to your heart. His sacrifice was not dependent on you deserving it. He didn't wait until you were perfect and all cleaned up to love you in this way.

How will you respond to His surrender? Can you allow it to draw you deeply into His love? Can you offer Him your heart in return? Surrendering to God in response to His limitless love is the key to living a life of freedom. The following prayer of surrender is taken from the booklet *Miracle Hour: A Method of Prayer That Will Change Your Life*. If you are ready to take the journey from the head to the heart, these words will help you to offer the Lord what He deeply desires.

A Prayer of Surrender

Loving Father, I surrender to You today with all my heart and soul. Please come into my heart in a deeper way. I say "yes," to You today. I open all the secret places of my heart to You and say, "Come on in." Jesus you are Lord of my whole life. I believe in You as my Lord and Savior. I hold nothing back. Holy Spirit, bring me to deeper conversion to the person of Jesus Christ. I surrender all to You: my health, my family, my resources, occupation, skills, relationships, time management, successes and failures. I release it, and let it go. I surrender my understanding of how things ought to be, my choices and my will. I surrender to You the promises I have kept and the promises I have failed to keep. I surrender my weaknesses and strengths to You. I surrender my emotions, my fears, my insecurities, my sexuality. I especially surrender _____, _____, _____.
Lord, I surrender my entire life to You, the past, the present, and the future. In sickness and in health, in life and in death, I belong to You.[54] *Amen.*

JULY 23

"For I know the plans I have for you, says the Lord, plans for welfare and not for evil, to give you a future and a hope." (Jeremiah 29:11)

God has a plan for your life. If you are feeling aimless and purposeless, it is not because your life is meaningless. It's because you haven't yet heard what God desires most for you.

In one sense, God has a plan for *all of mankind*. This plan is for us to glorify Him. Not because He needs an ego boost—God doesn't need anything—but because He knows that we are made to worship, not to be worshipped. Anytime we put ourselves on the pedestal (or others put us there), we are sure to disappoint. Being saturated with attention and glory can become addictive. There's a little tyrant in each one of us that wants to be in charge. This tyrant needs to be starved, not fed. Bringing glory to God is our first and most important purpose.

Then God has a plan for *women*. He has gifted us in certain ways, and His plan is for us to share those gifts with the world. Our ability to nurture, create beauty, bring life, and share a spirit of graciousness is something to be celebrated, not squelched. Many of our homes and gathering places are suffering neglect because too many women are ignoring this important aspect of who we are. We do not achieve equality with men by being exactly what they are. We achieve equality when our unique feminine gifts are equally valued as the masculine ones.

God has also given each of His children spiritual gifts. These are given to us for the benefit of others. When we discover our spiritual gifts and the needs in the world that we care about passionately, we are well on our way to discovering our specific calling. But if we take our gifts and focus on how we can use them to benefit ourselves, God's plan for our lives will remain elusive.

God's plan for us is always good. Even when circumstances make us question what He is up to, we can be assured that He is weaving together every heartache and breakthrough to create a unique, beautiful life. Because of this, there is always hope.

Dear Lord,
May I take the time to ask You what Your plan is for my life and to check my motives with my current pursuits. Am I doing what I'm doing for my own glory or for Yours? Amen.

Be Still

 JULY 24

"Give thanks in all circumstances; for this is the will of God in Christ Jesus for you."
(1 Thessalonians 5:18)

Practicing gratitude regardless of your circumstances is one of the most significant things you can do to increase your happiness. During a recent season when my life felt full of things I didn't want and not full at all of the things I wanted, I put this to the test. I committed to writing a typed page of gratitude each morning. Filling the page sometimes took some effort. I had to look beyond the obvious and dig a little deeper. But as I went through this exercise, something shifted within me, and my attitude visibly improved.

I asked myself, "Which is more likely to make me a saint? All my circumstances being just the way I want them to be, or things not going according to my plans?" This reminded me that often my real problem is that I want my own will to be done more than I want God's will to be done. Discontent is evidence of this.

All circumstances, even those we hate, are giving us the opportunity to grow more like Christ. We're being stretched, and this is increasing our capacity to love. It's up to us if we're going to fill that extra space with complaining or with an increase of love.

To check out whether gratitude works, I challenge you to take ten minutes each day for the next week to write down five things you are grateful for. Don't just think about them—actually write them down. If you want to really boost your happiness, share that gratitude with someone else. Think of someone in your life whom you are grateful for. Then write that person a letter telling him or her why. To take your happiness factor to a whole new level, bring the thank-you letter to the person and read it to him or her. I know it sounds odd and awkward. But the resulting joy will make a big difference for you, and to your loved one.

Dear Lord,
Give me eyes to see beyond the obvious and recognize the deeper lessons that are on offer to me. May I not miss a single opportunity to give thanks and grow in joy. Amen.

JULY 25

"Christ in you, the hope of glory." (Colossians 1:27)

In the Old Testament, the Holy Spirit would come upon a certain person, at a certain time, for a certain task. It was not a gift offered to all the Israelite people. It was rare and temporary.

Everything changed after Jesus died and rose again. He had told His disciples that it would be better for them if He left, which must have been terribly confusing. What could be better than having Jesus right next to you each minute of the day? But Jesus knew that only after He ascended into heaven would the Holy Spirit come to dwell in the hearts of believers.

The Holy Spirit is sent to dwell inside God's children, and in that sense, Christ is in us. In John 14:20, Jesus said, "in that day you will know that I am in my Father, and you in me, and I in you." The indwelling Spirit of Christ changes everything. It is because of the Holy Spirit that we can endure beyond what we think, love with divine love, and receive comfort straight from God and power to do all things through Christ who gives us strength.

We experience "Christ in [us], the hope of glory" most powerfully when we receive Him in the Eucharist. If we understood better the significance of His presence within us through the sacrament, we would never mindlessly sing the hymn after Communion or start thinking ahead to what we need to do after Mass. We'd be fervently praying, knowing that in those moments, Christ is actually praying with us, within us. This is the time to pray about all the things that matter most to you. Your prayers will be turbocharged and potent.

Without the Holy Spirit within us, we have no hope of glory—at least not the glory that is promised us in heaven. The Holy Spirit is divine life, and without the Spirit inside us, we won't be able to breathe divine air. Whatever glory substitute the world might offer us—social media followers, a nice bank account, a good reputation—will pale in comparison to heavenly glory. It is worth the wait. We get a little taste of it now, but there, the whole banquet.

Dear Lord,
Help me to recognize the incredible privilege it is to have Your Spirit dwelling within me and Your presence through the Eucharist. May I wake up and grab hold of the hope that is on offer to me each and every day. Amen.

Be Still

JULY 26

"Do not be conformed to this world but be transformed by the renewal of your mind, that you may prove what is the will of God, what is good and acceptable and perfect." (Romans 12:2)

The more we know about God and about our faith, the more we will love Him. The more we know what He expects of us, what the guidelines are that He has laid out for us in the Bible and in the teachings of the Church, the more we're going to make the right choices. Those right choices will correlate directly to our happiness. If we don't take the time to study our faith, we'll be blown around by whatever the current trends are in our culture, which may take us far from where God wants us to be. And being in the center of God's will is the safest and most satisfying place in the world.

Romans 12:2 calls us to give time to growing in knowledge of the faith. We need to pay attention to what we feed our minds. What are we watching on television? What movies do we see? What books and magazines do we read? To check yourself in this area, ask yourself, "Do I know more about my faith this year than I did last year?"

Dwelling on the truths of our faith will change our outlook on life and the decisions we make. We are promised in John 8:32 that when we know the truth, it will set us free. Once we are dwelling on what is true, we need that truth to enter our hearts. We become fully alive to the extent that truth has taken root deep within. Lies keep us dead in despair. Truth reminds us that a fresh start is always possible and that we have spiritual strength that can carry us through.

Dear Lord,
I recognize that I'm in the midst of a battle. But You have not left me to fight alone. You are with me—behind me, before me, all around me, and most important, within me. I can be fearless—not because of my innate strength, but because You dwell within me through the Holy Spirit. You can walk me through anything. Help me to remember that shrinking back, stepping off the path that You have set me on, will not result in blessing. My compromise won't bring safety or protection; it simply means I am walking away from Your will. I want to stay under the umbrella of Your protection. Help me to stay faithful. I need Your grace.

JULY 27

"And do not get drunk with wine, for that is debauchery, but be filled with the Spirit."
(Ephesians 5:18)

Debauchery is excessively indulging in some sensual pleasure. What we're indulging in isn't necessarily bad in moderation, but when it's overused, it becomes destructive. When we find ourselves reaching for more alcohol than we should, it's worth asking ourselves what we are after. Is there an emptiness that we are trying to fill? Are we so unhappy with our lives that we are wanting to numb out? Are we so stressed that we need something artificial to bring us down to a place where we feel calm? Are we self-medicating with alcohol?

Anytime we treat symptoms without getting down to the underlying issue, we are just delaying true healing. In other words, things are not going to get better. In fact, the very thing that you think is helping you will quickly turn around and grab hold of you. What you think you are controlling can rapidly start controlling you.

If this is where you find yourself today and you cannot stop, I encourage you to share this truth with one trusted person. The enemy wants to keep you in bondage. He is the one whispering, "You can't tell this to anyone. They will lose all respect for you." That is one of his favorite lies. And if he can keep us quiet, he can keep us enslaved. The truth is, you are loved, and people around you want to help you experience freedom. They don't think you are perfect, so there is no cover for you to blow. What you will be doing is taking a very important step toward freedom.

What might change if you started digging a little deeper instead of just reaching for the quick fix? What might happen if you called on the Holy Spirit to satisfy your deepest cravings and fill you with true joy? Real life is on the other side of the decision to stop letting alcohol play such a big role in your relaxation and fun. You don't need a drink. You need Jesus. He is the only one who will truly satisfy.

Dear Lord,
Help me to be brave enough to be honest about where I am going to satisfy my cravings and my need to relax. May I turn to a trusted friend—may I turn to You and speak my truth. Please set me free. Amen.

Be Still

 JULY 28

"For to me, to live is Christ, and to die is gain." (Philippians 1:21)

Many people look pulled together on the outside, but on the inside they feel a quiet desperation. "Is this all there is?" they wonder. Saint Paul assures us that *this life is not all there is*. There is so much more. It's as if we are standing watching a parade. We want to see what is just around the corner—then we can determine if it's worth sticking around. But God stands above all. He can see the beginning and what is just around the corner. He knows that there are better things ahead, both here on earth and in heaven.

Saint Paul clearly did not have a fear of death. To consider death a "gain" meant that He could see something beyond the grave that was far superior to what could be experienced on earth. Saint Ignatius of Antioch agreed with him: "It is better for me to die in Christ Jesus than to reign over the ends of the earth. Him it is I seek—who died for us. Him it is I desire—who rose for us. I am on the point of giving birth . . . Let me receive a pure light; when I shall have arrived there, then shall I be a man."[55]

Heaven is a real place. We can't understand what it's going to be like any more than a baby can imagine life outside the womb. Understandably, we prefer the known to the unknown. But the more we know Christ on a personal level, the more excited we will become about heaven, because we know He is there. In the words of Peter Kreeft, "We do not have to know what we do not need to know about Heaven. It should be our goal but not our distraction."[56]

Dear Lord,
Help me to focus on getting to know You more and more so that my longing for heaven increases. May I feel homesick for You while I am here on earth. May I never settle for less than what You have for me. Amen.

JULY 29

"He who has prepared us for this very thing is God, who has given us the Spirit as a guarantee." (2 Corinthians 5:5)

"This very thing" that God has prepared us for is our eternal destiny. This life on earth is not all there is; in fact, it's just the place of preparation for eternity. God wants us to arrive in heaven wearing the right clothes. He knows that we do not want to "be found naked" (2 Corinthians 5:3). Through baptism, we are clothed in Christ's robe of righteousness.

Why does it matter what we are wearing? We have been invited to the wedding supper of the Lamb. Heaven is a wedding banquet beyond anything you can imagine.

God has prepared everything we need for heaven and issues us an invitation. It is up to us to accept. He will not force the wedding clothes or the destination on us. In 2 Corinthians 5:5 we are told that when we say yes to the invitation, God gives us the Holy Spirit as a guarantee.

To understand what this means, we need to look at the meaning of the word *guarantee*. It comes from the Greek word *arrhabon*, which means "a partial payment." The modern Greek word, *arrhabona*, means "engagement ring." God gives us the Holy Spirit as a pledge. He promises that there is more to come at the wedding supper.

You might be wondering who is getting married. We discover the identity of the groom (the Lamb) in John 1:29, when John the Baptist saw Jesus walking toward him and said, "Behold, the Lamb of God, who takes away the sin of the world!" The groom is Jesus Christ, but who is the bride?

In 2 Corinthians 11:2, Saint Paul wrote to the Church, "I betrothed you to Christ to present you as a pure bride to her one husband." The Church is the bride of Christ, and you are a part of the Church.

What should the bride be doing as she waits? Revelation 19:7 says that "the bride has made herself ready; it was granted her to be clothed with fine linen, bright and pure—for the fine linen is the righteous deeds of the saints." Nothing is more beautiful on a woman than holiness.

Dear Lord,
May I focus on making myself ready to meet You in eternity. Instead of being distracted by temporal pursuits that will burn away after death, may I invest in what lasts: holiness. Amen.

Be Still JULY 30

"But seek first his kingdom and his righteousness, and all these things shall be yours as well." (Matthew 6:33)

One of the most important things I had to learn as a waitress was how to lift up and balance a large tray filled with plates of food. I had to get it up and over my shoulder, which I always found a little challenging. If I had my hand a little too far to the left or right, the whole tray would come crashing down. I needed to keep my hand right in the center in order to balance everything.

That is the place God needs to have in our lives. When He is at the center, everything else stays in balance. When we let other things take center stage, it all comes crashing down.

If we are going to seek God first, it is essential that we get to know Him. We need to know His character in order to determine if He is worthy of our trust. There is a big difference between getting to know who God really is and getting to know Him as we *think* He is. This was a real issue for the religious leaders during Jesus' day. They had certain preconceived notions of what He would be like. When Jesus didn't match up with their list they rejected Him and missed the Savior.

If we want to get to know God, we need to get to know Jesus Christ. Hebrews 1:3 says that Jesus "reflects the glory of God and bears the very stamp of his nature." Jesus is an exact representation of God. That is one of the reasons Bible study is so important, and especially the study of the Gospels. As we read the stories of Jesus' life, we begin to get to know Him. We see how He relates to people, the things He considers most important, and how much He loves us.

Getting to know God takes time. But at some point, we need to take a leap of faith. It's always a temptation to paddle to the edge of the wave, take one look, and then retreat to what we know, to what we can control. But faith is believing in what we don't see, and without faith, no one can please God. Faith means we trust God, even when we don't have satisfactory answers to all our questions.

Dear Lord,
Help me to have the humility to recognize that if I could understand everything about You, if all my questions were answered, if there was no need for faith or mystery, You'd be a pretty small god, one my mind could contain. Amen.

JULY 31

"She was deeply distressed and prayed to the Lord and wept bitterly." (1 Samuel 1:10)

Your heart matters to God. There is not a tear you shed that He does not see and consider sacred and precious. He is not a disinterested bystander who waits for you to get your act together. He is a savior who weeps with you and bleeds for you.

You have perhaps been sold the lie that the contents of your heart are just too much. Maybe your emotions have overwhelmed people close to you, so you have decided to close off your heart.

Perhaps you have ignored your heart because there's just so much to do. You worry that if you slow down and get introspective, your life will come off the rails and a mess will result. There always seems to be a reason, big or small, for just staying superficially in the present.

But perhaps there is something you want more than the familiar discomfort. Do you want to really live? Do you want to feel deeply and love passionately? Do you want to be fully present, right here, right now? Do you want to know who you are and whose you are, and be at peace with that? It is time to stop expecting people and things to deliver the very stuff that only God can do. But it begins with opening our hearts to Him and being honest.

I have a secret weapon. It's my prayer journal. Each morning, I start my day by talking to God about how I am feeling. He is my safe place to unload. In my journal, I let it all out. Then I thank Him for who He is and what He's done. I ask Him for what I need and ask Him to take all my emotions and order them. I ask Him to bring my emotions under His control, and to heal what is hurting and broken within me.

This journal is full of my letters to God. And when I look back at old entries, I can see how faithful He has been to me, that He has never left me. Writing it all down has helped me to remember. Saint Ignatius said, "We must speak to God as a friend speaks to a friend." He is waiting for you.

Dear Lord,
Instead of coming to You with my list of things I'd like You to do for me, I want to start bringing You my heart. Help me to have the strength to drop the walls I have built around it and to invite You in. Please come as a balm and a gentle healer. Amen.

August

Now to HIM who is ABLE to do IMMEASURABLY MORE than all we ask or IMAGINE according to HIS POWER that is at work within US.

EPHESIANS 3:20

AUGUST 1

"He brought me forth into a broad place; he delivered me, because he delighted in me." (Psalm 18:19)

Summer invites me to slow down, to settle into the here and now. This doesn't come easy to me. I have to fight to stay in the present moment.

My default is to spend time in the past, mulling over what was said, what I could have done better, what I missed. Or I live in the future. Instead of being rooted in the now, my eyes are looking ahead to what is next. This robs me of the joy of the ordinary day.

Is it possible to live in ordinary time? Yes, but I won't make that shift until I take a hard look at what lies beneath my hustle. I am so grateful to author Kate Bowler for revealing it to me through her beautiful writing in *Everything Happens for a Reason*. Kate writes while eyeing the clock, knowing that her life hangs in the balance as she battles stage 4 colon cancer in her midthirties. She reflects on how she lived in the apocalyptic future: "If I were to invent a sin to describe what that was—for how I lived—I would not say it was simply that I didn't stop to smell the roses. It was the sin of arrogance, of becoming impervious to life itself. I failed to love what was present and decided to love what was possible instead."[57]

"Becoming impervious to life itself"—what a thought. But isn't this what happens when we trade accomplishments for relationships? *Life* isn't the checked box, the money in the bank, the whirl of activity. *Life* is seeing the freckles on your child's nose, listening to the dreams of your spouse, laughter, gripping someone's hand when they suffer, serving in the hidden places, breathing in the new morning.

The enemy wants us to be consumed by the pain of the past and the fear of the future, and to miss the sacredness of the present. Saint Paul challenges us to "hold our ground" (Ephesians 6:13), to be rooted right here, right now. It isn't all up to you. It isn't all up to me. This means we can rest. We can slow down and return to a childlike rhythm made possible by trust.

Dear Lord,
Help me to pause and delight in the ordinary. May I grasp hold of this one wild and beautiful life that I've been given and love what is present and right in front of me. Amen.

Be Still

AUGUST 2

"Above all else, guard your heart, for everything you do flows from it." (Proverbs 4:23)

A friend once said it looked like I was treading water while trying to keep a bunch of balls in the air. It was an accurate observation. Then she said something that stopped me in my tracks. "I think that at the same time, you are kicking your heart away from you. Not because you think your heart doesn't matter. You just don't have time to stop and take care of it."

I know that above all else, I need to guard my heart. I believe wholeheartedly that everything we do flows from the heart. The heart is the essence of *who I am*, not *what I do*. It's where joy is found.

Joy does not reside in a life that is all about checking the boxes, even if the boxes are for really good things like spiritual growth, service, and loving your family. When most of what we do is preceded by "I should" or "I must," then there's a pretty good chance that we are lacking in the joy department. But this is a tricky thing. God asks us to obey Him, and so a ton of things get put on our "I must" list. People around us need to be actively loved, and that makes the "I should" list a million miles long.

I want to love people tangibly, and I want to obey God completely. But I want to figure out how to do those things in a way that doesn't feel like one enormous *should*. Not just because it doesn't feel good, but because the motivation isn't right. And when we operate for too long simply because we *must* and we *should*, we become robotic, and a little bit dead inside.

I want to fight for joy, because "the joy of the Lord is my strength" (Nehemiah 8:10). If I don't have joy, I'm weak—prone to burnout, discouragement, and frustration. I believe "the joy of the Lord" comes from knowing we are God's beloved daughters and living out of that reality. As a loving father, God wants us to experience getting lost in pure delight. He wants us to be replenished. He wants the blinders off our eyes so that we can see all that we have to be grateful for. He wants us to take time to rest. He knows us completely—we are the apple of His eye (Zechariah 2:8). He wants us to take the time to figure out what truly brings us joy—not what numbs us, distracts us, or just keeps us busy. Let's commit to tending to our hearts *each day*.

Dear Lord,
I hold out my heart to You, and ask You to pour Your love and grace over it. Amen.

AUGUST 3

Be Still

"But even if you do suffer for righteousness' sake, you will be blessed. Have no fear of them, nor be troubled." (1 Peter 3:14)

Romanian pastor Josef Tson was arrested and imprisoned several times for his faith. While being interrogated by six officials, he said:

> What is taking place here is not an encounter between you and me. This is an encounter between my God and me . . . My God is teaching me a lesson [through you]. I do not know what it is. Maybe He wants to teach me several lessons. I only know, sirs, that you will do to me only what God wants you to do and you will not go one inch further—because you are only an instrument of my Lord.[58]

During an earlier interrogation, an official had threatened to kill him. Pastor Tson replied:

> You should know your supreme weapon is killing. My supreme weapon is dying. Now here is how it works, sirs: You know that my sermons are on tape all over the country. When you shoot me or crush me, whichever way you choose, [you] only sprinkle my sermons with my blood. Everybody who has a tape of one of my sermons will pick it up and say, "I had better listen again. This man died for what he preached." Sir, my sermons will speak 10 times louder after you kill me and because you kill me. In fact, I will conquer this country for God because you killed me. Go on and do it.[59]

There is something incredibly powerful about a person who loves Jesus enough to suffer with grace and without fear. A life lived on a platform of suffering is challenging, and there are certainly days when it feels unbearable. But one thing it most definitely is *not* is meaningless.

A woman who suffers graciously leaves people utterly dumbfounded. Everyone expects her to fall apart, to be bitter, to give up. But when she stares down fear, people begin to wonder if her God is real. They wonder if she's drawing from a different source of strength than what they are accessing. They sense that there's something *more* in her life, something more than what they are experiencing.

Dear Lord,
May I not waste an ounce of my suffering. May I encounter challenges and turn them into opportunities to shine in the darkness. People I love are watching to see what makes me different. May my words, actions, and attitudes quietly reveal that You are real, and Your grace is enough. Amen.

Be Still

AUGUST 4

"Have no anxiety about anything." (Philippians 4:6)

Have you ever woken in the middle of the night with worry and then can't get back to sleep? Has it followed you around all day and become a filter that clouds everything? What can free us from the grip of anxiety?

When I am worrying, I'm projecting myself into the future and envisioning how things could turn out. The problem is, God is not there in my fantasy worst-case scenario. The majority of the things I worry about will never happen. The truth is, the present moment is rarely intolerable. What's miserable is to have your body here, right now, but your mind dwelling in the future. This dichotomy is unsettling and robs us of peace. God calls us to live in the present moment.

If we can get it through our heads that all God is asking is for us to obey Him and love like Christ for *these next five minutes*, we realize that step by step, we can move forward. It reminds me of the proverb "Worry is like a rocking chair—it gives you something to do but it doesn't get you anywhere." This is really a description of being stuck. Far better to stay in the present moment and ask the Lord, "*In this moment*, are you asking me to *act*—to do something specific? Or are you asking me to *accept*—to acknowledge that my current situation is beyond my control and therefore needs to be placed in Your hands?"

God provides grace and strength for us to do what He asks us to do. He does not provide grace for worry. This means that when we are dwelling in the land of what-ifs, we are envisioning an outcome without the miracle, without the inexplicable peace that surpasses understanding, and without the divine strength that enables us to persevere beyond our normal limitations. God steps into reality and transforms bad circumstances into something beautiful, but He *does not* step into the worries in our heads. When we focus on our worries, the best we've got is our own solution to the problem. And if we're worrying, we've probably already realized that our own "best solution" is either out of our control or simply not good enough. As someone wisely said, "Worry doesn't empty tomorrow of its troubles; it empties today of its strength." And we need all the strength we can get.

Dear Lord,
I am passing the burden over to You. You are already in the future, taking the threads of my life and weaving them into a beautiful tapestry. I trust You. Amen.

Be Still

AUGUST 5

"We have this hope as an anchor for the soul, firm and secure." (Hebrews 6:19)

My parents gave our kids kayaks for their birthdays, and every day of the summer my dad reminded them to tie up their kayaks to the dock. "One of these days, you're going to wake up in the morning and your kayaks will be gone," he'd warn. But tying up a kayak takes *forever*, so more often than not, the kayaks were just dragged onto the dock and turned upside down.

One night, a storm hit Camden as we slept. Sure enough, when we woke in the morning, one of the kayaks was missing. My dad didn't need to say a word; everyone knew that the kayak should have been tied up. The kids searched and when it was finally found, it was dirty and banged up. They didn't enjoy taking time to search for the kayak, but probably the hardest thing for them was the knowledge that they'd disappointed their grandfather. He'd sacrificed to give them such a generous gift, and they hadn't valued it enough to take care of it.

The untethered kayak makes me think about my spiritual life. God's given me the incredible gift of a close relationship with Him. It cost Him everything to offer me that gift. How does He ask me to take care of it? The answer is found in John 15:5: "I am the vine; you are the branches. If a man remains in me and I in him, he will bear much fruit; apart from me you can do nothing." Remaining in Christ, being as grafted to Him as a branch is to the vine, is like tightly tying the kayak's rope to the dock.

But remaining in Him takes time. All too often, we settle for pulling the kayak up on the dock instead of tethering ourselves to God. We talk *about* God instead of talking *to* Him. We get our *bodies* to church, but keep our *hearts* somewhere else. We sit down to read the Bible, but end up reading about someone else's experience of God instead.

When the day runs smoothly, we'll probably feel that this is a good enough spiritual life. The kayak will stay on the dock and will be there in the morning. Unless the storm hits. And it will. It's at those times that we need an anchor for the soul. Christ is our hope, and He is the anchor for our souls. The daily disciples of prayer, Bible reading, receiving the sacraments—these are the ropes that connect us to the anchor.

Dear Lord,
May I remain tethered, every day, to the anchor of my soul. Amen.

Be Still

 **AUGUST 6**

"May the God of hope fill you with all joy and peace in believing, so that you may abound in hope by the power of the Holy Spirit." (Romans 15:13)

A friend of mine shared the questions she was prayerfully journaling, and I decided to give them a try. One stopped me in my tracks, because I didn't know how to answer. The question: "What are you dreaming about right now?" What was I hoping for personally? I couldn't think of anything, and that felt really weird, and somehow wrong. I was cautious when it came to praying big dreams. That felt like I was setting myself up for disappointment.

The journey back to hope begins with taking a close look at the heart of the Father. Does He love us with the kind of attention that cares about every detail of our lives? Is He only concerned with us as an "end product of holiness," or does He care about our passion and purpose, too? Does He care how we feel in the midst of our struggle, or is He just waiting for us to learn the lessons that come from hard knocks?

Here is a truth we need to grasp: Your Father loves to give. He waits to be asked. Perhaps He is whispering James 4:2 to you, "You do not have because you do not ask." He wants you to come to Him like a little child. Think about the way children ask. They ask for the moon. They don't stop to think about what is possible. And how do most parents respond? We want to give. When what is requested is for their good, we want to move heaven and earth to give it. "If you then, who are wicked, know how to give good gifts to your children, how much more will your heavenly Father give good things to those who ask him?" (Matthew 7:11)

Your Father has already proven that He is *for you*. He has already proven that He will hold nothing back if it's for your good. You only need to look at the cross to see that proven. But *keep looking*. The cross isn't the only place you can see evidence of your Father's heart. Where have you seen evidence of Him taking care of you? What answers to prayer have you experienced?

Cultivating a spirit of gratitude will help you to keep your eyes on the heart of the Father. It will break the hold of cynicism on your heart. It will open you up to the possibility of hoping again. It will give you the courage to dream.

Dear Lord,
Teach me to hope again. Amen.

AUGUST 7

"When Peter saw him, he said to Jesus, 'Lord, what about this man?' Jesus said to him, 'If it is my will that he remain until I come, what is that to you? Follow me!'" (John 21:21–22)

Has God ever asked something of you that feels really hard and you look around and feel a little singled out? Do you see other people who seem to have it easier, and you wonder why He's asking so much of you and seemingly letting them get away with doing less?

God loves us too much to leave us where we are. He always draws us closer to Him, and in doing so, He gently reveals things that need to go or need to be gained in order for us to make that journey. This is the process of growing in spiritual maturity. It's an intensely personal process; no two journeys are alike. What God asks of one might not be what He is asking of another, and as a result, obedience can sometimes feel lonely.

In John 21, Jesus had just described Peter's particular journey. He shared that Peter was going to be used to shepherd the early Church, and that he would ultimately be led somewhere he didn't want to go. Then Jesus looked Peter in the eye and said, "Follow me."

Did Peter jump up and say, "Yes, Lord—I'm going to fix my eyes on You and run the race You have marked for me"? No. Peter gestured to John and said, "What about him, Lord?"

Jesus didn't satisfy Peter's curiosity by filling him in on what John's journey was going to look like. He spoke firmly to Peter and said, "What concern is it of yours? You follow me."

He says the same to you. Don't look to the left or the right. Fix your eyes on Jesus. Focus on your unique journey.

Will there be times you feel lonely? Yes, there will.
Will some of your surrenders be unique? Yes, they will be.
Will some of the people you love most question whether it's necessary for you to be so "sold out"? Yes, they will.
Will some even think you have taken things way too far? Yes, that will happen.

But God will see and note every sacrifice and surrender. He sees them as a sweet offering to Him. It isn't necessary that everyone around you applaud your decisions. Live for the pleasure of the One who made you and who gives you your every breath.

Dear Lord,
May I stop comparing my journey with that of others. Help me to sacrifice and surrender willingly, knowing that You never ask more of me than what is for my good and growth. Amen.

Be Still

 **AUGUST 8**

"Therefore, since we have a great high priest who has gone through the heavens, Jesus the Son of God, let us hold firmly to the faith we profess. For we do not have a high priest who is unable to sympathize with our weaknesses, but we have one who has been tempted in every way, just as we are—yet was without sin. Let us then approach the throne of grace with confidence, so that we may receive mercy and find grace to help us in our time of need." (Hebrews 4:14–16)

Sometimes we just desperately need someone who understands us when we are at our weakest—to be met with an *I understand* instead of a *Pull yourself together*. This is what Jesus does. He sympathizes with us in our weakness, because He knows what it feels like. He "has been tempted in every way, just as we are."

He knew that there would come a point for all of us when the best we had just wouldn't be enough. Nowhere is that more true than when it comes to our eternal salvation. No amount of effort makes us perfect enough to stand in God's presence. There will always be a gap between the best a person can offer and the perfection God requires. "The wages of sin is death" (Romans 3:23), and even a good deed done with selfish motive is enough to keep us separated from God.

Thankfully, "we have a great high priest who has gone through the heavens, Jesus, the Son of God." After His crucifixion and death, Jesus entered His Father's presence in heaven, offering His blood in place of ours. God the Father saw Jesus' sacrifice, and was satisfied with the price He paid for our sin. Because of Jesus, we can draw near.

But when our failings are front and center in our minds, we can be tempted to run away from God. It's at those times that we need to be reminded that we can approach the throne of God with confidence instead of fear. Why? Because Jesus sits on a throne of grace, not a throne of condemnation. When a voice tells us that we have to get ourselves fixed up before we can come to God, we can be certain the voice is not God's. He invites us to bring Him our questions, doubts, fears, and failures.

God doesn't ask you to perform for Him. He asks you to be in relationship with Him.

Dear Lord,
Thank You for letting me drop the burden of performance and just let You wrap Your arms around me in unconditional love. Amen.

AUGUST 9

Be Still

"My grace is sufficient for you, for my power is made perfect in weakness."
(2 Corinthians 12:9)

It's a rare privilege to see heroic openness to God's will up close. Over the years, I've watched an incredible woman welcome child after child with her openness to life. Just six weeks after she and her husband welcomed their ninth child, the child joined the saints in heaven. Days after the loss of their son, they sent out a letter with the following quote:

> The everlasting God has in His wisdom foreseen from eternity the cross that He now presents to you as a gift from His inmost heart. This cross He now sends you He has considered with His all-knowing eyes, understood with His divine mind, tested with His wise justice, warmed with His loving arms, and weighed with His own hands to see that it be not one inch too large and not one ounce too heavy for you. He has blessed it with His holy name, anointed it with His consolation, taken one last glance at you and your courage, and then sent it to you from heaven, a special greeting from God to you, an alms of the all-merciful love of God. —Saint Francis de Sales

We attended the visitation, where we were invited to join their son and adore our Lord during the Holy Hour. He was worshipping the Lord in heaven, and we would be worshiping Him here. We would be together in adoration. When I arrived at the visitation, I saw her and her husband standing at the foot of the cross, with the little coffin by their side. With every moment that followed, during the visitation and then at the funeral the next day, this beautiful couple showed us all what it means to grieve as Christians.

In the weeks that followed, this tender mother simultaneously grieved and offered encouragement to others. She reminded friends that there's no point in imagining what cross Christ might ask them to carry. "Don't waste your time imagining it. You don't have the grace for it now. But when it does come, the grace *will* be there," she said. She encouraged those around her not to fear the cross, and instead to embrace it as one of the main ways we can grow in holiness, the holiness that we all pray will be seen in us and in our families.

God didn't spare my friend pain and heartache. There were prayers during this journey that weren't answered the way she hoped. But God answered the cry of her heart with *His presence*. And her witness proves that His presence is enough.

Dear Lord,
May my life display Your all-sufficient grace shining forth in my weakness. Amen.

Be Still

AUGUST 10

"The Lord is near to the brokenhearted, and saves the crushed in spirit." (Psalm 34:18)

Perhaps you are experiencing a season of life when it feels like the rug has been pulled out from under you. Just when you feel you've reached your limit, something else happens that's really overwhelming. There are hardships that we can make sense of, and then there are circumstances that leave us utterly perplexed as to God's plan, and that is a weary, achy place to be.

As much as I don't want to hear it, the truth is, God's plan is bigger and better than my own. His vision for you and me is far greater than the best game plan we can come up with. God is building within us a palace that is fit for a king. The beautiful thing is, He doesn't wait until it's perfect to move inside. He takes up residence when it's still messy and under construction, and starts to do a transforming rebuild from the inside out.

So what should we do in the midst of the pain and discomfort? These are the three tips that are keeping my head above water at the moment:

1. **Do whatever it takes to spend time alone with God every day, first thing in the morning.**
   Without this time of filling up and connecting with the One who loves us, we are *toast*. We might make it through the day, but we won't do it graciously or with inner peace. The following verses might be consoling: Psalm 18:2, 34:18; Isaiah 63:9; Lamentations 3:22–26; Romans 8:18; 1 Corinthians 10:13; and 1 Peter 4:12–19, 5:6–10.

2. **Remember that the people around you aren't the enemy.**
   When our circumstances are overwhelming, the smallest things start to irritate us much more than they normally would, and blaming others is pretty tempting. It's important to remember that everyone is just doing the best they can and everyone's got their own pain. Within a family, we need to remember that we're all on the same team. Cutting each other slack and giving each other the benefit of the doubt is really important during stressful times.

3. **Have a good cry and then do something delightful.**
   It's amazing how much better you can feel after a good cry. Sometimes you just need to be alone, have an ugly sob fest, then wash your face and freshen up, and look for some little happy thing you can do. It doesn't have to be big, but try to build something into each day that simply brings delight.

Dear Lord,
Help me to remember that this too shall pass, and that each thing I endure does have a purpose, and is being used by You for something good. Amen.

AUGUST 11

"When I declared not my sin, my body wasted away through my groaning all day long." (Psalm 32:3)

Feel free to question my sanity, but I scheduled my son's graduation party for the day before we were leaving at six a.m. for a family vacation. My parents were staying with us the following night, which meant that one of my boys had to move out of his bedroom. His room had already been cleaned, so I asked him to sleep on the blow-up mattress in his brother's room.

The morning of the party dawned, and I walked into my son's bedroom only to find . . . my son. My boy, in his bed. Clothes were strewn everywhere, empty potato chip bags were on the floor, and a dog with muddy paws was curled up on the duvet. And I lost it. All the frustration of a too-busy week found an outlet in this one moment.

What did I want from my son? A simple apology. But the apology didn't come. Instead, he avoided eye contact with me throughout the morning and tried to make up for his actions by doing all sorts of unpleasant tasks, like changing the baby's diaper, cleaning out the refrigerator, and mowing the lawn. I appreciated his efforts, but what I really wanted was for him to simply say he was sorry.

How often do I respond to God in the same way my son responded to me? I owe God an apology, but I avoid Him instead. I try to make up for my sin by doing other good things, hoping that God will notice those things and ignore my need for confession. How much better it would be if I would just own my mess and tell Him I'm sorry.

It isn't as if God doesn't already know what we've done. Our confession will not surprise Him. But until we say the words, our sin creates a chasm between us and God. When we confess, a bridge back to Him is created. Unconfessed sin saps our spiritual strength. As David said in Psalm 32, "When I declared not my sin, my body wasted away . . . my strength was dried up as by the heat of summer."

When we confess, He forgives. When He forgives, He wipes the slate clean. What results? We have a spring in our step and a lightness in our spirit that feels as good as a breeze on a hot summer day.

Dear Lord,
Thank You for always meeting my humble confession with open arms of mercy. Amen.

Be Still

AUGUST 12

"Do you not know that in a race all the runners compete, but only one receives the prize? So run that you may obtain it." (1 Corinthians 9:24)

It's hard to remain steadfast with the little things—the thankless tasks that we're tired of. Do you feel tempted to procrastinate or quit even though you know that God is asking you to persevere and finish well? When we feel the urge to settle for mediocrity, the following tips can help us refocus.

1. **Keep your priorities straight.** When I'm sitting on the couch at five p.m. instead of staying faithful in the little things, it's often because I'm worn out. I've been going all day, and I don't feel I have anything left to give. That's when I need to ask myself where I've spent my best efforts. Has all my energy been sapped by activities outside my home so that all I have left for my family is my leftovers? Who gets my best? I say that my highest priority is my relationship with God, then my husband, then my children. I'm convicted by Psalm 101:2: "I will walk *in my house* with blameless heart." It's going to be hard for me to apply this verse if I've used up all my best efforts elsewhere.

2. **Focus on your long-range purpose.** When I'm feeling tired and bored with my responsibilities, it's time for me to look up and look ahead. What is it that I'll want to have accomplished in five, ten, or twenty years? In what way is this small task a part of a bigger vision? Proverbs 29:18 reminds me, "Without vision the people perish." We don't achieve our long-range purpose or vision through one heroic self-sacrificing event. Purposeful living is made up of many little decisions—small steps of faithfulness. The little things matter.

3. **Finish well.** "I do not run aimlessly; I do not fight as if I were shadowboxing. No, I drive my body and train it, for fear that, after having preached to others, I myself should be disqualified" (1 Corinthians 9:26–27). This verse can be applied over a lifetime, and also to every day. At the close of each day, I ask myself, "Have I finished well? Have I given time to the things that matter most? Am I leaving undone things that are going to make tomorrow more difficult?"

Dear Lord,
I resolve to remain steadfast with what You have placed before me. My rest will be all the sweeter when I've given my best to what matters most. Amen.

AUGUST 13

"Charm is deceptive and beauty fleeting; the woman who fears the LORD is to be praised. Acclaim her for the work of her hands, and let her deeds praise her at the city gates." (Proverbs 31:30–31)

My sophomore year of high school, we had a certain hall that most of the girls avoided whenever possible. Daily, a group of boys would gather and hold up numbers as girls walked by, giving a score based on their appearance. There was a list that circulated in our choir, passed among the tenors and basses. It gave scores to girls in a number of categories, mainly different body parts. Back then—and now—girls and women starved themselves to look like the airbrushed models in the magazines.

We need to take a look at the way our culture has shaped our values and our definition of what has true worth. Our culture measures us according to accomplishments: how much money we have, what we look like, and so on. The world celebrates the homecoming queen, the Harvard grad, and the woman with the biggest house.

But God is different. God looks at how we love. He places great value on generosity, on putting others' needs before our own. He sees the things that no one else sees: a mother getting up in the middle of the night with a sick child; a wife who overlooks the raised toilet seat. He sees the silent sacrifice. The times you bite your tongue instead of lashing out. The times your work and contribution go unnoticed by others. He sees.

Who and what do *you* see? Who are the women in your life who love and serve heroically? Can you think of a woman who is invisible to many but continues to quietly give behind the scenes? Who is the unsung hero in your midst? Her achievements may not be the ones that our culture applauds, but God sees what she does, and considers it of the greatest worth.

It has been said that one of the keys to happiness is cultivating gratitude. The deep pleasure that comes from gratitude is magnified when we take the time to not just feel grateful interiorly, but to express it to the person we are grateful for. Take time this week to write a letter of gratitude and admiration to a woman who loves heroically. Acclaim her for the works of her hands. And then deliver the letter, in person, and read it to her. You will be amazed at the joy it brings her, and you.

Dear Lord,
Help me to build a habit of calling out the goodness I see in others. Amen.

Be Still

AUGUST 14

"So we know and believe the love God has for us. God is love." (1 John 4:16)

An appeal to the heart of God never goes unanswered. It's always met with goodness, mercy, and grace. He is so much kinder than we give Him credit for. So why do we so often behave as if God is a harsh taskmaster? The lover of our souls wants to shower us with His love, and we run in the other direction, afraid of His disapproval.

Does the phrase "never enough" describe how you feel? Do you wake up and think, "I didn't get enough sleep"? Do you race through the day and crawl into bed thinking, "I didn't get enough done"? Never perfect enough. Never thin enough. Never beautiful enough. Never happy enough. Never enough.

Whose voice is this? Who whispers in your ear, "You're not enough"? Let me tell you emphatically, it is *not* God. God looks at you with kindness, and His heart fills with pride. This is the good kind of pride; it rejoices in the wonder of who you are. He says to you, "You have been given fullness in Christ! You are complete in Christ!" (Colossians 2:10).

So who is creating these expectations? Is it possible that we have heard what God desires from us and then added our own expectations and those of other people? Could it be that the feeling of being overwhelmed and inadequate is coming from trying to do things that God hasn't called us to do?

When the voice whispers, "You're not enough," speak the words, "I choose love." I choose to stand under the shower of God's love and just soak it up. I choose to be measured by God's love for me, and it's unconditional, limitless, and steadfast. I choose love instead of perfection, love instead of expectations, love instead of a never-ending rat race of busyness.

We can choose to be defined by love. We can choose to love God in return by admitting that we don't have nearly as much control over things as we imagine. We can confirm our love for Him by telling Him we're glad that *He's* got it all under control. As we fill up with His love, we can ask Him to let it overflow into the lives of those around us. On our own, we're not enough. But "Christ in you, the hope of glory" (Colossians 1:27)—now, that's a different story.

Dear Lord,
May I choose love over perfectionism, love over comparison, love over busyness. Amen.

AUGUST 15

The Assumption of the Blessed Virgin Mary

"Arise, O Lord, and go to your resting place, you and the ark of your might." (Psalm 132:8)

In Mary, we have a mother who will never leave us, one who is totally dedicated to our well-being. She knows that nothing will bring us greater fulfillment and satisfaction than being close to her Son. She "continues to intercede for her children, to be a model of faith and charity for all, and to exercise over [us] a salutary influence deriving from the superabundant merits of Christ" (*Compendium of the Catechism of the Catholic Church* 197).

Jesus, who held nothing back from us, offers us His mother. She is one of His most precious gifts, and He longs for us to know her, admire her, and become more like her. There's a love that only a mother can give, and He wants us to experience that love at its best.

Her fiat, her yes, changed the world. Her life quietly reminds us that sacrificial love is the only love that really makes a difference. Loving with abandon can involve risk, loss of reputation, and letting go of a comfortable life. It isn't a safe love, but it's the kind that brings light to the darkness around us.

As Saint John Paul II said, "She, more than any creature, shows us that the perfection of love is the only goal that matters, that it alone is the measure of holiness and the way to perfect communion with the Father, the Son, and Holy Spirit."[60]

Nestle into your place in the family. Let Mother Mary love you, pray for you, and challenge you to love radically, sacrificially, and wholeheartedly. You are not an orphan. You belong; you are cherished. This family is the safe place to land, refuel, and then launch into a world that needs your yes. May your time "at home" give you the strength to hold nothing back, and to echo Mary's words, "Let it be to me according to your word" (Luke 1:38).

Hail Mary, full of grace; the Lord is with thee; blessed art thou among women, and blessed is the fruit of thy womb, Jesus. Holy Mary, Mother of God, pray for us sinners, now and at the hour of our death. Amen.

Be Still

AUGUST 16

"Why are you cast down, O my soul, and why are you disquieted within me?" (Psalm 43:11)

At a time when Western women have more privilege and opportunity than ever before, our feelings of discontent and dissatisfaction have skyrocketed. Could it be that we are looking for answers to our longings in the wrong places? Could it be that we have become seekers of comfort instead of seekers of truth? Is it possible that instead of being open to God when He has shown us the way to go, we've insisted on our own way?

Jesus holds the answers to the deepest longings of the human heart, but we'll never discover the key to happiness until we stop trying to save ourselves. We have to admit that we need a savior.

Without a savior, we'll never be able to experience freedom from the grip of sin. No matter how we might try to save ourselves through good behavior and a desire to do the right thing, we will always fall short of the holiness that God requires.

The more we recognize our own weaknesses, the more we are reflecting the beatitude "Blessed are the poor in spirit, for theirs is the Kingdom of God" (Matthew 5:3). We do this when we acknowledge that we aren't perfect supersaints but actually need God to pick up the pieces of our lives and do with us what we cannot. When we admit this, God is delighted. In Isaiah 57:15, God tells us, "I live in a high and holy place, but also with him who is contrite and lowly in spirit, to revive the spirit of the lowly, and to revive the heart of the contrite." God promises to fill the hearts of the broken who authentically seek Him. It's His greatest desire to save everyone, but He can only save those who acknowledge their need.

Dear Lord,
Please give me the humility to set down my preconceived notions of who You are and what is true, in order to hear and accept Your perspective. Help me to shed my complacency so I can truly live the life I was created for. May my heart's deepest longings be satisfied by my relationship with You. Amen.

AUGUST 17

*God is faithful; he will not let you be tempted beyond what you can bear."
(1 Corinthians 10:13)*

I could hear the coins jangling in her pocket as she climbed up the stairs to my room. Some small change was missing, and I had just asked who had taken it. Greeted with silence and no admission of guilt, I told the kids I was going upstairs to wait. Whoever took it could come to me in their own time, but we weren't going anywhere until the truth had come out.

With tears in her eyes, my daughter admitted that she had taken the money. I asked why she felt it was OK to take money that she hadn't earned. She burst into tears. "I took it because the five dollars I had earned working in the garden is gone! I can't find my money, so I took it."

We talked about how hard it is to do the right thing when life is unfair. We talked about 1 Corinthians 10:13, which says, "No temptation has overtaken you except what is common to mankind. [We all get tempted.] And God is faithful; he will not let you be tempted beyond what you can bear. [When we say we just couldn't help it, that's not true. In our own strength we can't, but God will always help us make the right choice.] But when you are tempted, he will also provide a way out so that you can endure it." I asked my daughter what was the other option that she could have chosen.

I told her choices have consequences, and that she would have to give the money back (it belonged to her brother) and then ask him how she could serve him to show him she really was sorry. I asked her if she felt like it was hard, maybe impossible, to be as good as God wanted her to be. She gave a big nod of agreement. And then we got to the good news.

Every time our children (or we) mess up, it's an opportunity to be drawn to the cross. She was right—it is impossible to be as good as God wants us to be. So what is the solution? God expecting less of us? Us expecting less of our children? It's always tempting to lower the standards when we can't measure up. But when we do that, we miss out on a wonderful opportunity to see our need for God. Situations that cause our children (and us!) to see how desperately we need Christ and His grace can be the very things that lead to an authentic relationship with Him.

*Dear Lord,
It is hard. That's why we need You. May I rely on You instead of falling into the trap of self-sufficiency. Amen.*

Be Still

AUGUST 18

"Encourage one another and build one another up." (1 Thessalonians 5:11)

Have you ever had the experience of thinking the same old deflating and debilitating thoughts—listening to the same old lies that say you are worthless, not good enough, broken beyond repair? Have you ever looked in the mirror and seen nothing but the extra pounds or wrinkles? Have you ever wanted to just give up because the expectations scream so loud and no matter how hard you try, you know it'll never be enough?

You are not alone. Satan whispers these words to women all around the world. Do you know why? Because he is utterly terrified of what would happen if we actually believed the truth about who we are. If we saw ourselves as God sees us, if we stepped into our true identities and lived them out, if we as women called out the soul beauty in each other, we would unleash a torrent of divine love that would change the world.

When we are feeling discouraged about our worth, what we want more than anything is for someone to build us up. Considering this is out of our control—we can sit waiting for a long time—I suggest a different approach. What would you say to someone who is feeling the way you do? Write it down and read it back to yourself. Then find a woman who could use a kind word, and share with her how you see her and what you believe about her worth. People are emotionally starving for encouragement. A well-spoken word can change a person's day.

Even when we see that a loved one would be much happier if certain changes were made, saying so rarely has much effect, especially if the person hasn't actually asked us for advice. They may listen, but they will be unlikely to change.

Try this out: Walk into the room and say, "I respect you so much." Then walk out. I'll bet the person will follow you and ask you why. People need affirmation from those who love them because there is so much in the world that beats them down.

But don't just limit this to those you love—try it out with strangers. Let the woman know you like her outfit. Tell the mom that you think the way she smiles at her kids is beautiful. Tell the little girl that you are impressed she's being kind to her brother. "A word fitly spoken is like apples of gold in a setting of silver" (Proverbs 25:11).

Dear Lord,
May I spend more time complimenting others than thinking about what I don't like about myself. Amen.

AUGUST 19

"Be renewed in the spirit of your minds and put on the new man, created after the likeness of God in true righteousness and holiness." (Ephesians 4:23)

If we want to experience true freedom, it will begin with the renewing of our minds. How are our minds renewed? When we learn to recognize the difference between the truth of God's Word and the lies of the enemy of our soul. So how can we tell whose voice we are hearing?

When the American Bankers Association trains their tellers to recognize counterfeit money, they don't do it by having them study counterfeit bills. All they do, hour after hour, day after day, is handle authentic currency until they are so familiar with the true that they cannot possibly be fooled by the false.

This is how we are to experience renewal of our minds: We saturate our minds with what is true—and that truth is found in Scripture. This is God's love letter to us. The more we study it, the more we will recognize the voice of our loving Father. Romans 8:1 tells us, "There is therefore no condemnation for those who are in Christ Jesus." The voice that condemns is not the voice of God.

There is a difference between condemnation from the enemy and conviction from the Holy Spirit. The Holy Spirit works within us, convicting us of sin. This is sin that we have not yet confessed. We feel uneasy and guilty, and God uses these feelings to draw us to confess. That is conviction in action.

By contrast, the enemy of our soul condemns us. He focuses our attention on sin that we have already confessed and been forgiven for. Conviction and condemnation are two very different voices. Don't let the enemy's voice of condemnation keep you away from the throne of grace.

Jesus wants you to experience total freedom, and as He said in John 8:31, "If you remain in my word, you will truly be my disciples, and you will know the truth, and the truth will set you free."

It has been said that a Bible that is falling apart likely belongs to a person who isn't. Getting God's words off the page and into our minds and hearts is a huge step toward freedom and the life we desire.

Dear Lord,
Help me to value Your words more than the opinions of those around me. May I take the time to read them so I can recognize Your voice. Amen.

Be Still

AUGUST 20

"But now in Christ Jesus you who were once far off have been brought near in the blood of Christ." (Ephesians 2:13)

In the Old Testament, the average Israelite had no personal access to God. The very architecture of the temple made it clear that not just anyone could approach God. When you approached the temple, you first encountered the Court of the Gentiles (anyone could be there). The Temple got more restrictive the closer you got to the Holy of Holies, which was where God dwelled.

The Holy Place was separated from the Holy of Holies by a veil. The Mishnah (the recorded oral tradition of Jewish law) says that the veil was around six inches thick. It was sixty feet high—almost six stories—and twenty feet wide. It took three hundred priests to hoist it and move it into place. It was imposing and delivered a strong message: DO NOT ENTER.

Only one person was allowed to enter the Holy of Holies: the high priest. He was allowed to enter once a year, on Yom Kippur, the Day of Atonement. On this day, he entered with blood from sacrificed animals, asking forgiveness for the people's sin.

Fast-forward to Jesus hanging on the cross. He "cried out again in a loud voice, and gave up his spirit. And behold, the veil of the sanctuary was torn in two from top to bottom. The earth quaked, rocks were split . . ." (Matthew 27:50). God tore the veil right down the middle. This isn't something a man could have done. It was said that even horses tethered to its corners couldn't rip it apart.

Can you imagine the chaos that resulted from this gaping tear? For hundreds and hundreds of years, hardly anyone had seen behind this curtain. The torn veil symbolized a monumental change in the way God was to relate to man. Everything had changed.

Jesus wants you to draw near. You have been granted access. If you still feel there's a wall between you and God, is it possible that you have built it and are leaning on it? Have you shut down emotionally? Have you learned to meet heartache with frozenness? Have you learned to meet it alone?

This is not God's plan for you. This is not the freedom Christ died to offer you. While it's true that the people in your life may not be able to handle all your emotions and your story, God can. Nothing shocks Him. Nothing overwhelms Him. Let Him uncross your arms and take your hands in His.

Dear Lord,
I want to come out of hiding and allow You to access my heart. Amen.

AUGUST 21

"Let us then with confidence draw near to the throne of grace, that we may receive mercy and find grace to help in time of need." (Hebrews 4:16)

Too many of us are missing out on resting in God's presence at the throne of grace. We're stuck outside the walls because we have become defined by our sin.

We've gone to confession. We've laid it all out. But we feel like the sin still sticks to us like tar. We continue to feel train-wrecked. There's no peace. No matter what we do, we can't get rid of the sense that *what we did* has become *who we are.*

This feeling can leave us with a profound sense of hopelessness. We are afraid to believe that we can truly have a fresh start because of Jesus. We are so afraid of opening ourselves up to this possibility and then being disappointed.

But there's something else at play here, and we don't usually realize it. When we define ourselves by our sin, we have set ourselves up as a higher authority than God. God has said we are forgiven. In 1 John 1:9 we read, "If we confess our sin, He is faithful and just and will forgive our sins." We learn from Psalm 103:12 that "as far as the east is from the west, so far has He removed our transgressions from us." When we are unwilling to forgive ourselves, we are saying that *our* standards are the ones that really matter. While this is masked as humility, it's really pride. And this pride keeps us from confidently approaching God's throne of grace and mercy.

It is time for us to take God at His word. Are you ready to let God be God—to be the final authority, the One in charge? "If the Son makes you free, you will be free indeed" (John 8:36). Drop the shackles in the confessional. Breathe in God's grace. Let it penetrate from the top of your head to the tip of your toes. Invite His mercy to fill you and transform you. God promises to make you new. The only thing standing in the way is your unwillingness to accept it. There is no sin beyond the reach of His mercy. You are not the exception to the rule.

Dear Lord,
Forgive me for setting myself up as a higher authority than You. That wasn't my intention—I just feel so unworthy of forgiveness. But I don't want to layer more sin on top of the old ones by being prideful. So I ask You to forgive me, and I make an act of faith that Your forgiveness is real and works. Amen.

Be Still

AUGUST 22

"[Jesus] entered once for all into the sanctuary, not with the blood of goats and calves but with his own blood." (Hebrews 9:12)

Jesus entered the heavenly sanctuary with His own blood and appeared before God's throne on our behalf. He entered on behalf of all the people who had lived throughout the Old Testament, who looked forward to a redemption yet to come. He entered on behalf of the people who lived when He walked the earth—the very ones who had called out for His crucifixion. He entered on behalf of all those who would be born after the time of His incarnation—that's us. He appeared before the Father as the ultimate atonement. Another word for *atonement* is *satisfaction*. When God the Father looked on the blood of His perfect Son, Jesus, He was satisfied. He was satisfied with that sacrifice and offered forgiveness for anyone covered with Jesus' blood.

Do you want to approach God's throne of grace and rest in His presence? You need to enter His presence with blood, but it's not the blood of animals. You enter with the blood of your high priest, Jesus. We don't get to stand before the throne of grace because God has said that sin doesn't exist or doesn't matter. We don't approach Him because we've managed to adequately justify our actions. He never said that sin didn't require a price to be paid.

God has always known that we are broken and utterly unable to fix ourselves. We don't have to cover up our brokenness and hide from Him. We just need to take the solution He offers us. His solution—Jesus our high priest, dying in our place—is the faith we profess. This is the gospel of freedom.

"We do not have a high priest who is unable to sympathize with our weaknesses, but we have one who has been tempted in every way, just as we are—yet was without sin" (Hebrews 4:15). N. T. Wright says it well:

> So when we come to pray . . . we are not shouting across a great gulf. We are not trying to catch the attention of someone who has little or no concern for us . . . We may and must come boldly and confidently . . . This isn't arrogance, indeed . . . the real arrogance would be to refuse to accept his offer of standing before the Father on our behalf, to imagine that we have to bypass him and try to do it all ourselves.[61]

Dear Lord,
Help me to see that when I stand before the throne, I am utterly accepted. I am Yours. I am beloved. I belong. Amen.

AUGUST 23

"For a tent was prepared, the outer one, in which were the lampstand and the table and the bread of offering; it is called the Holy Place. Behind the second curtain stood a tent called the Holy of Holies." (Hebrews 9:2–3)

We are invited to draw near—to enter God's presence in the Holy of Holies. But some of us are hanging out in the Holy Place instead. This was the area in the temple where the Old Testament priests worked and worshipped. What are we doing in the Holy Place? We're giving the performance of our lives.

We are hoping that God will be impressed and will let us into the Holy of Holies. We're performing for God and for the people we love, and most of the time we feel like we will never measure up. This is a type of bondage in which we have surrendered a part of our personhood in order to be loved. When we start to believe that "good enough" never really is, we feel shame. This plants a seed of perfectionism that has sent roots deep into many of us. We act like performing orphans because we've forgotten *who* and *whose* we are.

Too many of us have substituted religiosity for resting in God's presence at the throne of grace. Or we may be standing at the throne with confidence, but we've placed our confidence in the wrong thing—we can delude ourselves into thinking that we deserve to stand before the throne of grace because of our exemplary behavior.

We can be very religious and look good from the outside. And at the same time, on the inside, we can be in bondage to a checklist of rules. God becomes someone who is very hard to please. Even if we do manage to check the boxes, we are at constant risk of becoming self-righteous.

We settle for being "religious" because it makes us feel safe. But feeling safe isn't the same as being free. We end up being in an invisible prison. We don't know the fresh air we are missing. We surround ourselves with people who think like we do and live like we do.

Religiosity, performing for God, defining ourselves by our sin, and shutting down emotionally are all forms of bondage. This is where Satan wants to keep us. God wants to set us free.

Dear Lord,
You want to see me free, filled with joy, and experiencing all the privileges I have as Your daughter. Help me to live like who I really am. I am not a performing orphan. I am Your beloved child. Amen.

Be Still

AUGUST 24

"Put off the old man that belongs to your former manner of life." (Ephesians 4:22)

We never meant to end up in bondage. We just adopted coping mechanisms or strategies to help us feel secure. This is especially true for those of us who deal with trauma in childhood. We needed something to create safety and sanity. We carried these coping mechanisms into adulthood, and at some point, they stopped working *for* us and started working *against* us. It's time to put off these old coping mechanisms. It's time to step into and truly live out our identities as daughters of the king.

Don't be afraid of the journey toward greater closeness to God. He has chosen it for you. It is safe, because He is the one leading you, and *He is good.* There will be times that feel uncertain, and you will be desperate to run back to your old coping mechanisms. Run to Him instead.

You are not Pandora's box. Opening up your heart and letting God inside will not release a torrent of chaos that will ruin you. That being said, you may be afraid to look at the core of who you are because every time you start to do it, you feel covered in shame.

Remember, shame is Satan's tool. It's his language. It's not God's. God created us with feelings, and feelings are neither right nor wrong. They are indicators of what is going on inside us. If we didn't have them, we wouldn't know ourselves and wouldn't be able to move to a place of greater freedom. Again, when we start to recognize what we are feeling, we can begin to feel shame. We say to ourselves, "I *shouldn't* feel this way," or "I *should* be able to just keep trucking.". And then we revert to the old coping mechanisms of denial, performance, taking things into our own hands, or whatever our MO has been.

And all the while, God is waiting for us to confidently approach the throne of grace and share what we are feeling with Him. He can handle it. He created us this way. He knows that if we ignore our feelings, they will just fester and smolder below the surface.

He wants us to feel the feelings *with Him* so that we can then start working on renewing our thinking. This will help us make choices that lead us to freedom and joy. This is not the same as wallowing in emotion. It's recognizing the feeling—feeling it, owning it—and then letting go through forgiveness.

Dear Lord,
Please help me let go of the secrets and rest. Amen.

AUGUST 25

"I have kept the faith." (2 Timothy 4:7)

How can we keep the faith? Every single day, we make sure that our minds are renewed. This is best done through Scripture study. If our minds aren't renewed, we just keep thinking the same old thoughts, and listening to the same old lies from the enemy. Your best ammunition against the lies of the enemy is God's Word loaded into your head. This will reprogram your thinking through the power of the Holy Spirit. It will remind you that you are loved and accepted in Christ.

Telltale sign that the enemy of your soul is messing with you:

- You feel shame
- You feel guilt over sin that you have already confessed
- Words of condemnation are on repeat in your head
- Despair

He plays dirty. When we get serious about following Christ, the enemy comes at us with all he's got. En route to yoga class or to meet a friend at Starbucks? He'll make sure you get a nice parking spot. Heading to Bible study? He'll send you rain and obstacles. His attacks are swift and often come out of nowhere.

When the obstacles come, we can feel tempted to think that this faith thing or this level of service or leadership just must not be for us. We take the obstacles as a sign that we should quit, instead of seeing them for what they are. What are they? Evidence that we are moving in the right direction.

But to remain faithful, we need to take advantage of the help God offers. Read His Word so you can recognize His voice. Get real in His presence to counter the lie that He is disinterested. Go to Mary for protection, and a phenomenal warrior will go to battle for you. The sacrament of confession will give you "an increase of spiritual strength for the Christian battle" (CCC 1496). The Eucharist will strengthen and feed you when you are weak.

I don't know what you are battling today, but I do know that you are a mighty warrior, and the enemy of your soul is *no match for you*. Go before God's throne. Kneel before Him today. And go confidently. Go covered in the blood of your Savior. This is the safe place you long for—God Himself.

Dear Lord,
I pray that the arrows meant for my destruction would be turned around and become a blessing because according to the prophet Isaiah, no weapon forged against me will prosper. I commit to stop focusing on the obstacles and the people involved, and praise You instead. Amen.

Be Still

AUGUST 26

"All who believed were together and had all things in common . . . and the Lord added to their number day by day those who were being saved." (Acts 2:44, 47)

People may have hundreds of friends on Facebook, but current research shows that 25 percent of Americans say they don't have anyone they can talk to about their personal troubles. We are growing increasingly socially isolated at the same time online social networks are exploding. We are too exhausted for social connection. A screen doesn't require any energy, while meaningful conversation does.

At first glance, it appears that our culture has nothing in common with the early Church. The apostles led a social revolution that turned the world upside down as they helped thousands connect with God. "Well, that was then, and this is now," we say. We don't expect a movement of the Holy Spirit to make that kind of impact. Sure, we'd like people to come to know God, but the obstacles are daunting.

But at their core, people have always been after the same thing. We want to know that we matter. We need to know that our lives have meaning. We seek connection.

We were created with an inner void so that we would search for that connection with our Creator. And during that search, we need earthly relationships that give us a taste of God's love. The human heart hasn't changed through the centuries; our needs and our hunger remain the same. So how did the early Church do it? And what can we learn from its members?

If we were to crack open the book of Acts (the story of the beginning of the Church), we'd see people choosing community over comfort and the well-being of that community over individual growth and prosperity. And what they were doing in their community mattered: They were praying. Every movement of the Holy Spirit, every breakthrough came about as a result of prayer.

The secret of setting the world on fire with love for God isn't found in programs or methods. All sorts of things can help us look more effective on the outside, but without a movement of the Holy Spirit, those things are empty. It might be slick, but walls won't break down in people's hearts. And without God's children being His hands and feet in the world, too much of God's goodness will remain in the Christian ghetto.

Dear Lord,
I am tired and weary. Could it be because I'm putting my energy into things that You're not asking me to do? Help me to see what changes I can make so I can build intentional community where I am. Amen.

AUGUST 27

Feast Day of Saint Monica

"What we have heard and known for ourselves must not be withheld from our descendants, but be handed on by us to the next generation." (Psalm 78:3–4)

Saint Monica took the call to pass her faith to her children very seriously. A woman of deep prayer, she suffered greatly as she watched her son, Augustine, explore everything the world had to offer while ignoring Christ and His grace. Many mothers today can relate to this heartache.

What can we learn from Saint Monica? She never gave up and persevered in prayer. Whenever possible, she facilitated connections between Augustine and faithful Christians. One of those people, Saint Ambrose, said to her, "Surely the son of so many tears will not perish." A friendship began between Ambrose and Augustine, and Augustine's conversion followed.

Who prayed for you like Saint Monica? Whose presence intersected your life and drew you to Christ? How can you be that person in someone else's life?

Something really important to remember is that we cannot control the timeline of someone's spiritual journey. If we really want people to encounter Christ, we have to give them the room to do so at their pace. Are you in it for the long haul? Will you persevere? Or are you going to give up when the journey starts to feel a little too long?

You might mistakenly think that in order to be that significant person in someone's life, you need to be full of knowledge. Nothing could be further from the truth. You need to be full of love and do whatever you can to be easy to love. When a person is drawn to you, you can in turn point that person to Christ. You don't do that by knowing more than he or she does. You accomplish it by being transparent and admitting your flaws. You do it by pulling back the curtain, dropping the mask, and letting him or her see that you really need God, and that He comes through for you. No one needs you to be perfect. But you will be much easier to love if you can be honest about your mistakes and failings.

There is simply no substitute for your physical presence in the life of your loved one. There's no substitute for time—time spent listening, and when God gives you the nudge, time spent pointing to Him. It doesn't have to be with a big theological explanation. But if you never mention Him at all, the person who is drawn to you will have no idea *why* you are different.

Dear Lord,
May I take seriously Your call to share my faith. May I be easy to love, authentic, available, and most important, prayerful. Amen.

Be Still

AUGUST 28

Feast Day of Saint Augustine

"O God, you are my God, I seek you; my soul thirsts for you; my flesh faints for you, as in a dry and weary land where no water is. So I have looked upon you in the sanctuary, beholding your power and glory." (Psalm 63:1–2)

Saint Augustine is one of the most influential Christians of history. We owe him a debt of gratitude for all he has explained about our faith. His writings endure and are as impactful today as they were centuries ago. But his journey wasn't linear. The detours were full of sex, sin, and searching. But Saint Augustine wasn't the only one searching. Jesus came to seek and save the lost (Luke 19:10), and He never gave up on Augustine.

Augustine wrote in *Confessions* what it was like to finally encounter Christ: "You called and cried out loud and shattered my deafness. You were radiant and resplendent, you put to flight my blindness. You were fragrant, and I drew in my breath and now pant after you. I tasted you, and I feel but hunger and thirst for you. You touched me, and I am set on fire to attain the peace which is yours."[62]

We may run, but God pursues us. He is the hound of heaven, never giving up on the children He loves. He waits, knowing that nothing will satisfy us until we rest in His embrace.

Are you praying for a loved one who appears far from God? Trust that God is near. The Lord does not wish "that any should perish, but that all should reach repentance" (2 Peter 3:9). Are you grieved over difficult circumstances in your loved one's life? Could it be that God is allowing him or her to exhaust the possibilities, to come to the end of his or her resources, so that the need for a savior is finally seen?

Dear Lord,
I know that no one can come to Jesus unless the Father draws them. May You draw my loved one to You [John 6:44]. May You overwhelm my loved one with the reality of Your love, so that he or she can "grasp how wide and long and high and deep is the love of Christ, and to know this love that surpasses knowledge" [Ephesians 3:18–19]. I pray that You would give my loved one a new heart and a new spirit . . . that You would remove his or her heart of stone and replace it with a heart of flesh [Ezekiel 11:19]. Amen.

AUGUST 29

"Two are better than one, because they have a good reward for their toil. For if they fall, one will lift up his fellow; but woe to him who is alone when he falls and has not another to lift him up." (Ecclesiastes 4:9–10)

As unpleasant as it is, getting to a place where we recognize our limits can be a gift from God. It's often only then that we will reach for God at a deeper level. Because of this, God allows us to experience situations, people, events, and conflicts that we can't fix, so we will turn to Him. When we recognize that we are not in control, it can cause us to look at Him with fresh eyes.

Sometimes we have caused those tough circumstances because of our own dumb choices. God created us with a deep desire for happiness. We are so hungry that we often look to satisfy this desire in the wrong places. Other times, the circumstances have nothing to do with anything we've done; we are not to blame. The temptation then is to blame God, become bitter, or give up.

Regardless of why we find ourselves in the pit, when it all falls apart, we are in a great position for spiritual growth. But it all depends on how we respond. The same circumstance can cause two very different faith decisions in a person's life, depending on who was there at the time and who helped shape his or her view of the circumstance. Will we grow bitter and blame God? Will we feel so guilty because of our dumb choice that we mistakenly believe that there's no way back? Or will we allow the difficulty to reveal our need for God and help us to use the pivotal circumstance to draw us to Him?

Who is there when you fall? What advice do your friends give you when you are in dire straits? Do they lift you up to God or point you away from Him? What kind of advice do *you* give?

Dear Lord,
People's forevers are at stake. I want to be a conduit of Your love and mercy. I am available. I stand ready and willing to step toward the pain when someone experiences a pivotal life experience that is hard. May I lift others up and point them to You. Amen.

Be Still

AUGUST 30

"Take delight in the LORD, and he will give you the desires of your heart." (Psalm 37:4)

What are you dreaming about and wishing for right now? Do you wonder if you're supposed to have desires that go beyond serving Jesus? Rest assured, when you follow Christ, He does not want to destroy what makes you unique. He is not in the business of turning His children into carbon copies of each other.

God didn't create us to be automatons—people without passions, dreams, and desires. In fact, He gives us healthy and wholesome desires because He wants us to experience joy. The devil tells us that following Christ is boring, and that we know best what will make us happy. God wants to explore our desires *with* us, to redeem the ones that He knows will ultimately not satisfy, and to help us achieve the ones that He knows will be good for us. He wants us to be the authentic women He created us to be, in touch with the desires of our hearts.

Women often worry that thinking about what brings them joy, what they dream of, and what they hope for is self-centered. But knowing who you are is simply being authentically *you*. That is healthy. What's unhealthy is making the achievement of these things your primary goal. Living selfishly occurs when you are determined to achieve these things at a cost to other people. Sometimes we'll have to say no to what we most desire, and although it's difficult, it's a part of surrendering our lives to Christ. But when we don't even know what we hope for, we've lost touch with who we are. And that's not living authentically.

We will not achieve every one of our dreams and hopes. Not every moment in the day will be joy-filled. But being aware of these desires in our hearts will help us to be on the lookout for the times when God delights us by bringing these things to pass. It'll help us to develop the virtue of gratitude. And we'll feel more fully alive as a result.

Dear Lord,
Help me to explore my desires with You and to avoid the pitfalls of ignoring them or pursuing them selfishly. Please bring the balance and wisdom I so desperately need. Amen.

Be Still

AUGUST 31

"When his breath departs he returns to his earth; on that very day his plans perish." (Psalm 146:4)

An Australian nurse, Bronnie Ware, has spent years caring for patients in the final weeks of their lives. She was so struck by her observations that she wrote a book called *The Top Five Regrets of the Dying.* Common themes emerged that remind us of the importance of living authentically.

Here are the top five regrets of the dying, as witnessed by Ware:

1. I wish I'd had the courage to live a life true to myself, not the life others expected of me.
2. I wish I hadn't worked so much.
3. I wish I'd had the courage to express my feelings.
4. I wish I had stayed in touch with my friends.
5. I wish that I had let myself be happier.[63]

Suppressed feelings had led to bitterness and often physical illness. The busyness of life had crowded out time with friends, and in the end, loneliness resulted. Many people had spent their lifetimes assuming that circumstances determined the course of their lives, not realizing that *choices* are what truly shaped them. Much of life had been spent pretending to be content, when dreams, desires, hopes, and preferences had never been truly owned and embraced.

If we want to live without regrets, it's clear that we need to embrace authenticity. It'll require leaving our comfort zones and dealing with some conflict. It means we don't settle for false peace, and instead do the hard work of reaching for the real thing. Is it easy? No. But the alternative, in the words of author and speaker Christine Caine, is becoming "actors in a drama rather than pilgrims on a journey." Let's not settle for that. Reach out and grab hold of your life—the messy, wonderful, imperfect, and authentic one you were created to live.

Dear Lord,
Help me to drop the mask and speak truth honestly. May I be honest with myself, acknowledging my hopes and dreams, even while recognizing I have no right to experience their fulfillment. May I be honest about my failings instead of covering up my sin. May my relationships improve as I pursue authentic living. Amen.

September

For I know the plans I have for you, says the Lord. Plans for welfare not evil to give you a hope & a future.

— Jeremiah 29:11

SEPTEMBER 1

"And God saw everything that he had made, and behold, it was very good." (Genesis 1:31)

In the beginning there was perfect balance. There was enough time to do what was needed. The pace of life wasn't frenzied. Everything the eye could see was beautiful. Equality and peace characterized the male and female relationship. There was no hunger or weariness. Life was good.

This perfect balance created a world of freedom. There was no need to worry. Absolute trust in God's goodness took away all fear of the future. Only one thing was required of the people living in paradise: They were not to eat from one particular tree. That was it. Just one thing needed to be avoided. God knew that if they ate from that tree, they would think they knew everything and would forget to trust Him.

The comfort of a perfectly balanced life was enjoyed until a lie tipped the scales. A serpent persuaded the woman that she knew better than God. Believing the lie that God was holding out on her, she became convinced that she was missing out. She was the first to question God's unconditional love for her, but certainly not the last. The perfect balance was lost.

That balance had been held in place by man's right relationship with God. It wasn't just God's rule that had been broken. His heart broke, His relationship with His children was damaged, and the perfect world He'd created to delight them was now going to be full of things that didn't work. Life would feel messy, stressful, unbalanced.

But God loved too deeply to leave things un-mended. A rescuer was promised and a journey began. Generation after generation waited. Long years passed. Then in an unexpected way, in the most unlikely of places, when very few realized it, *He came*. The rescuer was born to a woman who succeeded where the first woman had failed. Although the rescue plan wasn't what she had expected, she *trusted*. She put God first. She made pleasing God her highest priority—above her reputation, her security, her plans. This supreme act of faith released the lover of our souls into the mess of our existence. He came to help us find the way back to God, back to the life we were created for.

Dear Lord,
I am longing for a more balanced life. Help me to trade my priorities for Yours. I invite You into the chaos and ask You to order it. Amen.

Be Still

SEPTEMBER 2

"Worthy are you, our lord and God, to receive glory and honor and power for you created all things, and by your will they existed and were created." (Revelation 4:11)

If we want to live balanced lives, putting God first is the starting point. This lays the foundation, and if we miss it or try to diminish its importance, our lives will become shaky very quickly.

In the Old Testament book of Exodus, we read the story of God rescuing His people from slavery in Egypt. When God led the Israelites out of slavery, He gave them rules that they would need to follow if they were going to fully experience freedom. They didn't know how to be free; all they had known was slavery. And what would be sadder than being free but still acting like slaves? To help His people walk in freedom, God said, "I am the LORD your God, who brought you out of the land of Egypt, out of the house of bondage. You shall have no other gods before me. You shall not make for yourself a graven image" (Exodus 20:2–4). In other words, God was to be their first priority. This was the key to living in freedom.

We've been delivered from slavery, too. We weren't enslaved by Egyptians; we were slaves to sin. Our freedom wasn't earned; it was given to us as a gift, grace from a loving God. Because of the suffering and death of Jesus in our place, we are "through God . . . no longer a slave but a son, and if a son then an heir" (Galatians 4:7). We've been given freedom, but if we don't make God the first priority in our lives, we risk submitting ourselves to slavery again.

Anything or anyone we place as a higher priority than God will create pressure He never intended. How many of us feel enslaved to pressure? If we make financial stability or achievement the highest priority, we'll find that we never have enough. Even when we're experiencing success, fear of losing it all will nip at our heels. If we make a person our highest priority, the pressure put on that relationship will guarantee dissatisfaction and conflict. We cannot expect any person, no matter how wonderful, to be to us what only God has promised to be.

Dear Lord,
Help me to identify any area of my life where I am experiencing pressure because I have made something a higher priority than You. Amen.

SEPTEMBER 3

"You shall love the Lord your God with all your heart, and with all your soul, and with all your mind. This is the great and first commandment. And a second is like it, you shall love your neighbor as yourself." (Matthew 22:37–39)

Jesus cuts through the chaos, giving us some basic principles that we can apply to our heaving to-do lists. Two things are crucial. We're to give God the place of highest priority. After God, people come next.

Take a minute to think about the most important "neighbors" that God has placed in your life. These are the key people whom you sense God would like you to pour your life into. We're wise to check whether those priority people are receiving our best, or our relational leftovers.

It's so easy to let tasks and to-dos crowd out time for loved ones. Remember, when Jesus talked about love in Matthew 22, the word was used as a verb. We can feel love in our hearts but fail to show it in our actions. The love Jesus calls us to involves more than good intentions. It requires movement.

If we measure success by what we accomplish, then we'll have a hard time putting people ahead of our tasks. But at the end of our lives, God isn't going to ask about all that we have accomplished. He will look at how we've loved. This is the true measure of significance. Have we loved well? Sacrificially? With abandon?

Loving well requires time, as well as dependence on God. More often than not, the love required of us will exceed what we feel we have to give. This is why it's so essential that we put God first, by starting our day in prayer. We come to Him in prayer, believing Jesus' words to us in John 15:5: "I am the vine, you are the branches. He who abides in me, and I in him, he it is that bears much fruit, for apart from me you can do nothing." We attach ourselves to Him, and ask Him to fill us with His divine love. When the demands we feel are greater than our own resources, something beautiful happens. The divine love spills out, and it's like the fine wine that Jesus saved for last at the wedding at Cana. Instead of giving people our leftovers, we give them what is best—God's love, released because of our weakness and dependence on Him.

Dear Lord,
May I take the time to identify the priority relationships in my life, and then intentionally plan time in my calendar to invest in those relationships. Amen.

Be Still

SEPTEMBER 4

"She looks well to the ways of her household, and does not eat the bread of idleness." (Proverbs 31:27)

While organization and order shouldn't be our first priorities, they keep things running smoothly. We pursue order not so that we can feel proud of how pulled-together we are. Instead, these routines and systems free us up to focus on what really matters: how we love—God first, then others.

One of the obstacles to order is clutter. Is it possible that we simply have too much stuff? Buying more boxes to achieve order isn't always the solution. Sometimes a bunch of things just need to go out the door.

Money management is another big component in keeping things running well. How are you doing in that regard? Are your credit cards maxed out? Do you overspend? Do you shop out of boredom or to escape?

Meal preparation is an area where organization is a huge help. When we find ourselves at the grocery store without menus planned in advance, our bills go up because of impulse purchases. Not to mention the time wasted when we find ourselves staring into the fridge at five p.m., hoping for inspiration but lacking a plan.

Unfortunately, houses don't clean themselves. Do you have a regularly scheduled time to clean, or do you wait until the mess is just too much to bear or someone is coming over? Do you need help getting your family to pitch in? Developing a system with housecleaning can make a huge difference in how we feel in our homes.

Developing systems to bring the chaos of home into order requires the skill of time management. Do you have trouble saying no? Do you have difficulty following through on your commitments? Are your children overscheduled? All those things get in the way of living the life we deeply desire.

Jesus came into the mess of our world for the purpose of reaching into the midst of all of the sin and disorder to bring us to a place of peace. In our quest for order, we need to let Him into the mess of our lives. Skipping prayer time to get more done never gets us ahead. We actually get less done when we fail to pray.

Dear Lord,
I invite You into the areas of my home life that feel chaotic. Show me women I can learn from who are stronger than I am in this area. Help me to be self-disciplined with systems, doing the things that I don't feel like doing so that I am freed up to love well. Amen.

SEPTEMBER 5

Feast Day of Saint Teresa of Calcutta

"We ourselves feel that what we are doing is just a drop in the ocean. But the ocean would be less because of that missing drop." —Saint Teresa of Calcutta

God never intended for us to feel the pressure of "doing it all." He made us, and He knows our limits. Each day, He waits for us to turn to Him so He can reveal to us the things that are most important and those we can let go of. This is very hard for us to discern without the Holy Spirit's guidance. So much in life feels urgent. We fear the consequences of leaving things undone. God has the big picture, and longs to help us out of this place of pressure.

Come to God in the morning (or right now) with your calendar. Ask Him to reveal to you the things that are most important from His perspective. Ask Him to help you to be sensitive to His still, small voice throughout the day so that you can see interruptions as divine appointments. At the end of the day, place all the things that didn't get done in His very capable hands. Trust Him with all that you cannot carry or solve.

It's so easy to fall into the trap of looking at everything at once, as if it all has equal importance and needs to be done immediately. All the events of the day will not be crowded into one hour. All the goals of a lifetime will not be achieved in a year.

One of the greatest mistakes we can make is to try to do in one season of life what God has meant for a later one. When we come at life full of enthusiasm, dreams, plans, and goals, it can be hard to say no to the good in order to say yes to the best. But that is exactly the self-discipline that we must have if we are going to be able to live out our priorities.

It's so much better if we can take each day as it comes, considering whatever is at hand to be God's will for that moment. You can receive your day from Him piece by piece. God will give you work to do. He recognizes that you need strength to carry out His plan. This is what He provides.

Dear Lord,
Help me to live the way Saint Teresa of Calcutta did. She didn't set out to change the world, just to pour as much love as she possibly could into each moment and interaction. I want to follow You and love well. Amen.

Be Still

SEPTEMBER 6

"Take my yoke upon you and learn from me; for I am gentle and lowly in heart, and you will find rest for your souls." (Matthew 11:29)

The word *yoke* comes from the Greek word *zugos*, which can also be translated as "a pair of scales." It's as if Jesus was saying, "Take off your old yoke. It represents a way of weighing what's most important, and it's a broken scale. Replace it with my yoke. Replace it with my pair of scales. You'll find rest when you measure things as I do. What I consider most important each day isn't burdensome."

There are times when our expectations for ourselves are in areas that are not important to God. Failure in those areas gives us an opportunity to evaluate what matters most. Perhaps those expectations weren't worth pursuing in the first place.

Sometimes we have expectations in areas that God does care about. He wants us to grow in intimacy with Him and in holiness. It isn't wrong for us to have expectations and hopes in the area of spiritual growth, and the problem isn't always the expectation itself. Often, it's how we react when we fail. Do we wallow in self-pity? Do we quit? Do we turn to escapism? God wants us to get back up and persevere on our journey of growth.

It's very hard to let go of our expectations when we continue to measure our worth with a faulty scale. If our worth is tied to what we achieve, then the drive to be acceptable, good enough, or extraordinary will kick into gear, impacting our actions and attitudes. Good days will be ones when we meet all our expectations. They will be rare.

Grace-healed eyes look at life differently. They recognize that our worth was measured in one place: the cross. When Jesus died in our place, He declared us worth everything. Our worth isn't tied to what we do; it's tied to whose we are. We are God's beloved daughters. Toss out the old scales. They are only making you miserable.

Make a list of some of the things you are expecting of yourself right now. Are any of those expectations unrealistic during this season of life? Circle the expectations that you believe matter to God. To help you discern this, ask yourself, "If I don't meet this expectation, will Christ be upset?"

Dear Lord,
May Your grace do its healing work in me. I am resting in Your arms, closing my eyes, and just sitting in Your presence. Amen.

SEPTEMBER 7

"[God] is not far from each one of us." (Acts 17:27)

One of the reasons it's important to know Scripture is because it contains God's promises to us. Often, we expect things of God that He never promised. We can make the mistake of taking a Bible verse out of context, basing an expectation of God on that verse and later being disappointed when things don't go the way we expected them to. We need to know the whole truth. We need to know what God promised and what He *didn't* promise and adjust our expectations accordingly.

Did God promise that Christians wouldn't suffer if they were faithful to Him? No. But in Isaiah 43:2, He did promise that "when you pass through the waters, I will be with you; and through the rivers, they shall not overwhelm you."

Did God promise that His children would be healed from illness if they prayed hard enough and had faith? No. But He did promise in Psalm 23:4 that "even though [you] walk through the valley of the shadow of death, [you can] fear no evil; for [God is] with [you]; [His] rod and your staff, they comfort [you]."

In the face of our need, what God promises over and over again is Himself. He promises His presence. We cry out for relief, better finances, health, comfort, a miracle, and He promises: I am here for you. And He proves enough. Regardless of what we feel, we can count on the promise that God is not far from each one of us.

According to CCC 397, questioning God's goodness in the face of unmet expectations is caused by a lack of trust. It's hard to trust God when you can't see or feel Him. Author Ravi Zacharias says it well:

> This longing to be touched is also the reason many Christians question God when they struggle to live life well and in a manner that brings glory to God, especially when they are going through a time of darkness or fear . . . We would love to feel the embrace of the Almighty when we are feeling abandoned and alone. How many times have we wished we could just hear his voice? To the true seeker, sooner or later God comes through, even though his touch may not be recognized until much later. You see, instead of spectacular manifestations of power, the same God who used the human hand to write the Scriptures and preserve the written Word uses the human touch of his children to restore broken lives around them.[64]

Dear Lord,
May I be a conduit of Your love to those who are hurting. Amen.

Be Still **SEPTEMBER 8**

"Put on then, as God's chosen ones, holy and beloved, compassion, kindness, lowliness, meekness, and patience, forbearing one another and, if one has a complaint against another, forgiving each other; as the Lord has forgiven you, so you also must forgive." (Colossians 3:12–14)

If only it was our natural instinct to behave in this way. But all too often, circumstances derail us and we react in ways we later regret. If we were to take the time to analyze where our reaction came from, we'd often find that unmet expectations triggered our behavior. This is why it's an important exercise to get to know ourselves and recognize our often unspoken expectations.

Expectations can have such a hold on us that we often feel our reactions can't be helped. We might say, "I'm just so disappointed. I can't help how I reacted." "I can't control my emotions." "I just can't take it anymore." Is this true? Can we not help it? Or is it possible that God has provided the strength and courage we need to do the right thing, but we aren't asking for the Holy Spirit's help?

Our reactions to unmet expectations have a ripple effect, impacting the atmosphere in our homes and in our work environments. We don't always notice this. Recognizing how others are affected by our unmet expectations requires humbly asking, "What's it like to be on the other side of me? Are there any times my mood is changing the tone of our environment?"

What difference would it make, not just in our own hearts but in the lives of others, if we could let go of unrealistic expectations? If you feel that your reaction to unmet expectations has not reflected the Christian character described in Colossians 3:12–14, could you ask forgiveness from God and from the person who has been hurt by your reaction? Could you take the next step and ask someone to hold you accountable to grow in this area?

Remember that God's mercies never fail. We can be changed by the power of the Holy Spirit. We can break free from the chains of past responses. Freedom awaits.

Dear Lord,
Forgive me for the way I allow my expectations to rule my heart and home. Please change me so that the peace of Christ reigns. Amen.

SEPTEMBER 9

"He has showed you, O man, what is good; and what does the Lord require of you but to do justice, and to love kindness, and to walk humbly with your God." (Micah 6:8)

Expectations are so powerful that we often become enslaved to them. We can feel as if we are suffocating under our own expectations and those of others. But we have a choice. We can let go of unhealthy expectations and choose to live freely according to what God desires and expects of us.

What does God expect of us? This is summarized well in Micah 6:8. God doesn't expect perfection; He knows that we are human and prone to failure. Instead of perfection, He asks us to pursue holiness. And how does God measure holiness? By how we love. Primarily, He wants us to love Him. Then He wants to see that authentic love well up in our hearts and spill over into the lives of those He places in our paths.

If we imagine the soul as a flower, many of us are tightly closed buds. There's great beauty within, but we haven't yet begun to open up to reveal all that's there. Our souls begin to bloom, one petal at a time, as expectations are surrendered to the master artist's hand. This growth is painful. We hold tightly to expectations because they are tied to our hopes, dreams, standards, and the way we believe life should be. It's hard to let go.

The only way we'll be willing to surrender our expectations is if our trust in God's love is greater than our desire to do things our own way. Our trust will grow in direct proportion to the amount of time we spend with God. A heightened awareness of Him causes us to see how He smooths the way for us each day. The alternative is to rush through our lives, focusing on the execution of our expectations. When we go at this pace, we're too busy to notice God's hand guiding, protecting, and blessing us. As a result, our trust in Him stagnates. We forget that He has the whole picture and the best plans. Our prayer time can quickly become the appointment in which we give God His marching orders for the day. This is a sure recipe for disappointment.

Dear Lord,
I am grateful that because of the indwelling Holy Spirit, no matter how much I may feel my expectations are hardwired within me, I can break old habits. I can see the flowering of my soul to the beauty of its perfection, one step at a time. As my soul bursts into bloom, I'll be able to spread everywhere the sweet fragrance of Christ. Amen.

Be Still

SEPTEMBER 10

"Bear one another's burdens, and so fulfil the law of Christ." (Galatians 6:2)

"For each man will have to bear his own load." (Galatians 6:5)

A *burden* is something oppressive or worrisome.[65] It's hard to bear a burden alone. By contrast, a *load* is an amount that can be carried at one time.[66] Loads are made up of the things we're all expected to do for ourselves. We are to help one another with burdens, but be responsible for our own loads. When do we get into trouble? When we find ourselves either carrying others' loads or refusing to compassionately help others carry their burdens.

Many of us have been in a relationship with a controlling person. Establishing boundaries with such a person can feel scary. This is because neither option is very appealing—you either set the boundary and risk losing the relationship, or remain imprisoned to his or her demands. "God's plan is for us to be loved enough by him and others, to not feel isolated—even when we're alone."[67] We need to know in the depth of our being that *we are loved and not alone* in order to have the courage to set boundaries.

We were created to love, and when we fail to love, we fail to measure up to our greatest potential (see John 13:35). Difficulties arise when we equate love with meeting every need we encounter. Even Jesus didn't meet every need or heal every disease, and He is God. We all have limits, and as a result, we need to discern what God is asking us to do and what we are tempted to do out of guilt, fear, or other wrong motives. If we can't say no, there will come a point when we are unable to say yes to something God wants us to do. There are only so many hours in the day.

When we fill up on God's love, we are less apt to make decisions based on a fear of losing relationships or of making someone angry. God fills us up through the indwelling Holy Spirit, and "where the Spirit of the Lord is, there is freedom!" (2 Corinthians 3:17) We're free to love. Boundaries give us the space to make decisions based on freedom and love.

Dear Lord,
In which of my relationships do I lack healthy boundaries? Help me to discern which of my actions are motivated by fear and which are motivated by genuine love. Amen.

SEPTEMBER 11

Be Still

"May the Lord give strength to his people! May the Lord bless his people with peace!"
(Psalm 29:11)

We need God's strength in order to experience peace in our relationships. Author Gary Thomas shares the following insight into an alternative way to approach a common frustration in relationships:

> . . . instead of focusing your energy on resentment over how sparsely [someone] understands you, expend your efforts to understand him or her. As a spiritual exercise, find out what [his or her] day is really like. Ask her. Ask him. Draw them out—what is the most difficult part of your day? When do you feel like just giving up? Are parts of your day monotonous? Is there something you constantly fear? Take time to do an inventory of [their] difficulties rather than [their] shortcomings.[68]

It's all about perspective. The more we grow in empathy, the more we'll reflect Christ in our relationships. Who more than Jesus understands how difficult people can be? He was hassled, misunderstood, betrayed, battered physically and emotionally, and killed for something He didn't do. When we are frustrated in relationships, He gets it. But He never lets us off the hook in terms of how we should respond. He went before us, setting an example of speaking the truth in love, truly listening in order to understand what was in each person's heart, and engaging instead of getting offended. He didn't meet every temporary need He encountered, but He met the deepest need of every human heart. His love went the distance. He loved to the death, not because He was a doormat, but because His sacrifice meant that we would never have to be alone again.

Jesus has not left us to manage our relationships alone. His very nature has been placed within us and is made effective in us, by the indwelling Holy Spirit. This is our hope. This is what keeps us from giving up. When we say we can't speak the way that God desires, He replies, "I know you can't. That's why I inspired Saint James to write, 'No human being can tame the tongue—a restless evil, full of deadly poison' [James 3:8]. No *human being* can tame the tongue, but *I* can. I am inside you through the Holy Spirit. And that is the difference maker. My Son, Jesus Christ, the Word,[69] will powerfully speak His words through you because He is in you. And that changes everything."

Dear Lord,
I am grateful that nothing and no one is beyond the reach of Your hand. Move freely within me, Holy Spirit, letting me know when I should stay silent and when I should speak. May my words be Yours. Amen.

SEPTEMBER 12

"We love, because He first loved us." (1 John 4:19)

"To worship is to quicken the conscience by the holiness of God, to feed the mind with the truth of God, to purge the imagination by the beauty of God, to open the heart to the love of God, to devote the will to the purpose of God."
—William Temple

Worship is more than good liturgy, or great music, or eloquent prayers. It's really about a human heart opening up and reaching out to connect with God. It's a turning of the face to soak up the richness of who God is. It's pouring out our love to God (however imperfectly it might be done), knowing that He receives what we give with open arms. It's basking in His presence. Worship is about intimacy.

And it sounds good, in theory. But then we have to stop for gas on the way to Mass and we arrive late, the homily's lame, and the music is dismal. So we quickly conclude that this kind of worship must be for a select few who are destined for beatification, but not for the rest of us.

So what should we do? Give up? Coast along? Be grateful that no one can read our thoughts, so no one's the wiser if we mindlessly rush through our prayers and mentally plan our grocery lists during Mass?

These questions make me think about a wonderful book called *The 5 Love Languages*, by Gary Chapman. In it, he explains that each of us has a preferred way of receiving love: through acts of service, words of affirmation, receiving gifts, physical touch, or quality time. If we want to effectively love someone, we're wise to find out which of those expressions of love is most meaningful to him or her.

So what is God's love language? Because God desires intimacy and connection with us, I'd guess that quality time is pretty important to Him. And that's another way to look at worship. It's quality time that we offer to God, because we want Him to know that we love Him. But we don't want to come to Him out of obligation. That's better than nothing, but as far as motivations go, it's not what we're aiming for. How do we purify our motives? We ask for His help. Even in our offering of worship, we need His movement within us.

Dear Lord,
The only reason I can love is because You first loved me. Please help me to love You better, so that my worship becomes my way of telling You that You have my heart. Amen.

SEPTEMBER 13

"The God who made the world and everything in it, being Lord of heaven and earth, does not live in shrines made by man, nor is he served by human hands, as though he needed anything, since he himself gives to all men life and breath and everything." (Acts 17:24–25)

Does God command us to worship because He needs it? Acts 17 tells us that God doesn't need anything. We need Him; He doesn't need us. He commands our worship for our good. God created us in such a way that we are made to worship. We are the creatures, not the Creator. It's not a question of whether we'll worship, it's a question of whom or what we will worship. Worshipping God will orient us to reality and bring healing and perspective to our days.

Colossians 1:16 tells us that all things were created through Christ and for Christ. But all too often, we act as if God was created for us—to do what we want Him to do, to bless us and those we love. Worship gets us in a posture in which we recognize that God doesn't owe us anything. Because He is the Creator and sustainer of the universe, He has the right to do whatever He pleases. In the words of Pastor Francis Chan, "To put it bluntly, when you get your own universe, you can make your own standards. When we disagree, let's not assume it's [God's] reasoning that needs correction."[70]

When we worship, we are focusing on *who God is*, not *what He gives*. A. W. Tozer writes:

> What comes into our minds when we think about God is the most important thing about us. . . . Worship is pure or base as the worshipper entertains high or low thoughts of God. For this reason the gravest question before the Church is always God Himself, and the most portentous fact about any man is not what he at a given time may say or do, but what he in his deep heart conceives God to be like.[71]

Dear Lord,
I confess the times when I have felt that You owe me an explanation. Please give me the gift of humility so I can trust You even when I don't understand You. Amen.

Be Still

SEPTEMBER 14

"Thereby put me to the test, says the LORD of hosts, if I will not open the windows of heaven for you, and pour down for you an overflowing blessing." (Malachi 3:10)

Every moment of the day can be an act of worship. I'm not suggesting that we spend all our time in a church; rather, that we live with the awareness that God is always by our side. No matter what is going on in our lives, we can always turn our hearts toward Him. When we lift our faces to God with a spirit of expectancy, we are continually looking for opportunities to connect with Him. Miracles will flow out of that intimate relationship. Supernatural strength will be given. Time will be stretched. Healing will take place.

In 1 Thessalonians 5:17, we are told to pray constantly. This doesn't mean spending every minute on our knees, but living with a steady awareness of our dependence on God. We thank Him for the good things that come our way, whisper frequent requests for help, and stay conscious of the fact that everything we say and do can be either an offering of worship or a step away from God. As we go through the day, we can ask God, over and over again, "What would You like me to do in this minute?" This is an act of worship.

We can pray and worship God in the midst of our activities, but there's also great benefit in turning off the noise and sitting in silence. A Desert Father, Ammonas, wrote, "Behold, my beloved. I have shown you the power of silence, how thoroughly it heals and how fully pleasing it is to God. . . . It is by silence that the saints grew . . . it was because of silence that the power of God dwelt in them, because of silence that the mysteries of God were known to them."[72]

God will never be outdone in generosity. When we offer Him the sacrifice of worship, we should have a holy expectancy that what He'll give in return will be worth any price. God longs to open the floodgates of heaven for us, to pour down upon us blessing without measure. Don't let anything get in the way of this. Sin, noise, and busyness all can block the flow of these gifts. Take some time to examine your heart, looking for anything that God is asking you to remove so that there is room for Him to give you what you need.

Dear Lord,
I am quieting my heart, and sitting with a spirit of expectancy. Please speak to me; I am listening. Amen.

SEPTEMBER 15

"Come, bless the Lord, all you servants of the Lord, who stand by night in the house of the Lord!" (Psalm 134:1)

It may seem strange to worship throughout the night. This is an image of offering God the sacrifice of praise in the midst of the darkness of our sorrows, and it isn't an easy thing to do. Nevertheless, as Scottish minister George Matheson writes below, this is the time when our faith is perfectly tested:

> It is easy for me to worship in the summer sunshine . . . But when the songbirds cease and the fruit falls from the trees, will my heart continue to sing? Will I remain in God's house at night? Will I love Him simply for who He is? Am I willing to "keep watch for one hour" (Mark 14:37) with Him in His Gethsemane? Will I help Him carry His cross up the road of suffering to Calvary? . . .
>
> If I can do these things, then my worship is complete and my blessing glorious. Then I have indeed shown Him love during the time of His humiliation. My faith has seen Him in His lowest state, and yet my heart has recognized His majesty through His humble disguise. And at last I truly know that I desire not the gift but the Giver. Yes, when I can remain in His house through the darkness of night and worship Him, I have accepted Him for Himself alone.[73]

How can we turn away from the One who gave everything to save us? What cost could be too great? How can we allow distractions to get in the way of offering God the worship He is due? And isn't it just like Him, the giver of all good things, to return with blessing upon blessing anything that we've lifted up to Him?

It is only during our lifetimes that we are able to offer God this gift of worship in the darkness.

Dear Lord,
It is easy to worship You when everything in my life is going well. But when circumstances are really hard, my desire to understand why can feel overpowering—yet I know that because of the Holy Spirit, it is possible for me to worship in spite of conflicting emotions. In my darkest days, the best I can offer is empty hands, lifted to You. But I know that You are pleased with my turning to You. You see this offering as the widow's mite. So I will not withhold it and turn away, no matter how grim my day and heavy my heart. Amen.

Be Still

SEPTEMBER 16

"The earth is the LORD's and the fulness thereof, the world and those who dwell therein." (Psalm 24:1)

There is an enormous difference between being an owner and being a steward. Because owners' resources belong to them, it's fully within their right to use them as they please. By contrast, stewards have been placed in charge of something that belongs to someone else. Good stewards are always aware of how the owner would like his or her resources used, and then they use them accordingly. Decisions are based on what the owner would prefer, not what feels pleasant to the steward.

While the world tells us that we own all we have, Scripture says that God is the real owner and we are the stewards. In 1 Corinthians 6:19–20, Saint Paul wrote, "Do you not know that . . . you are not your own; you were bought with a price." That price was Christ's own life. He gave it in exchange for our freedom. Everything we have is an undeserved gift from Him. One of the most precious of those gifts that God has entrusted to us is time; we are to steward it well.

Jesus described a faithful steward in the following way: "Who then is the faithful and wise steward, whom his master will set over his household, to give them their portion of food at the proper time? Blessed is that servant whom his master when he comes will find so doing" (Luke 12:42–43). A good steward is the one whom God finds doing the things that matter to the master. Take a look at the upcoming week on your calendar. What things in your schedule matter most to God?

God is all about relationships. This is important to keep in mind, or we can make the mistake of assuming that as long as we're serving God, He's pleased with how we are spending our time. God doesn't just want us to pour our time into serving Him and others. He wants us to cultivate a relationship with Him, which means spending time with Him in prayer. You may wonder exactly how much time He wants us to spend with Him. The answer? As much time as it takes to maintain intimacy.

Spending time with God should be the primary goal of each day. There's no better time to do this than at the start of the day, because once we get going, distractions start to fill our minds. We head off into the day, having decided to handle things on our own without the game-changing help of God's grace. This may not be a conscious decision, but regardless, it's the decision we've made. God is a gentleman and won't force Himself into our schedules. We need to invite Him in.

Dear Lord,
I rise before dawn and cry for help; I hope in Your words. Amen.

SEPTEMBER 17

Be Still

"Look carefully then how you walk, not as unwise men but as wise, making the most of the time." (Ephesians 5:15–16)

A time-management expert taught an important principle, beginning by placing a gallon-sized mason jar on a table. He filled it to the brim with fist-sized rocks, and then asked the class, "Is this jar full?" They all agreed it was. He disagreed, and proceeded to pour gravel into the jar. The gravel settled into the spaces between the rocks, and he posed his question again: "Is this jar full?" A little less certain this time, the students said the jar *was* full now. Shaking his head, he poured sand into the jar. The sand found little crevices, and proved that the jar still had room. "Is this jar full?" he asked yet again. The students felt it had to be—there wasn't any room left in the jar. Out came a pitcher of water, and it was added to the mixture in the jar. "What was the point of my illustration?" asked the expert.

An enthusiastic student said, "It makes the point that if we organize ourselves well and do the big things first, we can always fit in a little bit more!"

"No," said the time-management expert. "It means that if we don't put the big rocks in first, we'll never be able to fit them."

We all have limits. Every day, there will be things that we wish we could have done that are left unfinished. We can't always fit in a little bit more. A life well lived is made up of days when the things that are most important are done first and many good things remain undone. As businessman and author Stephen R. Covey wisely wrote, "The key is not to prioritize what's on your schedule, but to schedule your priorities."[74]

God deserves to be our highest priority. When we find that we've spent hours without paying any attention to Him, all we have to do is inwardly turn back to Him. We can pray, "I'm so sorry that my mind has been so far away from you! Thank You for being there for me even when I'm not paying attention. Help me to tune in to You as I go forward." We can practice the constant presence of God in any season of life.

"The main thing about Christianity is not the work we do, but the relationship we maintain and the atmosphere produced by that relationship. That is all God asks us to look after, and it is the one thing that is being continually assailed."
—Oswald Chambers, 1874–1917, Scottish preacher

Dear Lord,
May I make You the highest priority in my life, placing You at the helm and heart of it all. Amen.

Be Still

SEPTEMBER 18

"[God] has appointed a time for every matter, and for every work." (Ecclesiastes 3:17)

For most of us, there is more expected of us than we can possibly get done in a day. Distractions come and can easily cause us to lose sight of what is most important. Dorothy Haskin, author of *A Practical Guide to Prayer*, wrote the following story of a concert violinist who was asked the secret of her mastery of the instrument:

> The woman answered the question with two words: "Planned neglect." Then she explained. "There were many things that used to demand my time. When I went to my room after breakfast, I made my bed, straightened the room, dusted, and did whatever seemed necessary. When I finished my work, I turned to my violin practice. That system prevented me from accomplishing what I should on the violin. So I reversed things. I deliberately planned to neglect everything else until my practice period was complete. And that program of planned neglect is the secret of my success."[75]

Just like the concert violinist, we need to deliberately plan to neglect those nonessentials that get in the way of our doing what is most important. If we do not determine which of our activities are the most important and *do those first*, then we will make choices based on circumstances, pressure, and our current mood.

Whenever I get overwhelmed and am tempted to say that I do not have enough time, I tell myself, "There is enough time in the day to accomplish everything *God* wants me to do. If I am harried, it is because I am doing things that God has not asked of me." When I take the time to analyze why I am doing a certain activity, I often find that I am doing things because they are personal goals and I want to accomplish them for my glory, or I'm doing things that God doesn't expect of me so that people will think more highly of me, or I'm doing what I feel like doing because it's comfortable.

The key to figuring out where you should spend your time lies in your motivation and your priorities. Do things have eternal value? If you were to cut out certain activities, would you be able to find more time to do the things that really matter to you?

Dear Lord,
Help me to practice planned neglect and tend to the eternally important things first. Amen.

SEPTEMBER 19

"For God is at work in you, both to will and to work for his good pleasure." (Philippians 2:13)

Once we've made sure our priorities are on our calendar and have determined to make each minute in the day count, we often hit a barrier. *We don't feel like doing what we know is right.* Our will is powerful, and it can derail the best laid plans. Thankfully, God hasn't left us alone to battle our wills. He's placed the game-changing Holy Spirit into our hearts. The Holy Spirit gives strength to Christians, helping us to do what we should, even when we don't feel like it.

Who is the Holy Spirit? The Holy Spirit is not an impersonal force or a warm feeling. He is a divine person who has thoughts, emotions, and a will (Romans 15:30, Ephesians 4:30). He is the helper sent by God who advocates for us (John 15:26). He convicts us of sin (John 16:8), leads us (Romans 8:14), reveals truth to us (John 16:13), strengthens and encourages us (Acts 9:31), and comforts us (John 14:16).

Saint John Paul II shared his perspective on how the Holy Spirit gives strength to Christians:

> The Spirit intervenes with a deep, continuing action at every moment and under all aspects of Christian life in order to guide human desires in the right direction, which is the direction of generous love of God and neighbor, following the example of Jesus. For this purpose the Holy Spirit strengthens the will, making the person capable of resisting temptations and of gaining victory in internal and external struggles. The Spirit enables the Christian to overcome the power of evil and especially Satan, like Jesus who was led by the Spirit into the desert (cf. Luke 4:1) and of fulfilling the demands of a life according to the Gospel.[76]

The Holy Spirit is living and active. This means that He can move with the ups and downs and ebb and flow of our lives. Even when we feel that we are running at breakneck speed, He can keep up. But we want to get to a place where we are letting the Holy Spirit set the pace. We want to follow the Spirit's lead, rather than just asking Him to bless us in what we think is best.

Dear Lord,
I give You control of my calendar. Please lead me and set the pace. I want to keep in step with the Spirit instead of trying to run ahead of You. Amen.

Be Still

SEPTEMBER 20

"Come away by yourselves to a lonely place, and rest a while." (Mark 6:31)

The Holy Spirit is sometimes called the "gentle guest of our souls." One of the gifts that the Holy Spirit places within us is gentleness. God loves to see us draw on the Holy Spirit's gift of gentleness, which helps us to be kind to others even when our natural inclination is to be harsh. But God isn't only concerned about us treating *others* with gentleness. He wants us to treat *ourselves* gently. He sees us ruled by expectations, overload, and stress. We push ourselves as if we are limitless, but we are not. The Holy Spirit gives us the strength to do things we would have thought were impossible, but it's not for the purpose of our keeping an unhealthy schedule fueled by an inability to say no.

If we're going to treat ourselves gently, we'll need to learn to live with margin. Why are we so reluctant to carve out room for margin in our lives? How unhappy do we have to be with our schedules before we'll make choices that bring some relief? Part of the trouble lies in the fact that the pain caused by lack of margin isn't always manifested outwardly. It's something felt—an inner ache for something different or better. Because we can't always put our finger on the specific problem, we're slower to solve it.

Joshua 24:15 says, "Choose this day whom you will serve." Many of us are serving a harsh taskmaster and are enslaved to schedules driven by people-pleasing, performance, and an addiction to busyness. God is a gentle leader and is not the one demanding this relentless pace. Our schedules can become our idols.

Putting our schedules under God's control requires carving out some buffer time. This is because God desires our availability. How many of us have schedules so tight that there's no time for relationships? God may have a divine appointment planned—a person He wants to place in our path for their benefit and ours—but we rush by, late to the next appointment. God wants us to be available to walk the second mile with someone in need (Matthew 5:41). He asks us to always be ready with an explanation for the hope within us (1 Peter 3:15). He wants us to carry one another's burdens (Galatians 6:2). The people God wants us to meet are often unexpected; these meetings can't be scheduled. We need margin on the calendar so that we can be available to God. The other option is to tune out the needs around us. But in doing so, do we tune out God?

Dear Lord,
I choose this day to bow down to You instead of to my relentless schedule. Amen.

SEPTEMBER 21

"Observe the sabbath day, to keep it holy as the Lord your God commanded you. Six days you shall labor and do all your work; but the seventh day is a sabbath to the Lord your God; in it you shall not do any work . . ." (Deuteronomy 5:12–14)

For hundreds of years in Egypt, the Israelites had been forced to work without stopping. Their value was based entirely on their productivity. When God led them to the Promised Land, He began to teach them that their value wasn't based on what they produced; it was rooted in their identity as God's beloved children.

God gave the Israelites the Ten Commandments to help them learn to walk in freedom. These rules were intended to clarify which choices would lead them back to captivity and which would help them experience the liberty of being God's children. Honoring the Sabbath was a critical part of experiencing freedom.

In the words of author Susan K. Rowland, "The Jews' insistence on keeping their laws, especially the Sabbath law, has irritated despots and dictators down through history. Slave masters, whether ancient or modern, know that people who feel free to take one day out of seven to rest and pray, are people that are truly free the other six days of the week."[77]

The Ten Commandments weren't only for the Old Testament Israelites; we're to obey them, too. It's interesting that the Sabbath commandment is the only one that has to do with how we are to care for ourselves. And it's interesting how quickly we ignore it. A well-known philosopher and physician, Albert Schweitzer, said, "Do not let Sunday be taken from you. If your soul has no Sunday, it becomes an orphan."

Are you feeling the effects of a fast-paced life with no time to rest? Take some time now to talk to God about the way you usually spend Sunday. Is He calling you to rest? Talk to Him about the barriers that prevent you from stopping your work. Ask Him to help you walk in freedom as His daughter—one valued because of who she is, not what she does.

Dear Lord,
You have given me the Sabbath as a day when I can exhale and breathe deeply. Help me to establish a healthier rhythm, trusting that it doesn't all depend on me, and that You have everything under control. Amen.

SEPTEMBER 22

"Truly, I say to you, unless you turn and become like children, you will never enter the kingdom of heaven." (Matthew 18:3)

We were able to lose track of time as we played as children. But now that we're older, many of us have forgotten what brings us joy and delight. Our days have become full of activities, and in the midst of all the *do*ing, we have lost the art of *be*ing.

The result? We are losing track of who we really are. Too many of us are waiting for permission to stop. When illness or emotional collapse comes, we know we have no choice but to slow down. God is asking us to slow down and stop *now*, rather than waiting for crisis to hit. Slowing down gives us a chance to become, to invest in what delights us and makes us unique.

If we want to experience wholeness, then we need to build play into our week. This requires first identifying what we enjoy, what fills us, what causes us to lose track of time. When we figure out what those activities are, we need to put them on the calendar. Doing so will help us become like children, trusting that the Father is taking care of business while we rest and play. You are not God's workhorse; you are His child.

Well-loved children know how to play, and they delight in seeing their loving Father's face. We are told in 2 Corinthians 3:18 that as we behold the glory of our Father, we are being changed into His likeness. When we stop, rest, and delight in Him, we are becoming more and more like Christ. He is inviting each one of us to quiet down and enjoy His presence. This is where we'll find the space to become the women God is calling us to be.

In his sermon "On the Pure Love of God," Saint Augustine asked a probing question:

> Suppose God proposed to you a deal and said, 'I will give you anything you want. You can possess the whole world. Nothing will be impossible for you. . . . Nothing will be a sin, nothing forbidden. You will never die, never have pain, never have anything you do not want and always have anything you do want—except for just one thing: you will never see my face.'

> Did a chill rise in your hearts when you read the words "You will never see my face"? That chill is the most precious thing in you; that is the pure love of God.[78]

Dear Lord,
Please help my love of You to grow. May I slow down, learn to trust You like a child, and seek Your face. I want to rest in Your presence. Amen.

SEPTEMBER 23

"There is great gain in godliness with contentment; for we brought nothing into the world and we cannot take anything out of the world." (1 Timothy 6:6–7)

When our desires go unchecked, we soon discover that we are never satisfied. So many of us feel driven to keep achieving and acquiring. When something is accomplished, it seems the bar has simply moved and we have a new set of goals to shoot for. Sometimes we feel like it's a fight just to keep our heads above water. Stop working? Stop making money? Stop striving? It sounds impossible. But God speaks into our harried lives and invites us to a different way of living.

God's command that we honor the Sabbath is one of the ways He teaches us how to practice contentment. In the words of author Wayne Muller:

> Sabbath is a time to stop, to refrain from being seduced by our desires. To stop working, stop making money, stop spending money. See what you have. Look around. Listen to your life. Do you really need more than this? Spend a day with your family. Instead of buying the new coffee maker, make coffee in the old one and sit with your spouse on the couch, hang out—do what they do in the picture without paying for it. Just stop. That is, after all, what they are selling in the picture: people who have stopped. You cannot buy stopped. You simply have to stop.[79]

In her book *One Thousand Gifts*, Ann Voskamp reflects on a pastor's greatest life regret: "Being in a hurry. Getting to the next thing without fully entering the thing in front of me. I cannot think of a single advantage I've ever gained from being in a hurry. But a thousand broken and missed things, tens of thousands, lie in the wake of all the rushing. . . .Through all that haste I thought I was *making up time*. It turns out I was *throwing it away*."[80]

Dear Lord,
Help me to stop and grow in appreciation for what I already have. Amen.

Be Still

SEPTEMBER 24

"Remember the sabbath day, to keep it holy." (Exodus 20:8)

What did we lose when Sunday became a day just like every other day of the week? As Saint John Paul II said, "When Sunday loses its fundamental meaning and becomes merely a part of a 'weekend,' people stay locked within a horizon so limited that they can no longer see 'the heavens.'"[81]

We have got to learn how to live according to the rhythm we were created for. Our bodies are crying out for rest. Our relationships are longing for greater depth. Our emotions need a sabbatical. We are living wrong when all we want is for something to take the edge off, to help us disengage from our current reality. It's watching the clock for that point in the day when we can have a glass of wine to anesthetize our emotions. It's equating rest with entering into a life other than our own through television and books. It's filling our minds and feasting our eyes on things that we don't have but we want on the internet. That isn't really living. That's living numb.

Could it be that in being able to check more things off the to-do list, we lose something more important—time to take a walk with a friend, bringing that relationship to a deeper place?

Could it be that in being able to make more money by working more hours or sealing the big deal, we lose something more important—time to refresh our souls and hear God's guiding, comforting voice?

Could it be that what your child gains in being able to play on a more competitive sports team (which always seems to require Sunday attendance) means he or she loses something more important—downtime with a mother who can pass on her faith in an unrushed, natural way?

There's so much to lose, yet so much to gain if we obey God and accept His offer of rest. When we slow down, we can delight in the people whom God places in our paths. We'll be able to look at people—really look at them—and try to imagine who they truly are. What might their dreams be? Their hopes? Their hurts? Exhale and see.

The greatest benefit comes from spending our Sabbath day not just relaxing, but remembering that God is always beside us, enjoying the day and our presence.

Dear Lord,
You have said, "Come to me . . . and I will give you rest" [Matthew 11:28]. I am committing to obey the third commandment—to rest on the Sabbath. Give me the fortitude to follow through on this commitment. Amen.

SEPTEMBER 25

"If I then, your Lord and Teacher, have washed your feet, you also ought to wash one another's feet." (John 13:14)

One of the barriers to serving the Lord is our sense that for it to be worth it, we have to do some far-reaching, noteworthy task. As a result, we delay. We tell ourselves that we haven't said no to God, we're just waiting for the right opportunity to come along. Or perhaps we see the copious need in the world, and doubt that the little bit we could do would make much difference.

Theophan the Recluse, desiring to challenge and comfort a woman who was searching for purpose, wrote the following:

> If each one of us did what was possible to do for whoever was standing right in front of our eyes, instead of goggling at the community of mankind, then all people, in aggregate, would at each moment be doing that which is needed by those in need, and by satisfying their needs, would establish the welfare of all mankind, which is made up of haves and have-nots, the weak and the strong.[82]

Every day God places people directly in our paths, and He asks us to show our love for Him by actively loving them. Saint Teresa of Calcutta wisely observed, "Loneliness and the feeling of being unwanted is the most terrible poverty." Service to the *heart* of another person is a true sharing of the love of God. One of the most overlooked places where significant ministry can occur is in our homes. Real healing happens in the context of authentic, real relationships. When we invite someone into our personal space, despite the mess or perceived lack of beauty there, hearts open and connect.

God understands the things that keep us from serving our neighbor, but He loves us too much to let us remain content with such an isolated life. He encourages us to not get overwhelmed by the mountain of need in the world, and to grow in our sensitivity to His gentle nudges as He prods us to reach out to those He places in our path each day. In the words of Brother Lawrence, "We ought not to be weary of doing little things for the love of God, who regards not the greatness of the work, but the love with which it is performed."[83]

Dear Lord,
Take the blinders off my eyes so I see the needs around me. Help me to see interruptions in my day as opportunities to serve. I may never see how significant these little acts of kindness are, but You see. You know. And that is enough. Amen.

SEPTEMBER 26

"Abide in me, and I in you. As the branch cannot bear fruit by itself, unless it abides in the vine, neither can you, unless you abide in me." (John 15:4)

Jesus is the vine, and we are the branches. If we want our lives to bear fruit, our highest priority should be to abide in Him. When we do this, His grace courses through us and does in and through us what we could never do on our own.

Author Mary Poplin wrote *Finding Calcutta* after spending a period of time serving alongside Saint Teresa of Calcutta. She had this to say about this saintly woman's perspective on her calling and service:

> Saint Teresa of Calcutta often referred to herself as a "pencil in God's hand." She believed that everything she was able to do was done by God's power working through her. Many people perceive Saint Teresa of Calcutta as someone who looked out at the poor and responded to their suffering with her own kindness, love and energy. This is not at all how Mother saw her calling. When anyone complimented Saint Teresa of Calcutta, she would always say, "It is him, his work." She meant this literally—God did the work through her.[84]

The call we receive from Christ will always go beyond what we can do in our own strength. God has designed it this way to ensure that we don't turn our service for Him into a source of personal pride that draws our hearts far from Him.

God wants our service for Him to be what overflows from a heart filled with His grace. He pours in; we pour out. If we leave Him out of the picture, we'll settle for less than what we were created to do. We'll miss out on the abundant life He planned for each one of us personally.

There are specific works that God is calling each of His daughters to step out and do. We are His hands and feet in a broken world. But He insists that we not do this alone. Take a few moments to place your open hands in His.

Dear Lord,
Infuse me with all I need to answer Your call to serve. I trust that as I pray and ask You to fill me, You will come with power and strength. Come, Lord Jesus, come! Amen.

SEPTEMBER 27

"[Gideon] said, 'How can I deliver Israel? Behold, my clan is the weakest in Manasseh, and I am the least in my family.'" (Judges 6:15)

These words from Gideon were spoken at a time when the Israelites lived in constant fear and at risk of starvation, because the Midianites would attack at harvest time and completely ransack the harvest, leaving nothing behind. The attacks caused them to cry out to God, asking Him to rescue them. God chose Gideon as His instrument to defeat the enemy.

What was God's response to Gideon's feelings of inadequacy? He didn't say, "Come on, Gideon. You're so amazing! You just need to take a better look at all your talents and gifts!" He simply said, "I will be with you." God's presence is the game changer.

Once Gideon had established that God was truly calling him to step out to fight the Midianites, he gathered an army. But God felt that the army was too large, and He sent thousands home. The Israelites had gone from thirty-two thousand soldiers to ten thousand, but God continued to strip Gideon of resources. He kept cutting down the numbers until there were just three hundred soldiers left. Then He handed out the weapons—a trumpet, a jar, and a torch.

Gideon faced impossible odds. He couldn't think of a person less likely to lead his people to deliverance than himself. And God kept stripping things down even further so that to the human eye, victory looked utterly unattainable. But Gideon trusted God and His methods. The soldiers crept down to the outskirts of the enemy's camp, and at Gideon's command, they blew their trumpets and smashed their jars to the ground. Chaos ensued, and the enemy was defeated. The broken jars symbolized each soldier's brokenness before God. But out of that brokenness, God brought victory.

Be comforted by Gideon's story, because the principles in it are true for you as well. It is your very brokenness, your limitations, and your inadequacies that God will redeem and use for your benefit. This is what He does. He takes the little we have to offer and infuses it with His limitless power. Your brokenness is just the beginning of the story.

Don't look at the size of the mountain before you. All the resources needed to scale it belong to your heavenly Father, and He will shower them upon you and share them with you because He is crazy about you. Don't hold back. *Arise*, for the Lord has delivered victory into your hands.

Dear Lord,
I will keep my eyes on You—not the mountain. I ask You to turn my brokenness into victory.
Amen.

Be Still  **SEPTEMBER 28**

"Not that I complain of want; for I have learned, in whatever state I am, to be content." (Philippians 4:11)

Note that Saint Paul did not say, "I was born with an extraordinary ability to be content in the midst of suffering." He said, "I have learned." This should greatly encourage us. Contentment can be learned. It doesn't depend on our circumstances. No matter where we are, regardless of our track record, we can grow in the area of contentment.

Lack of purpose is a barrier to contentment. When we don't know why we are here on earth, we often seek fulfilment and purpose in the wrong places. Sometimes we experience discontent because we don't seem to be doing anything that really matters. This can discourage us, causing us to settle for mediocrity instead of the great purpose God created us for. Other times we experience discontent because we *have* measured up and achieved our goals, but they were the wrong goals. We now realize that having achieved them doesn't satisfy us the way we expected. Contentment is intricately tied to recognizing the *true* purpose of our existence and spending our time accordingly. To discover it, we must start with the One who created us.

What is the purpose of your life? It's bigger than personal fulfilment, feeling an inner peace, or being happy. It's bigger than raising a family or having a career. Your purpose here on earth is to know God and become more like Him. Every longing, disappointment, and circumstance needs to be filtered through that truth. "The desire for God is written in the human heart, because man is created by God and for God; and God never ceases to draw man to himself. Only in God will he find the truth and happiness he never stops searching for" (CCC 27).

Contentment comes when we know we're living right in the middle of God's will. When we are able to look at all our circumstances as a means to fulfill our true purpose—knowing God and becoming more like Him—we are able to go through life thankfully. Our circumstances don't change, but our perspective does.

Dear Lord,
I offer You this area of discontent: _____. Will You please achieve Your purpose for me through this difficulty? I want to know You and become more like You. May my suffering not be wasted. Amen.

SEPTEMBER 29

"Therefore do not be anxious about tomorrow, for tomorrow will be anxious for itself. Let the day's own trouble be sufficient for the day." (Matthew 6:34)

Anxiety grips our emotions, harms our health, and leads our thoughts down a path that culminates in fear. Often we feel we can't get out from under our anxious thoughts, which take on a life of their own as we imagine worst-case scenarios. These thoughts omit God from the picture. In the words of author Linda Dillow, "Anxiety is that which divides and distracts the soul, that which diverts us from present duty to weary calculations of how to meet conditions that may never arrive. It's the habit of crossing bridges before we reach them."[85]

God goes ahead of us. In His timelessness, He is already in our tomorrows. There is nothing we will face that He has not evaluated before He allows it to touch us. And He promises that He'll never allow us to face things that are beyond our ability to bear, provided we lean on Him for grace.

When an anxious thought comes into our minds, we have a choice regarding how we will respond. Will we play with it? Will we travel with it into the future in our imaginations? Or will we stop it in its tracks, grab hold of the thought, and offer it to Christ? This is what is meant by 2 Corinthians 10:5: "Take every thought captive to obey Christ." We take it captive by replacing the worry with a truth that builds our trust in God.

Read the following words from the devotional *Jesus Calling* as if they were Jesus' words to you:

> Anxiety is the result of envisioning the future without Me. So the best defense against worry is staying in communication with Me. When you turn your thoughts toward Me, you can think much more positively. Remember to listen, as well as to speak, making your thoughts a dialogue with Me.
>
> If you must consider upcoming events, follow these rules: 1) Do not linger in the future, because anxieties sprout like mushrooms when you wander there. 2) Remember the promise of My continual Presence, include Me in any imagery that comes to mind. This mental discipline does not come easily, because you are accustomed to being a god of your fantasies. However, the reality of My Presence with you, now and forevermore, outshines any fantasy you could ever imagine.[86]

Dear Lord,
Help me to discipline my mind to stay in the present moment. But when I need to think about the future, may I always do so with a picture of You in the midst of anything I might face. Amen.

Be Still

SEPTEMBER 30

"And the whole congregation of the people of Israel murmured against Moses and Aaron in the wilderness, and said to them, 'Would that we had died by the hand of the Lord in the land of Egypt, when we sat by the fleshpots and ate bread to the full.'" (Exodus 16:2–3)

The book of Exodus describes the Israelites' four hundred years of slavery in Egypt. They were mistreated terribly and cried out to God. God sent them a rescuer, Moses, who led them out of Egypt and toward true freedom. The memories of God's mind-blowing miracles should have stayed fresh in their minds, but travel to the Promised Land proved to be a little tougher than they'd expected. There was nothing to eat or drink.

God met the Israelites in their place of need and provided manna for them to eat as they wandered in the wilderness. The problem was, that was *all* He provided. And they got sick of manna. Manna for breakfast, lunch, and dinner got pretty old. They began thinking Egypt hadn't been so bad and started to complain again.

In essence, the Israelites shook their fists at God and said, "We were better off when we didn't know you!" We might be shocked by how quickly they failed to remember God's goodness, but aren't we often guilty of the same forgetfulness?

When we find ourselves stuck in circumstances that we want to escape, we can wrongly conclude that nothing good can happen there. We look back, or fantasize about a different life, and we see fertile ground where great things could grow. Then we look at our current place and see barrenness, loss, heaviness. When we're in these stuck places, we have to guard our hearts, because there is something about those circumstances that can lead us to conclude that we would be better off without God. And nothing could be further from the truth.

The truth is, when we are stuck, we are deep in fertile ground. This is rich soil for transformation and growth. It's in this place that we can see God's provision and care for us in a whole new way. He may not provide an emergency exit from our problems; He may instead give us the grace to keep walking through them, day by day, hour by hour, minute by minute. Regardless of how He provides, He will be faithful. And we will see Him in a whole new light, and be forever changed because of it—if we cooperate. If we trust.

Dear Lord,
Help me to see a new facet of who You are through my current circumstances. Amen.

October

Be firm, steadfast, always fully devoted to the work of the Lord, knowing that in the Lord your labor is not in vain. 1 Corinthians 15:58

OCTOBER 1

Feast Day of Saint Thérèse of Lisieux

"Those who seek the Lord lack no good thing." (Psalm 34:10)

I've noticed something interesting about what gets me *on* and what gets me *off* of social media. Boredom gets me on, and I can lose track of time as I scroll mindlessly. What gets me off social media is discontent. I see something or someone that makes me feel bad, less than, or inadequate, so I turn it off. I think I could be spending my time a little better than this.

I'm reminded by Theodore Roosevelt that "comparison is the thief of joy." I'm tired of allowing my happiness to be robbed by something so preventable. We all know that everything presented on social media is the curated and filtered version. So why do we get caught in the trap of comparing our worst with others' best? Because who really knows what's behind that perfect picture on Facebook? Photos don't show the whole story.

Underlying our discontent is the sense that there is something better out there, and the belief that if we had it we'd be happier. But if you look back on your life, isn't it true that as soon as you get that one thing you've been dreaming of, a new desire takes its place? The appetite for more is never satisfied.

There is a different way to live. God created you as a one-of-a-kind, creative, difference-making masterpiece. Yes, you. You are not the exception to the rule. Don't equate that description with success in your career, breathtaking Instagram photos, or accolades. Being a world changer simply means that you take seriously the call to run *your* race without looking to the left or right and comparing yourself to others. It means trusting that you are exactly where you are meant to be, and being faithful right there.

The baton has been passed to you, and if you refuse to run, the world will miss out on the unique gifts you have to offer.

Today is the feast day of a woman who ran her race well: Saint Thérèse of Lisieux, the patron saint of Walking with Purpose. Instead of comparing herself to others, she trusted that God had her exactly where she was meant to be. She flourished in that place, despite its limitations and suffering. May we cultivate content hearts like hers.

"May you trust God that you are exactly where you are meant to be."
—Saint Thérèse of Lisieux

Dear Lord,
Help me to trust that I am exactly where I am meant to be. Amen.

Be Still  **OCTOBER 2**

"By his great mercy we have been born anew to a living hope . . . and to an inheritance which is imperishable, undefiled, and unfading, kept in heaven for you . . ." (1 Peter 1:3–4)

In the words of C. S. Lewis:

> If we consider the unblushing promises of reward and the staggering nature of the rewards promised in the Gospels, it would seem that our Lord finds our desires not too strong, but too weak. We are half-hearted creatures, fooling about with drink and sex and ambition when infinite joy is offered us, like an ignorant child who wants to go on making mudpies in a slum because he cannot imagine what is meant by an offer of a holiday at the sea. We are far too easily pleased.[87]

We find it hard to delay immediate gratification in order to gain a better eternity because of our poor understanding of what heaven will be like. In heaven, we will all be able to see God, and this will fill us with indescribable joy. But we will not all experience the same level of happiness in heaven. In the words of Frank Sheed:

> This happiness, though total for each, will not be equal in all. Will and intellect will be working at their highest, with no element in them unused or unfed. But how high will my highest or yours be? As high as our co-operation with grace in this life has made it. It is in this life that the soul grows; every piece of truth, every channel of grace, can be used by us, if we will, for growth. Whatever capacity the soul has grown to at death, that capacity will be filled in the glory and the joy of heaven.[88]

Never forget that a part of your inheritance is experienced on earth. It is "the immeasurable greatness of his power in us who believe, according to the working of his great might, which he accomplished in Christ when he raised him from the dead and made him sit at his right hand in the heavenly places, far above all rule and authority and power and dominion, and above every name that is named, not only in this age but also in that which is to come" (Ephesians 1:19–21).

Think about the resurrection power that was strong enough to raise Jesus from the dead. That's the power He offers us every day. This power can help us say no to immediate gratification when something greater will be gained through resisting temptation.

Dear Lord,
Forgive me for settling for mud pies. May my heart be filled with awareness of all You've given me and gratitude for the way You love me with abandon. Amen.

OCTOBER 3

"God has no other reason for creating than his love and goodness: 'Creatures came into existence when the key of love opened his hand.'" (CCC 293)

You are so dearly loved. It was God's personal love for you that caused Him to call you into existence. You are here on earth to experience a journey that originates in His hand (opened with the key of love), reflects that love throughout a lifetime, and then returns to His embrace in heaven.

Our purpose on earth is to prepare for the place where we'll experience the deepest contentment. "For here we have no lasting city, but we seek the city which is to come" (Hebrews 13:14). Through the riches of Christ Jesus, we have been given everything we need to make that journey.

And what a vision is waiting for us there! What fullness we'll experience when we come face-to-face with our rescuer. There we'll find that "the Lamb in the midst of the throne will be [our] shepherd, and he will guide [us] to springs of living water; and God will wipe away every tear from [our] eyes" (Revelation 7:17).

What are our rescuer's words for us today, when we are in the midst of this journey? Personalize these words from the book of Revelation: "I know your works. Behold, I have set before you an open door, which no one is able to shut; I know that you have but little power, and yet you have kept my word and have not denied my name. . . . Because you have kept my word of patient endurance, I will keep you from the hour of trial. . . . I am coming soon; hold fast what you have, so that no one may seize your crown" (Revelation 3:8–11).

Dear Lord,
I hold fast to You as the All-Sufficient One. May Your fullness fill me. True contentment is found in You, so I look to You for all I need. Amen.

Be Still

OCTOBER 4

"For God is not a God of confusion but of peace." (1 Corinthians 14:33)

We live in a time when simplicity seems elusive. Even when we agree that less is more, we feel overwhelmed at the thought of paring down. Simplifying takes time, and our schedules are one of the many things that need to be simpler.

How can we hear God over the noise? How can we find Him through the clutter? Could it be that we don't have much room for God because we're so full of everything else?

Have we bought into the American dream that true happiness comes from pursuing prosperity and success—and that it is our right? Are we so full of comfort, self-focus, and stuff (the buying of it, the taking care of it, and then the updating of it) that there is no room, no sacred space to behold God's greatness and glory? So we keep Him small so He fits into the little compartment in our lives that we've allocated to Him, and we head into the rat race.

Before we give up and assume that simplicity is never going to be possible for us, let's remember who is in control. We read in Acts 17:26 that when God made us, He determined the times set for us and the exact places where we would live. When and where we live is no mistake. And why did God pick this particular time in history and this place geographically for each one of us? We find the answer in Acts 17:27. He tailor-made each of our circumstances, "that [we] should seek God, in the hope that [we] might feel after him and find him. Yet he is not far from each one of us."

If all of this is a part of God's plan, then we can take heart. We can find hope. God knows what we're up against. He never asks anything of us that He doesn't equip us to accomplish.

God doesn't want us to simplify our lives so they are empty and boring. He wants us to clear space so that we can know Him more. Not only that, He wants us to *enjoy* Him. There is so much in creation and so much He puts in our days just to delight us. If we're rushing around, we're going to miss it.

A simplified life leaves room for joy. There's time to be gentle. There's margin. There's sacred space for God. A simplified life, a magnified God. Less of me, and more of Him.

Dear Lord,
Please help me simplify my life so I can discover the deeper pleasures You desire to give me. Amen.

OCTOBER 5

"Then Jesus told his disciples, 'If any man would come after me, let him deny himself and take up his cross and follow me.'" (Matthew 16:24)

What does it mean to deny ourselves? Does it mean that who we are (our personalities, interests, and unique qualities) doesn't matter and should be squelched? No. God created us, and He delights in who we are. But it does mean that we take our eyes off ourselves and put them on others. We let go of the need to be right, the need to be understood, the need to be comfortable, the need to have every craving satisfied.

This is done on a moment-by-moment basis. Each moment, we try to become conscious of what we are focusing on. Are we motivated by our own wants, or are we seeking to please God and do what He wants? Some call this "dying to self."

There's no better time to begin than right now. Each day, we can look for an opportunity to die to self. It could be not becoming defensive when someone questions us. Or saying no to some material comfort so that another person can be blessed. Or passing up an evening glass of wine so that we feel fresher in the morning and are more able to get up early to pray. What dying to self looks like in each of our lives will be unique. The important thing is to take the first step, "for whoever loses [her] life for [Christ's] sake will find it" (Matthew 16:25).

Christ does not ask anything of us that He has not already done. As we read in 2 Corinthians 5:15, "[Christ] died for all." The verse continues by telling us how Christians should respond: "that those who live might live no longer for themselves but for him." Denying ourselves for the Lord's sake goes against our natural instincts, and the only way we'll be able to do it is by fixing our eyes on Him, taking the time to behold His glory. But in order to behold God's glory, we have to let go of our own. And this, my friend, is hard to do. This is radical living. It involves abandoning all sorts of behaviors that we are quite comfortable with.

If we want to behold God's glory and there's no room, no sacred space for Him—if we're keeping Him small in our lives—there's just one solution: less of us and more of God.

Dear Lord,
What would less of me and more of You look like in my life? Please reveal to me how I can be freed from self-focus and fix my eyes on You. Amen.

Be Still

 OCTOBER 6

"One of the multitude said to [Jesus], 'Teacher, bid my brother divide the inheritance with me.'... And he said to them, 'Take heed, and beware of all covetousness; for a man's life does not consist in the abundance of his possessions.'" (Luke 12:13–14)

When the man brought his request to Jesus, Jesus didn't fix the problem. Instead, He drew attention to the issue in the man's heart. Jesus challenged him to explore his motives. When we present our problems to God, we're usually looking for a quick fix, and God often responds to us as He did to the man in Luke 12. Why? He is concerned with our steady growth and transformation on the heart level.

When we're longing for a simpler life, we might call out to God in prayer, asking Him to relieve the stress. Sometimes He does, but more often, He asks us to look within and explore why we continue to make decisions that get in the way of our pursuit of simplicity. The problem isn't "out there." It's in our hearts.

Jesus continued by telling the man a parable. He described a rich man financially planning for his life before death. With so many possessions and nowhere to go with them, the man concluded that building more barns to store it all would fix the problem. God's response to the man: "Fool! This night your soul is required of you; and the things you have prepared, whose will they be?" (Luke 12:20).

Can you see any parallels between the rich man's building of barns and the amount of time we put into caring for and updating our possessions? What causes us to consume at such an alarming rate? Why are we able to justify buying luxuries when others lack basic necessities?

Meditate on the following excerpt from Jen Hatmaker's book *7* and respond to God in prayer. Ask Him if He's calling you to have a different attitude toward your possessions, and how that attitude should translate into action.

> A child says "me." An adult says "us." Maturity deciphers need from want, wisdom from foolishness. Growing up means curbing appetites, shifting from "me" to "we," understanding private choices have social consequences and public outcomes. Let's be consumers who silence the screaming voice that yells, "I WANT!" and instead listens to the quiet "we need," the marginalized voice of the worldwide community we belong to.[89]

Dear Lord,
Help me to decipher my needs from my wants, and to stop trying to fill the void within me with more possessions. May I turn to You instead. Amen.

OCTOBER 7

"In returning and rest you shall be saved; in quietness and in trust shall be your strength." (Isaiah 30:15)

Isn't this the opposite of what we usually hear? We're told that we get ahead through our own hard work and tenacity. As life speeds up and gets noisy, we are terrified of the consequences of slowing and quieting down. But God promises us that it's exactly in the quiet that we'll be strengthened and saved.

What would it take for you to fully embrace simplicity? What kinds of changes would need to be made? Unquestionably, these sorts of changes require courage. It seems so much safer to just keep going, doing the same thing day after day. Maybe we lack the courage to make radical changes because we can't picture how amazing life would feel if it all became simpler.

What are we missing out on in the complexity of our lives? With all the hurry, multitasking, and anxiety, are we settling for superficial relationships, meaningless activity, and lack of peace? In the words of musician Audrey Assad, "Love moves slow." But we rush past, and the opportunities to love are lost.

It all begins with small choices: the decision to say no to things that might be good but will complicate our lives to a degree that we'll lose inner peace; the decision to live with margin in our use of time, our emotions, our finances, our relationships; the decision to stop pursuing the life that the world promises will bring us satisfaction, and instead pursue the things that God says matter most.

God will give us the grace for that first small step. As we obey, the grace will continue to be poured into us, and we'll discover that God is providing us the strength we need to swim upstream to a better life, a different ending.

Take a few moments to sit quietly before God. This could be in an adoration chapel (the quiet is truly restorative) or in your own home. Turn off the phone, the music, the television. Still your voice and listen instead. Focus on your breathing. Slow down. Just be available to God.

Dear Lord,
Help me to slow down. I am listening. Amen.

Be Still

 **OCTOBER 8**

"When [Jesus] had ceased speaking, he said to Simon, 'Put out into the deep and let down your nets for a catch.'" (Luke 5:4)

"The way Jesus shows you is not easy. Rather, it is like a path winding up a mountain. Do not lose heart! The steeper the road, the faster it rises towards ever wider horizons. May Mary, Star of Evangelization, guide you! Docile like her to the Father's will, take the stages of history as mature and convincing witnesses."[90]
—Saint John Paul II

The path to holiness will never be the easier one. Temptations to go back to the simpler road will be offered to you in the very moment when you most need to dig in and press forward. But if we refuse to settle for mediocrity, there will be no limit to the impact of your life. God will be able to work in and through you, and the pages of history being written in your lifetime will be changed.

When we are willing to stand as Christians despite the possible unpopularity of our beliefs, we move on to a platform of influence. We are being observed, and a watching world looks at our lives to see if Jesus makes much of a difference. If we refuse to shrink back, if instead we press closer to Christ, then He infuses us with supernatural strength to persevere. People around us will find it hard to deny the power of God when we are able to respond in ways that are not our natural bent.

Are you naturally critical? You evangelize when you stay silent or say something positive.
Do you naturally dominate a conversation? You evangelize when you listen well.
Are you naturally a worrier? You evangelize when you pray instead of talk about your fears.
Are you naturally timid? You evangelize when you speak up.
Are you naturally driven toward perfection in yourself and others? You evangelize when you give yourself and others grace.

When we ask God to transform our natural reactions into holy responses, people around us recognize that we are putting God above our own desires. We are acknowledging the supremacy of Jesus over our own comfort and wishes. Can you see how different it would be if we proclaimed the greatness of Jesus not so much through our words about Him as by our obedience to Him?

Dear Lord,
Instead of running back to the easy path when obedience is costly, I want to answer Your call in Luke 5:4 to "put out into deep water." May my radical obedience draw a watching world to You. Amen.

OCTOBER 9

"[Jesus] is not ashamed to call them 'brothers.'" (Hebrews 2:11)

"Jesus is God, but he humbled himself to walk with us. He is our friend, our brother." —Pope Francis

In order to fully appreciate what it means for Jesus to be our brother, we should never lose sight of the fact that He is God. At any moment during His time on earth, He could have called down legions of angels to rescue Him, yet He endured the worst suffering imaginable to come to our rescue. Why was He willing to do this?

He was falsely accused and condemned so we could be declared not guilty.
He was bound so that we could be set free.
He was given a crown of thorns so that we could receive the crown of life.
He was flogged so that we could be embraced and held.
He was stripped of His clothing so we could wear His robe of righteousness.
His arms were stretched open on the cross so that no one would be past the reach of His mercy.
His hands were nailed to the cross so our hands could receive the riches of divine grace.
He was separated from the Father so we could be ushered into the throne room of God.
He absorbed our sin so we could be filled with His divinity.
He was pieced with a spear in His side so we could draw near to His heart.

The best response to the mercy and faithfulness of Jesus is to follow the path of the spear, and connect with His heart. It's through intimacy with Jesus that we discover there is no enemy He hasn't conquered already. There's no trial we face that He hasn't endured. There is no cross we carry that He doesn't carry alongside us.

You are never alone. You are beloved. You are rescued. You are free. You are saved by your brother, your captain, your king.

Dear Lord,
May I never lose sight of what You sacrificed and endured for my sake. Thank You for being a big brother who comes to my rescue and never leaves me undefended. Amen

Be Still

OCTOBER 10

"But if you are patient when you suffer for doing what is good, this is a grace before God."
(1 Peter 2:20)

Is there something that God is asking you to patiently suffer and surrender? Is it possible that as hard as it is to surrender, doing so could usher in the grace that you so desperately desire?

There is no limit to the miracles that God can do in our lives. But we hamper His efforts when we cling to our own plans, desires, dreams, and worries. God works best when our hands are open and ready to receive.

Surrendering to God is hard. He understands this, so for Him, our letting go is the greatest gift we can offer Him. Father Wilfrid Stinissen describes it this way:

> If we are subject to trials here on earth, if we must struggle to say Yes to God, it is because in eternity, God wants to say to us: "You have given me something. It is not only I who give, but rather we give to each other. I give myself in gratitude because you have given me something that you could have refused to give. Now you can no longer give me anything, but at one time you did, and it has an eternal value. I never forget."[91]

The time to give these gifts to God is now. In heaven, we'll no longer have the opportunity. Our immediate sufferings, the very things we most want to change, are the perfect opportunity for us to let go and surrender to God's will. Yes, this is costly. But God is never outdone in generosity. As we are promised in 2 Timothy 2:11, "If we have died with him we shall also live with him." Real life, true freedom, and joy are not found in perfect circumstances. They're found in the release of control, the unclenched fist, the surrender, the fiat.

Let's allow our shoulders to relax. May we surrender to His hands, and let God move our heads and hearts, directing us where He deems best. In the words of Fr. Stinissen, "God is like a specialist in relaxation who works with the patient's head, turning it in different directions. The fact that it causes pain is not the specialist's fault. He does not turn it too far. No, it is because the patient's neck muscles are tense."[92] We tense up when we carry the weight of the world on our shoulders, mistakenly thinking it's all up to us.

Dear Lord,
I release control to You, the only One who has the power to bring the miracle, raise the dead, and usher in hope. Amen.

OCTOBER 11

"Say to all the people of the land and the priests, 'When you fasted and mourned in the fifth month and in the seventh, for these seventy years, was it for me that you fasted? And when you eat and when you drink, do you not eat for yourselves and drink for yourselves?'" (Zechariah 5:6–7)

If certain foods or eating habits have a hold on us, then we need something to help us break through to a place of freedom. Fasting is a wonderful spiritual tool that can release God's power and loosen the shackles of irresistible cravings. The practice of fasting flies in the face of a culture that insists that every single desire we feel should be satisfied.

We shouldn't fast to mindlessly and heartlessly follow a rule. The purpose of a spiritual fast shouldn't be to lose weight, either. In fasting, as in all things, our motives matter. When we fast, we are getting rid of excess and making space for God. Our focus needs to be on Him, not on the secondary benefits of fasting.

When we fast, a space is created that allows us to hear God better. It gives Him the room to reveal things to us that we desperately need to learn. This benefit of fasting is described by Richard Foster in his book *Celebration of Discipline*:

> More than any other discipline, fasting reveals the things that control us. This is a wonderful benefit to the true disciple who longs to be transformed into the image of Christ. We cover up what is inside us with food and other good things, but in fasting these things surface. If pride controls us, it will be revealed almost immediately. David writes, "I humbled my soul with fasting" (Ps. 69:10). Anger, bitterness, jealousy, strife, fear—if they are within us, they will surface during fasting. At first we will rationalize that our anger is due to our hunger; then we will realize that we are angry because the spirit of anger is within us. We can rejoice in this knowledge because we know that healing is available through the power of Christ.[93]

Dear Lord,
I want to experience freedom. These are the things that hold me back from fasting: [share them with Him]. I ask You to give me Your mind and thoughts on the matter of fasting, and to help me keep my motives pure when I fast. Amen.

Be Still  **OCTOBER 12**

"A man without self-control is like a city broken into and left without walls." (Proverbs 25:28)

Self-control is absolutely foundational to growing in balance. If we lack this essential trait, our lives will continually be out of kilter. We'll become enslaved to our passions and desires, and easy targets for temptation.

Without it, we stay in our cozy beds instead of getting up to pray.
Without it, we skip Mass when Sunday looks too busy.
Without it, we avoid confession like the plague, because we don't like talking about our sins.
Without it, we watch TV or surf the internet instead of reading the Bible.
Without it, we do what feels fun, comfortable, easy, and relaxing instead of what's good for us.
Without it, our thoughts run wild and the worries of tomorrow rob today of its joy.

Self-control is like a muscle that is built up by many small decisions to say no to what we feel like doing or thinking and yes to what we know is best and right. Exercising self-control strengthens the intellect so it can rule over the will.

Focusing on self-control is not without pitfalls, however. As we grow in our ability to make decisions based on what we know to be right instead of what we feel like doing, we'll be tempted to credit ourselves with this progress. This is the fatal mistake of thinking that all we've accomplished has been due to our own strength and ability. This was the error made by a British monk named Pelagius (AD 354–420), who denied original sin and insisted that if a man knew what was good, he could become self-controlled through sheer determination. Pelagius was denounced as a heretic at the Council of Carthage in AD 418. Vestiges of this heresy remain in our belief that all we need to live a self-controlled life is willpower. Nothing could be further from the truth. Any progress we make is due to God's work in us. Self-help books that leave God out of the picture fall into this trap.

Another pitfall is to view self-control as an end in itself. Self-control is not the goal of the Christian life. Our goal is growing in our relationship with Christ and becoming more like Him.

God wants to work within us to make us holy, but He won't force Himself on us. Self-control gets us into a position of opening our hearts to God's power and strength so that He can work in and through us.

Dear Lord,
Help me to grow in self-control, making the small decisions that will put me in a position for You to accomplish in me far more than I could ask or imagine. Amen.

OCTOBER 13

"About this we have much to say which is hard to explain, since you have become dull of hearing. For though by this time you ought to be teachers, you need some one to teach you again the first principles of God's word. You need milk, not solid food." (Hebrews 5:11–12)

It was difficult for the writer of Hebrews to lead his readers to a place of spiritual maturity because they had picked up the bad habit of not listening. Perhaps the truth seemed boring. Maybe they were feeling apathetic toward their faith. This sluggishness put them in a dangerous position. In 2 Timothy 4:3–4 we read that when people become dull of hearing, they "will not endure sound teaching, but having itching ears they will accumulate for themselves teachers to suit their own likings, and will turn away from listening to the truth."

A diet of milk is necessary for a baby. In that same way, someone new to his or her faith needs to be taught the basics. The author of Hebrews was talking to people who needed to progress and graduate to solid food. By this point, his listeners should have been teachers.

The story is told of an experienced teacher who applied for a promotion after twenty-five years in the classroom. She was passed over for a teacher with only one year of experience. Frustrated, she asked the principal why. The principal replied, "You haven't actually had twenty-five years of experience, as you claimed. You've actually had only one year of experience twenty-five times." Sadly, the same thing can often be said for many Christians.

While we all will not have equal teaching ability, all Christians should be able to pass on their faith. Everyone who has encountered Christ in a life-changing way has something to share. When we do nothing because we can't figure out what to say, we are missing an opportunity to grow. If we step out and share the difference Christ has made in our lives, we will be stretched and we will mature. Sometimes we'll make mistakes, which we'll learn from, and that's OK. What's not OK is to not bother trying.

We will stagnate in the spiritual life if we fail to apply the lessons we have been taught. Is there a lesson God has taught you, but you have failed to apply to your life? What is something specific you can do to discipline yourself to act on that lesson? Can you commit to *do it now*, instead of putting it off for later?

Dear Lord,
Please shed light on any areas of spiritual immaturity in my life. Help me to desire the truth, even when it isn't what I want to hear. Amen.

OCTOBER 14

"So the men partook of their provisions, and did not ask direction from the Lord." (Joshua 9:14)

Anytime we read that someone didn't ask direction from the Lord, it's likely that things aren't going to turn out well. In this case, God had told the Israelites to destroy the enemies living around them. One of those neighboring enemies came up with a survival plan: dressing up as weary travelers, coming to the Israelites as if they lived far away, and asking for a treaty. They *looked* like they'd traveled far with their moldy bread, torn shoes, and worn-out clothes. Because it *seemed* like the right thing to do, the leaders figured they could just go with their gut and make the treaty. They later greatly regretted skipping the step of asking God for His opinion when they realized that they'd been conned.

In our own lives, we face countless decisions of greater and lesser importance. Decision fatigue can cause us to either avoid making decisions or make hasty ones just to get it done. Unmade decisions weigh on the soul and suck the energy out of us. How can we be decisive and move forward? What's the balance between going with our gut and waiting for a signal from God?

It all starts with what we think of God, what kind of a Father we believe Him to be. If we think He hides His will from us, we'll probably give up before consulting Him. But if we believe Him to be a good Father, one who doesn't play games with us and wants to guide us, we'll be far more likely to go to Him for direction.

Discernment can feel like groping in the darkness, but there are some lights we can switch on to dispel the shadows. One light is God's perspective. We find out what that is by reading Scripture and learning what the Church teaches, praying, and asking Him to reveal His will to us. Often we are trying to figure something out, and God has already given the answer. Another light is the advice of godly people. When you are facing a decision, pay attention to whom you are listening to. Is it someone living a moral life who will be willing to speak the truth in love, or is it a friend who always tells you what you want to hear? The third light is your gut. This is the sense of inner peace or unrest that you feel. Turn all three of these lights on to dispel the darkness.

Dear Lord,
You are just as concerned with who I am during the decision-making process as You are with what I ultimately choose to do. I promise to go to You for direction with an attitude of trust. Amen.

OCTOBER 15

"Every athlete exercises self-control in all things. They do it to receive a perishable wreath, but we an imperishable one." (1 Corinthians 9:25)

Growing in self-control starts with little decisions that have big consequences. Developing the following habits strengthens our ability to make those smart choices:

- Do the hard things first. Procrastination is a barrier to self-discipline. Force yourself to set aside the pleasurable (often lower-priority) tasks and get the tough stuff out of the way.
- Be on time. When we're rushing around, we're more apt to make decisions based on convenience rather than what is wisest or best.
- Follow through. Strive to finish whatever project you start. Switch-tasking (switching back and forth between two tasks) will get in the way of this goal. It's inefficient and often means that two tasks are done halfway instead of one being done thoroughly.
- Be faithful to your word. This requires being careful about what you commit to. Before making the commitment, carefully consider what your yes will involve. Do you have what it takes to follow through and be faithful to your word?
- Keep your eye on the goal. Nothing gets in the way of this like our desire to be entertained. Let entertainment be your reward for a job well done, not the one thing in your day you refuse to give up.

In the words of Saint Paul, "I have fought the good fight, I have finished the race, I have kept the faith. From now on there is laid up for me the crown of righteousness, which the Lord, the righteous judge, will award to me on that Day, and not only to me but also to all who have loved his appearing" (2 Timothy 4:7–8). When he wrote those words, Saint Paul was facing death. The way he had lived prepared him for a beautiful eternity. His life was the compilation of countless small decisions—decisions to do what he knew to be right even if it didn't feel good in the moment. He lived purposefully, knowing that his time on earth was so short compared to eternity. Any pain on earth was worth his heavenly reward.

Dear Lord,
Please give me insight into how my decisions today are preparing me for heaven. Amen.

Be Still

OCTOBER 16

"Another said, 'I will follow you, Lord; but let me first say farewell to those at my home.' Jesus said to him, 'No one who puts his hand to the plow and looks back is fit for the kingdom of God.'" (Luke 9:61–62)

Gary Player, an incredibly successful international golfer, had lost count of how many times someone said to him, "I'd give anything if I could hit a golf ball like you." He usually gave a polite thank-you and moved on. But on a particularly hard day, he gave the more candid reply, "No, you wouldn't. You'd give anything to hit a golf ball like me, if it were easy." He then went on to explain the cost of his success: "You've got to get up at five o'clock in the morning, go out and hit a thousand golf balls, walk up to the club house to put a bandage on your hand where it started bleeding, then go and hit another thousand golf balls. That's what it takes to hit a golf ball like me."[94]

 How often do we do the same in the spiritual life? We look at someone who is a spiritual giant in our eyes and wish that we'd had her parents, or her advantages, or her knowledge. What we fail to see is the many small decisions she's made in secret that have cost her something. We see the end result. The saint knows the sacrifice that got her there.

Why we pursue greater spiritual depth has an enormous impact on whether we'll be willing to pay the price to get there. Do we want just enough of Jesus to make us feel good, but not so much that we have to make radical changes? How do we tend to react when following Jesus involves sacrifice?

All too often, when we know that saying yes to God is going to be costly, we say, "Yes, God, I want to follow and obey you, but . . ." And then we insert some qualification that lessens our degree of commitment. Our yes-but holds us back from spiritual maturity.

Jesus asks us to cross the line between a life of casual commitment to Him and one in which we offer Him everything. He asks us to hold nothing back. He asks us to count the cost, and to consider Him worth everything.

Dear Lord,
Please give me the strength and power to relinquish my yes-but. I want to give You my undivided heart. Amen.

Yes but I am angry, depressed, etc and this doesn't seem to be working. Help me Lord to quiet the voices in my head to hear your voice and your mother's.

OCTOBER 17

"Will you also go away?" (John 6:67)

When Jesus told His followers that unless they ate His flesh and drank His blood they had no eternal life in them, many of them "no longer walked with him" (John 6:66). What He was asking them to accept was a little too much. It was too radical. They didn't necessarily walk away from Him and toward a life of depravity. They just went back to what was considered normal. As a result, they missed living the life they were created for.

Do you also want to go away? Do you feel tempted to do the "slow fade," in which you take little steps away from the Lord when what He asks seems too much?

The call to follow Christ requires self-discipline. It means laying aside what we feel like doing in order to do what God has said is right. And it's costly. Following Christ means entering into a mutually self-giving relationship. There's nothing casual about it. It's an intimacy that grows as we say, "I want what You want, when You want it, how You want it," and then act on that commitment.

But may we never make the mistake of thinking this is accomplished through pure willpower—gritting our teeth and powering through. The obedience of self-discipline is brought about through our surrender to the Holy Spirit. He does in and through us what we can't do ourselves. When we pray, "Give me the strength to do what I know is right even though I don't feel like it," the Holy Spirit comes through for us.

This was Saint Teresa of Calcutta's secret. Early in her life, she made a pact with God to refuse Him nothing. She said, "If God imparts himself fully to us, shall we answer with just a fraction of ourselves?"[95] She determined to "do His bidding without delay" and "to be found faithful in the little practices." And what resulted from her Spirit-fueled self-discipline? The world was changed, one heart at a time. There is no limit to what God can do in and through a woman who has this kind of relationship with Him.

Dear Lord,
May my yes to You be without reservation, holding nothing back. You gave me Your all. May I give You nothing less. Amen.

Be Still  **OCTOBER 18**

"And he said, 'Abba, Father, all things are possible to you; remove this chalice from me; yet not what I will, but what you will.'" (Mark 14:36)

It isn't easy to surrender. It's hard to let go of what we want and instead embrace what God has given. Jesus walked the path before us, and gave us an example to follow.

Because God is good, He will never ask us to surrender anything unless it is for our benefit. His motives are always pure. His love for us combined with His ability to know all things means that He can look ahead and know exactly what will be best for us today and tomorrow. When we struggle with doubt, wondering if God is trustworthy, we need to look at the cross. That's where He proved the extent of His love. He holds nothing back that is for our good.

The enemy of our soul does all he can to convince us otherwise. He does his best to make us think that God is out to steal all our joy and fun. C. S. Lewis highlights this in his book *The Screwtape Letters*. In the book, Screwtape (the devil) trains his nephew in the best ways to keep Christians from experiencing the wonderful lives God has planned for them. Screwtape describes surrender in the following way: "When [God] talks of their losing their selves, He means only abandoning the clamour of self-will; once they have done that, He really gives them back all their personality, and boasts (I am afraid, sincerely) that when they are wholly His they will be more themselves than ever."[96]

Only a fool would surrender to someone he or she knew nothing about. God doesn't ask us to surrender to some unknown force or being. He asks us to surrender to *Him*—our loving Father whose greatest desire is to see us safe, fulfilled, and experiencing supernatural peace. When we are struggling to surrender to God, we need to shift our focus away from what we are clinging to and trying to keep, and instead focus on God. The more we know Him, the easier it will be to trust Him and release our lives into His capable hands. He is unchanging—"always the same, faithful and just, without any evil" (CCC 2086). This is one of the reasons it's so important to study the Bible, because He reveals His character through His Word.

Dear Lord,
Your attributes—Your character—make it clear that You are worthy of my trust. Thank You for Your unchanging goodness toward me. Amen.

OCTOBER 19

"But now that you have been set free from sin and have become slaves of God, the return you get is sanctification and its end, eternal life." (Romans 6:22)

Most people reading this verse will have an adverse reaction. Who wants to be called a slave? We'd rather hear about being God's beloved children. Make no mistake, we *are* God's beloved children and have "received the spirit of sonship. When we cry 'Abba, Father!' it is the Spirit himself bearing witness with our spirit that we are children of God" (Romans 8:15–16). But Scripture also says that we are God's slaves. Both *slave* and *child* describe our true identity.

Recognizing ourselves as slaves or servants of God may not feel warm and fuzzy, but we need to accept this truth. If we don't acknowledge God's greatness and superiority to us, we'll justify all sorts of compromise. When He asks something of us that is hard or seems unnecessary, we'll assume that we have the right to react any way we feel like. In the words of pastor Kyle Idleman:

> My concern is that many of our churches in America have gone from being sanctuaries to becoming stadiums. And every week all the fans come to the stadium where they cheer for Jesus but have no interest in truly following him. The biggest threat to the church today is fans who call themselves Christians but aren't actually interested in following Christ. They want to be close enough to Jesus to get all the benefits, but not so close that it requires anything from them.[97]

God is neither a celebrity we admire nor the captain of a successful sports team. He is *Lord*, which literally translated means He is the master. He doesn't need fans; He wants followers. As the King of the Universe, He requires that we follow Him by releasing to Him all that we are and all we possess.

When we surrender all we have to Christ, we are simply giving Him what He deserves. He gave us His life; we respond by giving Him ours. In addition, when we surrender, we are on the surest path to both holiness and happiness.

Dear Lord,
May I hold nothing back from You, trusting that the best plan for my life is Yours. Amen.

Be Still

OCTOBER 20

"He who loves his life loses it, and he who hates his life in this world will keep it for eternal life." (John 12:25)

Jesus said that it is only those who surrender their lives—who die to self—who will keep their lives eternally. In the words of Saint Teresa of Ávila, "Whoever makes a habit of prayer should think only of doing everything to conform his will to God's. Be assured that in this conformity consists the highest perfection we can attain, and those who practice it with the greatest care will be favored by God's greatest gift and will make the quickest progress in the interior life. Do not imagine there are other secrets. All our good consists in this."[98]

If we aren't willing to surrender our desires and needs to God, we'll become convinced that the only way we can be happy is to have those desires and needs satisfied. This places us on very shaky ground. Our circumstances will always be subject to change, and as a result, our happiness will rise and fall. But when we submit our will to God's, when we want what He wants, we can receive anything from His hand as a gift.

One of the most common excuses we use to avoid surrendering to God doesn't sound like an excuse at all. We might express enthusiasm over the idea of surrender, or we might acknowledge how right it is that God would ask this or that of us, but we determine to do it later. We haven't outright refused, so we figure God appreciates our good intentions. We're sure we'll do it tomorrow.

If we really want to grow in the spiritual life, we'll determine to obey God immediately when He calls. We'll recognize that He has every right to ask anything of us. "You are not your own; you were bought with a price" (1 Corinthians 6:19–20). We weren't purchased "with perishable things such as silver or gold, but with the precious blood of Christ" (1 Peter 1:18–19).

Ask God if there is something He wants from you. Sit in quiet to allow Him the chance to impress some thoughts on your heart. When you know that God is asking you to surrender and obey, do it straightaway. Don't put off something until tomorrow that could be done today.

Dear Lord,
What are You asking of me? What is the next right thing? [Take the time to listen to Him.] I commit to accepting Your will, and will take a step of obedience immediately. Amen.

OCTOBER 21

"My son, give me your heart, and let your eyes observe my ways." (Proverbs 23:26)

More than anything, God wants us to surrender our hearts to Him. What is the heart? The heart is the place where we keep our dreams, our love, our agendas. It's the driving force behind what we do. It's where our motives are rooted. When we offer our hearts, we open ourselves up to His transforming power. We are changed in the core of our being so that we begin to want what God wants, when He wants it, how He wants it. In the words of K. P. Yohannan, "By choosing to come into His presence, we leave aside our agenda and prepare ourselves to submit to His yoke. In His presence we are changed; the independent spirit is substituted for His will and His ways. Our hearts change as a deep transformation takes place within."[99]

The story is told of an unusual baptismal practice involving the Knights Templar. When the knights were baptized, they carried their swords with them. Their bodies would be immersed, but they held their swords above the water. In doing so, they offered God much of who they were, but held back the sword. That part of their lives would remain under their control.[100] What are you tempted to hold out of the water? What is the hardest thing for you to surrender to Christ?

We read in the Old Testament of Job, a man who suffered like no other. After losing his possessions and all his children, he was able to say, "Naked I came from my mother's womb, and naked shall I return; The LORD gave, and the LORD has taken away; blessed be the name of the LORD" (Job 1:21). Could we say the same? If God allowed us to lose the one thing that we'd hold out of the water, could we still say, "Blessed be the name of the Lord"? Do we love Him for who He is or for what He gives us? Take some time to meditate on this question. Ask God to help you have a heart like the Blessed Mother's when she said, "Behold, I am the handmaid of the Lord; let it be to me according to your word" (Luke 1:38).

Dear Lord,
I want to give You my all. My desire is to completely surrender, but I feel a war within me. One part of me desires Your will, and the other wants my own way. Please do the work within me of conforming my will to Yours. I cannot do it myself, but with You, all things are possible. Amen.

Be Still

OCTOBER 22

Saint John Paul II

"Love does no wrong to a neighbor; therefore love is the fulfilling of the law." (Romans 13:10)

We owe a debt of gratitude to Saint John Paul II for his role in the ending of communism in Europe, for igniting a fire of spiritual renewal among young adults, for repairing relationships between the Catholic Church and other religions, and, borrowing his own words, for "opening wide the door to Christ." His teaching on what it means to love changed the way we look at our bodies and one another. Saint John Paul II rejected the culture of use, writing, "Anyone who treats a person as the means to an end does violence to the essence of the other . . . We must never treat a person as a means to an end."[101]

None of us would like to admit that we treat people as a means to an end, but our true motives can be hard to recognize. Use is subtle. Our desire for pleasure, control, achievement, and comfort is intense. God invites us to let go of expectations. He asks us to look to the needs of others before our own. The purification of our motives is a long process and one that requires a humble heart before God. Asking Him to reveal why we do the good we do to others is a good first step. Noting how we react when people disappoint us is another.

In his book *Love and Responsibility*, Saint John Paul writes, "Love, in the full sense of the word is a virtue, not just an emotion, and still less a mere excitement of the senses . . . Love as a virtue is oriented by the will towards the value of the person."[102] Love is willing the good of the other. This is exactly how Saint John Paul II tirelessly loved. He remains greatly beloved—a truly sacrificial leader, a modern saint who taught us that mountains can be scaled, walls can be broken down, and love can conquer even the hardest hearts.

Dear Lord,
Please help me to see the times my love is conditional. May I recognize my tendency to use others for my own benefit. Purify my heart. May I go to You with my deepest needs and receive the filling of the Holy Spirit. May this allow me to step into our broken world, able to meet the needs of others instead of hoping that others will meet my needs. No one satisfies like You. May I turn to You first and wait for the outpouring of Your blessing. Amen.

OCTOBER 23

"And hope does not disappoint us." (Romans 5:5)

The Christian life is full of paradoxes. The least shall be greatest.[103] A life of self-denial is the fullest life.[104] We are strongest when we're weakest.[105] Then there is the paradox of surrender: We experience freedom when we embrace our limitations. Father Jacques Philippe wrote the following about this seeming contradiction in his book *Interior Freedom*:

> To achieve true interior freedom we must train ourselves to accept, peacefully and willingly, plenty of things that seem to contradict our freedom. This means consenting to our personal limitations, our weaknesses, our powerlessness, this or that situation that life imposes on us, and so on. We find it difficult to do this, because we feel a natural revulsion for situations we cannot control. But the fact is that the situations that really make us grow are precisely those we do not control.[106]

Fr. Philippe goes on to describe the various ways we can respond to these situations that we find undesirable. We can **rebel** against them, refusing to accept our current circumstances. We might move on from rebellion to a place of **resignation**. While this is progress, it still falls short of how God wants us to respond. "Resignation doesn't include hope. Resignation is a declaration of powerlessness that goes no further."[107] Father Philippe challenges us to move on to a place of **consent**. This is an attitude of the heart that accepts the situation and looks for the good hidden in it. The key to consent is the virtue of hope. When we are struggling to surrender a circumstance that we desperately wish would change, hope is the virtue we need to focus on and develop.

When our hearts are filled with hope, we can look past our current circumstances to the good that will come in the future. Embracing hope is a choice. The opposite of the virtue of hope is worry or anger over current circumstances. While those are natural reactions to situations that we hate, they lead us down a path toward darkness and discouragement.

Hope allows us to look beyond what is right in front of us to see potential, to continue dreaming, and to patiently wait for God to act. It isn't a passive wishfulness; it's an active forward focus that believes in God's promises. We can rest with a spirit of expectation because "he who promised is faithful" (Hebrews 10:23).

Dear Lord,
When I am in the midst of hard circumstances, may I look for the hidden treasure. May I find more of You then than ever before. Amen.

Be Still  **OCTOBER 24**

"So the soldiers did this. But standing by the cross of Jesus were his mother, and his mother's sister, Mary the wife of Clopas, and Mary Magdalene." (John 19:25)

The cross marks the moment of deepest surrender in the life of the Blessed Mother. Although Mary couldn't rescue her Son, she could have rebelled in her heart against the reality of this unimaginably horrific situation. She could have screamed out to Jesus to call on the angels to rescue Him. But this isn't how she responded. She stayed. She didn't leave His side. She offered Him strength and comfort through her surrender to God's will. She allowed Him the freedom to obey God without having to worry about what His obedience would cost her. There was nothing she loved more than her Son, and she offered Him back to the One who gave Him to her in the first place.

In order to surrender to God what we love most, we have to trust that He will take care of who or what we offer. In order to trust Him, we need to acknowledge the truth of God's words in Isaiah 55:8–9: "For my thoughts are not your thoughts, neither are your ways my ways. . . . For as the heavens are higher than the earth, so are my ways higher than your ways and my thoughts than your thoughts."

We hesitate to surrender what we love to God because we are afraid. We fear that He will allow something other than what we would choose. Think of something that's hard to surrender to God. Then read Jesus' words to Peter, receiving them as His words for you: "What I am doing you do not know now, but afterward you will understand."[108] Can you exercise hope today even though you can't see the why behind God's actions?

In order to place what is most precious to us in God's capable hands, we have to keep our focus on His sacrificial, never-diminishing love. When we rest under His tender, pure, compassionate, and true love, we feel secure. That security reminds us that we don't need to be afraid. God is in control. He loves us. He has the big picture. We do not.

Dear Lord,
My life and that of all I hold most dear are safe with You. I know that You came to rescue me, and You want to rescue those I love most, as well. They are each on their own journey, and the way You will capture their hearts is between You and them. I release my loved one into Your care. There's no safer place than in Your hands. Amen.

OCTOBER 25

Be Still

"The righteous gives and does not hold back." (Proverbs 21:26)

Surrendering is a lifelong process. We do it with little decisions and big ones. We step forward in faith, and sometimes step back in fear. Through it all, Jesus stays by our side, joyful beyond measure when our surrender reveals our trust in Him. It's the best thank-you we can give Him for all He's done for us, and He receives it as such.

We're also surrounded by the saints who cheer us on from heaven. They've walked the road of surrender before us and promise us that it's worth every obedient step. One of those saints is Thérèse of Lisieux. Her words in *Story of a Soul* can both comfort us in our weakness and challenge us to progress in the process of yielding our will to God. She describes the following interaction with her sisters in a way that reminds us that we're all works in progress. If she could change, so can we! Leonie, the older sister, gave her old doll clothes to Thérèse and Celine, telling them to take what they'd like. Celine carefully took one silk braid, but Thérèse declared, "I choose everything," and took it all. She went on to write:

> This episode sums up the whole of my life. Much later, when I understood what perfection was, I realized that to become a saint one must suffer a great deal, always seek what is best, and forget oneself. I understood that there were many kinds of sanctity and that each soul was free to respond to the approaches of Our Lord and to do little or much for Him—in other words, to make a choice among the sacrifices He demands. Then, just as when I was a child, I cried: "My God, I choose all. I do not want to be a saint by halves. I am not afraid to suffer for You. I fear only one thing—that I should keep my own will. So take it, for I choose all that you will."[109]

This is the secret of the saints. This is what Saint Paul was talking about when he said, "It is no longer I who live, but Christ who lives in me" (Galatians 2:20). It's the path to holiness, and the source of true happiness. It's the abundant life God is just waiting for you to live.

"One does not surrender a life in an instant. That which is lifelong can only be surrendered in a lifetime." —Elisabeth Elliot, Christian author and missionary

Dear Lord,
May I hold nothing back, but surrender all to You. I commit to paying special attention to my decisions and my attitudes, with the goal of uniting my will to Yours in all things. Amen.

Be Still  **OCTOBER 26**

"I know your works: you are neither cold nor hot. Would that you were cold or hot! So because you are lukewarm, and neither cold nor hot, I will spew you out of my mouth." (Revelation 3:15–16)

God doesn't want us to float through life without direction or purpose. Our life is a journey with eternity at its end. When we settle for mediocrity, we're unlikely to finish well. We'll be less than who God created us to be. We'll settle for comfort and ease, but miss out on heavenly reward.

The word *mediocre* is an interesting one; it comes from the Middle French term *mediocris*, "in a middle state"; literally, "at middle height." It is a combination of *medi (us)* "mid" + *ocris* "rugged mountain." In its most literal interpretation, it means "halfway up the mountain." What should be understood in this is that [we stop at the halfway point], and have no desire to go any farther. It is not a matter of halfway on a continuing journey, but a contentment to be at the halfway point.[110]

Saint Paul never advocated settling halfway up the mountain. It's certainly not what Jesus modeled for us with His relentless pursuit of our salvation. We are to give our best to the One who gave everything He had for us.

What is your greater tendency—looking down the mountain and contenting yourself with how far you've come (while comparing yourself favorably with those who are farther down) or looking up the mountain with discouragement and a focus on your inadequacies? Have you sat down halfway up?

When we think our mediocre efforts to follow Christ are better than nothing, we often ignore the impact our actions have on others. Countless people are watching us. Our actions speak louder than our words, and Christians are being observed to see if God really does make a difference. When we claim to follow Christ but refuse to remain faithful when the road gets rocky and obedience is hard, people question whether we really are who we claim to be.

But every day offers a fresh opportunity to pursue excellence. And when we make mistakes, which we are bound to do, all we need to do is ask forgiveness, and start again tomorrow.

Dear Lord,
You are calling me upward. I confess these areas of my life where I am settling for mediocrity: _____. Holy Spirit, please give me the strength to get up and move forward to the higher ground of commitment and maturity. Amen.

OCTOBER 27

"I have loved you with an everlasting love; therefore I have continued my faithfulness to you." (Jeremiah 31:3)

How do you measure your worth? No matter where you go, you are continually receiving messages about what our culture says matters most. Airbrushed images of models cause you to make outward beauty the measure. Pinterest and glossy magazines tempt you to measure your worth by the perfection of your home. The achievement-oriented culture tells you that your worth is measured by your accomplishments.

The checklist is long: Have a perfect body, perfect health, perfect clothes; be a perfect mother; have a perfect marriage and a perfect career; and consistently give back to those less fortunate. The result? Pressure, and a nagging sense that no matter what, you'll never be enough.

Author Richard Winter describes the consequence of living under this pressure: "The core of the problem is that when a person's self-worth depends on reaching those high standards, it is an inevitable script for self-defeat and their own personal hell of repeated failure and eternal regret."[111]

If you wonder if your self-image is tied to these standards and measures, ask yourself the following:

- Does my sense of worth fluctuate when I'm fifteen pounds overweight?
- Does my sense of worth fluctuate depending on what I've accomplished in a day?
- Would my sense of worth fluctuate if I had to downsize or scale back because of financial difficulties?

God wants you to be freed from these faulty measures of your worth. He already measured your worth when Jesus hung on the cross, and He declared *you* worth dying for. He loves you, and wants you to be rooted in that unconditional love. Perhaps you were loved conditionally in the past. God's love is different. Receiving and soaking up His unconditional love is the antidote to the bondage of trying to measure up to the perfect standard that the world says matters.

Sometimes it's hard to believe that you are treasured and loved by God. But you have to decide—whose voice are you going to listen to? Whom will you believe?

Dear Lord,
Your love for me is everlasting. It is unconditional, and doesn't fluctuate depending on what I accomplish in any area of my life. Even "spiritual achievements" don't cause You to love me more or less. May I let go of the try-hard life, which ends in defeat and heaviness of heart. Instead, may I be rooted and grounded in Your faithful love. Amen.

Be Still **OCTOBER 28**

"Deep within his conscience man discovers a law which he has not laid upon himself but which he must obey. Its voice, ever calling him to love and to do what is good and to avoid evil, sounds in his heart at the right moment. . . . For man has in his heart a law inscribed by God. . . . His conscience is man's most secret core and his sanctuary. There he is alone with God whose voice echoes in his depths." (CCC 1776)

It would be far easier to know what we should and shouldn't do if God's voice in our conscience were the only one we could hear. Unfortunately, our heads can become full of other voices, many coming from expectations of other people. It has been said that the way parents talk to their children becomes their children's inner voice. A child can equate a *parent's* approval or disapproval with *God's* approval or disapproval. When people are important to us, their expectations of us can become a litany we listen to whether they are speaking out loud or not. These voices compete for our attention and cause us confusion. Can you identify any expectations (think of the times you say "I should," "I must," or "I have to") that have become an inner voice, competing with God's voice within you?

Richard Winter describes the conscience of a perfectionist in the following way: "Unhealthy perfectionists tend to have very sensitive and sometimes distorted consciences. They often feel acute pangs of guilt or shame if they do not live up to their own, or others', expectations. Fear about what others will think about their decisions and actions becomes their central concern."[112]

We must accept the fact that we'll never measure up to the expectations of everyone around us. Nor should their approval be what we are pursuing. Our highest desire must be to please God. In order to know what He is asking of us, we need to quiet the voices of expectations so that we can hear God's voice echoing in the depths of our hearts.

Dear Lord,
I am laying the expectations that press in on me at the foot of Your cross. I release them to You. The weight of sin's consequence fell on You so it wouldn't fall on me. It cost You everything for me to be able to walk in grace. May expectations not keep me from the freedom You died to give me. Amen.

OCTOBER 29

"Pride goes before destruction, and a haughty spirit before a fall." (Proverbs 16:18)

Pride is often at the root of a perfectionist's need to reach an unrealistically high standard with no mistakes allowed. We tend to picture pride as a person looking down his or her nose at someone else. That is one manifestation, but often it operates in a far subtler way. Pride causes us to desire control at all costs. Being limited by human weakness is incredibly frustrating to someone who struggles with pride. When a perfectionist focuses on her "inner checklist" of how to do everything perfectly, she hopes it will help to keep her life under control. It's hard for her to relinquish control to God, but it's her only hope of living in freedom.

A perfectionist who struggles with pride dislikes unpredictability. She wants to control potential outcomes so she can keep it all together. The first step for her to break free of pride's grip is to recognize that the only control she'll ever gain will be an *illusion* of control. Life, by definition, is unpredictable and full of uncertainty. Like it or not, you are not in control of your own destiny. There is much you can do to shape it, but ultimately, there are things you cannot predict or change. Only God is truly in control.

We will feel pride loosen its grip in direct proportion to how much we trust God. According to Psalm 9:10, "Those who know [God's] name put their trust in [Him]." In the Bible, a person's name reveals something about his or her character. Knowing God's name means that we know who He is. The more we know Him, the better we'll be able to trust Him.

We cannot control everything, because we are not God. We can control a lot more than our ancestors did, but there will always be a gap between what we'd like to control and what is out of our hands. The more we trust God, the easier this will be to accept. Read the following Hebrew names of God and their descriptions. Which name reveals something about God that helps you trust Him? Pray to Him using that name. Ask Him to give you more faith to believe in what you cannot see.

El Shaddai (Genesis 17:1): All-sufficient one, Lord God almighty
Jehovah-Rapha (Exodus 15:26): The Lord who heals
Yahweh-yireh (Genesis 22:14): The Lord who provides
Jehovah Mekoddishkem (Exodus 31:13): The Lord who sanctifies you
Jehovah Shalom (Judges 6:24): The Lord is peace
Jehovah Raah (Psalm 23): The Lord my shepherd

Dear Lord,
You are God, and I am not. And that is a good thing. Amen.

Be Still  **OCTOBER 30**

"Fear not, for I have redeemed you; I have called you by name, you are mine." (Isaiah 43:1)

If we were to peel back the top layer of perfectionism, we would find fear underneath. A common fear that drives a perfectionist's behavior is the fear of failure. Failing to perfectly accomplish goals can feel like failing as a person. Underneath that fear is a deep desire to be unconditionally loved and accepted, but it's hard for the perfectionist to believe that love doesn't have to be earned.

Isaiah 43:1 says that God has redeemed us. The word *redemption* means "atonement for a fault or mistake; rescue; deliverance."[113] It's important to note that our "perfect" behavior is not what has earned our redemption. Our faults and mistakes aren't atoned for because we manage to work extra hard and almost always get things right. In Ephesians 1:7, Saint Paul writes, "In him we have redemption through his blood, the forgiveness of our trespasses, according to the riches of his grace which he lavished upon us." God has planned ahead for our failure. Nothing surprises Him. Even the most colossal personal failure will not place us out of reach of redemption. Redemption, forgiveness, and grace are always offered to us.

Because of the desire to control things and not make mistakes, perfectionists can fear commitment. Procrastination in decision making is common because perfectionists want to be absolutely certain of which decision is most likely to bring the desired outcome. While we are wise to think and pray before we act, at some point a leap of faith is often required.

"But what if I've made the wrong choice?" the perfectionist cries. Richard Winter describes the perfectionist's motto as "Nothing ventured, nothing lost."[114] While procrastinating may seem like the safest way to behave, what we actually lose is the opportunity to learn from our mistakes. This is one of God's favorite ways to teach us. Our mistakes don't derail Him; He uses them for our good.

When we aren't sure of the perfect way to go forward but we have prayed and asked for God's direction, we can pray the following:

Dear Lord,
I'm stepping forward in this particular direction. I've drawn on the wisdom of my past experiences and the things You've taught me through Scripture and the teachings of the Church. If this course of action is not the direction You want me to go in but I didn't hear You clearly, I pray You will teach me something through my mistake. I am going to walk through this door, and I pray that You would close it before I get there if it isn't Your will. Amen.

OCTOBER 31

"Take every thought captive to Christ." (2 Corinthians 10:5)

Can you imagine how mortifying it would be if all our thoughts were broadcast live and anyone could hear them? Sure, we have plenty of good thoughts, and we wouldn't care if people knew some of those, but what if they could hear all the negative ones, too? Thankfully, our thoughts are contained within us. They are private. They are ours, and no one can access them without our consent.

But does that mean what we do with them doesn't matter? As long as thoughts just stay in our heads, are they harmless? Does it matter what we think?

Jesus answers these questions with the following words: "Love the Lord your God with all your heart, and with all your soul, and with all your mind" (Matthew 22:37). If the thoughts in our minds aren't the ones God wants us to dwell on, we're going to have a hard time loving Him and the people He places in our paths. Our thoughts directly impact our actions. They matter a great deal to God.

Jerusha Clark, author of *Every Thought Captive*, writes:

> We sin, in large part, because we hold on to and live out of toxic beliefs. So whether we are aware of the depths and brokenness of our thoughts or not, they are very real, and they influence us more than we ever know. Many of our thoughts, unfortunately, are both negative and untrue. At different points in their lives, most women have believed poisonous lies such as these: I'm not good enough. What others think about me defines who I am. I am the sum of my accomplishments and my relationships. We have believed a multitude of other self-defeating falsities as well, lies that have hijacked and poisoned our minds.[115]

Even when we recognize that our thoughts matter, we might feel that we just can't help thinking certain things. We may feel powerless to get a grip on the fears that prey on our minds. Perhaps we don't know how to keep our emotions from ruling our thoughts. Many of us feel a constant barrage of negative thoughts about ourselves, and we just don't know what to do about it.

The good news is we are not victims of our thought patterns. We have a choice, and with God's help, we can come to a place where we learn to control what we hold in our minds. We do not need to be slaves to our emotions, our past, or our worries. Our minds can be transformed.

Dear Lord,
Please teach me how to bring my thoughts under Your control. May I compare what I'm thinking to the truth of Your words and reject any thoughts that aren't consistent with Yours. Amen.

November

Let us rid ourselves of every burden & sin that clings to us and persevere in running the RACE. Keeping our eyes fixed on JESUS.

Hebrews 12:1-2

NOVEMBER 1

Be Still

Solemnity of All Saints

"The four living creatures and the twenty-four elders fell down before the Lamb . . . with golden bowls full of incense, which are the prayers of the saints . . ." (Revelation 5:8)

Today is All Saints' Day, the day we honor all the saints who have died and are now resting in the satisfaction and joy of heaven. Those honored as saints aren't necessarily the people who had flashy résumés while on earth. Their accomplishments were often hidden and overlooked. But God saw every sacrifice and every radical choice made to love heroically. He gave them the highest title we could desire, "saint," and ushered them into His presence in heaven.

Before we write them off as being the lucky few, it's important to remember that we are *all* called to be saints. They are our examples to follow, but not in some unattainable sense. In fact, their lives are meant to remind us that holiness is possible.

Many of the saints obeyed in ways that made them stand out. Saint Maximilian Kolbe gave his life in exchange for another prisoner's in a WWII concentration camp. Saint Joan of Arc led the country of France to victory. Saint Damien died of leprosy, contracted during his ministry to the lepers of Hawaii. Saint Catherine of Siena was a mystic and a doctor of the Church who was key in restoring the papacy to Rome. We might hear their stories and think, "Well, good for them, but there's nothing so special about me."

Not so fast. What makes a saint holy isn't his or her extraordinary circumstances, but living obediently and faithfully, day by day, minute by minute. This is the true test of our faith—our ability to remain open to God's will in the small, seemingly insignificant moments. As my pastor recently said, "Saints aren't made by the glory of Mount Tabor but in the darkness of Calvary." It's during those moments in the shadows, when what is required is hard and hidden, that a saint is made. There won't be any accolades here, but God is watching. He misses nothing.

Dear Lord,
Help me to remain consistent in my relationship with You—praying whether or not I feel like it, loving sacrificially even when I'm worn out, and staying faithful even when it all feels boring. May my love for You be as persistent in the small moments as in the bigger, more noticeable ones. Amen.

Be Still

NOVEMBER 2

"When he lies, he speaks according to his own nature, for he is a liar and the father of lies." (John 8:44)

There is a battle that rages every day in our minds. God wants us to think the thoughts that will lead to good actions and attitudes. We also have an enemy who pulls us in the opposite direction. "Evil is not an abstraction, but refers to a person, Satan, the Evil One, the angel who opposes God. The devil . . . is the one who 'throws himself across' God's plan and his work of salvation accomplished in Christ" (CCC 2851). Satan is a liar and the father of lies. This gives us insight into the types of thoughts he will tempt us to dwell on.

So how do we determine whether a thought is the truth or a lie? The more we attune our ears and hearts to God's voice, the easier it will be to identify truth. Our ability to recognize God's voice will grow in direct proportion to our knowledge of Scripture and our sensitivity to the prompting of the Holy Spirit. We grow in sensitivity to the prompting of the Holy Spirit through confession (breaking down the barrier of sin), through prayer (asking God to give us greater sensitivity to the Holy Spirit), and then through obedience (acting immediately on what God has shown us to do).

What negative thought do you struggle with most often? Take that thought to its furthest point. For example, you may often find yourself thinking, "I'm overwhelmed with too much to do." Take that thought to the next point by asking, "So what will happen if I don't get everything done?" You might reply, "I'll fail. I'll let people down." Take it to the next point by asking, "So what happens if I fail?" You might reply, "I'll feel like a loser. Like I can't get my act together. Like I'm worthless." That final thought is the toxic one. That's the thought that needs to be battled and compared to the truth. *Is it true* that if I fail I am worthless? Is that thought consistent with what I read in Scripture? It's at this furthest point of the thought that we begin to find the deeper issue, the issue that needs to be held up to the truth of God's Word. Take your negative thought to its furthest point. Identify the toxic thought at its root. Compare that thought to God's truth.

Dear Lord,
Help me take my negative thought to the furthest point and take a look at the toxic lie that comes at the end. I reject that lie, and replace it with the truth of Your love, forgiveness, and provision. Amen.

NOVEMBER 3

"Light rises in the darkness." (Psalm 112:4)

Although we aren't to dwell on our worries, I would be remiss if I left you with the impression that we should always live on the surface of our emotions, never diving deeper to address what's going on in our hearts. Some of the wounds that we have experienced in the past (or are experiencing in the present) are deep and painful. When thoughts of intense hurt surface, am I suggesting that we ignore them and exchange them for thoughts of rainbows and sunshine? No. There is a big difference between dwelling on negative thoughts that are not true and facing real pain that needs healing.

Satan loves to play in the shadows. He loves when things stay hidden and confused. God wants to shine light into the darkness. Sometimes the light hurts our eyes; we don't want to look back and address painful memories. But God promises He will never leave our side, and that He wants to lead us to a place of healing and freedom. When we can name the pain in our past, its power over us starts to lessen. We realize that we can decide how we are going to respond. What happened in the past is beyond our control, but how we react to that reality today is very much in our control.

As we process our pain, God is very near, and always tender. "A bruised reed he will not break, and a dimly burning wick he will not quench; he will faithfully bring forth justice" (Isaiah 42:3). "The Lord is near to the brokenhearted and saves the crushed in spirit" (Psalm 34:18).

It can be scary to journey back to our place of woundedness. We might prefer to just not think about it. But God wants us to be able to think about what was true and real without those thoughts having a hold on us. He wants us to walk in freedom. Sometimes that means we have to go back and process the past. But He never leaves us to do that alone. And when we feel too weak and afraid to go there, He reminds us, "My grace is sufficient for you, for my power is made perfect in weakness" (2 Corinthians 12:9). And remember, there is nothing weak about asking for help. Taking advantage of professional help is not only wise; it's often God's chosen means to bring us to a place of healing.

God never tells His suffering children to "snap out of it" or "get it together." He realizes that the solution isn't always just to pray more, read the Bible more, or go to church more. He comes close to us in our sorrow and pain, and offers healing. Sometimes the first step of healing feels like the washing of a cut that's filled with gravel. It hurts, and we just want to slap on a Band-Aid instead of suffering the pain of getting rid of the dirt. But if we'll trust God, He'll only do what's necessary to bring us to a place of wholeness. And remember, you're in good company. Many saints have been just where you are today. Your story isn't finished. The best is yet to come.

Dear Lord,
Help me bring my pain into the healing light of Your love. Amen.

Be Still

 **NOVEMBER 4**

"Judge not, that you be not judged. For with the judgment you pronounce you will be judged, and the measure you give will be the measure you get. Why do you see the speck that is in your brother's eye, but do not notice the log that is in your own eye? Or how can you say to your brother, 'Let me take the speck out of your eye,' when there is the log in your own eye? You hypocrite, first take the log out of your own eye, and then you will see clearly to take the speck out of your brother's eye." (Matthew 7:1–5)

A common response to the moral decay observed in the culture is to see the main problem as out there as opposed to in here, in our own hearts. This leads to an us versus them mentality. From this perspective, the purity of us must be protected and preserved, and the sin of them is to be separated and pointed out. In his book *The Gulag Archipelago*, Aleksandr Solzhenitsyn explains why he believes this is a problematic way of looking at life: "If only it were all so simple! If only there were evil people somewhere insidiously committing evil deeds, and it were necessary only to separate them from the rest of us and destroy them. But the line dividing good and evil cuts through the heart of every human being. And who is willing to destroy a piece of his own heart?"[116]

Fear often lurks behind judgment. One of the reasons Christians have become better known for what they are against than what they are for is because we are afraid of truth being compromised. We want to defend the Church. We are afraid that if we don't speak loudly about what is wrong, the dark side will win.

But God doesn't need our protection. He is far greater than that. The chief objective of the Church is not self-preservation. This is not to be our concern, because Jesus has promised us that God will always do a good job of protecting the Church. In other words, we aren't allowed to ignore His command not to judge in Matthew 7 in the name of fighting on His behalf.

This is not to say that there is no place for our voices to speak truth within the culture. But the way in which we do it really matters, as does the motive behind our words. Does it come from compassion for those who need Jesus or fear of them and their influence?

Dear Lord,
May I spend more time interceding for those whom I think are the source of our culture's problems than I do complaining about them. Amen.

Be Still

NOVEMBER 5

"Let him who is without sin among you be the first to throw a stone at her." (John 8:7)

Who are the people who are often made to stand in the midst of Christians' judgment? We may not physically drag a person into our presence, but we circle him or her with the judgment of our words, written and spoken. Writer and speaker Sibi Riffer describes what it felt like for her to come to church as an unwed mother with a baby on her hip:

> I wondered if they would embrace me. Accept me. Allow me in—in spite of my circumstances and in spite of my mistakes. I'm sorry to share that I walked into a sea of judgment and condemnation during that season of my life. And unfortunately it caused me to leave the church for nearly a decade.
>
> Because when you are struggling with the lie that is "there is no way that a holy God could love a girl like me." And you are hanging on by a thread because life has just been too much . . .
>
> Every moment counts.
> The way you are received and welcomed or not.
> The way the caregivers receive your child with kindness or not.
> The way a seat is made available for you or not.
> The way you are looked down upon, questioned or *interrogated* by church members or *hopefully not*.
> The way someone took the time to speak with you or not.
> The way you are shamed and condemned or accepted and loved.
> All of those things and so much more are some of the reasons that people will give church and ultimately Jesus another chance.
>
> But one of the biggest reasons I walked away was this. *I didn't want what they had*. They made it loud and clear to me what they were against. *But they failed to demonstrate what they were for.*[117]

It's time for us to put down our stones. In a world that seeks to objectify women, we need to come alongside one another. Instead of judging one another, let's lead each other to Christ. Let's leave it to Him to point out the sin. He can be trusted to do this! We don't have to worry that if we stop shouting through our megaphones about what's sinful, humanity will go over the edge into the abyss. God can be trusted to convict people of sin. That's the Holy Spirit's job, not ours.

Dear Lord,
Please reveal to me which stone is in my hand. Give me the grace to put it down and instead offer love and mercy. Amen.

Be Still

 NOVEMBER 6

"Conduct yourselves wisely toward outsiders, making the most of the time. Let your speech always be gracious, seasoned with salt, so that you may know how you ought to answer every one." (Colossians 4:5–6)

Earning the right to be heard is critical if we're going to engage our culture and draw others closer to Christ. One way to do this is to build genuine relationships with people instead of treating them as projects in need of improvement. Another is to live in such a way that we earn people's respect and trust.

Sometimes we mistakenly think that we have to be in full-time ministry in order to really make a difference in the world for Christ. Nothing could be further from the truth. The issue isn't what job we are doing. The issue is how we live out our vocations, whether we're at home, in business, in politics, or anywhere else. It is in the context of day-to-day relationships and connections that real mission work takes place.

The late Chuck Colson, founder of Prison Fellowship, described it this way: "We must enter into the stories of the surrounding culture, which takes real listening. . . . We connect with the literature, music, theater, arts, and issues that express the existing culture's hopes, dreams, and fears. This builds a bridge by which we can show how the gospel can enter and transform those stories."[118]

Earning the right to be heard requires living a life of integrity, listening before speaking, and sharing your views with graciousness, gentleness, and reverence.

It isn't easy to listen when we are so certain that what we have to say will help. And sometimes it's hard to articulate what we believe, let alone to do it graciously and gently. God wants to help us. When we don't know what to say or how to say it, He wants us to call upon the Holy Spirit. When Jesus was speaking to the disciples about this very issue, He told them, "Do not be anxious about how you are to speak or what you are to say; for what you are to say will be given to you in that hour; for it is not you who speak, but the Spirit of your Father speaking through you" (Matthew 10:19–20). Which of your upcoming conversations needs to be sprinkled with salt? Ask God to speak through you.

"If we, each doing our own part, if we do good to others, if we meet there, doing good, and we go slowly, gently, little by little, we will make that culture of encounter: we need that so much. We must meet one another doing good."
—Pope Francis

Dear Lord,
Please help me ask more questions and listen better. When I open my mouth, may You speak through me. Amen.

NOVEMBER 7

"Go therefore and make disciples of all nations, baptizing them in the name of the Father and of the Son and of the Holy Spirit." (Matthew 28:19)

Cultural withdrawal is not an option for Christians if they are going to be obedient to Christ's command to spread the good news of the gospel. In the words of Pope Francis:

> We need to avoid the spiritual sickness of a church that is wrapped up in its own world: when a church becomes like this, it grows sick. It is true that going out on to the street implies the risk of accidents happening, as they would to any ordinary man or woman. But if the church stays wrapped up in itself, it will age. And if I had to choose between a wounded church that goes out on to the streets and a sick, withdrawn church, I would definitely choose the first one.[119]

In his book *Unfashionable: Making a Difference in the World by Being Different*, author Tullian Tchividjian shares his take on this passage of Scripture: "Christ has called his followers to be in the world yet distinct from it, to live against the world, for the world. The truth is, if you follow Jesus in this way, you will seem too pagan for your Christian friends and too Christian for your pagan friends."[120]

Dear Lord,
It's uncomfortable to follow You. When I'm obedient to You, I sometimes feel that I don't fit in anywhere. There can be an element of loneliness in faithfulness. Help me to remember that this earth isn't my home; heaven is. That's where I truly belong—with You. When I feel I don't blend in here, may it remind me that I was made for more. That "more" is eternity. Help me to remember that the goal of my life isn't to be comfortable or happy. Help me to persevere with whatever You are asking, even if it seems like no matter what I do, someone is unhappy with me. Help me to remember that it's a real gift that I can just be with You. It's not a performance. You just want the real me. Amen.

Be Still

 NOVEMBER 8

"The Good News of Christ continually renews the life and culture of fallen man; it combats and removes the error and evil which flow from the ever-present attraction of sin. It never ceases to purify and elevate the morality of peoples. It takes the spiritual qualities and endowments of every age and nation, and with supernatural riches it causes them to blossom, as it were, from within; it fortifies, completes, and restores them in Christ." (CCC 2527)

What a difference it would make if Christians revealed the power of the gospel by restoring culture with a fearlessly positive spirit instead of critiquing it. Author Austen Ivereigh has this to say about the positive manner in which we should engage culture: "Catholic Voices should be idealists and radicals, inviting society to another, better way. Pro-Lifers should sound like anti-slavery campaigners, not admonishing moralists, just as opponents of assisted dying should be campaigners for hospices on every corner. Don't be a grim reaper; be the angel that points to the brighter horizon."[121]

A negative outlook on the world can indicate a lack of confidence in Christ's power to overcome obstacles. Pope Francis addresses this in *The Joy of the Gospel*:

> One of the most serious temptations which stifles boldness and zeal is a defeatism which turns us into querulous and disillusioned pessimists, "sourpusses." Nobody can go off to battle unless he is fully convinced of victory beforehand. If we start without confidence, we have already lost half the battle and we bury our talents. While painfully aware of our own frailties, we have to march on without giving in.[122]

We can be fully confident that no matter how bad things get, God will have the victory in the end. He has already won the battle against sin and death! As Saint Paul wrote in Romans 8:31–39:

> So, what do you think? With God on our side like this, how can we lose? If God didn't hesitate to put everything on the line for us, embracing our condition and exposing himself to the worst by sending his own Son, is there anything else he wouldn't gladly and freely do for us? And who would dare tangle with God by messing with one of God's chosen? Who would dare even to point a finger? The One who died for us—who was raised to life for us!—is in the presence of God at this very moment sticking up for us. Do you think anyone is going to be able to drive a wedge between us and Christ's love for us? There is no way.[123]

Dear Lord,
I claim the promise of Romans 5:8:37: *"In all these things we are more than conquerors through him who loved us."* Amen.

NOVEMBER 9

"Let every man be quick to hear, slow to speak, slow to anger." (James 1:19)

We have countless opportunities to talk with people whose opinions differ from ours. How do we interact with them? Are we gracious or judgmental? Do we listen to or talk at people? Do we treat those who are different as "them" and thank God that we are "us"?

There is so much at stake. A cultural retreat into a Christian bubble is not an option. This means we have got to learn how to communicate winsomely with people who believe differently than we do. This doesn't mean that we compromise or blend in. It means we engage in a positive way that invites *dialogue*. This is going to require listening. All too often, when we "listen" we are actually preparing to make our next point. People can sense this, and it usually shuts down the discussion pretty fast.

I think it would make a big difference if we started saying things like, "Please tell me more about that." Or, "I don't know, let me give that some thought and come back to discuss it later." Or, "I'd really like to learn from you in this way." People rarely remember our arguments, but they always remember if they felt respected or belittled in our presence.

It's always a help when we continuously look for ways we can create a connection to people with whom we disagree. For example, although we might have a very different way in which we feel the dignity of life should be protected, it's possible that a bridge can be built by discussing our mutual desire to see people experience freedom, respect, and dignity. We can search for values that we share with others and build on that.

If the person we are talking to begins to get heated and defensive, it's worth at least considering the possibility that his or her reaction is related to a trigger, a painful event previously experienced. We have the opportunity to love and listen compassionately. This will be remembered far longer and more positively than us managing to get a couple more of our points made.

The truth is, people remember a story far better than an argument. Anytime we can simply share the difference that Christ has made in our lives, walls tend to come down. It's hard to argue with someone's personal experience.

There's too much at stake for us to keep winging it. It's time to educate ourselves in terms of meeting people in the middle with both truth and love. "By this all men will know that you are my disciples, if you have love for one another" (John 13:35).

Dear Lord,
May I be quick to listen and slow to speak. Amen.

Be Still

NOVEMBER 10

"But I am afraid that as the serpent deceived Eve by his cunning, your thoughts will be led astray from a sincere and pure devotion to Christ." (2 Corinthians 11:3)

Satan began his temptation of Eve with a question: "Did God really say . . . ?" He whispers questions to us, too. They might seem harmless. What is the danger in playing around with a question in our minds? That depends on the question. One of his favorites is "What if . . . ?" "What if you had married someone else?" "What if you had more money?" "What if God hadn't allowed that loss?" Would life be better? The question plants a seed of doubt in our minds regarding God's goodness. Underlying the subtler question is the real one: "Is God holding out on you? Does He *really* want what's best for you?"

Satan was subtle. Instead of inviting Eve to rebel against God, he asked questions, planted seeds of doubt, and mixed truth with lies. He caught her off guard. He does the same today.

The enemy of our soul wants us to doubt God's unconditional love for us. He wants us to doubt our dignity based on who we are in Christ. He wants us to doubt that sin has consequences. He wants us to doubt that God will forgive anything if we ask with a contrite heart. He wants us to doubt that inner beauty matters more than physical beauty. He wants us to doubt that *God is enough*, that *He is all we need*.

When we are faced with temptation, we can learn from Eve's mistakes:

1. She conversed with temptation. If Eve had kept her eyes on God and all He'd given her, she would have avoided the conversation with the serpent, which is what led her down the wrong path.
2. She was careless with God's Word. Her words, "You must not touch it," were her addition—not God's words.
3. She looked at the temptation. Once she started dwelling on the forbidden fruit, her eyes came off of God and His goodness. This weakened her resolve to obey.
4. She allowed her desires to drive her decision making. She saw that the tree was good, pleasing to the eye, and desirable. Her desires—rather than God's commands—became her focus.

Dear Lord,
Please reveal to me the area of my life where I am experiencing temptation, alerting me to any ways in which I am following Eve's pattern. Amen.

NOVEMBER 11

"You may freely eat of every tree of the garden; but of the tree of the knowledge of good and evil you shall not eat, for in the day that you eat of it you shall die." (Genesis 2:16–17)

Satan managed to get Eve to shift her focus from all she had been given to the one thing that was withheld. His message to her was, "Are you longing for something more? More knowledge? More wisdom? Then you should be able to have it! Why should you have to experience unfulfilled longings? Take matters into your own hands!" Satan's message is the same to us today. Do you want something you can't afford? Put it on a credit card. Are you longing for affirmation and attention? Dress seductively to get it. Are you discontent in your marriage? Satisfy your emotional needs with another man.

In Genesis 1:26, God said, "Let us make man in our image." Satan promised Eve that if she ate the fruit, she would be like God. Do you see what he did? He tempted Eve to sin in order to gain something that she *already had*. She was already made in God's image. God had already graciously and lovingly provided this for her. Yet Satan managed to get Eve to take her eyes off the freedom she had and focus instead on the one thing she couldn't have. When her focus shifted, she forgot who she was. She was God's beloved child, made in His image. She was deceived into believing that sinning against God would give her greater dignity, wisdom, and strength.

Before we are too hard on Eve, can we see times in our own lives when this has happened? How often do we forget that we are beloved daughters of God, and instead seek to earn dignity in ways other than resting in His grace and mercy? We forget that nothing we can do or give can make God love us more. He already is crazy about us. He already has given us dignity.

Dear Lord,
Help me to remember that the only place all my longings and desires will be fulfilled is in heaven, when they've been purified by Your love. Help my unfulfilled desires to draw me toward a longing for heaven with You. Thank You for meeting the deepest longing of my heart. I know I don't have to wait until heaven to experience something of Your presence and Your filling of my empty places. Help me to cultivate a heart of gratitude. There is much for which I am thankful. These are some of the blessings I acknowledge as coming from Your generous hands: [List them.]. Amen.

Be Still

NOVEMBER 12

"And he said, 'I heard the sound of thee in the garden, and I was afraid, because I was naked; and I hid myself.'" (Genesis 3:10)

Adam and Eve hid because they were naked. They felt exposed and vulnerable. When we feel those things, we hide, too. Often it is guilt that causes us to hide. *Guilt* is the act or state of having done a wrong or committed an offense.[124] When faced with our guilt, we have two choices. We can confess it and accept the consequences, or we can hide and try to sweep it all under the carpet. The first option leads to healing. The second can lead us to shame. Shame is defined as "a painful emotion caused by a strong sense of guilt, embarrassment, unworthiness, or disgrace."[125]

Shame can develop from guilt over a specific act, but we can also carry shame when we feel we don't measure up. It isn't always that we can point to a specific thing we've done wrong. We may just have a sense that we are walking under a cloud of discouragement, and we don't like ourselves very much. We are vulnerable to this anytime we base our dignity on the wrong things. It's then that we will be tempted to hide behind masks of performance, fake pleasantries, or tough exteriors that communicate, "I don't care."

Our dignity comes from being created in God's image and being adopted as His precious daughters. Does this mean we'll be perfect? No. We'll make mistakes. But when we're aware that we are less than we'd hoped, we have a choice. We can hide behind masks, or we can hide somewhere else. God invites us to hide in the shadow of His wings (Psalm 17:8) and to see Him as our hiding place and shield (Psalm 119:114). Colossians 3:3 says that our lives are hidden with Christ in God. This means that we no longer have to create our own safe places. We can drop the masks that hold us back from healing and wholeness.

Jesus promises to be a tender healer. We are safe with Him because His love for us is pure and devoid of any self-interest. All He does for us and in us is for our good. But He is a gentleman, and waits to be invited in.

Dear Lord,
I want to come out of hiding. I invite You in. I'm nervous to do it because there's so much in me that isn't good. But I've gotten to the point where I know that I can't fix myself. Jesus, I trust in You, and I ask You to take the mess of my heart and make it new. Amen.

Be Still

 ## NOVEMBER 13

"Man, tempted by the devil, let his trust in his Creator die in his heart and, abusing his freedom, disobeyed God's command. This is what man's first sin consisted of. All subsequent sin would be disobedience toward God and lack of trust in his goodness." (CCC 397)

What virtue could have protected Eve from all the trouble she got into? It's the same virtue that can keep us from despair, or from taking matters into our own hands. It's the virtue of trust. Underneath Eve's discontent and susceptibility to temptation was a lack of trust in God. Did He really want the best for her or was He holding back? Was His way truly the one that would lead to freedom and fulfillment? Was He worthy of trust?

Have you ever been in a situation of real need, only to discover that the friend you thought you could count on was nowhere to be found? While you may have continued with the friendship, no doubt your trust in that person was eroded. We trust those who we know are with us and for us, and who will stay by our side in the hard times.

Trust in Christ is never misplaced. He proved to us that He is in it for the long haul, *for our sake*, when He suffered and hung on the cross. He could have taken the easy way out, but He didn't. He stayed on the cross for *you*.

In the times when people might desert us, that is when He is nearest. It's a comfort to know that He hears each spoken need. Every detail of our life matters to Him. He cares. We don't always perceive His work, but He always acts on our behalf.

When life seems too much and disappointments weigh heavily on our hearts, when the future seems scary, God invites us to trust Him enough to hide in Him. He encourages us to shed the masks that conceal our true selves, crawl into His lap, and let Him shelter us in His love.

Don't make Eve's mistake. Don't forget who you are. You are God's beloved daughter. He gave everything so that you could have that privilege. The intimacy that Eve lost in the garden is available to you. God calls to His tired, weak, and wandering daughters, "Come home and rest in my love! Your strength will return as you rest in me. I call you by name. You are mine. All you long for can be found in me. I am worthy of your trust. Hide yourself in my love."

Dear Lord,
I am tired and weary. The effort it takes to shield myself is exhausting me. I am ready to hand over the reins to You. Jesus, I trust in You. Take care of everything. Amen.

lack of trust — I looked and shouldn't and it was for sure and a lack of trust. Please forgive me Lord. 11/13/24

Be Still

NOVEMBER 14

"Now Sarai, Abram's wife, bore him no children." (Genesis 16:1)

Have you ever wanted something so much you were utterly consumed by it? Even though much can be out of our control, what we do as we wait is really up to us. We can manipulate to get our way. We can break rules to get what we want. We can make everyone around us miserable because misery loves company. Or we can let our longing and waiting drive us closer to the heart of Christ. It's up to us.

Sarai was a woman who longed for something with every fiber of her being. Her arms were empty, and she wanted nothing more than for them to be filled with a baby. Women who lived during that time felt that if they didn't produce children, they had failed. Watching other women enjoying what she lacked was painful. There were many times when she felt alone in her struggle. "Why?" she must have asked. "Why am I being denied something that is so freely given to everyone else? Isn't it a good thing for me to want a baby? I'm willing to pour out my life for the sake of another. Shouldn't my good desire result in an answer to my prayer?"

Why didn't God just give Sarai what her heart desired? Why did she have to experience this unfulfilled longing? Why did she have to wait? If we're honest, we often want to ask God these same questions about our own situations.

Perhaps the following words from Pope Emeritus Benedict XVI can shed some light on why we suffer:

> Pain is part of being human. Anyone who really wanted to get rid of suffering would have to get rid of love before anything else, because there can be no love without suffering, because it always demands an element of self-sacrifice, because, given temperamental differences and the drama of situations, it will always bring with it renunciation and pain.
>
> When we know that the way of love—this exodus, this going out of oneself—is the true way by which man becomes human, then we also understand that suffering is the process through which we mature. Anyone who has inwardly accepted suffering becomes more mature and more understanding of others, becomes more human. Anyone who has consistently avoided suffering does not understand other people; he becomes hard and selfish.[126]

We long to be mature, faith-filled women. This requires learning how to suffer and wait well. A lifetime spent avoiding suffering leaves us stagnant and unable to cope. May this not be our story.

Dear Lord,
Help me to suffer well, recognizing times of waiting and self-denial as opportunities for refinement and growth. Amen.

NOVEMBER 15

"When [Abram] was about to enter Egypt, he said to Sarai his wife, 'I know that you are a woman beautiful to behold; and when the Egyptians see you, they will say, "This is his wife"; then they will kill me, but they will let you live. Say you are my sister, that it may go well with me because of you, and that my life may be spared on your account.' When Abram entered Egypt the Egyptians saw that the woman was very beautiful. And when the princes of Pharaoh saw her, they praised her to Pharaoh. And the woman was taken into Pharaoh's house." (Genesis 12:11–15)

Sarai was taken into Pharaoh's palace, and Abram benefited from her ascent in position. He received flocks, herds, slaves, donkeys, and camels. But God wasn't pleased. He rescued Sarai, even if Abram had dropped the ball. *When* God did this is not clear. He responded by striking Pharaoh and his household with plagues. The pagan ruler was inflamed by Abram's lack of integrity. May this serve as a warning to us: We are to display character even when it involves risk. That's what it means to be a follower of Christ.

Before we judge Abram too harshly, let's recognize our own tendency to lie when we feel threatened. No matter how hopeless our situation may seem, God can be trusted to see us through. If doing the right thing means that we are put in a position of greater risk, then it's time to call on God's promises to provide for us! We may not see a solution, but God, who knows all things, can always provide a way out. "No temptation has overtaken you that is not common to man. God is faithful, and he will not let you be tempted beyond your strength, but with the temptation will also provide the way of escape, that you may be able to endure it" (1 Corinthians 10:13). We have a choice. We can look at God through our difficulties, and the difficulties will make obedience seem impossible. Or we can look at our difficulties through God, knowing that He provides the strength and wisdom we need when we are at the end of our own resources. Put God between you and your difficulty. It'll create a space that helps you realize His perspective on your problems. Wait and see how He displays His power in your life! Take some time to look at your difficulties and temptations in light of God's power to deliver you.

Dear Lord,
I ask You for a rescue. I affirm my trust in Your faithfulness and love. "[You] who promised [are] faithful" [Hebrews 10:23]. Amen.

Be Still

 NOVEMBER 16

"Now Sarai, Abram's wife, bore him no children. She had an Egyptian maid whose name was Hagar; and Sarai said to Abram, 'Behold now, the Lord has prevented me from bearing children; go in to my maid; it may be that I shall obtain children by her.' And Abram hearkened to the voice of Sarai." (Genesis 16:1–3)

Abram and Sarai remained childless, despite the fact that God had promised to give them a child. Instead of continuing to wait, Sarai took matters into her own hands, and gave her maid, Hagar, to Abram. The plan was for the baby to be born and for Sarai and Abram to adopt the baby as their own. Although this would be the *last* solution a modern-day woman would suggest ("Hey honey, why don't you go sleep with a younger woman?"), this was an accepted practice at that time. According to the *New International Commentary*, "an old Assyrian marriage contract" gave the following instructions: "If within two years she has not procured offspring for him, only she may buy a maid-servant and even later on, after she procures somehow an infant for him, she may sell her wherever she pleases."[127] Since Hagar was her slave, she was Sarai's property. As a result, Hagar's child would belong to Sarai.

The consequence of Sarai's decision to take matters into her own hands would be felt throughout the generations. Ishmael, the son of Abram and Hagar, would later be the father of several prominent Arab tribes, and an ancestor of Muhammad. The relationship between Isaac's and Ishmael's descendants continues to be tense to this day.

Our instinct as women is to help. God created us this way (Genesis 2:18). But there's a fine line between helping and manipulating. Sarai took matters into her own hands and manipulated the situation. Her motives may have been good, but her methods were not.

Waiting is hard, especially when we feel as if there's nothing we can do to help the situation. We can choose to wait passively or actively for God. Actively waiting means that we pray and exercise the muscle of faith by focusing on God's promises and learning more about His character, which will help us remember how reliable and powerful He is. Remember, "not one word has failed of all His good promises" (1 Kings 8:56). So "trust in the Lord with all your heart, and do not rely on your own insight. In all your ways acknowledge Him, and He will make straight your paths" (Proverbs 3:5–6).

Dear Lord,
I cast my anxieties on You. I am finding it hard to wait. Please grow my trust and faith, because "without faith it is impossible to please [You]" [Hebrews 11:6]. Amen.

NOVEMBER 17

"[The angel of the Lord] said, 'Hagar, maid of Sarai, where have you come from and where are you going?' She said, 'I am fleeing from my mistress Sarai.'" (Genesis 16:8)

Although it had been Sarai's idea to have her maid Hagar sleep with Abram to conceive a child for the two of them, once Hagar was pregnant, Sarai reconsidered. She found Hagar's attitude and "fortune" to be too much and sent her away into the wilderness.

God was in search of Hagar. She was significant to Him; He cared about her plight. He revealed Himself to Hagar in a personal way. In response, she called Him "a God of seeing."

This phrase, "a God of seeing," is translated *El Roi* in Hebrew. This name for God reveals His character as the God who sees. This revelation was life-altering for Hagar. Suddenly she knew that she was not alone. Someone could see her and her difficult circumstances. Someone was watching out for her. And that someone cared about her present and future.

What difference does El Roi make in our lives today? This name of God reminds us that when trials and distress enter our lives, He *sees*. Some of us have experienced circumstances that make us wonder if God has forgotten us, if He's gotten busy watching over His other children and missed the tragedy that visited our door. If these thoughts have played in your mind, remember, God's character does not change. God is the same yesterday, today, and forever. The same God who saw Hagar sees you. He sees the hurt that you are experiencing. One day, justice will be served. He promises this in 2 Thessalonians 1:5–10. It is not for us to judge. That is His job. But rest assured, He sees it all.

It's also a comfort to know God as El Roi if you have a loved one who is far from you. It's difficult not knowing what is going on in his or her life, but rest in the knowledge and truth that El Roi is watching over your loved one. He sees.

Dear Lord,
Help me to know You better. Help me grasp this important aspect of Your character. I have hurts that make my heart cry out for justice. Sometimes I long even for revenge. I recognize how this eats me up inside, and I don't want to be this way. Help me to hand over my past to You. Help me to release my anger and hurt to You. You saw it all, and You promise to hold every person accountable for his or her actions. Help me to stop being the judge. Flood my heart with healing. Help me to forgive. Help me to trust. Amen.

Be Still

NOVEMBER 18

"And God said to Abraham, 'As for Sarai your wife, you shall not call her name Sarai, but Sarah shall be her name. I will bless her, and moreover I will give you a son by her; I will bless her, and she shall be a mother of nations; kings of peoples shall come from her.'" (Genesis 17:16)

After Sarai and Abram took matters into their own hands by taking Hagar's child as their own, God again promised them their own child. Abraham responded by saying, "Oh that Ishmael [his son by Hagar] might live in your sight!" He couldn't conceive of the possibility of Sarai having a baby, and no wonder. Genesis 18:11 tells us that her body was no longer capable of childbearing. Perhaps that's why God changed both Abram's and Sarai's names to Abraham and Sarah. Maybe they both needed to look at each other through fresh eyes. They likely needed a reminder that God can do anything, even when hope is gone. God said again, "Sarah your wife shall bear you a son, and you shall call him Isaac. I will establish my covenant with him as an everlasting covenant for his descendants after him."

In Genesis 18:1–15, angels came to visit Abraham and Sarah, and told Abraham that by springtime, Sarah would have had a child. Sarah's response was to laugh to herself at the absurdity of the thought. One of the angels said in reply, "Is anything too hard for the Lord?" (Genesis 18:14).

God did the impossible for Sarah. Her son Isaac's birth is recorded in Genesis 21. It wasn't according to Sarah's timetable, and it wasn't in the way that she expected. But He came through for her. Scripture is full of promises for you and for me. How He'll choose to fulfill them in our lives is unlikely to be the way we would predict. "For my thoughts are not your thoughts, neither are your ways my ways, says the Lord. For as the heavens are higher than the earth, so are my ways higher than your ways and my thoughts than your thoughts" (Isaiah 55:8–9). We may not understand His methods or timing, but we can be assured that His way is always best.

Is there something in your life that seems impossible? Talk to God about it. Ask Him to purify your heart so that your desires are in keeping with His will.

Dear Lord,
Please align my desires with Your will. Only when this takes place will all my prayers be answered. Help me to remember that when Your response to my prayer is no or to wait, it isn't because You are holding out on me. It is because You are bringing something better. Amen.

Be Still

NOVEMBER 19

"By faith Sarah herself received power to conceive, even when she was past the age, since she considered him faithful who had promised." (Hebrews 11:11)

Clearly, something happened between the time Sarah laughed at the thought of giving birth to a child (Genesis 18:12) and the actual conception. Hebrews 11:11 tells us that she was given the power to conceive because she considered God faithful. The moving of God's hand to bless her was connected to her faith. Scripture doesn't record exactly how that change in Sarah's heart occurred. Perhaps her laughter wasn't rooted in doubt over what *God* was capable of doing but in what He could do through *her*. Sometimes that's what blocks our faith. It isn't that we doubt that God is powerful and able to perform miracles. We just don't feel worthy of them, or we think He would never choose to do those things in our lives.

Sarah made some big mistakes. People were hurt in the process, and the consequences were long term. We can look at her in judgment, or we can look in the mirror to conclude that there's no such thing as a perfect person. But fortunately, there is a perfect God with a perfect plan.

God's perfect plan wasn't thwarted even when Sarah and Abraham made mistakes. His love and faithfulness weren't based on their performance. Yes, consequences of their wrong actions were felt, but God wasn't limited by them.

We can receive both a warning and hope as we reflect on Sarah's life. We aren't the only ones who feel the consequences of our actions. They affect our families, sometimes for generations to come. Our influence can be for good or ill. We can pass a baton of faith, wisdom, and contentment, or we can pass one of judgment, anger, unforgiveness, and a critical spirit. How will we be remembered? What kind of legacy are we passing along?

Any of us who have messed up, who look back on life decisions with regret, can receive hope when observing what God did in spite of Sarah's mistakes. He can do the same with our mixed-up lives. God enters our imperfection, and if we let Him, He takes all the broken pieces and makes them into something beautiful. He has a perfect plan for each of our lives, and if we want to experience it, we need only surrender the reins to Him. When we try to take matters into our own hands, we rarely end up with the happy ending we desire. But if we allow God to order our steps, He promises to guide us to what will bring us the greatest fulfillment and joy.

Dear Lord,
I offer You my life—as is—with its disorder, unmet desires, sin, dreams, and hopes. I give You all of it and ask You to put it in order. Please take over and write my story. Amen.

Be Still

NOVEMBER 20

"Give thanks in all circumstances; for this is the will of God in Christ Jesus for you."
(1 Thessalonians 5:17)

Isn't it strange that we need to be reminded to be grateful—we who live in the most privileged of circumstances? Most of us are wealthy by the world's standards. Do you make $35,000 a year? Then you are in the top 4 percent of wealth in the world. Fifty thousand? Top 1 percent.

In the words of Jen Hatmaker:

> Excess has impaired perspective in America; we are the richest people on earth, praying to get richer. We're tangled in unmanageable debt while feeding the machine, because we feel entitled to more. What does it communicate when half the global population lives on less than $2 a day, and we can't manage a fulfilling life on twenty-five thousand times that amount? Fifty thousand times that amount? It says we have too much, and it is ruining us.[128]

We are invited in 1 Thessalonians 5:17 to change our perspective—to focus on what we already have, and express our gratitude for it. November asks to be remembered as its own month, and to stop letting December creep in and switch the focus to Christmas and all the shopping and planning it entails. Don't get me wrong, no one loves Christmas more than I do, but let's give November its moment in the sunshine.

The most impactful place for us to practice gratitude is in our relationship with God. Thanking Him for what He gives us is really important, but true praise means thanking Him for *who He is*. This lifts our focus to a higher plane, and reminds us that it's not all about what we have and what's going on here on earth. There is an eternal perspective that we need in our daily living, one centered on God—His goodness, His mercy, His steadfast love, His holiness, His unchanging nature, His faithfulness, and so much more.

What might change if we began our days by breathing in the fresh air and just thanking God for sustaining us, for the fact that we are *alive*? What if we followed that act of gratitude with the remembrance that with our generous God, "The steadfast love of the Lord never ceases; His mercies never come to an end; they are new every morning" (Lamentations 3:22–23)?

Dear Lord,
Thank You for being so patient with me when I behave like a spoiled child. Despite all You have given me, still I want more. Help me to be content with what I have. Amen.

NOVEMBER 21

"He who is you is greater than he who is in the world." (1 John 4:4)

Because the indwelling Holy Spirit is more powerful than our enemy, we can gain victory over our thoughts. That being said, our enemy doesn't go down without a fight. One of the ways he gets us to believe lies is by convincing us that if we *feel* something, it must be true. The truth is, we can't always trust our feelings. We read in Jeremiah 17:9 that "the heart is deceitful above all things, and desperately corrupt; who can understand it?" Of course, with God, all things are possible and nothing is without remedy. But the verse does illustrate that we're going to have to put in some effort if peace is going to reign in our hearts.

Instead of seeking to determine if something is true based on our feelings, we need to hold up a thought and compare it to God's truth. If the thought isn't consistent with God's truth, we need to reject it and replace it with a different one.

It's critical to recognize that we are in the midst of a spiritual battle. We are told in 2 Corinthians 10:4 that our weapons "are not worldly but have divine power." Those weapons are truth, righteousness, the gospel, faith, salvation, and Scripture. They are exactly what we need to fight the good fight.

Nothing delights Satan more than a woman ruled by her untamed thoughts and emotions. But a woman who recognizes that she's got powerhouse weapons that are strong enough to tear down anything Satan seeks to throw in her path? That's the kind of woman he wishes would just stay in bed.

Do you realize the power that is within you? Do you recognize the "immeasurable greatness of his power"[129] that is in us through the indwelling Holy Spirit? Do you know this is the same power that raised Jesus from the dead? "He who is in you is greater than he who is in the world" (1 John 4:4).

But it's as we sit at God's feet that we soak up that power. This is one of the reasons we have got to make time for prayer. Skipping prayer means we're heading out into the day with feeble weapons that are no match for what our enemy might throw at us. Take some time today to be filled with the power of the Holy Spirit.

Dear Lord,
Please fill every part of me, from the top of my head to the tip of my toes. Empower me with Your Spirit so I can go out in Your strength! Amen.

Be Still

 **NOVEMBER 22**

"The eye is the lamp of the body. So, if your eye is sound, your whole body will be full of light; but if your eye is not sound, your whole body will be full of darkness. If then the light in you is darkness, how great is the darkness!" (Matthew 6:22–23)

This verse reminds us to check the entry points of our minds. The Trojan horse seemed like such a great spoil of war, but with Greek warriors hidden inside, it brought about the destruction of Troy. In that same way, we can either invite all sorts of garbage into our minds or wisely avoid the things that expose us to fresh negative material.

Matthew 6:22–23 reminds us to guard our eyes, because what is filtered through them is invited into the whole body. What are we watching? What are we reading? Are we inviting certain images or temptations into our lives through what our eyes are taking in?

Another way negative thoughts enter our minds is through the words of our friends. In 1 Corinthians 15:33 we are reminded that bad company corrupts good morals. We are a reflection of the people who are closest to us. What kind of qualities should tip us off that a person might not be the wisest choice of friend? Proverbs 22:24–25 tells us to keep an eye on the way that people deal with anger. Gossip is another thing to watch for. Proverbs 18:8 says that "The words of a whisperer are like delicious morsels; they go down into the inner parts of the body."

Which of the entry points to your mind are often left unguarded? What you look at? Whom you spend time with? What you listen to? Where you go? What can you do to better protect yourself?

Even though we have enormous spiritual power within us, we still need to guard the entry points to our minds. There are some situations that are guaranteed to take us down a bad mental path. Choosing to stay home rather than putting ourselves in a place where we're probably going to be filled with wrong thoughts isn't cowardly. It's wise. Recognizing that certain friends bring out the worst in us and reducing our time with them is prudent. This doesn't mean that we should retreat into a Christian bubble; we are meant to be the sweet fragrance of Christ to people who don't know Him. But we need to pay attention to whether we are being the influencers or the influenced.

Dear Lord,
Please help me identify anything that needs adjusting in this area of my life. Amen.

NOVEMBER 23

Be Still

"And which of you by being anxious can add one cubit to his span of life?" (Matthew 6:27)

When we are worrying, we are usually imagining the worst-case scenario apart from God's presence. Without realizing it, what we are often saying is, "I don't think You can help me through this, Lord. I think this problem is too big for You." This is a lie that we need to reject the minute it comes into our minds. Then we need to replace the lie with the truth.

A good truth to dwell on when we are in the grip of worry is found in Isaiah 43:1–2: "Fear not, for I have redeemed you; I have called you by name, you are mine. When you pass through the waters I will be with you; and through the rivers, they shall not overwhelm you; when you walk through fire you shall not be burned, and the flame shall not consume you." This promise from Scripture assures us that God will not allow us to be destroyed. He will be with us through anything we will face and will protect us in the unknown.

The key to trusting God is holding firm to this truth even when we can't see the future. This isn't easy, because we want to know so we can prepare. CCC 2115 speaks to this desire: "God can reveal the future to his prophets or to other saints. Still, a sound Christian attitude consists in putting oneself confidently into the hands of Providence for whatever concerns the future, and giving up all unhealthy curiosity about it. Improvidence, however, can constitute a lack of responsibility."

We can't know everything the future holds, but there are certain things we can count on. Here are some things we do know:

1. In this world we will have trouble, but Jesus has overcome the world (John 16:33).
2. God will strengthen and help us; He will uphold us with His victorious right hand (Isaiah 41:10).
3. God's steadfast love will not depart from us, and His promise of peace will not be removed (Isaiah 54:10).

Ask God to help you replace your worries with trust. "The prayer of the Psalms is the great school of this trust" (CCC 304). Psalms 23, 46, and 121 are great trust-building psalms. It can also be helpful to go to a friend for encouragement. "Anxiety in a man's heart weighs him down, but a good word makes him glad" (Proverbs 12:25).

Dear Lord,
I place my worries in Your hands and thank You for the fact that You alone are totally worthy of my trust. Amen.

Be Still

NOVEMBER 24

"Behold, I am standing by the spring of water, and the daughters of the men of the city are coming out to draw water. Let the maiden to whom I shall say, 'Pray let down your jar that I may drink,' and who shall say, 'Drink, and I will water your camels'—let her be the one whom thou hast appointed for thy servant Isaac. By this I shall know that thou hast shown steadfast love to my master." (Genesis 24:13–14)

This was Eliezer's prayer after he was tasked with going back to his master Abraham's homeland to find a suitable wife for Isaac. When Eliezer approached that land, a beautiful young woman came out and offered water. He saw this as an answer to his prayer and asked her father (Abraham's relative) if he would give his daughter, Rebekah, in marriage to Isaac.

One can imagine the thoughts that ran through Rebekah's head as she heard Eliezer describe the reason for his journey and his perspective on their meeting. But her heart was won over and she agreed to marry Isaac and move to a new place. As she prepared to become Isaac's bride, she was given beautiful gold and silver jewelry and fine clothing to wear.

In 2 Corinthians 11:2, we learn that we have been betrothed to Christ, to be presented as a pure bride to our one husband. We are invited to the wedding feast. Revelation 19:6–9 describes our preparations: "Let us rejoice and exult and give him the glory, for the marriage of the Lamb has come, and his bride has made herself ready; it was granted her to be clothed with fine linen, bright and pure—for the fine linen is the righteous deeds of the saints."

To prepare us to meet Him face-to-face at the wedding feast, Jesus has given us the gifts of redemption and forgiveness, "according to the riches of his grace which he lavished upon us" (Ephesians 1:7–8). What a beautiful image—God lavishing us with grace. I'm sure that Rebekah loved her gold and silver jewelry and fabulous clothes, but nothing compares to the riches that God pours out on each one of His beloved daughters.

Dear Lord,
Stepping into the unknown and leaving all that Rebekah loved required a leap of faith. Yet, she didn't hesitate. Where are You asking me to step out in faith? Help me to respond with immediate obedience, trusting that You have given me all I need to do things Your way. I ask You to help me to shift my perspective from the unknown and the things I fear and onto Your all-sufficiency and continuous provision of all that I need. Amen.

NOVEMBER 25

Be Still

"And Isaac prayed to the Lord for his wife, because she was barren; and the Lord granted his prayer, and Rebekah his wife conceived. The children struggled together within her; and she said, 'If it is thus, why do I live?' So she went to inquire of the Lord." (Genesis 25:21–22)

God answered Isaac's prayer, but that didn't mean that things were easy. Rebekah's pregnancy was uncomfortable and difficult. She made this clear when she said, "If it is thus, why do I live?" (Genesis 25:22). In other words, "If this miserable state I'm in is the way our prayer was answered, what's the point? I'm still unhappy!" Sometimes the answer to our prayers isn't what we expect.

Some time ago, I said the following to the Lord: "My heart's desire is to be totally abandoned to Your will. I want to be like Saint Thérèse of Lisieux. I want to be able to say (and mean it!), 'If the Lord offered me the choice, I would not choose anything: I want nothing but what He wants. It is what He does that I love.'"[130]

I asked God to work in my life to help me to abandon my will to His. He answered me, but not in the way that I would have planned. He brought a challenging circumstance into my life, one that affected my health, my emotions, my productivity, my pride, and my ability to control my life. At the same time, I was no longer experiencing many of the comforts of His presence. By this I don't mean that He left me, because His Word says that He will *never* leave us or forsake us (Hebrews 13:5), but I didn't feel or sense His presence as I usually did. I related to Rebekah's words. In this place of darkness, stripped of all the things I wanted to offer God (such as my service and beautiful prayers), all I could offer Him was empty hands of surrender. But wasn't that exactly the place I had wanted to go? The answer to my prayer was His plan, in His timing, in His way . . . but I didn't find it easy.

A dear friend wrote me the following: "Ask the Lord, 'What is it that You want to be to me in this situation that You could not be to me in any other?' He will show Himself to you in new ways through this."

Dear Lord,
What do You want to be to me in this situation that You could not be in any other? May I look for the unique opportunities to get to know You better in each season, especially the difficult ones. Amen.

Be Still

NOVEMBER 26

"And the Lord said to [Rebekah], 'Two nations are in your womb, and two peoples, born of you, shall be divided; the one shall be stronger than the other, the elder shall serve the younger.'" (Genesis 25:23)

God shared with Rebekah a prophecy about her two sons before they were born. Esau, the older, was born with his brother, Jacob, grasping his heel. As they grew, Esau became a hunter while Jacob preferred to be home. Isaac loved Esau best "because he ate of his game" (Genesis 25:28), but Rebekah preferred Jacob.

We may naturally feel a certain affinity toward one person over another, but if those feelings are likely to result in strife within our families, then we need to change the way we think in order to change the way we feel. Only by taking the time to dwell on what is true and right are we strengthened to do the God-honoring thing, regardless of what we are feeling in the moment. Disciplining the mind to dwell on a child's good characteristics helps to control the feelings that could drive a mother's behavior toward favoritism.

Esau was the firstborn, and that carried with it certain rights. But he didn't value his birthright and when he was famished, he gave it to his brother in exchange for a bowl of stew. *Halley's Bible Handbook* describes the deal as follows: "Esau's transfer of his birthright for a meal demonstrated that he was 'godless' (Hebrews 12:16), since at the heart of the birthright were the covenant promises that Isaac had inherited from Abraham. The owner of the birthright, generally the firstborn, also received at least a double portion of the father's wealth at the time of the father's death."[131]

Esau wasn't the last to struggle with long-term good versus short-term gain. God has given us "redemption through his blood, the forgiveness of our trespasses, according to the riches of his grace which he lavished upon us" (Ephesians 1:8). He then has placed the Holy Spirit in our hearts as a guarantee that we will receive an eternal inheritance (Ephesians 1:14 and 2 Corinthians 1:22). While we wait for our inheritance, He asks us to "Look carefully then how you walk, not as unwise men but as wise, making the most of the time, because the days are evil. Therefore do not be foolish, but understand what the will of the Lord is" (Ephesians 5:15–17).

But it's so tempting to forget all that and live in a way that makes us happy in the moment! It's truly difficult to delay gratification.

Dear Lord,
Strengthen me so I don't settle for instant satisfaction instead of the true blessing of holy living. Amen.

NOVEMBER 27

"When Isaac was old and his eyes were dim so that he could not see, he called Esau his older son, and said to him, 'My son'; and he answered, 'Here I am.' He said, 'Behold, I am old; I do not know the day of my death. Now then, take your weapons, your quiver and your bow, and go out to the field, and hunt game for me, and prepare for me savory food, such as I love, and bring it to me that I may eat; that I may bless you before I die.'" (Genesis 27:1–4)

Rebekah overheard this conversation between Isaac and Esau and set to work. God had promised that her younger son, Jacob, would receive the blessing, but instead of trusting God to work out His purposes with His timing and method, Rebekah took matters into her own hands. She helped Jacob disguise himself as Esau and tricked Isaac into blessing Jacob instead. In Rebekah's mind, the end justified the means.

God had already declared that Jacob would be the stronger and the blessing was to go to him. God had decided that the elder was to serve the younger. God's plan came to pass, and Jacob received the blessing. But had Rebekah not manipulated the situation and instead trusted God to work, she could have enjoyed seeing His will come to pass without personal heartache. The consequence of her manipulation was the loss of her favorite son. Esau got so angry that Jacob had to flee for his life and didn't return until after Rebekah's death. Taking matters into her own hands and manipulating the situation wasn't worth it. It never is. Even when the prize is so desirable, it's always better to trust God and wait.

Having faith means believing with all our hearts that it *can* be done. Trust is the assurance that it *will* be done. We have faith in God when we know that He can do all things for our good. And we trust Him when we rest in the assurance that He will do all things for our good, in His own way, in His own timing.

Dear Lord,
I feel tempted to take matters into my own hands and create the result I desire, no matter what it costs. I want to take control, but I know that this leaves You out of the picture. So I invite You into this particular circumstance and ask for Your perspective. I ask You to make it clear if I am to wait for You in trust, or if there is something specific You are asking me to do. May I not run ahead of You. Amen.

Be Still

NOVEMBER 28

"You hypocrite, first take the plank out of your own eye, and then you will see clearly to remove the speck from your brother's eye." (Matthew 7:5)

I recently shared one of my parenting struggles with a friend. I explained that my husband and I had caught one of our children in a string of lies. Simply saying "I'm sorry" wasn't going to be enough. We felt it was necessary for our child to talk through the specific ways in which we had been deceived. The response to our request? A door slammed in anger. I wasn't sure when, if ever, the true apology would come.

I confessed to my friend how I had controlled and manipulated my husband during these very same months. He had known our child was up to something, and the lengths I had gone to as I defended our child had crossed a line. I had undermined Leo and battled him at every turn. "I'm so disgusted with myself!" I said. "I've told him I'm sorry, but I haven't gone into all the details. It would just be too hard to lay it all out!"

My friend started to laugh. "Can't you see? You are expecting behavior from your child that you can't—or won't—do yourself!"

In Matthew 7:5, Jesus didn't say we are to do nothing about the speck in our child's eye. But He put things in the proper order, in hopes that we'll go to our child in the right spirit—a spirit of humility.

Dan Allender writes of this in his book *How Children Raise Parents*:

> It's one thing to admit failure . . . But to confess failure, truly, is to hunger for redemption. And redemption is not merely change, nor is it knowing that one is forgiven. There are some who change only to become proud and demanding of others to do the same. Others know they are forgiven and use that as an excuse to perpetrate the same harm again and again, expecting no personal consequences. True redemption involves being struck dumb by the enormity of our failure and then struck even dumber by the enormity of the heart of God that cancels our debt.[132]

God can make use of everything—even our mistakes—in His salvific plan. We all make poor choices sometimes. How we respond to them makes all the difference. Can we be authentic? Can we admit our failure? By doing so, we can give others hope for love in their brokenness.

Dear Lord,
I am grateful for Your enormous heart that cancels my debt and redeems my failures. May I extend that mercy to others. Amen.

NOVEMBER 29

Be Still

"Then the king of Jericho sent to Rahab, saying, 'Bring forth the men that have come to you, who entered your house; for they have come to search out all the land.'" (Joshua 2:3)

When this request was posed to Rahab, she had a split second to make a life-altering decision. She could either side with her countrymen or trust in God. The people of Jericho were all terrified of the Israelites' God, but there was something different about Rahab's response. While her profession (prostitution) left her stripped of dignity, something in her longed to be swept up and protected by the God who was coming. Would He care about her? Would she be disqualified from His love? In spite of everything stacked against her, she hoped there was a place for her with Him. She decided to hide the Israelite slaves instead of turning them in.

Rahab's split-second decision was shaped by her view of herself, of her world, and of God. What she believed gave her courage. Many times in our lives, we will be faced with choices that require a split-second decision. We won't always have the luxury of consulting a friend or mulling over the pros and cons. What we decide to do will be determined by what we have previously decided we most value in ourselves, what we believe about our world, and what we believe about God.

The following are some questions we can ask ourselves when faced with a decision: "What does God think about my decision?" "What character issues are at stake?" "Which decision is a better one if I look at it from an eternal perspective?"

Was it a mere coincidence that the two Israelite spies were drawn to the house of Rahab? No. God had seen past the walls of Jericho, through the ungodly culture surrounding her, beyond her bad choices, and into her heart. When He looked at her heart, He saw what pleased Him most: faith. Rahab's faith moved God's heart and hand, and she was promised rescue. But remember, her faith led to action. True faith is reflected in our decisions.

Dear Lord,
As Rahab said in Joshua 2:11: "The Lord your God is he who is God in heaven above and on earth beneath." There is no one and nothing higher or more important than You. I ask You for wisdom in my decision making, because You are the One I want to please—it is Your approval that matters to me. Please guide me. Instead of relying on my gut and human wisdom, I want to trust in You with all my heart and lean on You for understanding. Amen.

Be Still

 **NOVEMBER 30**

"By faith Rahab the harlot did not perish with those who were disobedient, because she had given friendly welcome to the spies." (Hebrews 11:33)

The Israelite spies had told Rahab to hang a scarlet cord from her window the day of the battle. By this sign, they'd know to rescue everyone in that house. When Rahab and her family (the only survivors of the attack) were brought out of the city, they were temporarily placed outside the Israelite camp. But with time, she and her family were invited to become a part of the community. It must have been beyond her wildest dreams. During her time of waiting in Jericho, she believed that God was real, but she also knew that she didn't belong to Him. The wait must have enhanced her ultimate joy. Rahab, who had made her living trading her dignity for money, became one of the chosen ones. God wanted her in spite of her past.

This was not the end of Rahab's story. She went on to have a son and is named in Matthew as one of Jesus Christ's ancestors. Who would have thought that Rahab would not only be rescued, but would be given one of the greatest honors possible among the Israelites? For a nation of people focused on genealogy, you would think that God would have chosen more pristine characters to be Christ's ancestors, but God doesn't look at things the way man does.

His choice of Rahab teaches us something very important: When He looks at us, He sees our potential. He knows that within each of us lies a destiny that will bring fulfillment and joy. He also knows that the key to discovering it is found in a relationship with Him. He looks for women hungering for closeness with Him. Our past does not disqualify us from a magnificent future with Him.

Rahab risked it all. What if she'd been caught hiding the spies? What if someone had noticed her hanging the scarlet cord out her window? She cast all her fears at His feet and hoped.

Where do we place our hope? Are we willing to trust God regardless of what He asks of us? Rahab let go not just of her old lifestyle, but of the things that gave her security. She practiced abandonment. Our past doesn't disqualify us, but when we cling to anything other than God for security, we miss out on the magnificent rescue that He desires for us.

Dear Lord,
I hand You control of my life, and ask You to create a masterpiece out of the broken pieces. Please make me whole. Amen.

December

the Truth will set you FREE.

JOHN 8:32

DECEMBER 1

"But when the time had fully come, God sent forth his Son, born of woman." (Galatians 4:4)

God has always had a plan. Everything He does and allows has a purpose. He is never asleep on the job. This is true globally, and it's true of your life, personally. He has always known that our greatest problem is our separation from Him. We were created for Him, which means we will never be happy apart from Him. We needed a bridge between man and God, and "God sent forth his Son," which was the beginning of the fulfillment of that plan. The coming of Christ set in motion the events that would allow us to be united to God again.

The phrase "when the time had fully come" lets us know that the timing of Jesus' birth was not arbitrary. God didn't suddenly get sick of the state of things and decide to step in. Everything that happened up to that point was getting people ready for the solution.

God prepared the Jewish people through the law. One of the most critical commands was to love the Lord their God, and not worship idols. This was a struggle for them and led to their fall from the height of world power into years of captivity. But when the Jewish people came out of that period of enslavement, lessons had been learned on the heart level. They emerged as a monotheistic people, unlike the pagan nations around them. The law did not make them perfect, but it had readied them for Christ's coming.

God also prepared the Gentile people, but it wasn't through the law. It was through allowing them to try everything else out, to see if it would bring peace and satisfaction. The pagan people at that time had tried it all, and had been left disillusioned and despairing.

In the words of author Frank Sheed, "The Law had brought Israel as far as it could, but it had brought it there trained in mind and will and filled with hope—ready for what was to come. If Israel's preparation was by way of vitality and hope, paganism's was by way of devitalization and despair. The Jew had learned the glory of God, the pagan the worthlessness of all else."[133]

The fullness of time has come. Are you ready to receive the solution to your greatest problem? Advent offers a perfect opportunity to recognize the worthlessness of all but Christ and the hope that lies in Him.

Dear Lord,
May I let go of all that is worthless so I can embrace You. Train my mind and will to be open to all You have for me. Amen.

Be Still

DECEMBER 2

"[Jesus] said to them, 'These are my words which I spoke to you, while I was still with you, that everything written about me in the law of Moses and the prophets and the psalms must be fulfilled.' Then he opened their minds to understand the Scriptures." (Luke 24:44–45)

Advent is a time of waiting, which brings to mind the centuries that the Jewish people spent waiting for the Savior. The Old Testament is filled with several dozen major prophecies regarding "the anointed one" ("Messiah" in Hebrew), the deliverer who was to be sent by God at some point in the future to rescue His people. These prophecies were hints of what was to come, which would make it easier to identify whether a person was the true Messiah or an impostor.

Spoiler alert: Jesus nailed every single one of them. Some of us take that fact at face value, but others have a bit more of a skeptical streak. Didn't Jesus already know what was said in the Old Testament, so couldn't He just choose to fulfill each one? Actually, no. Many of the prophecies were tied to events (some historical, some personal) that a person just couldn't control.

Next objection: Wasn't the Bible just put together to make Jesus look good? Couldn't the New Testament writers just have worked the facts to make it all fit? For example, there was an Old Testament prophecy that said the Messiah's bones wouldn't be broken, so couldn't the writer of the Gospel of John have just *said* that the legs of the two thieves on either side of Jesus were broken, but that Jesus was already dead so the soldiers didn't break His? A number of things make it unlikely that one of the Gospel writers would have fabricated the facts. Why would they later have been willing to be martyred for the honor of a fake messiah? Why wouldn't the Jewish community, which was full of eyewitnesses, have jumped all over falsified facts? While the Jewish Talmud never refers to Jesus positively, it also doesn't refute that the fulfillment of the prophecies took place. On that subject, there is silence.

Reading the Old Testament prophecies can build our faith as we recognize God's plan slowly unfolding with great precision. May seeing God's attention to detail with the unfurling of His plan increase our trust in what He is doing in our own lives. His work may be hidden, but it is taking place in and around us.

Dear Lord,
When Your intervention in my life is unseen, may my trust increase nonetheless. Amen.

DECEMBER 3

Be Still

"But you, O Bethlehem ... who are little to be among the clans of Judah, from you shall come forth for me one who is to be ruler in Israel, whose origin is from old, from ancient days." (Micah 5:2)

The Jewish people knew from the prophet Micah that the Messiah was to be born in Bethlehem. Mary might have wondered how that prophecy was to be fulfilled since she was living in Nazareth. But God had taken care of this detail. He prompted Caesar Augustus to decree that everyone in the world was to take part in a census. All people were to go back to their hometowns and be enrolled. This meant that Joseph, Mary's husband, needed to travel back to the city of David (called Bethlehem) because he was from the lineage of David. All happened exactly as Micah had prophesied.

Other Old Testament prophecies fulfilled include the massacre of the innocents in Bethlehem (prophesied in Jeremiah 31:15, fulfilled in Matthew 2:18); and Jesus bringing light to Galilee (prophesied in Isaiah 9:1–2, fulfilled in Matthew 4:12–16), being sent to heal the brokenhearted (prophesied in Isaiah 61:1–2, fulfilled in Luke 4:1–19), being betrayed (prophesied in Psalm 41:10, fulfilled in Luke 22:47–48), being falsely accused (prophesied in Psalm 35:11, fulfilled in Mark 14:57–58), and being betrayed for thirty pieces of silver (prophesied in Zechariah 11:12–14, fulfilled in Matthew 27:9–10).

Were these prophetic fulfillments just some kind of an accident? Analysis by mathematician Peter W. Stoner concludes that the probability of someone fulfilling just eight of the prophecies is one chance in one hundred million billion.[134] And Jesus fulfilled far, far more than eight! What do we do with numbers like that? We can't even wrap our heads around them. The response it should evoke in us is wonder and awe. At the very least, we should be pretty impressed with the fact that sending Jesus as the Messiah was God's intention from the get-go, and He didn't miss a detail in bringing it to pass exactly as He'd planned. Take a few minutes to praise God for being so far beyond anything we can wrap our heads around. Don't expect to figure Him out—just let Him know you find Him amazing. The One who holds history in His hands is listening to you.

Dear Lord,
My mind cannot contain you. You are infinite; I am finite. You control everything; my control is an illusion. Please increase my trust in and amazement by you. Amen.

Be Still  DECEMBER 4

"Therefore the LORD *himself will give you a sign. Behold, a virgin shall conceive and bear a son, and shall call his name Immanuel." (Isaiah 7:14)*

When Mary told Joseph she was pregnant, he was *not* thinking, "This is a sign from the Lord and we are so blessed!" He was far more likely stunned, perplexed, devasted, and a bit paralyzed. It took a visit from an angel to settle him and give him a new perspective. He didn't waver once he understood that this was all a part of God's plan, but to begin with, it rocked his world.

We all have those moments in life when the ground underneath us seems to shift. Perhaps it comes as a phone call in the middle of the night with tragic news, or an unwanted medical diagnosis, or the death of a precious dream, or the loss of a dearly loved one. Whatever the cause, the sure comfort is the same. We get a clue to what it is from the prophetic name of Jesus, spoken of in Isaiah 7:14.

Jesus was called Immanuel, which means "God with us." His name points to His deity (*God* with us) and His closeness (God *with us*). God *with us* will bring us comfort and strength only to the degree to which we are in awe of *God* with us. The greater our view of God, the more we will be helped and strengthened by His presence. If our image of God is small, we won't turn to Him for help. We'll rely on ourselves and other people instead.

When we are faced with heavy or heartbreaking circumstances, we are never alone or without resources. The Creator of the world is intimately acquainted with our problems. He dwells in us through the Holy Spirit, comes into our bodies in the sacrament of the Eucharist, and speaks to us through His Word. He offers us continuous comfort, enlightenment, protection, strength, and peace. All this is conveyed through His presence. *He is enough* for whatever we face.

Dear Lord,
Thank You for Your protection and presence. Thank You for being Immanuel, God with us. Amen.

DECEMBER 5

Be Still

"For we are the aroma of Christ to God among those who are being saved and among those who are perishing." (2 Corinthians 2:15)

In the rush to relocate the elf, deck the halls, plow through crowded shops, wrap, bake, and so on, we sometimes forget that Jesus is "watching the fun" as we prepare for His birthday. *Is it fun?* Or has the sparkle of Christmas grown dim because of the quantity of stuff, the steady activities, and the pressure to keep up with the latest electronic or name-brand gifts?

Do you ever get to the end of the Christmas season and find that your strongest emotion is relief that you got through it? Advent is supposed to be about preparing for the coming of Christ, but too often, all we're really preparing for is more stuff to shove in drawers and closets, and hefty credit card bills in January.

We are to be the "aroma of Christ among those who are being saved and among those who are perishing" (2 Corinthians 2:15). This means it's more important for me to be the scent of Christ to someone in need than for my house to smell like pine, gingerbread, and peppermint.

I can't solve world hunger. I can't build a well in every village that needs clean water. I can't hold every orphaned child who is longing for a mother's arms. But if all God's children decided to celebrate Jesus' birthday by doing justice and showing kindness in action, we would see change. That scent of Christ would fill the air and people would be drawn to Him. Now that would be a birthday gift fit for a king.

Can we spend less on gifts for loved ones who already have so much, and give to someone truly in need?
Can we forgo a luxury for ourselves in order to be more generous?
Can we practice kindness in unlikely places, like the mall parking lot and the long line in the store?
Can we walk humbly with God by prioritizing time with Him over creating the "perfect" Christmas?

The next time I relocate our Elf on the Shelf, I'm going to remind myself that Jesus watches the fun of Christmas, and nothing delights Him more than seeing love in action.

Dear Lord,
May I be the fragrance of Christ as I prepare for Your coming. Amen.

Be Still

DECEMBER 6

"It is the time to seek the Lord." (Hosea 10:12)

As Christmas approaches, I'm freshly inspired to create the perfect Advent setting in my home. I picture beautiful arrangements of greenery and berries by my front door, a lovely tree by the roaring fire, homemade cookies, and peace and harmony wafting through the house like the scent of cinnamon, cloves, and orange. Regardless of my good intentions, my reality never seems to match my ideal. Take, for example, the Advent calendar that I always forget to fill until mid-December. Why on earth I bought the Advent house with the tiny openings that hardly any candy actually fits in is beyond me. But now it's a tradition (although an empty one, literally), so each year I bring it out and hope that I'll get my act together a little earlier.

Thankfully, a meaningful Advent season isn't dependent on a perfectly decorated house, consistent traditions, homemade cookies, or Christmas cards sent out on time. What is Advent all about? It's about getting ready, *spiritually* preparing for the coming of Christ. As we wait to celebrate Christ's birth, we remember the long wait the Israelites had as they anticipated the coming of their rescuer, the Messiah. During their wait, God stretched out a long Advent calendar, in which from time to time, they were able to "open" a gift that reminded them they were drawing closer to the realization of the promise. These gifts were prophecies that pointed to Christ, and glimpses of God's plan of redemption. There are literally hundreds of Old Testament prophecies that were fulfilled by Jesus.

He continues to fill up a very personal Advent calendar for each one of us, every day. Jesus (who is the giver of all good gifts) sends us reminders of His love that are handpicked for His precious daughters. Pope Emeritus Benedict XVI described this in his apostolic letter, *Porta Fidei*, dated October 11, 2011: "Faith grows when it's lived as an experience of love received and when it is communicated as an experience of grace and joy." When we see God's love at work in our lives, our faith grows. Unfortunately, these graces often go unnoticed by us as we dash around, too busy to see.

Perhaps this Advent season can be different. Look for His unexpected gifts. How is God helping you to experience His love today? Did you listen to a beautiful piece of music? Did you receive an unexpected kindness? Did a piece of Scripture speak to your heart and encourage you? Did your child give you a surprise hug? What reminder of His love did He send you today?

Dear Lord,
You know what delights me. Help me to recognize what You've sent my way. Amen.

DECEMBER 7

"Thrones were placed and one that was Ancient of Days took his seat; his raiment was white as snow, and the hair of his head like pure wool; his throne was fiery flames, its wheels were burning fire. A stream of fire issued and came forth from before him; a thousand thousands served him, and ten thousand times ten thousand stood before him; the court sat in judgment, and the books were opened." (Daniel 7:9–10)

Advent is a time of waiting and preparation. As we prepare to encounter Jesus, I wonder how your heart is doing right now. So many of us have been deeply hurt, and what we are waiting for isn't the perfect gift wrapped under the tree. We're waiting for justice. And its delay makes it hard to prepare for Christmas, because our hearts are bleeding out. So often it seems that retribution will never come. We're tired of waiting.

We talk a great deal about God's mercy, and that's an important part of His character. But another aspect is that of judge. God sees. He is fair. One day, all wrongs and injustices will be made right. This is the side of God that we see in Daniel 7. Daniel was experiencing a vision in which he saw evil being judged and destroyed.

The Ancient of Days sat on His throne. He will be sitting on His throne the day we must all account for the way we have lived. The person who hurt you will be held responsible. Even if it seems that justice will never be served, be assured: God knows. One day, He will make everything right.

But one day we, too, will stand before Him. When our life passes before our eyes, how will we feel, looking at our choices in His presence? Will we have chosen to trust Him and let go of anger, or will we have clung to bitterness, impeding our ability to love? Will we have allowed God to work within our pain, teaching us things that we wouldn't otherwise have learned? Will we have welcomed His Spirit into our hearts, helping us to forgive?

God can bring beauty from ashes during our lifetime, but our full restoration will take place in heaven. All will be purified there, and we'll be able to see ourselves and God with clarity. Our dignity will be restored. We will be healed, and every tear will be wiped from our eyes, one day. Can you trust Him as you wait?

Dear Lord,
"It is in heaven that we shall know our titles of nobility."[135] May I wait well for that full unveiling of my dignity and Your justice. Amen.

Be Still  **DECEMBER 8**

The Immaculate Conception of the Blessed Virgin Mary

"And [the angel Gabriel] came to [Mary] and said, 'Hail, full of grace, the Lord is with you!'" (Luke 1:28)

The Catholic Church has always taught that Mary was conceived without sin. This belief, called the dogma of the Immaculate Conception, does not refer to Mary's conception of Jesus. It refers to the conception of Mary in the womb of her mother, Saint Anne. According to CCC 492, "The 'splendor of an entirely unique holiness' by which Mary is 'enriched from the first instant of her conception' comes wholly from Christ: she is 'redeemed, in a more exalted fashion, by reason of the merits of her Son.'"

Jesus redeemed Mary. He saved her, not from the pit of sin, but before she fell into it. She was saved not through her own merits, but through the merits of Jesus. You might ask how this is possible, since Jesus hadn't yet died on the cross or risen from the dead at the time of Mary's conception. We ask this because of our finite understanding of time. The Old Testament saints were saved by looking forward to the cross. They didn't have a perfect understanding of how their salvation would be won. They didn't have perfect sight, but they believed anyway. This is a description of faith. We look back at the cross; they looked forward. And in God's perfect plan, He saves in the timetable and manner that He chooses.

Many argue against the teaching of Mary's Immaculate Conception by pointing to Romans 3:23: "All have sinned and fall short of the glory of God." But does this verse say that there are no exceptions? What about a baby? Or a child below the age of reason? What about Jesus? Exceptions to this verse exist.

Have you ever thought, "It was easier for Mary to be obedient to God than it is for me. She was given the gift of being full of grace from birth." Meditating on Mary's dignity and holiness can inspire us, but if we don't have a clear understanding of our own dignity, it can cause us to feel discouraged. To avoid this, focus on your own dignity. You were filled with grace at baptism, when you became God's beloved daughter. You received the life of the Holy Spirit, who breathes love into you. You may feel like you can't love the way Mary loved, but God provides for what you lack. You have an inherent dignity.

Dear Lord,
I am grateful that I share in the grace that You bestowed on Mary. What radiance. What a privilege. What unmerited favor. Thank You. Amen.

DECEMBER 9

"Who knows whether you have not come to the kingdom for such a time as this?" (Esther 4:14)

When God calls us to take our place in our generation, when He calls our hearts to join Him in making this world a better place, He uses all of it to form us into women of strength, dignity, purpose, and healing—even the things that you worry disqualify you from serving Him. Those are the very things that make you authentic, human, and someone others can relate to when they are overwhelmed by their own weaknesses. God has promised never to leave you or forsake you. He has placed limitless beauty within you, and His presence is what allows that beauty to shine forth. When you invite Him into the tender places of your heart, He promises to make everything beautiful in its time. Perhaps if you could stop your striving and slow down, you'd hear His whisper, His still, small voice, beckoning you to a different path.

You are here for such a time as this. There is a holy destiny with your name on it. But it will take courage to take hold of it. It will require you to claim God's promise that the old things have passed away and all things are being made new in your life (2 Corinthians 5:17).

In the words of Amena Brown Owen and Ann Voskamp in their poem, "The Esther Generation":
Sometimes we imagine that God's voice is a disappointed hard lined teacher
Who is waiting to whack our knuckles with a ruler for any imperfections
But that isn't God's voice at all
That isn't God's heart at all
He speaks tenderly
He doesn't need to raise His voice
He speaks as if He's right next to us
Because He's right next to us
Because He goes before us
Because His Spirit lives inside us
He starts with love
And not because He is a hopeless romantic
But mostly because
He is all love and hope and second chances.[136]

This Advent, may the God of all hope soften us, strengthen us, and restore us. May we place our stories—our past, present, and future—into His hands. May all of it be used for His glory, for such a time as this.

Dear Lord,
Help me stop the striving, the consumption, the trying to keep up, and the determination to check everything off the list. This season is about You, not me getting it all done. Slow me. Soften me. Remake me. Amen.

Be Still

DECEMBER 10

"He had brought up Hadassah, that is Esther, the daughter of his uncle, for she had neither father nor mother; the maiden was beautiful and lovely, and when her father and her mother died, Mordecai adopted her as his own daughter." (Esther 2:7)

Esther was a heroine—brave, bold, brilliant... and broken. We know from Esther 2:7 that she was orphaned as a child. This would have caused her enormous pain, and no doubt ushered in wounds of abandonment and fear. Yet somehow, she overcame her obstacles and saved her people from genocide.

Even those of us who haven't lost our parents can feel the pain of abandonment, loneliness, and isolation. This may come from an experience of rejection or conditional love. When we feel insecure, self-protection is often our default response. We may put up walls around our hearts, and then set out to create our own security. Underlying these behaviors is a fear that if we don't perform, if we don't control our circumstances, we will be left alone. While the Christmas season can be full of cozy family time, for many it's a time when family dysfunction intensifies or loneliness feels especially acute and unbearable.

According to 1 John 4:18, it is perfect love that will drive fear from our hearts. God's love for us is perfect because it is utterly selfless and pure. He proved His love on the cross. What more could He have offered? Place His perfect love between you and your fear, and let it remind you that His presence makes all the difference.

Ephesians 1:4–5 (AMP) says, "[God] predestined and lovingly planned for us to be adopted to Himself [as His own] children through Jesus Christ, in accordance with the kind intention and good pleasure of his will." He chose *you*. He has always wanted you.

What a difference there is between a slave who earns her keep and a daughter who simply rests in her position in the family, confident that she belongs. "For you did not receive the spirit of slavery to fall back into fear, but you have received the spirit of sonship. When we cry, 'Abba! Father!'" (Romans 8:15)

Dear Lord,
I am Your daughter. I am not an orphan. I am beloved, and I don't need to perform in order to earn Your love. Help me to stop behaving like a performing orphan. That is not who I am. You have adopted me and made me Your own. I can call You Abba, just as Jesus did. I rest in this truth. Help me to enjoy the life of joy and fulfillment You offer to me simply because You love me. Amen.

DECEMBER 11

"Behold, the Lord's hand is not shortened, that it cannot save." (Isaiah 59:1)

As Christmas approaches, is your heart aching over a loved one who is far from God? Are you trying to trust God with the heart of the one you love, but finding it really hard?

Although God is all-powerful, He always respects human freedom. He doesn't force anyone to love Him. But what He *does* do is create opportunity after opportunity for people to see His goodness. He orchestrates people's paths to the cross so that His children can share about the difference He makes. He softens hearts. He breaks down barriers. God's heart and arm are moved toward these actions in response to our prayers.

You will have the greatest influence on people when they know that you love them. When they can rest in your unconditional love, when they trust that you are for them, when they don't feel like a "project," when they don't feel that you will love them only if they change—then, and only then, will barriers come down. And don't doubt the power of the unspoken word. We may pat ourselves on the backs, saying we love unconditionally because we bite our tongues and don't say what we are thinking. Oh, friend, *they know*. They sense the judgment. They see the disappointment in our eyes. We *earn* the right to be heard. We earn the right to speak truth into our loved ones' hearts. We earn it when we learn how to love without conditions. It's as we do this that we truly reflect the heart of God to those who desperately need to know His love.

No amount of manipulation, or orchestration of circumstances, or perfect words, or even the perfect example of godliness is going to open and change the hearts of our loved ones. When a heart softens and breaks open, that is the work of God. It is only He who can reach into the secret places of the heart, bringing healing, comfort, and a quenching of thirst.

Not only is God's arm not too short to reach into your loved one's heart, He has limitless patience and matchless love. Are you desperate for your loved one to know Christ? Be assured, God is even more desperate to be known. Go to the Lord in prayer for your loved one. Storm heaven. Don't give up. God wants this even more than you do, and He will not cease drawing hearts to Him.

Dear Lord,
"It is you who have made the heavens and the earth by your great power and by your outstretched arm! Nothing is too hard for you" [Jeremiah 32:17]. Amen.

Be Still

DECEMBER 12

"I will not leave you desolate." (John 14:18)

We all need a mother. No matter how old we are, we long to be nurtured, protected, and loved. Yet many of us, for various reasons, are not receiving this tender care. We may feel like a motherless daughter because our mother has died. Or perhaps our earthly mother wasn't able or willing to love us in a way that really satisfied our needs. We might be caring for our mothers as they age, and our roles have been reversed. Whatever the reason, we can end up in a place where we're doing all that we can just to hold it together. And needing to be strong all the time only intensifies the desire to find a place where we can arrive broken and needy and receive comfort.

Here's the good news: We are not orphans. We have a heavenly Father who is always there to heal, forgive, restore, and redeem us. We have a heavenly mother who longs to spread a blanket (her mantle of protection) over us, to comfort us, to come alongside us in our times of need, to pray for us when we need strength, to help us stay on a path that leads us closer to Jesus.

Who needs Mary?
Those who don't feel known.
Those who are harsh.
Those who don't feel loved.
Those who are afraid that if they do too much, they'll be taken advantage of.
Those who are afraid of what obedience to God might cost.
Those who take care of everybody else and need someone to take care of them.
We all need a mother.

When Mary was asked to collaborate with God, she was given no guarantees—just the opportunity to love. The first thing the angel said to her was, "Do not be afraid" (Luke 1:30). These are Mary's words to us, as well. She led by example, showing total confidence in God when she said, "Let it be done to me according to your word" (Luke 1:38). She showed total confidence in Jesus when she turned to the servants at the wedding at Cana and said, "Do whatever He tells you" (John 2:5). She gives *us* the same message: "Do whatever He tells you." But we hesitate, wondering how much pain or sorrow such obedience might cause us.

Mary didn't know what suffering her yes—her fiat—might bring. And we don't know, either. But we do know that we don't walk that path alone. And we know that obedience, though costly, pays eternal dividends that make any sacrifice worth it.

Dear Lord,
Thank You for the gift of Your mother. May I follow Mary's example, uniting my will totally to Yours. Amen.

DECEMBER 13

Be Still

"And he sat down opposite the treasury, and watched the multitude putting money into the treasury. Many rich people put in large sums. And a poor widow came, and put in two copper coins, which make a penny. And he called his disciples to him and said to them, 'Truly I say to you, this poor widow has put in more than all those who are contributing to the treasury. For they all contributed out of their abundance; but she out of her poverty has put in everything she had, her whole living.'" (Mark 12:41–44)

The poor widow could certainly have justified keeping her money for herself, especially after seeing rich people putting large sums of money into the treasury. Very often, we resist the call to give generously because we are afraid that our own needs won't be met. Fear gets in the way of generosity. Greed is another real deterrent to radical giving, as we struggle to resist the urge to continually buy more and more, confusing needs with wants. Indifference is possibly the scariest emotion blocking generosity, as we don't even notice that it's within us. We're too busy paying attention to the list of Christmas gifts we need to buy. When we don't see the poor up close, it's very easy to ignore their needs and focus on blessing the blessed. I am preaching to myself here.

I have heard it said, "Our generosity isn't measured by how much we give, but by how much we keep." When we hear of large financial donations, our first reaction is often to elevate those gifts above all others. Large dollar amounts impress us because we can see the great good these financial gifts can accomplish. But as God measures our generosity, He is well aware of what we have held back for our own comfort. True sacrificial giving comes at a cost.

Certainly poverty isn't only an issue of finances. There is the poverty of food and water, but there is also the poverty of love, as well as deep loneliness. As Christians, we are called to alleviate both types of suffering. May our hearts stay tender to all the needs around us.

Dear Lord,
This Advent season, please free us from numbness, complacency, and indifference. All we have is Yours. May we seek to honor You with all we possess. Help us to differentiate between our wants and our needs. Help us to have the strength to forgo luxuries for the sake of those who don't have their most basic needs met. Amen.

Be Still

DECEMBER 14

"Abide in me." (John 15:4)

Does the thought of growing in intimacy with Christ ever feel like adding one more thing to an already overwhelmed schedule? How many of us rush through Advent with a constant inner dialogue of thoughts like these:

> *I'm never going to pull this off.*
> *I'm the only one who can do this.*
> *This isn't fair. I think I'm the only person working this hard.*
> *Lord, don't You care?*
> *I'm so tired.*
> *I'm sick of living like this.*

We get glimpses of other people's wholehearted living, and we recognize that there is something missing in our own lives. We wonder if we just need Christmas to be over. Or less on our plate. Or a different job. Or more money.

I think Martha maybe felt a little bit that way when she peeked into the living room at Mary settled in at Jesus' feet. But that longing in her heart quickly turned to irritation. "What is wrong with her?" she must have thought. Everyone knew that a woman's place was not in the middle of a religious gathering of men. Her next thought might have been, "Who does she think she is?"

Make no mistake—anytime a person ventures out of safety and decides to live life with exuberance and joy, there will be someone who says, "Who does she think she is?" If it isn't a voice from outside, our own thoughts chime in. "Who do you think you are? Temper your expectations. This is just life. Stop expecting it to feel great. Just keep on trucking. Just do the next thing on the list." The next thing on the list. And the next. And the next. And we trudge through life, halfheartedly and a little bit resentfully.

What if choosing the better part wasn't about something *more* being required of us? What if the key to wholehearted living was a trading of our current lists for the one Jesus offers us?

Here's an alternative to-do list for today: Explore who I am in Christ. Worry less. Be teachable. Taste freedom. Work with joy.

Dear Lord,
I had such good intentions at the start of Advent—to somehow do all the things required for the holidays and still spend time quietly at Your feet. I am feeling like I am not doing any of it well. Anxiety and expectations fill my heart and are robbing me of peace. Help me to set my list aside and just rest in Your presence. Just for a few minutes. May I breathe deeply and be reminded that only one thing is required of me. All the urgent things can wait, because You matter more. Amen.

DECEMBER 15

Be Still

"But Martha was distracted with much serving; and she went to him and said, 'Lord, do you not care that my sister has left me to serve alone? Tell her then to help me.'" (Luke 10:40)

Martha asked, "Lord, do you not care?" Mary's unwillingness to help seemed like such a selfish choice. The injustice appeared obvious. When Jesus responded by *defending* Mary's choice, Martha must have been taken aback. No matter how gently He said it, exhausted Martha must have been incredulous that somehow she was the one being criticized.

Jesus didn't side with Mary because He didn't care about Martha; He pointed to a different choice precisely because He cared about Martha *so much*. It was clear to Jesus that Martha defined her worth by her productivity. Every time her burst of energy and hard work resulted in a successful event or a sense of accomplishment, she felt like she mattered. She measured her worth by her performance.

Jesus was inviting Martha to sit at His feet, because that is the best place to learn *who we really are*. When we are in productivity mode, we remember *what we can do*. Those are two very different things.

We produce a lot and then we're likely to fall into the traps of self-sufficiency and pride. Or we don't produce enough and we feel like failures. Both responses leave us vulnerable to believing the wrong messages about who we are and what we're worth.

The world is constantly sending us messages about who we are. "You are what you produce." "You are what you eat." "You are what you wear." "You are what you make of yourself." Jesus invites us to sit at His feet and fill up our minds with His perspective. Sit at His feet and remember who you really are.

Dear Lord,
Help me to remember that You love me because I belong to You, not because I'm perfect or because of the things I do. Give me the mind of Christ so that I will live out the truth that I cannot earn Your love; it is unconditional. Help me to lift my eyes to Your face and see reflected back all the warmth, compassion, mercy, and grace that radiates from Your heart. Who am I? I am Your beloved daughter. When I fail, You fill in the gaps. When I see all I lack, You remind me that You, within me, are enough. When I'm tempted to beat myself up, You remind me that You took the beating so that I could rest in grace. Help me to do that. May I cease my striving, because my worth was defined and settled when You died for me on the cross. Amen.

Be Still

DECEMBER 16

"Martha, Martha, you are anxious and troubled about many things." (Luke 10:41)

"Wait a minute, Lord," Martha must have wanted to say. "You think that the problem is my worrying? Well, thank heavens I trouble myself about things. If I didn't, then what would everyone be unwrapping on Christmas? What's on my to-do list today? Oh, right—*everything*."

Of course, that's not what she said, because, after all, it was Jesus who was making the point. But just because she didn't say it doesn't mean she wasn't thinking it and justifying her actions. Because isn't that what we so often do? When someone tells us not to worry, it can almost make us more anxious, because we think we're the only people paying enough attention to realize what is at stake. When we feel that level of responsibility, the weight of it all can be paralyzing.

Are things not going according to your plan this Advent? Could it be that they are going *exactly* according to His, and He knows something that you do not? Could it be that He even desires that you fail at something so that a significant lesson is learned? Might He be saying no to one prayer in order to say yes to a far more important one?

As Pastor Todd Wagner says, "Worry is believing God won't get it right." Peace comes when we trust God and say, "I don't have a clue what to do about this, but I am going to live free and light because God is in control, and He knows what He's doing."

Jesus tells us to put on His yoke and learn from Him when we feel burdened (Matthew 11:29). When we put on Jesus' yoke, it doesn't mean that we sit down and abdicate all responsibility. We still need to move forward and do our part. The critical thing is to determine what we are responsible for and what part is out of our hands. We must trust God with what we cannot control.

Dear Lord,
As Corrie ten Boom wrote, "Worry is carrying tomorrow's load with today's strength—carrying two days at once. It is moving into tomorrow ahead of time. Worry does not empty tomorrow of its sorrow. It empties today of its strength."[137] Help me to see what You are asking me to do today, and everything that falls outside of that, I give to You. Amen.

Be Still

DECEMBER 17

"I believe that you are the Christ, the Son of God, he who is coming into the world." (John 11:27)

In John 11:1–44, Martha and Mary's beloved brother, Lazarus, was terribly sick. The sisters sent word to Jesus saying, "Lord, he whom you love is ill" (John 11:3). They knew that Jesus could heal Lazarus, and they knew He loved him. So they waited expectantly. And waited a little longer. They did the calculations. He should have been there by now. Doubt crept in. Many days later than they'd expected, Jesus arrived. But by then, Lazarus had died. Grief washed over the sisters like a tidal wave. Mary couldn't even come out and see Jesus when He arrived.

And what about Martha? This would be a defining moment for her. Would she crumple under the weight of doubt, questioning Jesus' love for her because He hadn't answered her request as she'd expected? Or would she remain rooted in the truth that Jesus loved her more than she could ever imagine, and that He was in control even if all circumstances suggested otherwise?

In Luke 10, Jesus had seen that Martha's identity was wrapped up in what she produced. Her worth was determined by her productivity. How did Martha respond to Jesus' correction? She *learned*. She *changed*. It's one thing to be humble in a general sense ("I'm such a hot mess"; "I'm flawed and broken"), but when something specific is pointed out in our lives, that's when we reveal whether we are truly teachable. Martha proved that she was.

In the midst of heartrending grief, Martha was able to say, "Yes, Lord. I believe that you are the Christ, the Son of God, he who is coming into the world." It's interesting that this powerhouse statement of faith came not from contemplative Mary, but from recovering workaholic Martha. Because that's what an encounter with Jesus can do—*if* we are teachable.

To be teachable, we need to listen, act on what we hear, and respond to correction. There is no greater key to freedom than being teachable. It will allow you to progress in the spiritual life by leaps and bounds. While others will be learning the same lesson over and over, you will be scaling new heights of holiness. The alternative to being teachable is spiritual stagnation. When we don't respond to the correction God has given us, we don't progress. We remain stuck, sluggish, stale.

Dear Lord,
Am I teachable? Or am I defensive? Please reveal to me any area where You have been trying to teach me something but I have not listened or not acted on what I've heard from You. Amen.

Be Still

DECEMBER 18

"Did I not tell you that if you would believe you would see the glory of God?" (Luke 11:40)

After declaring her faith in Jesus as the Messiah, Martha went back to the house and got her sister, Mary. The two (and all their fellow mourners) joined Jesus at their brother Lazarus' tomb. Jesus requested that they roll away the stone covering the tomb. Martha told Jesus that it would smell terrible; Lazarus had been dead for four days. But Jesus asked her to believe, promising that if she did, she'd see the glory of God.

Lazarus was raised from the dead by Jesus' simple words, "Lazarus, come out!" And out Lazarus came, bound with bandages, with his face wrapped in a cloth. He was alive, but he wasn't free. He could move forward in a halting way, but he couldn't see, run, or dance. His grave clothes had to be removed before he could really live.

In the same way, we can be given new life in Christ but still live in bondage. One of the things that can keep us in bondage is a poor understanding of the magnitude of what happened in John 11:43–44 and when Jesus Himself rose from the dead. In both cases, we see that Jesus has power over death. Critical observation: In neither the raising of Lazarus nor His own resurrection did Jesus need the assistance of a few good men (or women). Our sins were placed on Jesus, and He received the punishment due us. When He died on the cross, it meant that the debt we owed was *paid in full*.

We remain in bondage when we have a faulty understanding of what purchased our freedom. It wasn't Christ *plus* our efforts. It was Christ, and Christ alone. We must learn the same lesson Martha learned in Luke 10: Our identity isn't found in our productivity. But we must take it one step further and recognize that our salvation—our freedom—isn't found in our productivity either. Our salvation isn't something we *earn*. It has everything to do with what Christ already accomplished on the cross.

When we recognize this, we can follow Mary's example and rest at the feet of Jesus. We can ask Him to strip us of our burial clothes and to help us run in freedom. Do you ever feel bound up by expectations that seem unattainable? What burial clothes need to be removed in your life so that you can experience freedom?

Dear Lord,
Please unwrap my burial clothes, and clothe me with Christ. Help me to discern which thoughts are keeping me from resting in your grace and then running in freedom. Amen.

Be Still

"There they made [Jesus] a supper; Martha served, and Lazarus was one of those at table with him." (John 12:2)

Martha was back to serving dinner. She had learned a life-changing lesson from Jesus, she had been transformed, and she had seen God's glory show up and exceed her wildest expectations when her brother was raised from the dead. And then she went back to her normal tasks, serving others. Although Martha needed to avoid falling into the pit of rooting her identity in her productivity, that didn't mean she'd spend the rest of her life in contemplative prayer. Work was still required.

The same is true for us. We can experience spiritual awakening that makes us long to just stay in that place of worship and joy. But at some point, we need to go back to everyday life and do what is required. There are still tasks to do to prepare for Christmas. So how do we do this work in a way that pleases God? According to Brother Lawrence, being made holy "does not depend upon changing our works, but in doing that for God's sake which we commonly do for our own."[138]

Even with all the best attempts to lead balanced lives, there are times when our work gets overwhelming. When days like that start to get the better of us, it's helpful to stop and ask a very important question: What does God want?

God, more than anything, wants our hearts. When we do nothing but work, we become production machines. When this happens, without intending to, we live detached from our hearts. We become robotic, simply going through the motions. We're on the treadmill of productivity, and there's no time to step off and rest or worship or play. All the while, we know God wants something from us, so we offer Him our good deeds—all the results of our productivity—instead of our hearts. But that's not what He's after.

Our work most glorifies God when our heart is in it, not detached from it. Our heart is where our joy lives. It's where our motives come from. God wants your work to be infused with joy. That doesn't mean that every single second of it is exciting and fun. Redemptive work is one way we carry the cross and follow Jesus, and that is difficult. But all our work should not feel that way. Life should not feel that way. Take some time to meditate on what brings you joy. Make sure your work is balanced with those times.

Dear Lord,
Help me to balance work with activities that bring me joy. I offer it all to You as my worship. It's my offering of a full life well lived and saturated with gratitude. Amen.

Be Still

DECEMBER 20

"No eye has seen, no ear has heard, no mind has conceived what God has prepared for those who love him." (1 Corinthians 2:9)

The Advent season can be a hard time to hope. The lights, decorations, and smells create something beautiful. That beauty expands our hearts and makes us long for fulfillment. It can make us yearn for traditions we had in childhood. The deepest ache comes when we long for the presence of loved ones who were here in years past but are no longer with us.

These aches were placed in our hearts by our Creator to make us long for heaven. Our time on earth is not all there is. Our destiny is an eternal one, and it is only there that we will have all our longings satisfied. During our lifetimes, we'll get tastes of what that heavenly bliss is going to be like, but they are only meant to point us homeward, never to totally fill and satisfy us.

When we look to people, to circumstances, or even to answers to prayer to satisfy our longings, we will always be disappointed. We were made for more, and that *more* is not here. Yes, Jesus satisfies. Yes, His Holy Spirit fills us and makes all the difference in our lives. But there will always be a gap between what we experience on earth and the total union with God that we were created for.

What we think of heaven will have an enormous impact on how we feel about all of this. If we think of heaven as a place where we do nothing but play harps and sing all day, we're going to try to squeeze as much satisfaction out of this life as we can. We'll have the attitude of "Let's eat and drink and be merry because tomorrow we die (and everything gets really boring after that point)."

Oh, my friends. Nothing could be further from the truth. Heaven is *not* going to be boring. It's going to be the place where our emptiness is filled. Where our joy shoots through the roof to the point of ecstasy. Where all our longings will be satisfied. Everything wrong will be made right. Every tear will be wiped from our eyes. When Jesus left this earth, He went to get it all ready for us. Think about the ultimate Christmas experience. The most beautifully decorated home. Sublime smells. Food with the perfect blend of flavor and comfort. Unwrapping the gift that you've been hoping for but were sure was out of reach. Being surrounded by those you love. All of that is just a taste of what Jesus has prepared for us.

The story is told of a woman who lost her only child. Holding him in her arms, she turned her face toward heaven and said, "I give you joy, my sweet child." This is what awaits us—pure joy.

Dear Lord,
May I turn my heart to heaven, recognizing that all my longings will be satisfied there. Amen.

Be Still

DECEMBER 21

"Give instruction to a wise man, and he will be still wiser; teach a righteous man and he will increase in learning." (Proverbs 9:9)

The story is told of a young man in China who asked an older teacher if he would teach him. The older man invited the younger one to sit down and have tea. As the teacher spoke, he was continually interrupted by the student. "Oh, I already know that." "Oh, yes—that happened to me before and this is what I did." "Oh, I don't have that problem."

The teacher stopped talking and began to pour tea into the teacup. He poured and poured until the liquid began to run over the sides of the cup. "Stop! It's enough! My cup is full!" said the student.

"I see that," said the teacher. "Your cup is very full. And I cannot teach you anything until you empty your cup." Without teachability, truth and wisdom become like the tea being poured into the already full cup. They run all over, without actually doing any good.

If we are to become more than workhorses—if we are going to take hold of our lives and live with joy and exuberance—we must be open to change. We must open our hearts wide and embrace new thoughts and new ways of doing things. We must empty our cups of old habits that aren't serving us well anymore. Old habits die hard, but they *can* die. And on the other side of that death is freedom and joy. It is possible to change and to experience the wholehearted living that has been elusive. In nineteenth-century author George Eliot's words, "It's never too late to be what you might have been." What might change in the atmosphere of our homes if we gave everyone the gift of our humble teachability this Christmas?

A truly teachable spirit won't come from gritting our teeth, tensing our shoulders, and charging forward. It will come when we invite the Holy Spirit into the process. He is the One who whispers in our hearts who we are in Christ. He is the One who softens our hearts and makes us receptive to teaching. C. S. Lewis says it well: "It is not trying that is ever going to bring us home. All this trying leads up to the vital moment at which you turn to God and say, 'You must do this. I can't.'"[139]

We can't do it alone, but thank God, we are never alone. He is with us and He beckons us forward, toward a life of freedom and joy.

Dear Lord,
Soften my heart and help me to be open to instruction. This holiday season, may I be quickly convicted when I become defensive. May I invite people to speak truth into my life and learn from them. Amen.

Be Still

DECEMBER 22

"Martha received [Jesus] into her house. And she had a sister called Mary, who sat at the Lord's feet and listened to his teaching." (Luke 10:39)

While Martha was frustrated that Mary didn't get up and help, Jesus said that Mary had chosen "the good portion" (Luke 10:42). He commended Mary for her two actions: sitting and listening. This is a hard truth for those of us who love to cross things off the to-do list. And at no time of year is the list longer than in the days before Christmas.

But maybe our busyness and unwillingness to sit down are a part of a bigger issue, one we're very anxious to ignore. In the words of essayist Tim Kreider, "Busyness serves as a kind of existential reassurance, a hedge against emptiness. Obviously your life cannot possibly be silly or trivial or meaningless if you are so busy, completely booked, or in demand every hour of the day."[140]

We avoid slowing down and sitting at the Lord's feet because we're afraid of what we'll hear when it all gets quiet. There's nothing like people and tasks to distract us from acknowledging inner emptiness and pain. But when we kick our emotions and pain away and just get busy keeping the balls up in the air, we are leaving the One with the solutions out of the picture. We don't have the solution, but God does. Slowing down and acknowledging that there is something wrong inside doesn't mean we are failures. It means we're human, we're real, and sometimes life really, really hurts.

We don't have all the solutions. Instead of distracting ourselves and ignoring this reality, we can choose to follow Mary's example. Sitting at the feet of Jesus means we are in a posture of humility and openness before Him. We offer God access to the deep, hidden corners of our hearts. These are the parts of us that are aching, rebelling, justifying, and desperately needing His healing. These are the places that we know are holding us back, but we don't know what we're supposed to do about it.

When you sit at the feet of Jesus and gaze up at His face, you are reflected in His eyes. Make no mistake, He is not looking at you with disappointment. Lean in and look a little closer. What is reflected in His eyes is the you He had in mind when He created you. He not only sees you—the wrinkles, the wounds, the scars—He sees your potential. He sees who you can become.

Dear Lord,
It's hard to see myself through Your eyes, so please "help me understand what you had in mind when you made the original me."[141] Amen.

Be Still

DECEMBER 23

"Then Mary, when she came where Jesus was and saw him, fell at his feet, saying to him, 'Lord, if you had been here, my brother would not have died.'" (John 11:32)

When Mary and Martha had sent word to Jesus that their brother, Lazarus, was dying, He didn't come in time. We've all experienced a time when Jesus hasn't shown up in the way that we felt He should. Perhaps something happened in your past that you feel He should have prevented. Maybe you are in the midst of a crisis right now, and you can't figure out why Jesus isn't stepping in and stopping the madness. You look around at other people who seem to be having the time of their lives during the holidays, and all you feel is ache and weariness. Have you desperately wanted to experience a miracle in an area of your life? If the wait feels too long, perhaps you've asked, "Where are you, God?"

It's *there*, right there in that place, that He is meeting you. He may not have shown up in the way you think He should have, but I promise you, He is there. Just as He met Mary in her place of grief, He meets you, and weeps over what has hurt you. He grieves over all that sin has robbed from you.

God never encounters you with indifference. He comes with tenderness. He looks into your heart and recognizes that you have blocked some corners of it because you are desperately afraid of being hurt or out of control again. He understands, but He doesn't want you to stay in that place.

He knows why you have rolled a big stone in front of that part of your heart. When you, like Martha, say, "That stone cannot be removed! There'll be a stench," He understands why you are self-protecting. But He also knows that you can't self-protect and love at the same time. And when you can't love, you are held back from experiencing the full life He created you for.

So here is what He's asking. He's asking if you will let Him roll back that stone and place His healing hands over each area that is causing you pain. He's asking you to surrender those areas to Him, one at a time, step by step. This is the path to freedom.

Dear Lord,
I ask You to bring victory into this specific area of my life [name it], where I have up until now only experienced defeat. I invite You into this place and ask You to be Lord over it. Amen.

Be Still

DECEMBER 24

"And she gave birth to her first-born son and wrapped him in swaddling cloths, and laid him in a manger, because there was no place for them in the inn." (Luke 2:7)

When we were driving back to the airport after meeting our first grandson, my husband and I talked about the effect little Luke had on him. "When I just held him, sleeping on my chest, all the things I've been worried about just faded away. There was a power in that little baby. He commanded all the attention in the room, simply by being there."

It makes me think of a night thousands of years ago when another baby was born. It was the night that changed everything. Hope was ushered in just because of His presence. Suddenly, everything else faded in importance. The door between heaven and earth was opened, and a baby entered. God entered the world in the most vulnerable state possible. His fragility, His softness, His dependence . . . this was the beginning for the One who would love us to death. Mingled with the outpouring of His love is death—the incarnation and the cross. This self-giving is the price of true intimacy. It's always demanding and brings with it a feeling of vulnerability.

I wonder where this Christmas Eve finds your heart. Is it weary from giving? Is it apprehensive, wondering how family dynamics will play out over the next few days? Are you feeling tempted to self-protect, to draw back, to fall into old coping mechanisms? Stress does that to the best of us.

Can you pause and feel the power of the baby in your midst? The Christ child comes and reminds us that all else can fade in importance, if we will focus on Him. It's His birthday, but He comes to offer gifts to *us*. He offers us kindness, hopeful that we will use it to offer forgiveness to those who don't seem to deserve it. He offers us patience, hopeful that we will use it to listen to the relative's story that we have already heard a million times. He offers us goodness, hopeful that we will do small things with great love for the people who are sitting in their chairs when we think they should be helping us. He offers us gentleness, hopeful that we'll be the balm between frustrated loved ones. He offers us self-control so that we close our mouths when the quick retort is on the tip of our tongues.

Oh come, oh come Emmanuel, and breathe new life into our families and homes. This Christmas Eve, we welcome You. Amen.

Be Still

The Nativity of the Lord

"Be not afraid; for behold, I bring you good news of a great joy which will come to all the people; for to you is born this day in the city of David a Savior, who is Christ the Lord. And this will be a sign for you: you will find a baby wrapped in swaddling cloths and lying in a manger." (Luke 2:10–12)

This helpless baby, born without luxury or fanfare, was the solution to mankind's greatest problem. Most people weren't paying attention when He arrived, but those who noticed either felt threatened or responded in worship.

The same is true today. Most people think of Jesus with indifference, despite the fact that He would take the chaos of their lives and turn it into a powerful story if they turned to Him. Many are threatened. They understand exactly who He says He is—the king, the alpha and omega. But allowing Him to be that in their own lives would mean abdicating the throne themselves, and they like to be in charge of their own destiny. Then there are those who worship. The worship is imperfect, but it is an offering that nonetheless pleases God.

What are we able to offer God in worship? He doesn't need anything. Perhaps we can learn a lesson from the wise men. They brought Jesus gold, frankincense, and myrrh—three gifts symbolizing something more. The gold was a gift of beauty and worth, honoring Jesus as king. The frankincense honored Him as a priest, as it was used in the temple for worship (symbolizing prayers reaching to heaven). The myrrh, used for embalming bodies, pointed to Christ's sacrificial death.

Could we worship Jesus today with our gold, offering Him what is of most worth to us? This might be a gift of time, money, or best of all, of our hearts. We could worship Jesus with frankincense by spending some quiet time in prayer, despite all the festivities around us. We could worship by offering myrrh, a gift symbolizing death. Could you die to a selfish instinct today? Instead of doing or saying what feels easier, could you do what is sacrificial for another?

Before the night is done, could you sit with Him for a moment on His birthday and give Him the gift of your presence? He will meet you there, and bestow on you the deeply satisfying gift of grace.

Dear Lord,
I am so grateful that You came to earth, were willing to take on our human nature with all its limitations, and then offered Your very self in our place. Thank You for Your love and presence—the only thing that truly satisfies. Amen.

Be Still

 DECEMBER 26

"But Mary kept all these things, pondering them in her heart." (Luke 2:19)

Belief precedes action. Before we do something, we believe something. This was true for Mary, and it's true for women today. Whom we listen to, the books we read, the music we hear, and the movies we watch all influence us more than we realize. What we feed on will ultimately shape our opinions, beliefs, and actions.

"Believing is an act of the intellect assenting to the divine truth by command of the will moved by God through grace" (CCC 155). This means that when we expose ourselves to divine truth, when we soak up God's perspective on things, we are strengthening our intellect. When God's truth is up in our heads, it strengthens our will to make the right choice because we want to.

Mary was careful about what she allowed her mind to dwell on. She pondered things, "pondering on them in her heart" (Luke 2:19). Instead of just taking life as it came and reacting to circumstances in whatever way her emotions led her, she took the time to reflect on the big picture, on God's plan, on His faithfulness and goodness. The time she spent quietly pondering shaped her beliefs. With her beliefs rooted firmly in God's trustworthiness, faithfulness, and goodness, she was able to face enormous challenges with grace.

As the year comes to an end, you have a choice. What will you fill your mind with over the next year? What is the next book you'll pick up? How will you spend your leisure time? Mary challenges us to make it count, to soak up truth.

In the words of Pope Emeritus Benedict XVI, "I would like to suggest that you keep the Holy Bible within reach.... By so doing moments of relaxation can become in addition to a cultural enrichment also an enrichment of the spirit, fostering the knowledge of God and dialogue with him, prayer."[142]

Does this guarantee that we'll never make the wrong choice? No, but it increases the odds that we'll make the right ones. And for the times when we mess up, it's good to be reminded that "the steadfast love of the Lord never ceases, his mercies never come to an end; they are new every morning; great is your faithfulness" (Lamentations 3:22–23).

Mary reminds us of new beginnings. Fresh starts. Renewed hope. All because of the one who promises, "Behold, I make all things new!" (Revelation 21:5).

Dear Lord,
May I ponder positive and healthy things in my heart because I have intentionally filled my mind with truth and goodness. Amen.

DECEMBER 27

"My soul magnifies the Lord, and my spirit rejoices in God my Savior, for he has regarded the low estate of his handmaiden. For behold, henceforth all generations will call me blessed; for he who is mighty has done great things for me, and holy is his name." (Luke 1:47–49)

Mary's focus on God's goodness and greatness filled her heart with gratitude, which is the best antidote to discontent. A heart full of gratitude leaves no room for doubt, dissatisfaction, and unhappiness. In addition to her focus on God, Mary focused on who God had created her to be. She never lost sight of her God-given worth. She knew where her dignity came from and didn't allow anyone or anything to rob her of it.

Is there an area in your life where you are struggling to remain content? So often, we believe that if we could receive what we're longing for, we would feel more secure, peaceful, fulfilled, and self-confident. But what usually happens is that when we receive what we've waited for, it isn't long before another unmet desire feeds our discontent.

Just like Mary, you have a choice between dwelling on your if-onlys and what-ifs and focusing on what God has already done for you and what He is doing right now. You also have a choice in terms of how you determine your worth and identity. We will always be tempted to define ourselves by what we have, what we're accomplishing, or our reputations. Mary allowed herself to be defined by God, not by her circumstances.

We often don't realize how much our discontent is holding us back from being the women God created us to be. It's as if we're in a holding pattern, waiting for certain circumstances of our lives to change so that we can really start living the life that God has for us. But this is never His plan. He wants us to engage fully in the moment, trusting that whatever He is allowing, giving, or withholding is ultimately for our good. This is really hard to do. But our ability to follow Mary's example, saying, "I want what you want. I'll take your 'plan A' instead of all my own ideas," really will be impacted by what we choose to focus on.

Dear Lord,
May I remember that praise is a key that unlocks the door to gratitude and joy. Amen.

Be Still

DECEMBER 28

The Feast of the Holy Innocents

"Then Herod, when he saw that he had been tricked by the wise men, was in a furious rage, and he sent and killed all the male children in Bethlehem and in all that region who were two years old or under." (Matthew 2:16)

Herod had paid attention to prophecies of Jesus' birth, but instead of responding with worship, he felt threatened by this Jewish king. When the wise men didn't tell him who or where the baby was, Herod had all the male children in Bethlehem and in that region age two years old and under murdered. We remember the loss of these precious children today on the Feast of the Holy Innocents.

It's a horrific scene to imagine, and something we might want to turn away from. Focusing on the massacre of babies is the opposite of bringing Christmas cheer. But the Church insists that we not look away. Today, the number of people killed through genocide, gun violence, and abortion rises higher than that of the massacre of Bethlehem, and what we are encouraged to remember in all these cases is that each and every one of these souls matter to God. Their lives are not forgotten.

Things that go unnoticed or are hidden from the world are seen by God. There is no sorrow He doesn't see. Psalm 56:8 says that He holds all our tears in a bottle. When we are raw and hurting, God doesn't turn away. This is true on a personal and a global level. Where there is pain, God leans in. He is present and marks the loss, the injustice, wrongdoing.

In the moment when we wail, "God, why don't You do something?" He is at work redeeming the very things that the enemy intended to destroy us. But in order for God's work to be done—for beauty to come from the ashes—we have to open our hearts and cooperate with Him. There is nothing He cannot restore, but He is a gentleman, and will not force His way in. If we will pray, "Lord, have Your way with me," then He promises to transform even the most tragic circumstances into something that brings us good, not harm.

Dear Lord,
You are the potter, I am the clay. I don't know why You allow certain things to intersect my life, but I long to be molded into the masterpiece that You know I can be. So bend me, mold me, make me, move me. May my will be totally united with Yours. Amen.

DECEMBER 29

Feast of the Holy Family

"And [Jesus] went down with them and came to Nazareth, and was obedient to them; and his mother kept all these things in her heart. And Jesus increased in wisdom and in stature and in favor with God and man." (Luke 2:51–52)

Today we honor Mary, Joseph, and Jesus and the way they modeled family life for us during their years in Nazareth. We honor them by emulating them, by doing all we can to show the difference that Christ makes within a family. Let's be honest, it's a pretty tall order. The family is where we are most ourselves—where it all breaks down, where the masks come off—and things can get ugly. It is here that we rub against each other the most, and that can either refine us like a diamond or irritate and bring out the worst in us.

What has God asked us to do within the walls of our home? It says in Deuteronomy 6:5–9 that we are to love the Lord our God with all our heart and with all our soul and with all our strength. These commandments are to be upon *our* hearts. We are to impress them on our children, to talk about them when we sit at home and when we walk along the road, when we lie down and when we get up.

We can only pass to the next generation what we have ourselves. So we need to start with our own receptivity to God. We are to love the Lord, spend time with Him, develop and strengthen a relationship with Him, and *then* we are to teach these things to our children.

Raising children to know, love, and serve God is an enormous challenge. It takes a community. Spiritual mothering is something each of us is called to do. Hungry hearts abound. We are all needed.

We'll often find this call to be exhausting. Daily prayer for the children we love is critical. It will not only draw us closer to God and closer to the children as we pray for them, it will draw down God's strength and power on our behalf. In the Appendix, you will find the prayer list that I have used for years with my own children. May it serve as a springboard for your prayers.

Dear Lord,
As I share spiritual truths with the next generation, I am reminding myself of them. When I feel discouraged, I need to remember that You are my hope, and that You have placed Your Holy Spirit within me. Because of this, I can do all the things that You ask of me. Amen.

Be Still

DECEMBER 30

"In all these things we are more than conquerors through him who loved us." (Romans 8:37)

One of the favorite tactics of the enemy of our soul is to constantly preoccupy us with what we are not, so that we never fully encounter and embrace who God is. The more we focus on our inadequacies in a spirit of defeat, the less we appropriate the grace that God wants to pour into us.

When we sit at the feet of Jesus, He invites us to see ourselves through His eyes. He wants us to experience the mercy and unconditional love that He feels for us. But He also hopes our time together isn't all about what we feel. His desire is that we gaze on Him and see His greatness and power. He hungers for us to recognize that when we are honest about our weak spots, He comes with strength to fill in the gaps. He wants us to see that the only way we can conquer the things that hold us back from freedom and fullness in Him is to let Him do the work within us. Our strength alone is no match for hardwiring and patterns of sin. But with Christ? We conquer overwhelmingly through Him.

This posture of humility is the secret of the saints. They struggled with the same things we do. But moment by moment, they asked God to transform their natural tendencies into virtues. God is always patient. He doesn't expect us to be "finished" today. He just asks that we depend on Him and keep putting one foot in front of the other on the journey. Missionary Amy Carmichael gives good perspective on this pilgrimage toward spiritual maturity:

> Sometimes when we read the words of those who have been more than conquerors, we feel almost despondent. I feel that I shall never be like that. But they won through step by step, by little bits of wills, little denials of self, little inward victories. By faithfulness in very little things, they became what they are. No one sees those little hidden steps. They only see the accomplishment, but even so, those small steps were taken. There is no sudden triumph, no [sudden] spiritual maturity. That is the work of the moment.[143]

The people around us don't necessarily see the little hidden steps, but God does. He and the saints in heaven are cheering us on, encouraging us to keep going—to never give up.

Dear Lord,
May I never underestimate the importance of all the small decisions I make each day. May I choose You and others over my own comfort, knowing that these inner victories are investments in my eternity. Amen.

"Now to him who is able to keep you from falling and to present you without blemish before the presence of his glory with rejoicing, to the only God, our Savior through Jesus Christ our lord, be glory, majesty, dominion, and authority, before all time and now and for ever. Amen." (Jude 1:24–25)

We've come to the end of the year and are ready to turn the page of the calendar. There's a good chance we've eaten more than we should have during the holidays, spent too much, and are thinking about the ways in which we'd like to improve. Even if we don't make New Year's resolutions, our minds go there, wanting this next year to be better than the last.

Now is a great time to reflect on both the victories and the regrets of the past year—not to dwell on what went wrong, but to enter the New Year with intentionality. It's helpful to think about the different parts of your life that all contribute to your overall well-being. How are you doing physically? Emotionally? Relationally? Spiritually? Financially? Intellectually? Do you know God better now than you did a year ago? Setting a goal in each of these areas is a wise way to head into the year.

That being said, most people fail to follow through on their New Year's resolutions. Often it's because we are trying to do too many things at once. Listing all your goals but then choosing to focus on one at a time increases your chances of achieving them all. Writing them down in a journal each day, underlining the goal you are focusing on, can be a powerful exercise. This keeps your mind on all the goals, but reminds you of your main priority.

But nothing is more important than applying Jude 1:24–25 to your New Year's resolutions. What is going to keep you from stumbling? It's God. He's the One who is able to keep you from falling. Bring Him into the process. Pray about what His goals are for you, and ask Him to help you grow to be more like Jesus in the coming year. Think about why you are endeavoring to meet these goals. Is it for your glory? You'll be most likely to achieve the things that you are doing for *His* glory.

Dear Lord,
Over the next year, I want to grow in my resemblance to Christ. Give me the self-discipline I need to make changes. I commit to relying on You for help. Purify my desires so that I want what You want and do all things for Your glory. Amen.

Appendices

Topical Index

During Times of Suffering or Heartache

January 3	March 30	May 23	August 10
January 7	March 31	May 24	August 20
January 11	April 1	May 25	August 21
January 16	April 2	May 28	August 24
January 17	April 5	May 29	September 7
February 1	April 11	May 30	September 15
February 5	April 12	June 2	September 30
February 7	April 26	June 4	November 3
February 11	April 27	June 9	November 12
February 12	April 28	June 19	November 14
February 20	May 7	June 21	November 17
March 1	May 8	June 27	November 25
March 4	May 9	July 3	December 4
March 10	May 10	July 6	December 7
March 11	May 11	July 9	December 10
March 17	May 12	July 11	December 12
March 24	May 14	July 31	December 20
March 25	May 21	August 3	December 23
March 27	May 22	August 9	

When I Am Anxious

January 13	February 7	April 22	August 4
January 17	February 8	May 8	September 29
January 23	February 9	June 13	November 23
January 25	February 10	June 26	December 4
January 26	March 30	July 3	December 16
January 27	March 31	July 11	
February 6	April 11	July 12	

The Importance of Prayer and Listening to His Voice

January 1	March 1	June 4	July 9
January 2	March 13	June 5	July 21
January 4	March 23	June 13	July 30
January 5	April 5	June 18	July 31
January 6	April 24	June 22	August 5
January 8	May 5	June 23	August 6
January 9	May 7	June 24	August 10
January 10	May 8	June 30	August 19
January 11	May 9	July 1	August 25
January 14	May 10	July 4	August 26
January 20	May 18	July 5	August 27
February 3	May 20	July 7	September 12
February 4	May 21	July 8	September 13

Be Still

September 14	October 7	November 21	
September 15	October 14	December 17	
September 16	October 18	December 26	
September 17	November 2	December 29	

Surrender to His Will

January 1	May 14	July 5	October 19
January 4	May 18	July 8	October 20
January 16	May 21	July 10	October 21
January 17	May 29	July 13	October 23
February 1	June 1	July 20	October 24
February 11	June 2	July 22	October 25
February 18	June 3	July 24	October 30
February 21	June 4	August 3	November 14
February 22	June 5	August 9	November 19
February 25	June 14	August 10	November 25
March 1	June 15	August 21	November 27
March 7	June 16	August 29	November 29
March 19	June 17	August 30	November 30
March 21	June 18	September 9	December 4
March 23	June 20	September 20	December 16
April 3	June 24	September 28	December 17
April 17	June 27	September 30	December 23
April 28	June 28	October 2	December 27
May 2	June 29	October 5	December 28
May 3	June 30	October 6	
May 4	July 2	October 14	
May 11	July 4	October 18	

What It Means to Be a Disciple

January 8	March 8	May 24	July 14
January 9	March 16	May 26	July 15
January 12	March 23	May 28	July 17
January 15	March 29	May 30	July 18
January 18	April 5	May 31	July 24
January 19	April 14	June 4	July 28
January 21	April 16	June 6	July 29
January 31	April 17	June 15	August 1
February 2	April 18	June 16	August 5
February 17	April 19	June 17	August 7
February 22	April 23	June 22	August 9
February 23	April 24	June 23	August 15
February 27	April 28	June 25	August 24
February 29	May 3	June 28	August 26
March 3	May 6	June 29	August 31
March 5	May 16	July 1	September 2
March 6	May 17	July 11	September 3
March 7	May 18	July 13	September 13

Topical Index

September 21	October 22	November 6	December 14
October 2	October 26	November 7	December 17
October 6	October 31	November 8	December 19
October 13	November 1	November 9	December 21
October 15	November 4	December 6	December 25
October 17	November 5	December 13	December 27

Practical Advice for the Journey

January 10	March 20	July 31	September 21
January 14	April 5	August 4	September 24
January 17	April 24	August 10	September 29
January 18	May 8	August 11	October 7
January 23	May 15	August 12	October 8
February 10	May 17	August 18	October 15
February 15	July 1	August 19	October 31
February 23	July 7	August 25	November 2
March 1	July 12	September 4	November 10
March 2	July 13	September 5	November 22
March 3	July 14	September 6	November 23
March 6	July 15	September 10	November 29
March 9	July 24	September 16	December 31
March 13	July 26	September 17	
March 14	July 27	September 18	
March 15	July 30	September 19	

In Temptation

January 7	February 26	August 25	October 28
January 15	April 14	August 28	October 29
January 21	April 26	September 8	October 30
February 2	July 2	October 2	October 31
February 13	July 3	October 8	November 10
February 14	July 10	October 9	November 11
February 16	July 27	October 10	November 12
February 22	August 8	October 11	November 28
February 24	August 17	October 12	

When I Feel Lost and Without Purpose

January 3	April 15	June 15	October 26
January 6	April 18	June 16	November 19
March 18	April 24	July 23	November 24
March 19	May 4	July 28	November 30
March 22	May 5	August 30	December 1
April 4	May 16	September 25	December 2
April 6	May 31	September 28	December 3
April 13	June 7	October 1	December 6
April 14	June 11	October 3	December 9

409

Be Still

When I Need to Be Reminded of My Identity and God's Love for Me

January 10	April 1	May 29	August 30
January 14	April 6	June 2	September 21
January 19	April 7	June 7	October 1
January 24	April 9	June 8	October 3
January 25	April 10	June 9	October 27
January 28	April 11	June 10	November 11
January 29	April 15	June 11	November 12
February 3	April 17	June 12	November 13
February 8	April 18	June 18	November 24
February 12	April 20	June 26	November 30
February 13	April 21	July 16	December 8
February 15	April 25	July 17	December 10
February 17	April 26	July 21	December 12
February 24	May 1	August 6	December 15
March 3	May 6	August 14	December 17
March 6	May 12	August 15	December 20
March 14	May 19	August 18	December 27
March 15	May 21	August 22	December 30
March 24	May 22	August 23	
March 26	May 23	August 24	
March 27	May 24	August 28	

Radical Trust That God Can When I Cannot

January 1	February 24	May 7	July 12
January 2	February 25	May 11	July 17
January 3	March 1	May 14	July 19
January 7	March 2	May 18	July 20
January 11	March 4	May 28	July 25
January 13	March 5	May 29	July 29
January 17	March 10	June 2	August 6
January 22	March 11	June 10	August 8
January 27	March 21	June 14	August 16
January 30	March 26	June 17	August 17
February 1	March 31	June 18	August 22
February 5	April 1	June 19	August 28
February 6	April 2	June 21	August 29
February 7	April 3	June 24	September 1
February 9	April 4	June 27	September 5
February 12	April 12	June 29	September 6
February 14	April 19	July 2	September 8
February 15	April 27	July 5	September 11
February 16	May 2	July 6	September 14
February 17	May 3	July 8	September 19
February 20	May 4	July 9	September 22
February 21	May 5	July 11	September 26

Topical Index

September 27	November 19	December 11	December 23
October 17	November 21	December 17	December 24
November 6	November 25	December 18	December 30
November 8	December 4	December 21	December 31
November 18	December 8	December 22	

I Am Free and Forgiven

January 13	March 2	June 22	August 23
January 14	March 12	June 27	August 24
January 19	March 25	June 29	September 2
January 24	April 2	July 10	October 3
January 27	April 8	July 22	November 19
January 28	April 9	August 8	November 24
January 29	April 19	August 11	November 30
January 30	April 20	August 19	December 8
February 8	May 23	August 20	December 18
February 13	June 9	August 21	December 23
February 18	June 10	August 22	

When I Am Lonely

February 10	April 6	May 1	June 14
March 15	April 11	May 14	August 7
April 1	April 20	May 22	August 18

To Combat the World's Lies and Restlessness

January 15	March 28	June 7	August 29
January 18	March 29	June 11	August 30
January 21	April 12	June 21	August 31
February 10	April 14	July 3	September 2
February 15	April 16	July 25	September 6
February 17	April 21	July 26	October 1
February 18	April 22	August 1	October 20
February 19	April 23	August 2	November 20
March 7	April 25	August 13	December 1
March 22	May 5	August 14	December 5
March 23	May 19	August 16	December 20
March 24	May 27	August 19	
March 25	May 31	August 28	

What True Christian Friendship Looks Like

January 21	May 25	June 25	September 8
January 26	May 28	July 1	September 10
January 28	May 29	August 18	September 11
February 16	May 30	August 26	
March 16	June 6	August 27	
March 20	June 12	August 29	

To Break Free from the Hustle

January 2	April 21	August 16	November 20
January 5	April 22	August 23	December 5
January 11	May 15	August 31	December 6
January 20	May 19	September 1	December 14
January 27	June 1	September 5	December 15
March 13	June 22	September 9	December 16
March 26	June 28	October 4	December 18
March 27	June 30	October 7	December 19
April 12	August 1	October 27	December 21
April 13	August 2	October 28	December 22
April 16	August 14	October 29	December 31

The Spiritual Battle

January 10	February 24	May 20	July 10
January 21	February 25	May 21	July 12
January 30	February 26	June 3	July 26
February 4	March 14	June 8	August 25
February 14	April 26	June 10	November 2
February 15	April 27	June 13	November 21
February 16	May 8	June 26	

When I Need to Persevere

February 1	March 18	August 12	August 27
February 11	March 13	August 25	December 31

Old Testament Index

Genesis
January 19
May 25
September 1
October 29
November 11
November 12
November 14
November 15
November 16
November 17
November 18
November 19
November 24
November 25
November 26
November 27

Exodus
February 21
February 28
May 2
May 3
May 14
June 23
September 2
September 24
September 30
October 29

Numbers
March 1

Deuteronomy
January 13
February 9
February 26
March 10
April 26
May 16
May 24
July 3
July 18
September 21
December 29

Joshua
January 13
September 20
October 14
November 29

Judges
September 27
October 29

Ruth
January 16

1 Samuel
May 17
May 19
July 8
July 31

2 Samuel
May 8

1 Kings
May 8
June 22
November 16

Ezra
March 9

Nehemiah
August 2
March 12

Esther
December 9   December 10

Job
January 25   July 14   October 21

Psalms
January 4	May 6	July 9	August 31
January 5	May 7	July 10	September 7
January 9	May 10	July 11	September 11
January 14	May 11	July 12	September 15
January 23	May 12	August 1	September 16
January 28	May 23	August 10	October 1
February 6	June 1	August 11	October 29
February 7	June 9	August 12	November 3
March 30	June 14	August 15	November 12
April 12	June 21	August 16	November 23
April 15	June 25	August 21	December 3
April 24	June 26	August 27	December 28
April 26	June 30	August 28	
April 30	July 5	August 30	

Proverbs
January 10	April 13	August 12	October 25
January 12	April 23	August 13	October 29
January 21	May 5	August 18	November 16
February 8	June 12	September 4	November 22
February 16	June 25	October 12	November 23
March 3	August 2	October 21	December 21

Ecclesiastes
January 26   May 9   August 29   September 18

Song of Solomon
March 14

Isaiah
January 2	May 29	August 16	November 23
February 10	June 13	September 7	December 3
February 21	June 17	October 7	December 4
March 23	June 18	October 24	December 11
April 27	June 19	October 30	
May 21	July 22	November 3	
May 22	August 10	November 18	

Old Testament Index

Jeremiah
February 5	May 8	July 23	December 11
February 19	May 27	October 27	
March 23	July 15	November 21	
April 15	July 16	December 3	

Lamentations
March 4	August 10	November 20	December 26

Ezekiel
February 18	February 20	August 28
February 19	July 15	

Daniel
March 5	December 7

Hosea
February 3	April 6	December 6

Amos
May 16

Micah
January 6	March 22	December 3
March 3	September 9	

Nahum
April 1

Habakkuk
April 3

Zephaniah
April 11	June 26	June 27

Zechariah
January 7	April 5	August 2	December 3
February 25	July 10	October 11	

Malachi
September 14

New Testament Index

Matthew

January 9	March 25	June 22	October 5
January 22	March 30	July 30	October 31
February 6	April 17	August 6	November 4
February 17	April 22	August 16	November 6
February 19	April 24	August 20	November 7
February 23	April 25	September 3	November 22
February 25	April 26	September 6	November 23
March 6	May 4	September 20	November 28
March 8	May 19	September 22	December 3
March 11	May 21	September 24	December 16
March 19	June 6	September 29	December 28

Mark

February 14	March 21	September 20	December 13
February 15	April 2	October 18	
March 13	September 15	December 3	

Luke

January 1	May 31	September 19	December 16
January 3	June 2	October 6	December 17
January 27	June 3	October 8	December 18
February 22	June 4	October 16	December 22
March 2	June 5	October 21	December 24
March 12	June 24	December 2	December 25
March 15	June 25	December 3	December 26
March 21	August 15	December 8	December 27
April 19	August 28	December 12	December 29
May 27	September 16	December 15	

John

January 13	March 8	June 8	August 5
January 21	March 28	June 11	August 7
January 24	March 29	June 12	August 15
January 25	March 30	June 15	August 19
January 31	March 31	June 20	August 21
February 8	April 7	June 21	August 28
February 9	April 17	June 24	September 3
February 14	April 20	June 28	September 10
February 16	April 25	July 20	September 11
February 29	May 1	July 25	September 19
March 4	May 10	July 26	September 25
March 7	May 16	July 29	September 26

New Testament Index

October 17
October 20
October 24
November 2

November 5
November 9
November 23
December 12

December 14
December 17
December 18
December 19

December 23

Acts

July 20
August 26

September 7
September 13

September 19
October 4

Romans

January 3
January 6
January 15
January 18
January 27
February 2
February 16
March 7

March 17
April 10
April 30
May 18
June 9
June 10
June 17
July 17

July 19
July 22
July 26
August 6
August 8
August 10
August 19
September 19

October 19
October 22
October 23
November 8
December 8
December 10
December 30

1 Corinthians

January 8
February 10
February 13
February 16
February 24
March 16

April 18
April 30
June 7
July 2
July 3
August 10

August 12
August 17
September 16
October 4
October 15
October 20

November 15
November 22
December 20

2 Corinthians

January 2
January 10
January 11
January 22
February 13
February 14
March 20
April 9
April 14

April 27
May 8
May 20
May 24
May 25
May 28
June 9
June 18
June 29

July 5
July 8
July 21
July 29
August 9
September 22
September 29
October 5
October 31

November 3
November 10
November 21
November 24
November 26
December 5
December 9

Galatians

January 19
January 30
March 18

April 16
April 21
May 30

July 21
September 2
September 10

September 20
October 25
December 1

Ephesians

January 2
January 10

January 19
January 29

February 15
February 23

March 9
March 24

417

April 15	May 26	August 1	September 19
April 26	May 27	August 19	October 2
May 8	June 7	August 20	October 30
May 15	June 10	August 24	November 24
May 20	July 4	August 28	November 26
May 24	July 27	September 17	December 10

Philippians

January 2	April 4	June 25	September 19
January 10	April 14	June 29	September 28
February 16	May 4	July 28	
March 27	May 8	August 4	

Colossians

January 20	April 8	August 14	November 12
February 14	May 26	September 8	
March 25	June 6	September 13	
March 31	July 25	November 6	

1 Thessalonians

July 24	August 18	September 14	November 20

1 Timothy

September 23

2 Timothy

February 6	July 7	October 10
April 16	July 18	October 13
May 11	August 25	October 15

Titus

March 26

Hebrews

February 11	July 6	August 23	November 16
February 27	July 30	October 3	November 19
April 8	August 5	October 9	November 25
April 28	August 8	October 13	November 26
May 13	August 21	October 23	November 30
May 26	August 22	November 15	

James

January 14	February 21	July 1	September 11
January 17	May 18	July 13	November 9
February 4	June 20	August 6	

1 Peter

February 1	July 19	August 10	October 2
May 8	August 3	September 20	October 20

2 Peter

February 12	February 17	August 28

1 John

January 25	April 18	August 14	December 10
February 4	April 25	August 21	
February 24	April 26	September 12	
March 31	June 19	November 21	

Jude

December 31

Revelation

January 3	July 17	September 2	November 1
June 16	July 18	October 3	November 24
June 30	July 29	October 26	December 26

Monthly Prayers for Children

My heart is on fire to enable women to know Christ through Scripture. I want to do all I can to make sure that I have that same focus with my children. I long to see God shape, mold, and fill my children's hearts. These are the prayers that I use daily, month by month, as I lift up my children to their heavenly Father.

I recommend turning the Bible verses into prayers. Praying God's words back to Him is a very effective and powerful form of prayer.

January

Dear God, my children are being raised in a culture where truth and morals are relative. I pray that my children would know the truth about You and would follow You wholeheartedly. May they know and love the Bible.

Proverbs 7:1–3: "My son, keep my words and store up my commands within you. Keep my commands and you will live; guard my teachings as the apple of your eye. Bind them on your fingers; write them on the tablet of your heart."

February

Dear God, I pray for holy influences in the lives of my children. Please bring good friends into their lives who will hold them accountable and sharpen them.

Proverbs 12:26: "A righteous man is cautious in friendship, but the way of the wicked leads them astray."

Proverbs 27:17: "As iron sharpens iron, so one man sharpens another."

March

Dear God, I pray for my children's vocations. May they offer You their lives. If it is Your will that they marry, I pray they would choose a person of Christian faith and that the strength of their marriage would come from a mutual commitment to God. If it's Your will that they'd have a religious vocation, I pray they would say yes, offering You their very best. Either way, I pray they would seek out what Your plan is for their lives, and that You'd equip them to fulfill their unique calling.

Ephesians 2:10: "For we are his handiwork, created in Christ Jesus for the good works that God has prepared in advance, that we should live in them."

April

Dear God, please protect my children from evil. I ask for protection from sexual immorality, specifically pornography and promiscuity. Help them to use media wisely, especially internet social networking sites.

John 17:15: "I do not ask that you take them out of the world but that you keep them from the evil one."

May

Dear God, I pray that my children would be leaders in their generation, holding high the causes of Christ instead of the causes of the world.

1 Timothy 4:12: "Don't let anyone look down on you because you are young, but set an example for the believers in speech, in conduct, in love, in faith and in purity."

Philippians 2:12–16: "Do everything without complaining or arguing so that you may become blameless and pure, children of God without fault in a crooked and depraved generation, in which you shine like stars in the universe as you hold out the word of life."

June

Dear God, I pray that my children would respect authority. I pray they'd respect their father and me, teachers, the Church, and other authorities. I pray that their ultimate authority would be You, and that they would surrender their will to You.

Ephesians 6:1: "Children, obey your parents in the Lord, for this is right. 'Honor your father and mother.' This is the first commandment with a promise, 'that it may go well with you and that you may have a long life on earth.'"

Hebrews 13:17–18: "Obey your leaders and submit to their authority. They keep watch over you as men who must give an account. Obey them so that their work will be a joy, not a burden, for that would be of no advantage to you."

July

Dear God, I pray that any suffering in the lives of my children would be used to produce holy character. In my role as a mother, I desire to protect. Help me not to get in the way of Your work in my children's lives.

Romans 5:3–5: "We also rejoice in our sufferings, because we know that suffering produces perseverance; perseverance, character; and character, hope. And hope does not disappoint us, because God has poured out his love into our hearts by the Holy Spirit, whom he has given us."

August

Dear God, I pray that my children would be people of integrity (being the same person when no one is looking). Keep them from the faulty belief that you can be one person online and another in reality. Keep them from an obsession with image. May they find their identity in You.

Colossians 3:9–10: "Do not lie to each other, since you have taken off your old self with its practices and have put on the new self, which is being renewed in knowledge in the image of its Creator."

September

Dear God, as my children prepare for another school year, I pray that they would have strength of character so they can stand firm against peer pressure and the devil's schemes.

Ephesians 6:14–18: "Stand firm then, with the belt of truth buckled around your waist, with the breastplate of righteousness in place, and with your feet fitted with the readiness that comes from the gospel of peace. In addition to all this, take up the shield of faith, with which you can extinguish all the flaming arrows of the evil one. Take the helmet of salvation and the sword of the Spirit, which is the word of God. And pray in the Spirit on all occasions."

October

Dear God, I pray that my children would have hearts of compassion. May they desire to serve and meet the needs of the suffering and marginalized. May they be focused on others and free from the mentality that "it's all about me."

Proverbs 14:31: "He who oppresses the poor shows contempt for their Maker, but whoever is kind to the needy honors God."

November

Dear God, grant my children the wisdom to recognize God's truth and Satan's subtle lies. I specifically pray against the following lies:

"What I do on the internet is my business. It's harmless and doesn't hurt anyone."
"Beautiful people are worth more."
"I have to perform to be loved."

John 8:32: "You will know the truth, and the truth will set you free."

John 17:17: "Consecrate them in the truth. Your word is truth."

December

Dear God, I pray that my children would be careful with their words—not gossiping, exaggerating, lying, or speaking unkindly. I pray that their words would be pleasing to You not just out in public but also in the way they speak to their family members.

Proverbs 4:23–27: "Above all else, guard your heart, for it is the wellspring of life. Put away perversity from your mouth; keep corrupt talk far from your lips. Let your eyes look straight ahead, fix your gaze directly before you. Make level paths for your feet and take only ways that are firm. Do not swerve to the right or the left; keep your foot from evil."

"For to the one who has, more will be given"
Matthew 13:12

CHRIST'S LOVE IS ENDLESS.
And the journey doesn't end here.

Walking With Purpose is more than a Bible study, it's a supportive community of women seeking lasting transformation of the heart. And you are invited.

Walking With Purpose believes that change happens in the hearts of women – and, by extension, in their families and beyond – through Bible study and community. We welcome all women, irrespective of faith background, age, or marital status.

Connect with us online for regular inspiration and to join the conversation. There you'll find insightful blog posts, Scriptures, and downloads.

For a daily dose of spiritual nourishment, join our community on Facebook, Twitter, Pinterest and Instagram.

And if you're so moved to start a Walking With Purpose study group at home or in your parish, take a look at our website for more information.

walkingwithpurpose.com
The Modern Woman's Guide to the Bible.

Who We Are
Walking with Purpose is a ministry of Jesus Christ.

Why We Exist
We exist to enable women to know Jesus Christ personally through Scripture and the teachings of the Roman Catholic Church.

Our Mission
Our mission is to help every Catholic woman and girl in America to open her heart to Jesus Christ.

Our Vision
Our vision for the future is that, as more Catholic women deepen their relationships with Jesus Christ, eternity-changing transformation will take place in their hearts – and, by extension – in their families, in their communities, and ultimately, in our nation.

walking with purpose

You can support our mission through a tax-deductible gift.
Learn more at walkingwithpurpose.com/donate

Notes

1. St. Josemaria Escriva, *The Way* (New York: Doubleday, 1982), 33.
2. C. S. Lewis and Pauline Baynes, *The Lion, the Witch and the Wardrobe* (New York: HarperCollins, 2005), 146.
3. Carolyn Custis James, *The Gospel of Ruth* (Grand Rapids, MI: Zondervan, 2008), 84–5.
4. Jacques Philippe, *Interior Freedom* (New York: Scepter, 2002), 32.
5. Father Paul Farren, *Freedom and Forgiveness: A Fresh Look at the Sacrament of Reconciliation* (Dublin: Columba Press, 2013), 1.
6. Scott Hahn, *Lord, Have Mercy: The Healing Power of Confession* (New York: Doubleday, 2003), 175.
7. Philippe, *Interior Freedom*, 36.
8. Jolie Lee, "Biggest American Fear? Walking Alone at Night, Survey Finds," *USA Today*, October 22, 2014, http://www.usatoday.com/story/news/nation-now/2014/10/22/fear-study-chapman-university/17663861/.
9. Erin Hanson, "Just My Poems," The Poetic Underground, http://thepoeticunderground.com/post/87639964775/the-talent-of-all-of-you-astounds-me-this-a-quote.
10. Lynn Okura, "Brené Brown: 'Joy Is the Most Vulnerable Emotion We Can Experience,'" *HuffPost*, December 6, 2017, http://www.huffingtonpost.com/2013/10/18/brene-brown-joy-numbing-oprah_n_4116520.html.
11. C. S. Lewis, *The Problem of Pain* (New York: HarperCollins, 2001), 94.
12. Philip Yancey, *Where Is God When It Hurts?* (Grand Rapids, MI: Zondervan, 1997), 88.
13. Adrian Warnock, *Raised with Christ: How the Resurrection Changes Everything* (Wheaton, IL: Crossway Books, 2010), 143.
14. Tim Keller, *Counterfeit Gods: The Empty Promises of Money, Sex, and Power, and the Only Hope That Matters* (New York: Penguin Books, 2009), 149.
15. Philip Yancey, *Prayer* (Grand Rapids, MI: Zondervan, 2006), 36.
16. Barna Group and Jon Tyson, "Sacred Roots Outline," http://www.bibleresourcelink.com/frames/pdf/sacred-roots-outline.pdf.]
17. Father John Bartunek, *The Better Part* (Hamden, CT: Circle Press, 2007), 977.
18. Catholics Come Home, "2000 Years of Faith," https://www.catholicscomehome.org.
19. "Frequently Requested Church Statistics," Center for Applied Research in the Apostolate, http://cara.georgetown.edu/frequently-requested-church-statistics/.
20. Kevin Knight, "Science and the Church," New Advent, http://www.newadvent.org/cathen/13598b.htm.
21. Thomas E. Woods Jr., *How the Catholic Church Built Western Civilization* (Washington, DC: Regenery Publishing, 2012), 187, 198, 201.
22. Kevin Knight, "Universities," New Advent, http://www.newadvent.org/cathen/15188a.htm.

23 Thérèse of Lisieux, *Autobiography of a Saint*, trans. Ronald Knox (London, UK: Harvill, 1958), 235.
24 Lewis, *The Problem of Pain*, 92.
25 George Weigel, *Witness to Hope* (New York: HarperCollins, 2001), 517.
26 Ibid., 529.
27 Gary Smalley and Ted Cunningham, *From Anger to Intimacy: How Forgiveness Can Transform Your Marriage* (Ventura, CA: Regal, 2009), 137–8.
28 Gabe Lyons, *The Next Christians* (Colorado Springs, CO: Multnomah Books, 2010), 197.
29 Linda Dillow, *Calm My Anxious Heart* (Colorado Springs, CO: Nav Press, 2007), 161.
30 Father Jean C. J. d'Elbée, *I Believe in Love* (Manchester, NH: Sophia Institute Press, 2001), 17.
31 Presentation by Christopher West, *An Introduction to the Theology of the Body* (West Chester, PA: Ascension Press, 2008).
32 D'Elbée, *I Believe in Love*, 9.
33 Bartunek, *The Better Part*, 819.
34 John Paul II, *The Splendor of Truth* (Washington, DC: United States Conference of Catholic Bishops, 1993), 5.
35 Monsignor Charles M. Mangan, "Our Grave Obligation to Forgive," *Catholic Online*, January 29, 2006, http://www.catholic.org/featured/headline.php?ID=2950.
36 Bill Moyers, "A Conversation with Maya Angelou," *Bill Moyers Journal*, Public Broadcasting System, first aired November 21, 1973, https://billmoyers.com/content/conversation-maya-angelou/.
37 Henri Nouwen, *Making All Things New* (New York: HarperCollins, 1981).
38 "John Paul II Quotes," Goodreads, https://www.goodreads.com/author/quotes/6473881.Pope_John_Paul_II.
39 http://www.vatican.va/archive/compendium_ccc/documents/archive_2005_compendium-ccc_en.html
40 Scott Hahn, *Hail, Holy Queen: The Mother of God in the Word of God* (New York: Doubleday) 27–8.
41 Beth Moore, *Breaking Free* (Nashville, TN: LifeWay Press, 2008), 185.
42 Bob Schuchts, "Healing the Whole Person: Facing Our Brokenness" (lecture, Good Shepherd Catholic Church, Tallahassee, FL, March 14, 2017).
43 C. S. Lewis, *The Weight of Glory* (New York: HarperCollins, 2001), 161.
44 Henri Nouwen, *Making All Things New and Other Classics* (London, UK: HarperCollins Religious, 2000), 29.
45 N.T. Wright, *Hebrews for Everyone* (Louisville, KY: John Knox Press, 2004), 149.
46 N. T. Wright, *Hebrews for Everyone* (Louisville, KY: John Knox Press, 2003), 149.
47 D'Elbée, *I Believe in Love*, 76.
48 Charles Haddon Spurgeon, "The Believer a New Creature," The Spurgeon Center, https://www.spurgeon.org/resource-library/sermons/the-believer-a-new-creature#flipbook/.
49 Babylonian Talmud, Menachot 29A, in Brant Pitre, *Jesus and the Jewish Roots of the Eucharist: Unlocking the Secrets of the Last Supper* (New York: Doubleday, 2010), 130–1.

50 Michael Harter, ed., *Hearts on Fire* (St. Louis: Institute of Jesuit Sources, 1993), 9.
51 Peter Kreeft, *Practical Theology* (San Francisco: Ignatius Press, 2014), 124.
52 Life Application, ed., Romans 6:16–18 footnote in the New International Version Bible (Wheaton, IL: Tyndale House, 1991), 2038.
53 L. B. Cowman, *Streams in the Desert* (Grand Rapids, MI: Zondervan, 2007), 73.
54 Linda Schubert, *Miracle Hour* (Santa Clara, CA: Miracles of the Heart Ministries, 1991), 12–13.
55 Saint Ignatius of Antioch, *Ad Rom.*, 6, 1–2: *Apostolic Fathers*, II/2, 217–20.
56 Kreeft, *Practical Theology*, 326.
57 Kate Bowler, *Everything Happens for a Reason* (New York: Random House, 2018), 156.
58 Jeff Robinson, "Romanian Josef Tson Recounts God's Grace amid Suffering," *Baptist Press*, July 19, 2004, http://www.bpnews.net/18713.
59 Ibid.
60 Margaret R. Bunson, *Pope John Paul II's Book of Mary* (Huntington, IN: Our Sunday Visitor, 1996), 17.
61 Wright, *Hebrews for Everyone*, 45.
62 Saint Augustine, *Confessions* (Oxford, UK: Oxford University Press, 2008), 201.
63 Bronnie Ware, "Top Five Regrets of the Dying," Exposing the Truth, July 27, 2013, http://www.exposingthetruth.co/top-five-regrets-of-the-dying/#axzz2tEjmC2Sx.
64 Ravi Zacharias, *Has Christianity Failed You?* (Grand Rapids, MI: Zondervan, 2010), 87.
65 *Merriam-Webster Online*, s. v. "burden," http://www.merriam-webster.com/dictionary/burden.
66 *Merriam-Webster Online*, s. v. "load," http://www.merriam-webster.com/dictionary/load?show=0&t=1385405406.
67 Henry Cloud and John Townsend, *Boundaries: When to Say Yes, How to Say No to Take Control of Your Life* (Grand Rapids, MI: Zondervan, 1992), 67.
68 Gary Thomas, *Sacred Marriage: What If God Designed Marriage to Make Us Holy More Than to Make Us Happy?* (Grand Rapids, MI: Zondervan, 2000), 66.
69 John 1:1.
70 Francis Chan and Danae Yankoski, *Crazy Love: Overwhelmed by a Relentless God* (Colorado Springs, CO: David C. Cook, 2008), 34.
71 A. W. Tozer, *The Knowledge of the Holy* (San Francisco: HarperSanFrancisco, 1992), 1.
72 Thomas Merton, *Contemplative Prayer* (Garden City, NY: Doubleday, 1969), 42.
73 Cowman, *Streams in the Desert*, 460.
74 Stephen R. Covey, A. Roger Merrill, and Rebecca R. Merrill, *First Things First* (New York: Simon & Schuster, 1996), 161.
75 Dorothy C. Haskin, *A Practical Guide to Prayer* (Chicago: Moody Press, 1951), 32.
76 Saint John Paul II, "General Audience: The Spirit Gives Strength to Christians," June 26, 1991,

http://www.vatican.va/holy_father/john_paul_ii/audiences/alpha/data/aud19910626en.html.
77 Susan K. Rowland, "Sabbath Moments in a Busy World," AmericanCatholic.org, http://www.americancatholic.org/Newsletters/CU/preview.aspx?id=256.
78 Peter Kreeft, *Three Philosophies of Life* (San Francisco: Ignatius Press, 1989), 94-5.
79 Wayne Muller, *Sabbath: Finding Rest, Renewal, and Delight in Our Busy Lives* (New York: Bantam Books, 1999), 137.
80 Ann Voskamp, *One Thousand Gifts: A Dare to Live Fully Right Where You Are* (Grand Rapids, MI: Zondervan, 2010), 65–6.
81 Address of John Paul II to the Bishops of Australia on their "Ad Limina" visit, Friday, 26 March 2004.
82 St. Theophan the Recluse, *The Spiritual Life: And How to Be Attuned to It* (Platina, CA: St. Herman of Alaska Brotherhood, 1955), 87, 93.
83 Brother Lawrence, *The Practice of the Presence of God* (New York: Image Books, 1977), 29.
84 Mary Poplin, *Finding Calcutta: What Mother Teresa Taught Me About Meaningful Work and Service* (Downers Grove, IL: InterVarsity Press, 2008), 31.
85 Dillow, *Calm My Anxious Heart*, 120.
86 Sarah Young, *Jesus Calling: Enjoying Peace in His Presence* (Nashville, TN: Thomas Nelson, 2004), 304.
87 C. S. Lewis, "The Weight of Glory," in *The Weight of Glory and Other Addresses*, ed. W. Hooper (New York: Simon & Shuster, 1996), 25–6.
88 Frank Sheed, *Theology and Sanity* (San Francisco: Ignatius Press, 1978), 344.
89 Jen Hatmaker, *7: An Experimental Mutiny Against Excess* (Nashville, TN: B&H, 2012), 94.
90 The Holy See, "Message of the Holy Father Pope John Paul II for the XI World Youth Day," November 26, 1995, https://w2.vatican.va/content/john-paul-ii/en/messages/youth/documents/hf_jp-ii_mes_26111995_xi-world-youth-day.html.
91 Wilfrid Stinissen, *Into Your Hands, Father: Abandoning Ourselves to the God Who Loves Us* (San Francisco: Ignatius Press, 1986), 74.
92 Ibid., 85.
93 Richard J. Foster, *Celebration of Discipline: The Path to Spiritual Growth* (San Francisco: HarperSanFrancisco, 1988), 55.
94 James Emery White, *You Can Experience . . . A Spiritual Life* (Nashville, TN: Word, 1999), 201.
95 Mother Teresa, *Mother Teresa: Come Be My Light: The Private Writings of the Saint of Calcutta*, ed. Brian Kolodiejchuk (New York: Doubleday, 2007), 29.
96 C. S. Lewis, *The Screwtape Letters* (Old Tappan, NJ: Fleming H. Revell, 1979), 59.
97 Kyle Idleman, *Not a Fan: Becoming a Completely Committed Follower of Jesus* (Grand Rapids, MI: Zondervan, 2011), 25.
98 Father Jean Bauptiste San-Jure S.J. and Saint Claude de la Columbiere S.J. *Trustful Surrender to Divine Providence* (Charlotte, NC: TAN Books, 2012), 29-30.
99 K. P. Yohannan, *The Lord's Work Done in the Lord's Way* (Carrollton, TX: GFA Books, 2004), 38.

100 Idleman, *Not a Fan*, 202.
101 John Paul II, *Love and Responsibility* (New York: Farrar, Straus and Giroux, 1981), 27.
102 Ibid., 123.
103 Matthew 23:11–12.
104 Matthew 10:39.
105 2 Corinthians 12:10.
106 Philippe, *Interior Freedom*, 28–9.
107 Ibid., 30.
108 John 13:7.
109 St. Thérèse of Lisieux, *Story of a Soul: The Autobiography of St. Thérèse of Lisieux*, trans. John Clarke (New York: Doubleday, 2001), 9.
110 Glendale Church of Christ, "Fighting the Good Fight: Fighting Mediocrity," Truth & Reason, September 15, 2013, http://www.truth-reason.com/wp-content/uploads/2013/09/ftgf6-fightingmediocrity.pdf.
111 Richard Winter, "Perfectionism: The Road to Heaven—or Hell?" L'Abri Papers no. RW01, L'Abri Fellowship, http://www.labri.org/england/resources/05052008/RW01_Perfectionism.pdf.
112 ——— *Perfecting Ourselves to Death: The Pursuit of Excellence and the Perils of Perfectionism* (Downers Grove, IL: InterVarsity Press, 2005), 78.
113 Dictionary.com, s. v. "redemption," http://dictionary.reference.com/browse/redemption.
114 Winter, "Perfectionism."
115 Jerusha Clark, *Every Thought Captive* (Colorado Springs, CO: Th1nk, 2006), 14–5.
116 Aleksandr Solzhenitsyn, *The Gulag Archipelago* (New York: Harvill Press, 1974), 442.
117 Sibi Riffer, "The New Church Lady," *Pearls and Grace* (blog), February 6, 2014, http://pearlsandgrace.blogspot.com/2014/01/the-new-church-lady.html.
118 Charles Colson and Ellen Vaughn, *Being the Body* (Nashville, TN: W, 2003), 371.
119 "Pope Francis: In His Own Words," *Catholic Herald*, March 14, 2013, https://catholicherald.co.uk/news/2013/03/14/pope-francis-in-his-own-words/.
120 Tullian Tchividjian, *Unfashionable: Making a Difference in the World by Being Different* (Colorado Springs, CO: Multnomah Books, 2012), 82.
121 Austen Ivereigh, *How to Defend the Faith Without Raising Your Voice: Civil Responses to Catholic Hot-Button Issues* (Huntington, IN: Our Sunday Visitor, 2012), 156.
122 Pope Francis, *The Joy of the Gospel* (Dublin: Veritas Publications, 2013), 50.
123 "Romans 8:31–39 (The Message)," Bible Gateway, http://www.biblegateway.com/passage/?search=Romans+8%3A31-39&version=MSG.
124 *Webster's New World Dictionary* (New York: Prentice Hall Press, 1986), 622.
125 Jessica L. Tracy, Richard W. Robins, and June Price Tangney, *The Self-Conscious Emotions: Theory and Research* (New York: Guilford Press, 2007), 202.
126 Benedict XVI, *God and the World* (San Francisco: Ignatius Press, 2002), 322.
127 Victor P. Hamilton, *The Book of Genesis: Chapters 1–17* (Grand Rapids, MI: William B. Erdman, 1990), 444.
128 Hatmaker, *7*, 3.

129 Ephesians 1:19–20.
130 D'Elbée, *I Believe in Love*, 87.
131 Henry H. Halley, *Halley's Bible Handbook* (Grand Rapids, MI: Zondervan, 2007), 118.
132 Dan B. Allender, *How Children Raise Parents* (Colorado Springs, CO: Waterbrook Press, 2003), 104.
133 Sheed, *Theology and Sanity*, 230.
134 Peter W. Stoner, *Science Speaks* (Chicago: Moody Press, 1969), 109.
135 Saint Thérèse of Lisieux, *Story of a Soul*, 68.
136 Amena Brown Owen and Ann Voskamp, "This Is Us: The #Esther Generation [a Spoken Word Poem]," A Holy Experience, http://aholyexperience.com/2014/03/this-is-us-the-esthergeneration-a-spoken-word-poem/.
137 Corrie ten Boom, *Clippings from My Notebook* (Nashville, TN: Thomas Nelson, 1982).
138 Brother Lawrence, *The Practice of the Presence of God* (Virginia Beach, VA: Whitaker Distribution, 1982).
139 C.S. Lewis, *The Complete C.S. Lewis Signature Classics*, (NY, NY: Harper Collins, 2002), 120.
140 Tim Kreider, "The 'Busy' Trap," *New York Times*, June 30, 2012, https://opinionator.blogs.nytimes.com/2012/06/30/the-busy-trap/.
141 Tim Hansel, *Holy Sweat* (Waco, TX: Word, 1987), 79.
142 Pope Benedict XVI, "General Audience," The Holy See, August 3, 2011, http://w2.vatican.va/content/benedict-xvi/en/audiences/2011/documents/hf_ben-xvi_aud_20110803.html.
143 Hansel, *Holy Sweat*, 130.